FINLAND

INVESTMENT AND BUSINESS GUIDE

VOLUME 1

STRATEGIC AND PRACTICAL INFORMATION

International Business Publications, USA
Washington DC, USA - Finland

FINLAND

INVESTMENT AND BUSINESS GUIDE

VOLUME 1 STRATEGIC AND PRACTICAL INFORMATION

UPDATED ANNUALLY

We express our sincere appreciation to all government agencies and international organizations which provided information and other materials for this guide

Cover Design: **International Business Publications, USA**

2019 Edition Updated Reprint International Business Publications, USA
ISBN 1-4387-6757-9

For additional analytical, business and investment opportunities information, please contact Global Investment & Business Center, USA at (703) 370-8082. Fax: (703) 370-8083. E-mail: ibpusa3@gmail.com Global Business and Investment Info Databank - www.ibpus.com

Printed in the USA

For additional analytical, business and investment opportunities information, please contact Global Investment & Business Center, USA at (703) 370-8082. Fax: (703) 370-8083. E-mail: ibpusa3@gmail.com Global Business and Investment Info Databank - www.ibpus.com

FINLAND
INVESTMENT AND BUSINESS GUIDE
VOLUME 1
STRATEGIC AND PRACTICAL INFORMATION

TABLE OF CONTENTS

STRATEGIC AND DEVELOPMENT PROFILES

BASIC INFORMATION

Capital and largest city	Helsinki 60°10′N 24°56′E
Official languages	• Finnish • Swedish
Recognised regional languages	Sámi
Religion	• Evangelical Lutheran Church • Orthodox Church
Demonym(s)	• Finnish • Finn
Government	Unitary parliamentary republic
• President	Sauli Niinistö
• Prime Minister	Juha Sipilä
Legislature	Eduskunta/Riksdagen
Formation	
• Autonomy within Russian Empire	29 March 1809
• Independence from Russian SFSR	6 December 1917
• Civil War against Red Finland/FSWR	27 January – 15 May 1918
• Joined the European Union	1 January 1995
Area	
• Total	338,424 km^2 (130,666 sq mi) (64th)
• Water (%)	10
Population	
• September 2018 estimate	▲5,520,535 (114th)
• 2017 official	5,513,000
• Density	16/km^2 (41.4/sq mi) (213th)
GDP (PPP)	2018 estimate
• Total	$257 billion
• Per capita	$46,559
GDP (nominal)	2018 estimate
• Total	$277 billion
• Per capita	$50,068
Gini (2017)	25.3 low · 6th
HDI (2017)	▲ 0.920 very high · 15th
Currency	Euro (€) (EUR)
Time zone	UTC+2 (EET)

• Summer (DST)	UTC+3 (EEST)
Date format	dd.mm.yyyy
Driving side	right
Calling code	+358
ISO 3166 code	FI
Internet TLD	.fi[a]

Finland is a country in Northern Europe bordering the Baltic Sea, Gulf of Bothnia, and Gulf of Finland, between Norway to the north, Sweden to the northwest, and Russia to the east. Finland is a Nordic country and is situated in the geographical region of Fennoscandia. The capital and largest city is Helsinki. Other major cities are Espoo, Vantaa, Tampere, Oulu and Turku.

Finland's population is 5.52 million (2018), and the majority of the population is concentrated in the southern region. 87.6% of the population is Finnish and speaks Finnish, a Uralic language unrelated to the Scandinavian languages; next come the Finland-Swedes (5.2%). Finland is the eighth-largest country in Europe and the most sparsely populated country in the European Union. The sovereign state is a parliamentary republic with a central government based in the capital city of Helsinki, local governments in 311 municipalities, and one autonomous region, the Åland Islands. Over 1.4 million people live in the Greater Helsinki metropolitan area, which produces one third of the country's GDP.

Finland was inhabited when the last ice age ended, approximately 9000 BCE. The first settlers left behind artefacts that present characteristics shared with those found in Estonia, Russia, and Norway The earliest people were hunter-gatherers, using stone tools. The first pottery appeared in 5200 BCE, when the Comb Ceramic culture was introduced. The arrival of the Corded Ware culture in southern coastal Finland between 3000 and 2500 BCE may have coincided with the start of agriculture. The Bronze Age and Iron Age were characterised by extensive contacts with other cultures in the Fennoscandian and Baltic regions and the sedentary farming inhabitation increased towards the end of Iron Age. At the time Finland had three main cultural areas – Southwest Finland, Tavastia and Karelia – as reflected in contemporary jewellery.

From the late 13th century, Finland gradually became an integral part of Sweden through the Northern Crusades and the Swedish part-colonisation of coastal Finland, a legacy reflected in the prevalence of the Swedish language and its official status. In 1809, Finland was incorporated into the Russian Empire as the autonomous Grand Duchy of Finland. In 1906, Finland became the first European state to grant all adult citizens the right to vote, and the first in the world to give all adult citizens the right to run for public office.

Following the 1917 Russian Revolution, Finland declared itself independent. In 1918, the fledgling state was divided by civil war, with the Bolshevik-leaning Red Guard supported by the equally new Soviet Russia, fighting the White Guard, supported by the German Empire. After a brief attempt to establish a kingdom, the country became a republic. During World War II, the Soviet Union sought repeatedly to occupy Finland, with Finland losing parts of Karelia, Salla, Kuusamo, Petsamo and some islands, but retaining their independence.

Finland joined the United Nations in 1955 and established an official policy of neutrality. The Finno-Soviet Treaty of 1948 gave the Soviet Union some leverage in Finnish domestic politics during the Cold War era. Finland joined the OECD in 1969, the NATO Partnership for Peace in 1994, the European Union in 1995, the Euro-Atlantic Partnership Council in 1997, and finally the Eurozone at its inception, in 1999.

Finland was a relative latecomer to industrialisation, remaining a largely agrarian country until the 1950s. After World War II, the Soviet Union demanded war reparations from Finland not only in money but also in material, such as ships and machinery. This forced Finland to industrialise. It rapidly developed an advanced economy while building an extensive welfare state based on the Nordic model, resulting in widespread prosperity and one of the highest per capita incomes in the world. Finland is a top performer in numerous metrics of national performance, including education, economic competitiveness, civil liberties, quality of life, and human development. In 2015, Finland was ranked first in the World Human Capital and the Press Freedom Index and as the most stable country in the world during 2011–2016 in the Fragile States Index, and second in the Global Gender Gap Report. It also ranked first on the World Happiness Report report for 2018 and 2019. A large majority of Finns are members of the Evangelical Lutheran Church, and freedom of religion is guaranteed under the Finnish Constitution.

GEOGRAPHY

Location: Northern Europe, bordering the Baltic Sea, Gulf of Bothnia, and Gulf of Finland, between Sweden and Russia

Geographic coordinates: 64 00 N, 26 00 E
Map references: Europe
Area:
total: 337,030 sq km
land: 305,470 sq km
water: 31,560 sq km

Area - comparative: slightly smaller than Montana

Land boundaries:
total: 2,628 km
border countries: Norway 729 km, Sweden 586 km, Russia 1,313 km

Coastline: 1,126 km (excludes islands and coastal indentations)

Maritime claims:
contiguous zone: 6 nm
continental shelf: 200-m depth or to the depth of exploitation
exclusive fishing zone: 12 nm
territorial sea: 12 nm (in the Gulf of Finland - 3 nm)

Climate: cold temperate; potentially subarctic, but comparatively mild because of moderating influence of the North Atlantic Current, Baltic Sea, and more than 60,000 lakes

Terrain: mostly low, flat to rolling plains interspersed with lakes and low hills

Elevation extremes:
lowest point: Baltic Sea 0 m
highest point: Haltiatunturi 1,328 m

Natural resources: timber, copper, zinc, iron ore, silver

Land use:
arable land: 8% permanent crops: 0%

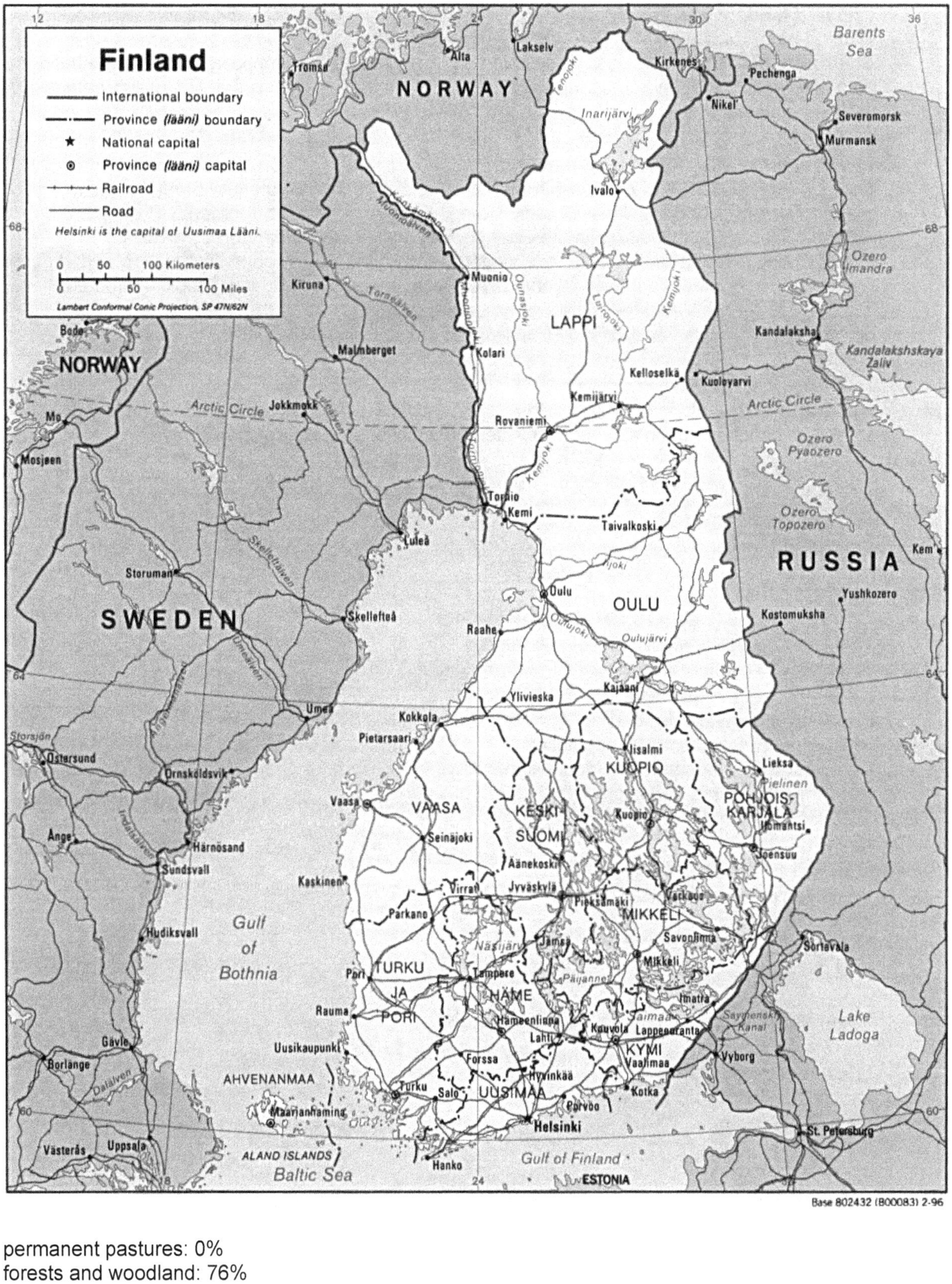

permanent pastures: 0%
forests and woodland: 76%
other: 16%

Irrigated land: 640 sq km
Natural hazards: NA
Environment - current issues: air pollution from manufacturing and power plants contributing to acid rain; water pollution from industrial wastes, agricultural chemicals; habitat loss threatens wildlife populations

Environment - international agreements:
party to: Air Pollution, Air Pollution-Nitrogen Oxides, Air Pollution-Sulphur 85, Air Pollution-Sulphur 94, Air Pollution-Volatile Organic Compounds, Antarctic-Environmental Protocol, Antarctic Treaty, Biodiversity, Climate Change, Desertification, Endangered Species, Environmental Modification, Hazardous Wastes, Law of the Sea, Marine Dumping, Marine Life Conservation, Nuclear Test Ban, Ozone Layer Protection, Ship Pollution, Tropical Timber 83, Tropical Timber 94, Wetlands, Whaling
signed, but not ratified: Air Pollution-Persistent Organic Pollutants, Climate Change-Kyoto Protocol

Geography - note: long boundary with Russia; Helsinki is northernmost national capital on European continent; population concentrated on small southwestern coastal plain

PEOPLE

Population: 5,167,486

Age structure:
0-14 years: 18% (male 478,497; female 459,646)
15-64 years: 67% (male 1,747,738; female 1,712,058)
65 years and over: 15% (male 295,177; female 474,370)

Population growth rate: 0.17%
Birth rate: 10.8 births/1,000 population
Death rate: 9.73 deaths/1,000 population
Net migration rate: 0.58 migrant(s)/1,000 population

Sex ratio:
at birth: 1.04 male(s)/female
under 15 years: 1.04 male(s)/female
15-64 years: 1.02 male(s)/female
65 years and over: 0.62 male(s)/female
total population: 0.95 male(s)/female

Infant mortality rate: 3.82 deaths/1,000 live births

Life expectancy at birth:
total population: 77.41 years
male: 73.74 years
female: 81.2 years

Total fertility rate: 1.7 children born/woman

Nationality:
noun: Finn(s)
adjective: Finnish

Ethnic groups: Finn 93%, Swede 6%, Lapp 0.11%, Roma 0.12%, Tatar 0.02%

Religions: Evangelical Lutheran 89%, Greek Orthodox 1%, none 9%, other 1%

Languages: Finnish 93.4% (official), Swedish 5.9% (official), small Lapp- and Russian-speaking minorities

Literacy:
definition: age 15 and over can read and write
total population: 100% (1980 est.)
male: NA%
female: NA%

GOVERNMENT

Country name:
conventional long form: Republic of Finland
conventional short form: Finland
local long form: Suomen Tasavalta
local short form: Suomi

Data code: FI
Government type: republic
Capital: Helsinki

Administrative divisions: 6 provinces (laanit, singular - laani); Aland, Etela-Suomen Laani, Ita-Suomen Laani, Lansi-Suomen Laani, Lappi, Oulun Laani

Independence: 6 December 1917 (from Russia)
National holiday: Independence Day, 6 December (1917)
Constitution: 17 July 1919

Legal system: civil law system based on Swedish law; Supreme Court may request legislation interpreting or modifying laws; accepts compulsory ICJ jurisdiction, with reservations

Suffrage: 18 years of age; universal

Executive branch:

chief of state: President Sauli NIINISTO (since 1 March 2012)
head of government: Prime Minister Juha SIPILA (since 29 May 2015); note - he resigned on 8 March 2019 after Parliament voted down his health program; President NIINISTO asked him to stay as a caretaker prime minister until after the 14 April 2019 new elections
cabinet: Council of State or Valtioneuvosto appointed by the president, responsible to Parliament

elections/appointments: president directly elected by absolute majority popular vote in 2 rounds if needed for a 6-year term (eligible for a second term); election last held on 28 January 2018 (next to be held in January 2024); prime minister appointed by Parliament
election results: Sauli NIINISTO reelected president; percent of vote Sauli NIINISTO (independent) 62.7%, Pekka HAAVISTO (Vihr) 12.4%, Laura HUHTASAARI (PS) 6.9%, Paavo VAYRYNEN (independent) 6.2%, Matti VANHANEN (Kesk) 4.1%, other 7.7%

Legislative branch:
description: unicameral Parliament or Eduskunta (200 seats; 199 members directly elected in single- and multi-seat constituencies by proportional representation vote and 1 member in the province of Aland directly elected by simple majority vote; members serve 4-year terms)

elections: last held on 14 April 2019 (next to be held on April 2023)
election results: percent of vote by party/coalition - Kesk 21.1%, PS 17.6%, Kok 18.2%, SDP 16.5%, Vihr 8.5%, Vas 7.1%, SFP 4.9%, KD 3.5%, other 2.6%; seats by party/coalition - Kesk 49, PS 38, Kok 37, SDP 34, Vihr 15, Vas 12, SFP 9, KD 5, Aland Coalition 1; composition men 117, women 83, percent of women 41.5%

Judicial branch:
highest courts: Supreme Court or Korkein Oikeus (consists of the court president and 18 judges); Supreme Administrative Court (consists of 21 judges, including the court president and organized into 3 chambers); note - Finland has a dual judicial system - courts with civil and criminal jurisdiction and administrative courts with jurisdiction for litigation between individuals and administrative organs of the state and communities
judge selection and term of office: Supreme Court and Supreme Administrative Court judges appointed by the president of the republic; judges serve until mandatory retirement at age 68

subordinate courts: 6 Courts of Appeal; 8 regional administrative courts; 27 district courts; special courts for issues relating to markets, labor, insurance, impeachment, land, tenancy, and water rights

Political parties and leaders:
Aland Coalition (a coalition of several political parties on the Aland Islands)
Center Party or Kesk [Juha SIPILA]
Christian Democrats or KD [Sari ESSAYAH]
Finns Party or PS [Jussi HALLA-AHO]
Green League or Vihr [Pekka HAAVISTO]
Left Alliance or Vas [Li ANDERSSON]]
National Coalition Party or Kok [Petteri ORPO]
Social Democratic Party or SDP [Antti RINNE]
Swedish People's Party or SFP [Anna-Maja HENRIKSSON]

International organization participation:
ADB (nonregional member), AfDB (nonregional member), Arctic Council, Australia Group, BIS, CBSS, CD, CE, CERN, EAPC, EBRD, ECB, EIB, EITI (implementing country), EMU, ESA, EU, FAO, FATF, G-9, IADB, IAEA, IBRD, ICAO, ICC (national committees), ICCt, ICRM, IDA, IEA, IFAD, IFC, IFRCS, IHO, ILO, IMF, IMO, IMSO, Interpol, IOC, IOM, IPU, ISO, ITSO, ITU, ITUC (NGOs), MIGA, MINUSMA, NC, NEA, NIB, NSG, OAS (observer), OECD, OPCW, OSCE, Pacific Alliance (observer), Paris Club, PCA, PFP, Schengen Convention, UN, UNCTAD, UNESCO, UNHCR, UNIDO, UNIFIL, UNMIL, UNMOGIP, UNRWA, UNTSO, UPU, WCO, WFTU (NGOs), WHO, WIPO, WMO, WTO, ZC

Diplomatic representation in the US:
chief of mission: Ambassador Kirsti KAUPPI (since 17 September 2015)
chancery: 3301 Massachusetts Avenue NW, Washington, DC 20008
telephone: [1] (202) 298-5800
FAX: [1] (202) 298-6030
consulate(s) general: Los Angeles, New York

Diplomatic representation from the US:
chief of mission: Ambassador Robert "Bob" Frank PENCE (since 24 May 2018) (2018)
embassy: Itainen Puistotie 14B, 00140 Helsinki
mailing address: APO AE 09723
telephone: [358] (9) 6162-50
FAX: [358] (9) 6162-5135

Flag description: white with a blue cross that extends to the edges of the flag; the vertical part of the cross is shifted to the hoist side in the style of the Dannebrog (Danish flag)

ECONOMY

Finland has a highly industrialized, largely free-market economy with per capita GDP almost as high as that of Austria and the Netherlands and slightly above that of Germany and Belgium. Trade is important, with exports accounting for over one-third of GDP in recent years. The government is open to, and actively takes steps to attract, foreign direct investment.

Finland is historically competitive in manufacturing - principally the wood, metals, engineering, telecommunications, and electronics industries. Finland excels in export of technology as well as promotion of startups in the information and communications technology, gaming, cleantech, and biotechnology sectors. Except for timber and several minerals, Finland depends on imports of raw materials, energy, and some components for manufactured goods. Because of the cold climate, agricultural development is limited to maintaining self-sufficiency in basic products. Forestry, an important export industry, provides a secondary occupation for the rural population.

Finland had been one of the best performing economies within the EU before 2009 and its banks and financial markets avoided the worst of global financial crisis. However, the world slowdown hit exports and domestic demand hard in that year, causing Finland's economy to contract from 2012 to 2014. The recession affected general government finances and the debt ratio. The economy returned to growth in 2015, posting a 0.3% GDP increase before growing 1.4% in 2016.

Finland's main challenges will be reducing high labor costs and boosting demand for its exports. In June 2016, the government enacted a Competitiveness Pact aimed at reducing labor costs, increasing hours worked, and introducing more flexibility into the wage bargaining system. The Government was also seeking to reform the health care system and social services. In the long term, Finland must address a rapidly aging population and decreasing productivity in traditional industries that threaten competitiveness, fiscal sustainability, and economic growth.

GDP (purchasing power parity):

$231.4 billion (est.)
$228.2 billion (2015 est.)
$227.6 billion (2014 est.)
note: data are in 2016 dollars
country comparison to the world: 63

GDP (official exchange rate):
$236.9 billion (est.)

GDP - real growth rate:
1.4% (est.)
0.3% (2015 est.)
-0.6% (2014 est.)
country comparison to the world: 167

GDP - per capita (PPP):
$42,200 (2015 est.)
$41,700 (2014 est.)
$41,800 (2017 est.)
note: data are in 2016 dollars
country comparison to the world: 41

Gross national saving:
20.9% of GDP (est.)
20.7% of GDP (2015 est.)
19.8% of GDP (2014 est.)
country comparison to the world: 88

GDP - composition, by end use:
household consumption: 55.1%
government consumption: 24.2%
investment in fixed capital: 20.2%
investment in inventories: -0.1%
exports of goods and services: 35.4%
imports of goods and services: -34.8% (est.)

GDP - composition, by sector of origin:
agriculture: 2.5%
industry: 26.9%
services: 70.6% (est.)

Agriculture - products:
barley, wheat, sugar beets, potatoes; dairy cattle; fish
Industries:
metals and metal products, electronics, machinery and scientific instruments, shipbuilding, pulp and paper, foodstuffs, chemicals, textiles, clothing

Industrial production growth rate:
0.8% (est.)
country comparison to the world: 152

Labor force:
2.675 million (est.)
country comparison to the world: 112

Labor force - by occupation:
agriculture: 4.5%
industry: 24%
services: 71.5% (2014)

Unemployment rate:
8.8% (est.)

9.4% (2015 est.)
country comparison to the world: 109

Population below poverty line:
NA%
Household income or consumption by percentage share:
lowest 10%: 4.2%
highest 10%: 21.5% (2015)

Distribution of family income - Gini index:
21.5 (2015)
26.8 (2008)
country comparison to the world: 149

Budget:
revenues: $128.5 billion
expenditures: $132.7 billion
note: Central Government Budget (est.)

Taxes and other revenues:
53.7% of GDP (est.)
country comparison to the world: 9

Budget surplus (+) or deficit (-):
-1.8% of GDP (est.)
country comparison to the world: 71

Public debt:
63.6% of GDP (est.)
63.7% of GDP (2015 est.)
note: data cover general government debt, and includes debt instruments issued (or owned) by government entities other than the treasury; the data include treasury debt held by foreign entities; the data include debt issued by subnational entities, as well as intra-governmental debt; intra-governmental debt consists of treasury borrowings from surpluses in the social funds, such as for retirement, medical care, and unemployment; debt instruments for the social funds are not sold at public auctions
country comparison to the world: 58

Fiscal year:
calendar year

Inflation rate (consumer prices):
0.4% (est.)
-0.2% (2015 est.)
country comparison to the world: 49

Central bank discount rate:
0.25% (31 December 2016)
0.3% (31 December 2010)
note: this is the European Central Bank's rate on the marginal lending facility, which offers overnight credit to banks in the euro area
country comparison to the world: 134

Commercial bank prime lending rate:

1.46% (31 December 2016 est.)
2% (31 December 2015 est.)
country comparison to the world: 182

Stock of narrow money:
$130.2 billion (31 December 2016 est.)
$123.7 billion (31 December 2015 est.)
note: see entry for the European Union for money supply for the entire euro area; the European Central Bank (ECB) controls monetary policy for the 18 members of the Economic and Monetary Union (EMU); individual members of the EMU do not control the quantity of money circulating within their own borders
country comparison to the world: 30

Stock of broad money:
$177.3 billion (31 December 2016 est.)
$174.1 billion (31 December 2015 est.)
country comparison to the world: 44

Stock of domestic credit:
$355.3 billion (31 December 2016 est.)
$357.9 billion (31 December 2015 est.)
country comparison to the world: 32

Market value of publicly traded shares:
$133.7 billion (31 December 2016 est.)
$NA (31 December 2015 est.)
$154.4 billion (31 December 2014 est.)
country comparison to the world: 38

Current account balance:
$-2.511 billion (est.)
$-968 million (2015 est.)
country comparison to the world: 155

Exports:
$59.6 billion (est.)
$57.45 billion (2015 est.)
country comparison to the world: 42

Exports - commodities:
electrical and optical equipment, machinery, transport equipment, paper and pulp, chemicals, basic metals; timber

Exports - partners:
Germany 13.9%, Sweden 10.1%, US 7%, Netherlands 6.6%, Russia 5.9%, UK 5.2%, China 4.7% (2015)

Imports:
$60.51 billion (est.)
$60.46 billion (2015 est.)
country comparison to the world: 43

Imports - commodities:

foodstuffs, petroleum and petroleum products, chemicals, transport equipment, iron and steel, machinery, computers, electronic industry products, textile yarn and fabrics, grains

Imports - partners:
Germany 17%, Sweden 16.1%, Russia 10.9%, Netherlands 9%, Denmark 4.1% (2015)

Reserves of foreign exchange and gold:
$10.6 billion (31 December 2016 est.)
$10 billion (31 December 2015 est.)
country comparison to the world: 73

Debt - external:
$544.7 billion (31 March 2016 est.)
$524.7 billion (31 March 2015 est.)
country comparison to the world: 20

Stock of direct foreign investment - at home:
$153.5 billion (31 December 2016 est.)
$135.9 billion (31 December 2015 est.)
country comparison to the world: 35

Stock of direct foreign investment - abroad:
$140.6 billion (31 December 2016 est.)
$141.1 billion (31 December 2015 est.)
country comparison to the world: 31

Exchange rates:
euros (EUR) per US dollar -
0.92 (est.)
0.89 (2015 est.)
0.89 (2014 est.)
0.76 (2017 est.)
0.78 (2012 est.)

ENERGY

Electricity - production:
70.34 billion kWh
country comparison to the world: 39

Electricity - consumption:
84.83 billion kWh
country comparison to the world: 36

Electricity - exports:
1.645 billion kWh
country comparison to the world: 46

Electricity - imports:
19.09 billion kWh
country comparison to the world: 9

Electricity - installed generating

capacity:
16.68 million kW
country comparison to the world: 43

Electricity - from fossil fuels:
52.3% of total installed capacity
country comparison to the world: 151

Electricity - from nuclear fuels:
16.2% of total installed capacity
country comparison to the world: 14

Electricity - from hydroelectric plants:
18.8% of total installed capacity
country comparison to the world: 93

Electricity - from other renewable sources:
12.7% of total installed capacity
country comparison to the world: 19

Crude oil - production:
13,530 bbl/day
country comparison to the world: 85

Crude oil - exports:
0 bbl/day
country comparison to the world: 110

Crude oil - imports:
214,700 bbl/day (2010 est.)
country comparison to the world: 32

Crude oil - proved reserves:
0 bbl
country comparison to the world: 130

Refined petroleum products - production:
282,300 bbl/day
country comparison to the world: 44

Refined petroleum products - consumption:
204,800 bbl/day
country comparison to the world: 57

Refined petroleum products - exports:

144,400 bbl/day
country comparison to the world: 38

Refined petroleum products - imports:
113,800 bbl/day
country comparison to the world: 48

Natural gas - production:
0 cu m
country comparison to the world: 129

Natural gas - consumption:
4.7 billion cu m
country comparison to the world: 64

Natural gas - exports:
0 cu m
country comparison to the world: 98

Natural gas - imports:
3.661 billion cu m
country comparison to the world: 39

Natural gas - proved reserves:
0 cu m
country comparison to the world: 136

Carbon dioxide emissions from consumption of energy:
54.06 million Mt

COMMUNICATIONS

Telephones - main lines in use:
890,000
country comparison to the world: 79

Telephones - mobile cellular:
9.32 million
country comparison to the world: 83

Telephone system:
general assessment: modern system with excellent service
domestic: digital fiber-optic fixed-line network and an extensive mobile-cellular network provide domestic needs
international: country code - 358; submarine cables provide links to Estonia and Sweden; satellite earth stations - access to Intelsat transmission service via a Swedish satellite earth station, 1 Inmarsat (Atlantic and Indian Ocean regions); note - Finland shares the Inmarsat earth station with the other Nordic countries (Denmark, Iceland, Norway, and Sweden)

Broadcast media:
a mix of publicly operated TV stations and privately owned TV stations; the 2 publicly owned TV stations recently expanded services and the largest private TV station has introduced several special-interest pay-TV channels; cable and satellite multi-channel subscription services are available; all TV signals have been broadcast digitally since September 2007; analog broadcasts via cable networks were terminated in February 2008; public broadcasting maintains a network of 13 national and 25 regional radio stations; a large number of private radio broadcasters

Internet country code:
.fi; note - Aland Islands assigned .ax

Internet hosts:
4.763 million
country comparison to the world: 22

Internet users:
4.393 million
country comparison to the world: 55

TRANSPORTATION

Railways:
total: 5,865 km
broad gauge: 5,865 km 1.524-m gauge (2,192 km electrified; 480 km double- or multiple-track)
Highways:
total: 77,895 km
paved: 49,853 km (including 473 km of expressways)
unpaved: 28,042 km
Waterways: 6,675 km total (including Saimaa Canal); 3,700 km suitable for steamers
Pipelines: natural gas 580 km
Ports and harbors: Hamina, Helsinki, Kokkola, Kotka, Loviisa, Oulu, Pori, Rauma, Turku, Uusikaupunki, Varkaus
Merchant marine:
total: 101 ships (1,000 GRT or over) totaling 1,185,966 GRT/1,153,089 DWT
ships by type: bulk 9, cargo 23, chemical tanker 6, passenger 1, petroleum tanker 11, rail car carrier 1, roll-on/roll-off 38, short-sea passenger 12
Airports: 157
Airports - with paved runways:
total: 69
over 3,047 m: 3
2,438 to 3,047 m: 26
1,524 to 2,437 m: 10
914 to 1,523 m: 20
under 914 m: 10
Airports - with unpaved runways:
total: 88
914 to 1,523 m: 6
under 914 m: 82

MILITARY

Finnish Defense Forces (FDF): Army (Puolustusvoimat), Navy (Merivoimat; includes Coastal Defense Forces), Air Force (Ilmavoimat)

Military service age and obligation:
18 years of age for male voluntary and compulsory - and female voluntary - national military and nonmilitary service; service obligation 6-12 months; military obligation to age 60

Manpower available for military service:
males age 16-49: 1,155,368
females age 16-49: 1,106,193

Manpower fit for military service:
males age 16-49: 955,151
females age 16-49: 912,983

Manpower reaching militarily significant age annually:
male: 32,599
female: 31,416

Military expenditures:
1.47% of GDP
1.42% of GDP (2011)
1.47% of GDP (2010)
country comparison to the world: 62

TRANSNATIONAL ISSUES

Disputes - international:
various groups in Finland advocate restoration of Karelia and other areas ceded to the Soviet Union, but the Finnish Government asserts no territorial demands

Refugees and internally displaced persons:

stateless persons: 2,293 (2014)

IMPORTANT INFORMATION FOR UNDERSTANDING FINLAND

Official Name: Republic of Finland

PROFILE

GEOGRAPHY

Area: 337,113 sq. km. (130,160 sq. mi.); about the size of New England, New Jersey, and New York combined.
Cities: Capital -- Helsinki (pop. 525,000). Other cities -- Tampere (182,700), Turku (164,700).
Terrain: Low but hilly, more than 70% forested, with more than 60,000 lakes.
Climate: Northern temperate.

PEOPLE

Nationality: Noun -- Finn(s). Adjective -- Finnish.
Population: 5.13 million.
Population growth rate: 0.3%.
Ethnic groups: Finns, Swedes, Lapps, Roma, Tartars.
Religions: Lutheran 89%, Orthodox 1%.
Languages: Finnish 93%, Swedish 6% (both official); small Lapp- and Russian-speaking minorities.
Education: Years compulsory -- 9. Attendance -- almost 100%. Literacy -- almost 100%.
Health: Infant mortality rate -- 3.8/1,000. Life expectancy -- males 72 yrs., females 80 yrs.
Work force (2.5 million; of which 2 million are employed): Public services -- 32%. Industry -- 22%. Commerce -- 14%. Finance, insurance, and business services -- 10%. Agriculture and forestry -- 8%. Transport and communications -- 8%. Construction -- 6%.

GOVERNMENT

Type: Constitutional republic.
Constitution: July 17, 1919.
Independence: December 6, 1917.
Branches: Executive -- president (chief of state), prime minister (head of government), Council of State (cabinet). Legislative -- unicameral parliament. Judicial -- Supreme Court, regional appellate courts, local courts.
Subdivisions: 12 provinces, provincial self-rule for the Aland Islands.
Political parties: Social Democratic Party, Center Party, National Coalition (Conservative) Party, Leftist Alliance, Swedish People's Party, Green Party.
Suffrage: Universal at 18.

HISTORY

The origins of the Finnish people are still a matter of conjecture, although many scholars argue that their original home was in what is now west-central Siberia. The Finns arrived in their present territory thousands of years ago, pushing the indigenous Lapps into the more remote northern regions. Finnish and Lappish -- the language of Finland's small Lapp minority -- both are Finno-Ugric languages and are in the Uralic rather than the Indo-European family.

Finland's nearly 700-year association with the Kingdom of Sweden began in 1154 with the introduction of Christianity by Sweden's King Eric. During the ensuing centuries, Finland played an important role in the political life of the Swedish-Finnish realm, and Finnish soldiers often predominated in Swedish armies. Finns also formed a significant proportion of the first "Swedish" settlers in 17th-century America.

Following Finland's incorporation into Sweden in the 12th century, Swedish became the dominant language, although Finnish recovered its predominance after a 19th-century resurgence of Finnish nationalism. Publication in 1835 of the Finnish national epic, The Kalevala -- a collection of traditional myths and legends -- first stirred the nationalism that later led to Finland's independence from Russia.

In 1809, Finland was conquered by the armies of Czar Alexander I and thereafter remained an autonomous grand duchy connected with the Russian Empire until the end of 1917. On December 6, 1917, shortly after the Bolshevik Revolution in Russia, Finland declared its independence. In 1918, the country experienced a brief but bitter civil war that colored domestic politics for many years. During World War II, Finland fought the Soviet Union twice -- in the Winter War of 1939-40 and again in the Continuation War of 1941-44. This was followed by the Lapland War of 1944-45, when Finland fought against the Germans as they withdrew their forces from northern Finland.

Treaties signed in 1947 and 1948 with the Soviet Union included obligations and restraints on Finland vis-a-vis the U.S.S.R. as well as territorial concessions by Finland; both have been abrogated by Finland since the 1991 dissolution of the Soviet Union (see Foreign Relations).

GOVERNMENT AND POLITICAL CONDITIONS

Finland has a mixed presidential/parliamentary system with executive powers divided between the president, who has primary responsibility for national security and foreign affairs, and the prime minister, who has primary responsibility for all other areas. Constitutional changes made in the late 1980s strengthened the prime minister -- who must enjoy the confidence of the parliament (Eduskunta) -- at the expense of the president. Finland's 1995 accession to the European Union has blurred the line between foreign and domestic policy; the respective roles of the president and prime minister are evolving, and plans are under consideration to rewrite the constitution to clarify these and other issues.

Finns enjoy individual and political freedoms, and suffrage is universal at 18. The country's population is ethnically homogeneous with no sizable immigrant population. Few tensions exist between the Finnish-speaking majority and the Swedish-speaking minority.

Elected for a 6-year term, the president:

- Handles foreign policy, except for certain international agreements and decisions of peace or war, which must be submitted to the parliament;
- Is commander-in-chief of the armed forces and has wide decree and appointive powers;
- May initiate legislation, block legislation by pocket veto, and call extraordinary parliamentary sessions; and
- Appoints the prime minister and the rest of the cabinet (Council of State).

The Council of State is made up of the prime minister and ministers for the various departments of the central government as well as an ex-officio member, the Chancellor of Justice. Ministers are not obliged to be members of the Eduskunta and need not be formally identified with any political party.

Constitutionally, the 200-member unicameral Eduskunta is the supreme authority in Finland. It may alter the constitution, bring about the resignation of the Council of State, and override presidential vetoes; its acts are not subject to judicial review. Legislation may be initiated by the president, the Council of State, or one of the Eduskunta members.

The Eduskunta is elected on the basis of proportional representation. All persons 18 or older, except military personnel on active duty and a few high judicial officials, are eligible for election. The regular parliamentary term is four years; however, the president may dissolve the Eduskunta and order new elections at the request of the prime minister and after consulting the speaker of parliament.

The judicial system is divided between courts with regular civil and criminal jurisdiction and special courts with responsibility for litigation between the public and the administrative organs of the state. Finnish law is codified. Although there is no writ of habeas corpus or bail, the maximum period of pre-trial detention has been reduced to four days. The Finnish court system consists of local courts, regional appellate courts, and a Supreme Court.

Finland has 12 provinces. Below the provincial level, they are divided into cities, townships, and communes administered by municipal and communal councils elected by proportional representation once every four years. At the provincial level, the 11 mainland provinces are administered by provincial boards composed of civil servants, each headed by a presidentially appointed governor. The boards are responsible to the Ministry of the Interior and play a supervisory and coordinating role within the provinces.

The island province of Aland is located near the 60th parallel between Sweden and Finland. It enjoys local autonomy by virtue of an international convention of 1921, implemented most recently by the Act on Aland Self-Government of 1951. The islands are further distinguished by the fact that they are entirely Swedish-speaking. Government is vested in the provincial council, which consists of 30 delegates elected directly by Aland's citizens.

Finland's defense forces consist of 34,700 persons in uniform (27,300 army; 3,000 navy; and 4,400 air force); the country's defense budget equals about 2% of GDP. There is universal male conscription under which all men serve from eight to 11 months. As of 1995, women were permitted to serve as volunteers. A reserve force ensures that Finland can field 500,000 trained military personnel in case of need.

Finland's proportional representation system encourages a multitude of political parties and has resulted in many coalition governments. Political activity by communists was legalized in 1944, and although four major parties have dominated the postwar political arena, none now has a majority position. The Social Democratic Party (SDP) gained a plurality in Finland's parliament in the general election of March 1995. But it won far less than an overall majority and so formed a five-party governing coalition.

The SDP won 28% of the vote in 1995, mainly among the urban working class but also with some support among small farmers, white-collar workers, and professionals. The Leftist Alliance (LA) -- the SDP's rival on the left -- gained 11% of the vote in 1995 and joined the SDP-led government. The LA was formed in May 1990 and replaced the People's Democratic League, the group that represented the Finnish Communist Party in the Eduskunta.

Finland's two other major parties are the Center Party, traditionally representing rural interests, and the National Coalition -- or Conservative -- Party, which draws its major support from the business community and urban professionals. The Center won nearly 20% and the Conservatives 18% of the vote in 1995. The Conservatives are the second-largest party in the SDP-led coalition, which is rounded out by the Swedish People's Party and the Green Party. The Center Party leads the opposition in Parliament.

PRINCIPAL GOVERNMENT OFFICIALS

Portfolio	Minister	Took office	Left office	Party
Prime Minister	Juha Sipilä	29 May 2015	Incumbent	Centre
Minister of Foreign Affairs Deputy Prime Minister	Timo Soini	29 May 2015	Incumbent	Finns
Minister of Finance	Alexander Stubb	29 May 2015	Incumbent	National Coalition
Minister for Foreign Trade and Development	Lenita Toivakka	29 May 2015	Incumbent	National Coalition
Minister of Justice and Employment	Jari Lindström	29 May 2015	Incumbent	Finns
Minister of Interior	Petteri Orpo	29 May 2015	Incumbent	National Coalition
Minister of Defence	Jussi Niinistö	29 May 2015	Incumbent	Finns
Minister of Local Government and Public Reforms	Anu Vehviläinen	29 May 2015	Incumbent	Centre
Minister of Education and Culture	Sanni Grahn-Laasonen	29 May 2015	Incumbent	National Coalition
Minister of Agriculture and the Environment	Kimmo Tiilikainen	29 May 2015	Incumbent	Centre
Minister of Transport and Communications	Anne Berner	29 May 2015	Incumbent	Centre
Minister of Economic Affairs	Olli Rehn	29 May 2015	Incumbent	Centre
Minister of Social Affairs and Health	Hanna Mäntylä	29 May 2015	Incumbent	Finns
Minister of Family Affairs and Social Services	Juha Rehula	29 May 2015	Incumbent	Centre

Finland's embassy in the United States is at 3301 Massachusetts Avenue, NW, Washington, DC 20008; tel: 202-298-5800; fax: 202-298-6030.

ECONOMY

Rank	41st (nominal) / 53rd (PPP)
Currency	Euro (EUR)
Fiscal year	calendar year
Trade organisations	EU, WTO and OECD
	Statistics
GDP	$194.1 billion (PPP est.) $244.3 billion (est.)
GDP growth	▼-1.4%
GDP per capita	▲$38,271 (PPP; est.)
GDP by sector	▼Agriculture: 2.8% ▼Industry: 25.9% ▲Services: 71.2%
Inflation (CPI)	▼3.2%
Population below poverty line	17.9% at risk of poverty or social exclusion
Gini coefficient	▲28.2
Labour force	▼2,385 million
Labour force by occupation	▼Agriculture and forestry 4.4% ▼Industry 15.5% ▼Construction 7.1% ▲Commerce 21.3% ▼Finance, insurance, and business services 13.3% ▲Transport and communications 9.9% ▼Public services 28.5%
Unemployment	▼8,5% (2014)
Average gross salary	▲3,190 € / 3,988 $, monthly
Average net salary	▲2,321 € / 2,901 $, monthly
Main industries	metals and metal products, electronics, machinery and scientific instruments, shipbuilding, pulp and paper, foodstuffs, chemicals, textiles, clothing
Ease-of-doing-business rank	▬12th
	External
Exports	▼$78.23 billion
Export goods	Electrical and optical equipment, machinery, transport equipment, paper and pulp, chemicals, basic metals; timber
Main export partners	Sweden 11.1% ▲Russia 10.0% ▼Germany 9.2% ▼Netherlands 6.3% ▲United States 6.3% United Kingdom 5.1% China 4.6%
Imports	▼$81.86 billion
Import goods	foodstuffs, petroleum and petroleum products, chemicals, transport equipment, iron and steel, machinery, textile yarn and fabrics, grains
Main import partners	▬Russia 17.8% ▼Germany 12.3% ▼Sweden 10.7%

	▼ Netherlands 5.7%
	▲ China 7.7%
	▼ Norway 3.6%
	▲ United States 3.4%
FDI stock	▲ $100.76 billion
Gross external debt	▲ $563.1 billion
Public finances	
Public debt	56.9% of GDP (est.), net debt 17.4% of GDP
Revenues	$129.4 billion
Expenses	$134 billion (2012 est.)
Economic aid	donor: ODA, $1.023 billion
Credit rating	AAA (Domestic) AAA (Foreign) AAA (T&C Assessment) (Standard & Poor's)
Foreign reserves	US$11.492 billion

Finland has a highly industrialised, mixed economy with a per capita output equal to that of other western economies such as France, Germany, Sweden or the United Kingdom. The largest sector of the economy is services at 65.7 percent, followed by manufacturing and refining at 31.4 percent. Primary production is 2.9 percent.

With respect to foreign trade, the key economic sector is manufacturing. The largest industries are electronics (21.6 percent), machinery, vehicles and other engineered metal products (21.1 percent), forest industry (13.1 percent), and chemicals (10.9 percent). Finland has timber and several mineral and freshwater resources. Forestry, paper factories, and the agricultural sector (on which taxpayers spend around 2 billion euro annually) are politically sensitive to rural residents. The Greater Helsinki area generates around a third of GDP.

In a 2004 OECD comparison, high-technology manufacturing in Finland ranked second largest after Ireland. Knowledge-intensive services have also ranked the smallest and slow-growth sectors – especially agriculture and low-technology manufacturing – second largest after Ireland. Investment was below expected. Overall short-term outlook was good and GDP growth has been above many EU peers. Finland has the 4th largest knowledge economy in Europe, behind Sweden, Denmark and the UK. The economy of Finland tops the ranking of Global Information Technology 2014 report by the World Economic Forum for concerted output between business sector, scholarly production and the governmental assistance on Information and communications technology.

Finland is highly integrated in the global economy, and international trade is a third of GDP. The European Union makes 60 percent of the total trade. The largest trade flows are with Germany, Russia, Sweden, the United Kingdom, the United States, Netherlands and China. Trade policy is managed by the European Union, where Finland has traditionally been among the free trade supporters, except for agriculture. Finland is the only Nordic country to have joined the Eurozone; Denmark and Sweden have retained their traditional currencies, whereas Iceland and Norway are not members of the EU at all.

Finland has a dynamic industrial economy based on abundant forest resources, capital investments, and technology. Traditionally, Finland has been a net importer of capital to finance industrial growth. In the 1980s, Finland's economic growth rate was one of the highest of industrialized countries.

In 1991, Finland fell into a deep recession caused by economic overheating, depressed foreign markets, and the dismantling of the barter system between Finland and the former Soviet Union. The same year, Finland devalued the markka to promote export competitiveness. This helped stabilize the economy, and the recession bottomed out in 1993.

Exports of goods contribute more than 20% of Finland's GDP; combined exports of goods and services amount to at least 25% of GDP. Exports and imports of goods equal about 40% of GDP. Timber and metalworking are Finland's main industries, but other industries produce manufactured goods ranging from electronics to motor vehicles. Finnish-designed consumer products such as textiles, porcelain, and glassware are world-famous.

Except for timber and several minerals, Finland depends on imported raw materials, energy, and some components for its manufactured products. Farms tend to be small, but sizable timber stands are harvested for supplementary income in winter. The country's main agricultural products are dairy, meat, and grains. Finland's EU accession has accelerated the process of restructuring and downsizing of this sector.

An extensive social welfare system, constituting about one-fifth of the national income, includes a variety of pension and assistance programs and a comprehensive health insurance program. Although free education through the university level also is available, only about one child in four receives a higher education in the highly competitive system. In the mid-1970s, the educational system was reformed with the goal of equalizing educational opportunities. Beginning at age seven, all Finnish children are required to attend a "basic school" of nine grade levels. After this, they may elect to continue along an academic (lukio) or vocational (ammat-tikoulu) line. But most pursue vocational studies, since the number of openings in higher educational institutions is less than the demand.

FOREIGN RELATIONS

Finland's basic foreign policy goal from the end of the Continuation War with the U.S.S.R. in 1944 until 1991 was to avoid great-power conflicts and to build mutual confidence with the Soviet Union. Although the country was culturally, socially, and politically Western, Finns realized they must live in peace with the U.S.S.R. and take no action that might be interpreted as a security threat. The dissolution of the Soviet Union in 1991 opened up dramatic new possibilities for Finland and has resulted in the Finns actively seeking greater participation in Western political and economic structures.

RELATIONS WITH RUSSIA

The principal architect of the post-1944 foreign policy of neutrality was J.K. Paasikivi, who was President from 1946 to 1956. Urho Kekkonen, President from 1956 until 1981, further developed this policy, stressing that Finland should be an active rather than a passive neutral. This policy is now popularly known as the "Paasikivi-Kekkonen Line."

Finland and the U.S.S.R. signed a peace treaty at Paris in February 1947 limiting the size of Finland's defense forces and providing for the cession to the Soviet Union of the Petsamo area on the Arctic coast, the Karelian Isthmus in southeastern Finland, and other territory along the former eastern border. Another provision, terminated in 1956, leased the Porkkala area near Helsinki to the U.S.S.R. for use as a naval base and gave free access to this area across Finnish territory.

The 1947 treaty also called for Finland to pay to the Soviet Union reparations of 300 million gold dollars (amounting to an estimated $570 million in 1952, the year the payments ended). Although an ally of the Soviet Union in World War II, the United States was not a signatory to this treaty because it had not been at war with Finland.

In April 1948, Finland signed an Agreement of Friendship, Cooperation, and Mutual Assistance with the Soviet Union. Under this mutual assistance pact, Finland was obligated -- with the aid of the Soviet Union, if necessary -- to resist armed attacks by Germany or its allies against Finland or against the U.S.S.R. through Finland. At the same time, the agreement recognized Finland's desire to remain outside great-power conflicts. This agreement was renewed for 20 years in 1955, in 1970, and again in 1983 to the year 2003.

The Finns responded cautiously in 1990-91 to the decline of Soviet power and the U.S.S.R.'s subsequent dissolution. They unilaterally abrogated restrictions imposed by the 1947 and 1948 treaties, joined in voicing Nordic concern over the coup against Soviet leader Mikhail Gorbachev, and gave increasing unofficial encouragement to Baltic independence.

At the same time, by replacing the Soviet-Finnish mutual assistance pact with treaties on general cooperation and trade, Finns put themselves on an equal footing while retaining a friendly bilateral relationship. Finland now is boosting cross-border commercial ties and touting its potential as a commercial gateway to Russia. It has reassured Russia that it will not raise claims for Finnish territory seized by the U.S.S.R., and continues to reaffirm the importance of good bilateral relations.

MULTILATERAL RELATIONS

Finnish foreign policy emphasizes its participation in multilateral organizations. Finland joined the United Nations in 1955 and the EU in 1995. As noted, the country also is a member of NATO's Partnership for Peace as well as an observer in the North Atlantic Cooperation Council and the Western European Union.

Finland is well represented in the UN civil service in proportion to its population and belongs to several of its specialized and related agencies. Finnish troops have participated in UN peacekeeping activities since 1956, and the Finns continue to be one of the largest per capita contributors of peacekeepers in the world. Finland is an active participant in the Organization for Security and Cooperation in Europe (OSCE).

Cooperation with the other Scandinavian countries also is important to Finland, and it has been a member of the Nordic Council since 1955. Under the council's auspices, the Nordic countries have created a common labor market and have abolished immigration controls among themselves. The council also serves to coordinate social and cultural policies of the participating countries and has promoted increased cooperation in many fields.

In addition to the organizations already mentioned, Finland is a member of the International Bank for Reconstruction and Development, the International Monetary Fund, the World Trade Organization, the International Finance Corporation, the International Development Association, the Bank for International Settlements, the Asian Development Bank, the Inter-American Development Bank, the Council of Europe, the Organization for Economic Cooperation and Development, and INTELSAT.

U.S.-FINLAND RELATIONS

The United States established diplomatic relations with Finland in 1919, following its 1917 declaration of independence from the Russian Empire. The United States severed diplomatic relations with Finland in 1944 during World War II, due to Finland's alliance with Nazi Germany. U.S.-Finland diplomatic relations were reestablished in 1945. Finland is bordered on the east by Russia and, as one of the former Soviet Union's neighbors, was of particular interest and importance to the United States both during the Cold War and in its aftermath. Before the Soviet Union dissolved in 1991, longstanding U.S. policy was to support Finnish neutrality while maintaining and reinforcing Finland's historic, cultural, and economic ties with the West.

The United States and Finland have enjoyed an enduring partnership and friendship. Finland has contributed to the advancement of technology and research, promotion of international economic development, and the defense of human rights and peace. The United States has welcomed Finland's integration into Western economic and political structures. In 1994, Finland joined the North Atlantic Treaty Organization's (NATO) Partnership for Peace program and was designated a NATO Enhanced Opportunity Partner at the 2014 Wales Summit. It became a full member of the European Union (EU) in 1995 and joined the EU's Economic and Monetary Union in 1999.

U.S. Assistance to Finland

The United States provides no development assistance to Finland.

Bilateral Economic Relations

Finland welcomes foreign investment. Exports from the United States to Finland include machinery, telecommunications equipment and parts, metalliferous ores, road vehicles and transport equipment, computers, peripherals and software, electronic components, chemicals, medical equipment, and some agricultural products. Imports from Finland to the United States include electronics, machinery, ships and boats, paper and paperboard, refined petroleum products, and telecommunications equipment and parts. Finland participates in the Visa Waiver Program, which allows nationals of participating countries to travel to the United States for certain business or tourism purposes for stays of 90 days or less without obtaining a visa.

Finland is a member of the European Union. The U.S. economic relationship with the EU is the largest and most complex in the world, and the United States and the EU continue to pursue initiatives to create new opportunities for transatlantic commerce.

Finland's Membership in International Organizations

Finland and the United States belong to a number of the same international organizations, including the United Nations, the Arctic Council, Euro-Atlantic Partnership Council, Organization for Security and Cooperation in Europe, Organization for Economic Cooperation and Development, International Monetary Fund, World Bank, and World Trade Organization. Finland also is an observer to the Organization of American States and is a NATO Enhanced Opportunity Partner.

Bilateral Representation

US EMBASSY HELSINKI (E) Itainen Puistotie 14, 00140 Helsinki, 358-9-6162-50,
Fax +358-9-6162-5135, Workweek: Monday-Friday 0830-1700,
Website: https://fi.usembassy.gov/

Officer Name
DCM OMS Seijefa Hauptmann
AMB OMS Rosi Smith
Co-CLO Nunzia Clouse
FCS Aaron Held

American Embassy
Address: Itäinen Puistotie 14 B, FIN-00140 Helsinki, Finland
Telephone: +358-9-171 931
E-mail: webmaster@usembassy.fi

U.S. TRADE IN GOODS WITH FINLAND

NOTE: All figures are in millions of U.S. dollars on a nominal basis, not seasonally adjusted unless otherwise specified. Details may not equal totals due to rounding. Table reflects only those months for which there was trade.

Month	Exports	Imports	Balance
January 2018	110.8	556.7	-445.9
February 2018	149.5	584.5	-435.0
March 2018	145.7	710.8	-565.0
April 2018	137.8	601.9	-464.0
May 2018	171.2	602.0	-430.7
June 2018	192.1	644.7	-452.6
July 2018	165.1	553.4	-388.3
August 2018	216.5	618.3	-401.8
September 2018	179.9	612.6	-432.7
October 2018	154.1	622.8	-468.7
November 2018	137.6	565.9	-428.3
December 2018	112.2	493.2	-381.0
TOTAL 2018	1,872.6	7,166.6	-5,294.0

TRAVEL AND BUSINESS INFORMATION

The U.S. Department of State's Consular Information Program provides Travel Warnings and Consular Information Sheets. **Travel Warnings** are issued when the State Department recommends that Americans avoid travel to a certain country. **Consular Information** Sheets exist for all countries and include information on immigration practices, currency regulations, health conditions, areas of instability, crime and security, political disturbances, and the addresses of the U.S. posts in the country. **Public Announcements** are issued as a means to disseminate information quickly about terrorist threats and other relatively short-term conditions overseas which pose significant risks to the security of American travelers. Free copies of this information are available by calling the Bureau of Consular Affairs at 202-647-5225 or via the fax-on-demand system: 202-647-3000. Travel Warnings and Consular Information Sheets also are available on the Consular Affairs Internet home page: http://travel.state.gov and the Consular Affairs Bulletin Board (CABB). To access CABB, dial the modem number: 301-946-4400 (it will accommodate up to 33,600 bps), set terminal communications program to N-8-1(no parity, 8 bits, 1 stop bit); and terminal emulation to VT100. The login is travel and the password is info. (Note: Lower case is required). The CABB also carries international security information from the

Overseas Security Advisory Council and Department's Bureau of Diplomatic Security. Consular Affairs Tips for Travelers publication series, which contain information on obtaining passports and planning a safe trip abroad, can be purchased from the Superintendent of Documents, U.S. Government Printing Office, P.O. Box 371954, Pittsburgh, PA 15250-7954; telephone: 202-512-1800; fax 202-512-2250.

Emergency information concerning Americans traveling abroad may be obtained from the Office of Overseas Citizens Services at (202) 647-5225. For after-hours emergencies, Sundays and holidays, call 202-647-4000.

Passport Services information can be obtained by calling the 24-hour, 7-day a week automated system ($.35 per minute) or live operators 8 a.m. to 8 p.m. (EST) Monday-Friday ($1.05 per minute). The number is 1-900-225-5674 (TDD: 1-900-225-7778). Major credit card users (for a flat rate of $4.95) may call 1-888-362-8668 (TDD: 1-888-498-3648).

Travelers can check the latest health information with the U.S. Centers for Disease Control and Prevention in Atlanta, Georgia. A hotline at 877-FYI-TRIP (877-394-8747) and a web site at http://www.cdc.gov/travel/index.htm give the most recent health advisories, immunization recommendations or requirements, and advice on food and drinking water safety for regions and countries. A booklet entitled Health Information for International Travel (HHS publication number CDC-95-8280) is available from the U.S. Government Printing Office, Washington, DC 20402, tel. (202) 512-1800.

Information on travel conditions, visa requirements, currency and customs regulations, legal holidays, and other items of interest to travelers also may be obtained before your departure from a country's embassy and/or consulates in the U.S. (for this country, see "Principal Government Officials" listing in this publication).

U.S. citizens who are long-term visitors or traveling in dangerous areas are encouraged to register at the U.S. embassy upon arrival in a country (see "Principal U.S. Embassy Officials" listing in this publication). This may help family members contact you in case of an emergency.

STRATEGIC INFORMATION FOR BUSINESS AND INVESMENTS

ECONOMIC DEVELOPMENT

Finland has a highly industrialised, mixed economy with a per capita output similar to that of other western European economies such as France, Germany and United Kingdom but slightly lower than Sweden. The largest sector of the economy is services at 72.7 percent, followed by manufacturing and refining at 31.4 percent. Primary production is 2.9 percent.

With respect to foreign trade, the key economic sector is manufacturing. The largest industries are electronics (21.6 percent), machinery, vehicles and other engineered metal products (21.1 percent), forest industry (13.1 percent), and chemicals (10.9 percent). Finland has timber and several mineral and freshwater resources. Forestry, paper factories, and the agricultural sector (on which taxpayers spend around 2 billion euro annually) are politically sensitive to rural residents. The Greater Helsinki area generates around a third of GDP.

In a 2004 OECD comparison, high-technology manufacturing in Finland ranked second largest after Ireland. Knowledge-intensive services have also ranked the smallest and slow-growth sectors – especially agriculture and low-technology manufacturing – second largest after Ireland. Investment was below expected. Overall short-term outlook was good and GDP growth has been above many EU peers. Finland has the 4th largest knowledge economy in Europe, behind Sweden, Denmark and the UK. The **economy of Finland** tops the ranking of Global Information Technology 2014 report by the World Economic Forum for concerted output between business sector, scholarly production and the governmental assistance on Information and communications technology.

Finland is highly integrated in the global economy, and international trade is a third of GDP. The European Union makes 60 percent of the total trade. The largest trade flows are with Germany, Russia, Sweden, the United Kingdom, the United States, Netherlands and China. Trade policy is managed by the European Union, where Finland has traditionally been among the free trade supporters, except for agriculture. Finland is the only Nordic country to have joined the Eurozone; Denmark and Sweden have retained their traditional currencies, whereas Iceland and Norway are not members of the EU at all.

GDP (in Bil. Euro)	GDP per capita (in Euro)	GDP growth (real)	Inflation rate (in Percent)	Unemployment (in Percent)	Government debt (in % of GDP)	
1980	33.7	7,059	▲5.7 %	▲11.6 %	5.3 %	10.9 %
2010	▲187.1	▲34,962	▲3.0 %	▲1.8 %	▲8.5 %	▲47.1 %
2011	▲196.9	▲36,625	▲2.6 %	▲3.3 %	▼7.8 %	▲48.5 %
2012	▲199.8	▲36,990	▼−1.4 %	▲3.2 %	▼7.7 %	▲53.9 %
2013	▲203.3	▲37,470	▼−0.8 %	▲2.2 %	▲8.2 %	▲56.5 %
2014	▲205.5	▲37,693	▼−0.6 %	▲1.2 %	▲8.7 %	▲60.2 %
2015	▲209.6	▲38,307	▲0.1 %	▼0.2 %	▲9.4 %	▲63.6 %
2016	▲215.8	▲39,322	▲2.1 %	▲0.4 %	▼8.8 %	▼63.0 %
2017	▲224.3	▲40,753	▲3.0 %	▲0.8 %	▼8.7 %	▼61.4 %

INCOME AND CONSUMPTION

Finland's income is generated by the approximately 1.8 million private sector workers, who make an average 25.1 euro per hour (before the median 60% tax wedge) in 2007. According to a 2003 report, residents worked on average around 10 years for the same employer and around 5 different jobs over a lifetime. 62 percent worked for small and medium-sized enterprises. Female employment rate was high and gender segregation on career choices was higher than in the US. In 1999 part-time work rate was one of the smallest in OECD.

Future liabilities are dominated by the pension deficit. Unlike in Sweden, where pension savers can manage their investments, in Finland employers choose a pension fund for the employee. The pension funding rate is higher than in most Western European countries, but still only a portion of it is funded and pensions exclude health insurances and other unaccounted promises Directly held public debt has been reduced to around 32 percent in 2007. In 2007, the average household savings rate was -3.8 and household debt 101 percent of annual disposable income, a typical level in Europe.

In 2008, the OECD reported that "the gap between rich and poor has widened more in Finland than in any other wealthy industrialised country over the past decade" and that "Finland is also one of the few countries where inequality of incomes has grown between the rich and the middle-class, and not only between rich and poor."

In 2006, there were 2,381,500 households of average size 2.1 people. Forty percent of households consisted of single person, 32 percent two and 28 percent three or more. There were 1.2 million residential buildings in Finland and the average residential space was 38 square metres per person. The average residential property (without land) cost 1,187 euro per square metre and residential land on 8.6 euro per square metre. Consumer energy prices were 8-12 euro cent per kilowatt hour. 74 percent of households had a car. There were 2.5 million cars and 0.4 other vehicles. Around 92 percent have mobile phones and 58 percent Internet connection at home. The average total household consumption was 20,000 euro, out of which housing at around 5500 euro, transport at around 3000 euro, food and beverages excluding alcoholic at around 2500 euro, recreation and culture at around 2000 euro. Upper-level white-collar households (409,653) consumed an average 27,456 euro, lower-level white-collar households (394,313) 20,935 euro, and blue-collar households (471,370) 19,415 euro

Finnish politicians have often emulated other Nordics and the Nordic model. Nordic's have been free-trading and relatively welcoming to skilled migrants for over a century, though in Finland immigration is a relatively new phenomenon. This is due largely to Finland's less hospitable climate and the fact that the Finnish language shares roots with none of the major world languages, making it more challenging than average for most to learn. The level of protection in commodity trade has been low, except for agricultural products.

As an economic environment, Finland's judiciary is efficient and effective. Finland is highly open to investment and free trade. Finland has top levels of economic freedom in many areas, although there is a heavy tax burden and inflexible job market. Finland is ranked 16th (ninth in Europe) in the 2008 Index of Economic Freedom. Recently, Finland has topped the patents per capita statistics, and overall productivity growth has been strong in areas such as electronics. While the manufacturing sector is thriving, OECD points out that the service sector would benefit substantially from policy improvements.

The IMD World Competitiveness Yearbook 2007 ranked Finland 17th most competitive, next to Germany, and lowest of the Nordics. while the World Economic Forum report has ranked Finland the most competitive country. Finland is one of the most fiscally responsible EU countries.

PRODUCT MARKET

Economists attribute much growth to reforms in the product markets. According to OECD, only four EU-15 countries have less regulated product markets (UK, Ireland, Denmark and Sweden) and only one has less regulated financial markets (Denmark). Nordic countries were pioneers in liberalising energy, postal, and other markets in Europe. The legal system is clear and business bureaucracy less than most countries. For instance, starting a business takes an average of 14 days, compared to the world average of 43 days and Denmark's average of 6 days. Property rights are well protected and contractual agreements are strictly honored. Finland is rated one of the least corrupted countries in Corruption Perceptions Index. Finland is rated 13th in the Ease of Doing Business Index. It indicates exceptional ease to trade across borders (5th), enforce contracts (7th), and close a business (5th), and exceptional hardship to employ workers (127th) and pay taxes (83rd).

JOB MARKET

According to the OECD, Finland's job market is the least flexible of the Nordic countries. Finland increased job market regulation in the 1970s to provide stability to manufacturers. In contrast, during the 1990s, Denmark liberalised its job market, Sweden moved to more decentralised contracts, whereas Finnish trade unions blocked many reforms. Many professions have legally recognized industry-wide contracts that lay down common terms of employment including seniority levels, holiday entitlements, and salary levels, usually as part of a Comprehensive Income Policy Agreement.

Those who favor less centralized labor market policies consider these agreements bureaucratic, inflexible, and along with tax rates, a key contributor to unemployment and distorted prices. Centralized agreements may hinder structural change as there are fewer incentives to acquire better skills, although Finland already enjoys one of the highest skill-levels in the world

TAXATION

Tax is collected mainly from municipal income tax, state income tax, state value added tax, customs fees, corporate taxes and special taxes. There are also property taxes, but municipal income tax pays most of municipal expenses. Taxation is conducted by a state agency, Verohallitus, which collects income taxes from each paycheck, and then pays the difference between tax liability and taxes paid as tax rebate or collects as tax arrears afterward. Municipal income tax is a flat tax of nominally 15-20%, with deductions applied, and directly funds the municipality (a city or rural locality). The state income tax is a progressive tax; low-income individuals do not necessarily pay any. The state transfers some of its income as state support to municipalities, particularly the poorer ones. Additionally, the state churches - Finnish Evangelical Lutheran Church and Finnish Orthodox Church - are integrated to the taxation system in order to tax their members.

The middle income worker's tax wedge is 46% and effective marginal tax rates are very high. Value-added tax is 24% for most items. Capital gains tax is 30-34% and corporate tax is 20%, about the EU median. Property taxes are low, but there is a transfer tax (1.6% for apartments or 4% for individual houses) for home buyers. There are high excise taxes on alcoholic beverages, tobacco, automobiles and motorcycles, motor fuels, lotteries, sweets and insurances. For instance, McKinsey estimates that a worker has to pay around 1600 euro for another's 400 euro service - restricting service supply and demand - though some taxation is avoided in the black market and self-service culture. Another study by Karlson, Johansson & Johnsson estimates that the percentage of the buyer's income entering the service vendor's wallet (inverted tax wedge) is slightly over 15%, compared to 10% in Belgium, 25% in France, 40% in Switzerland and 50% in the United States. Tax cuts have been in every post-depression government's agenda and the overall tax burden is now around 43% of GDP compared to 51.1% in Sweden, 34.7% in Germany, 33.5% in Canada, and 30.5% in Ireland.

State and municipal politicians have struggled to cut their consumption, which is very high at 51.7% of GDP compared to 56.6% in Sweden, 46.9 in Germany, 39.3 in Canada, and 33.5% in Ireland. Much of the taxes are spent on public sector employees, many of which are jobs-for-life and amount to 124,000 state employees and 430,000 municipal employees. That is 113 per 1000 residents (over a quarter of workforce) compared to 74 in the US, 70 in Germany, and 42 in Japan (8% of workforce). The Economist Intelligence Unit's ranking for Finland's e-readiness is high at 13th, compared to 1st for United States, 3rd for Sweden, 5th for Denmark, and 14th for Germany. Also, early and generous retirement schemes have contributed to high pension costs. Social spending such as health or education is around OECD median. Social transfers are also around OECD median. In 2001 Finland's outsourced proportion of spending was below Sweden's and above most other Western European countries. Finland's health care is more bureaucrat-managed than in most Western European countries, though many use private insurance or cash to enjoy private clinics. Some reforms toward more equal marketplace have been made in 2007-2008. In education, child nurseries, and elderly nurseries private competition is bottom-ranking compared to Sweden and most other Western countries. Some public monopolies such Alko remain, and are sometimes challenged by the European Union. The state has a programme where the number of jobs decreases by attrition: for two retirees, only one new employee is hired.

AGRICULTURE

Finland's climate and soils make growing crops a particular challenge. The country lies between 60° and 70° north latitude - as far north as Alaska - and has severe winters and relatively short growing seasons that are sometimes interrupted by frosts. However, because the Gulf Stream and the North Atlantic Drift Current moderate the climate, and because of the relatively low elevation of the land area, Finland contains half of the world's arable land north of 60° north latitude. In response to the climate, farmers have relied on quick-ripening and frost-resistant varieties of crops. Most farmland had originally been either forest or swamp, and the soil had usually required treatment with lime and years of cultivation to neutralise excess acid and to develop fertility. Irrigation was generally not necessary, but drainage systems were often needed to remove excess water.

Until the late nineteenth century, Finland's isolation required that most farmers concentrate on producing grains to meet the country's basic food needs. In the fall, farmers planted rye; in the spring, southern and central farmers started oats, while northern farmers seeded barley. Farms also grew small quantities of potatoes, other root crops, and legumes. Nevertheless, the total area under cultivation was still small. Cattle grazed in the summer and consumed hay in the winter. Essentially self-sufficient, Finland engaged in very limited agricultural trade.

This traditional, almost autarkic, production pattern shifted sharply during the late nineteenth century, when inexpensive imported grain from Russia and the United States competed effectively with local grain. At the same time, rising domestic and foreign demand for dairy products and the availability of low-cost imported cattle feed made dairy and meat production much more profitable. These changes in market conditions induced Finland's farmers to switch from growing staple grains to producing meat and dairy products, setting a pattern that persisted into the late 1980s.

In response to the agricultural depression of the 1930s, the government encouraged domestic production by imposing tariffs on agricultural imports. This policy enjoyed some success: the total area under cultivation increased, and farm incomes fell less sharply in Finland than in most other countries. Barriers to grain imports stimulated a return to mixed farming, and by 1938 Finland's farmers were able to meet roughly 90 percent of the domestic demand for grain.

The disruptions caused by the Winter War and the Continuation War caused further food shortages, especially when Finland ceded territory, including about one-tenth of its farmland, to the Soviet Union. The experiences of the depression and the war years persuaded the Finns to secure independent food supplies to prevent shortages in future conflicts.

After the war, the first challenge was to resettle displaced farmers. Most refugee farmers were given farms that included some buildings and land that had already been in production, but some had to make do with "cold farms," that is, land not in production that usually had to be cleared or drained before crops could be sown. The government sponsored large-scale clearing and draining operations that expanded the area suitable for farming. As a result of the resettlement and land-clearing programs, the area under cultivation expanded by about 450,000 hectares, reaching about 2.4 million hectares by the early 1960s. Finland thus came to farm more land than ever before, an unusual development in a country that was simultaneously experiencing rapid industrial growth.

During this period of expansion, farmers introduced modern production practices. The widespread use of modern inputs—chemical fertilisers and insecticides, agricultural machinery, and improved seed varieties—sharply improved crop yields. Yet the modernisation process again made farm production dependent on supplies from abroad, this time on imports of petroleum and fertilisers. By 1984 domestic sources of energy covered only about 20 percent of farm needs, while in 1950 domestic sources had supplied 70 percent of them. In the aftermath of the oil price increases of the early 1970s, farmers began to return to local energy sources such as firewood. The existence of many farms that were too small to allow efficient use of tractors also limited mechanisation. Another weak point was the existence of many fields with open drainage ditches needing regular maintenance; in the mid-1980s, experts estimated that half of the cropland needed improved drainage works. At that time, about 1 million hectares had underground drainage, and agricultural authorities planned to help install such works on another million hectares. Despite these shortcomings, Finland's agriculture was efficient and productive—at least when compared with farming in other European countries.

FORESTRY

Forests play a key role in the country's economy, making it one of the world's leading wood producers and providing raw materials at competitive prices for the crucial wood-processing industries. As in agriculture, the government has long played a leading role in forestry, regulating tree cutting, sponsoring technical improvements, and establishing long-term plans to ensure that the country's forests continue to supply the wood-processing industries.

Finland's wet climate and rocky soils are ideal for forests. Tree stands do well throughout the country, except in some areas north of the Arctic Circle. In 1980 the forested area totaled about 19.8 million hectares, providing 4 hectares of forest per capita—far above the European average of about 0.5 hectares. The proportion of forest land varied considerably from region to region. In the central lake plateau and in the eastern and northern provinces, forests covered up to 80 percent of the land area, but in areas with better conditions for agriculture, especially in the southwest, forests accounted for only 50 to 60 percent of the territory. The main commercial tree species—pine, spruce, and birch—supplied raw material to the sawmill, pulp, and paper industries. The forests also produced sizable aspen and elder crops.

The heavy winter snows and the network of waterways were used to move logs to the mills. Loggers were able to drag cut trees over the winter snow to the roads or water bodies. In the southwest, the sledding season lasted about 100 days per year; the season was even longer to the north and the east. The country's network of lakes and rivers facilitated log floating, a cheap and rapid means of transport. Each spring, crews floated the logs downstream to collection points; tugs towed log bundles down rivers and across lakes to processing centers. The waterway system covered much of the country, and by the 1980s Finland had extended roadways and railroads to areas not served by waterways, effectively opening up all of the country's forest reserves to commercial use.

Forestry and farming were closely linked. During the twentieth century, government land redistribution programmes had made forest ownership widespread, allotting forestland to most farms. In the 1980s, private farmers controlled 35 percent of the country's forests; other persons held 27 percent; the government, 24 percent; private corporations, 9 percent; and municipalities and other public bodies, 5 percent. The forestlands owned by farmers and by other people—some 350,000 plots—were the best, producing 75 to 80 percent of the wood consumed by industry; the state owned much of the poorer land, especially that in the north.

The ties between forestry and farming were mutually beneficial. Farmers supplemented their incomes with earnings from selling their wood, caring for forests, or logging; forestry made many otherwise marginal farms viable. At the same time, farming communities maintained roads and other infrastructure in rural areas, and they provided workers for forest operations. Indeed, without the farming communities in sparsely populated areas, it would have been much more difficult to continue intensive logging operations and reforestation in many prime forest areas.

The Ministry of Agriculture and Forestry has carried out forest inventories and drawn up silvicultural plans. According to surveys, between 1945 and the late 1970s foresters had cut trees faster than the forests could regenerate them. Nevertheless, between the early 1950s and 1981, Finland was able to boost the total area of its forests by some 2.7 million hectares and to increase forest stands under 40 years of age by some 3.2 million hectares. Beginning in 1965, the country instituted plans that called for expanding forest cultivation, draining peatland and waterlogged areas, and replacing slow-growing trees with faster-growing varieties. By the mid-1980s, the Finns had drained 5.5 million hectares, fertilized 2.8 million hectares, and cultivated 3.6 million hectares. Thinning increased the share of trees that would produce suitable lumber, while improved tree varieties increased productivity by as much as 30 percent.

Comprehensive silvicultural programmes had made it possible for the Finns simultaneously to increase forest output and to add to the amount and value of the growing stock. By the mid-1980s, Finland's forests produced nearly 70 million cubic meters of new wood each year, considerably more than was being cut. During the postwar period, the annual cut increased by about 120 percent to about 50 million cubic meters. Wood burning fell to one-fifth the level of the immediate postwar years, freeing up wood supplies for the wood-processing industries, which consumed between 40 million and 45 million cubic meters per year. Indeed, industry demand was so great that Finland needed to import 5 million to 6 million cubic meters of wood each year.

To maintain the country's comparative advantage in forest products, Finnish authorities moved to raise lumber output toward the country's ecological limits. In 1984 the government published the Forest 2000 plan, drawn up by the Ministry of Agriculture and Forestry. The plan aimed at increasing forest harvests by about 3 percent per year, while conserving forestland for recreation and other uses. It also called for enlarging the average size of private forest holdings, increasing the area used for forests, and extending forest cultivation and thinning. If successful, the plan would make it possible to raise wood deliveries by roughly one-third by the end of the twentieth century. Finnish officials believed that such growth was necessary if Finland was to maintain its share in world markets for wood and paper products.

INDUSTRY

Since the 1990s, Finnish industry, which for centuries had relied on the country's vast forests, has become increasingly dominated by electronics and services, as globalization lead to a decline of more traditional industries. Outsourcing resulted in more manufacturing being transferred abroad, with Finnish-based industry focusing to a greater extent on R&D and hi-tech electronics.

ELECTRONICS

The Finnish electronics and electrotechnics industry relies on heavy investment in R&D, and has been accelerated by the liberalisation of global markets. Electrical engineering started in the late 19th century with generators and electric motors built by Gottfried Strömberg, now part of the ABB Group. Other Finnish companies – such as Instru, Vaisala and Neles (now part of Metso) - have succeeded in areas such as industrial automation, medical and meteorological technology. Nokia was once a world leader in mobile telecommunications.

METALS, ENGINEERING AND MANUFACTURING

Finland has an abundance of minerals, but many large mines have closed down, and most raw materials are now imported. For this reason, companies now tend to focus on high added-value processing of metals. The exports include steel, copper, chromium, zinc and nickel, and finished products such as steel roofing and cladding, welded steel pipes, copper pipe and coated sheets. Outokumpu is known for developing the flash smelting process for copper production and stainless steel.

With regard to vehicles, the Finnish motor industry consists mostly of manufacturers of tractors (Valtra, formerly Valmet tractor), forest machines (f.ex. Ponsse), military vehicles (Sisu, Patria), trucks (Sisu Auto), buses and Valmet Automotive, a contract manufacturer, whose factory in Uusikaupunki produces Mercedes-Benz cars. Shipbuilding is an important industry: the world's largest cruise ships are built in Finland; also, the Finnish company Wärtsilä produces the world's largest diesel engines and has market share of 47%. In addition, Finland also produces train rolling stock.

The manufacturing industry is a significant employer of about 400,000 people.

CHEMICAL INDUSTRY

The chemical industry is one of the Finland's largest industrial sectors with its roots in tar making in the 17th century. It produces an enormous range of products for the use of other industrial sectors, especially for forestry and agriculture. In addition, its produces plastics, chemicals, paints, oil products, pharmaceuticals, environmental products, biotech products and petrochemicals. In the beginning of this millennium, biotechnology was regarded as one of the most promising high-tech sectors in Finland. In 2006 it was still considered promising, even though it had not yet become "the new Nokia".

PULP AND PAPER INDUSTRY

Forest products has been the major export industry in the past, but diversification and growth of the economy has reduced its share. In the 1970s, the pulp and paper industry accounted for half of Finnish exports. Although this share has shrank, pulp and paper is still a major industry with 52 sites across the country. Furthermore, several of large international corporations in this business are based in Finland. Stora Enso and UPM were placed #1 and #3 by output in the world, both producing more than ten million tons. M-real and Myllykoski also appear on the top 100 list.

ENERGY INDUSTRY

Finland's energy supply is divided as follows: nuclear power - 26%, net imports - 20%, hydroelectric power - 16%, combined production district heat - 18%, combined production industry - 13%, condensing power - 6%. One half of all the energy consumed in Finland goes to industry, one fifth to heating buildings and one fifth to transport. Lacking indigenous fossil fuel resources, Finland has been an energy importer. This might change in the future since Finland is currently building its fifth and approved the building permits for its sixth and seventh reactors. There are some uranium resources in Finland, but to date no commercially viable deposits have been identified for exclusive mining of uranium. However, permits have been granted to Talvivaara to produce uranium from the tailings of their nickel-cobalt mine.

FINLAND LEGAL SYSTEM BASICS

When the Finnish Parliament adopted the Declaration of the Independence of Finland on 6 December 1917, the new state already had a rich national culture and centuries of experience in managing its own affairs. The makings of an independent nation derived partly from the times of Swedish rule (from the 12th Century until 1809) and especially from the period when Finland was an autonomous Grand Duchy of the Russian Empire (from 1809 until 1917).

THE WESTERN INFLUENCES

For 700 years Finland was a Province of the Kingdom of Sweden, equal in status to any other Swedish Province. This common history is the basis of the similarities between the Finnish and Swedish societies - similarities that can be seen as well in the culture as in the political and legal structures. Swedish continues to be an official language in Finland, in addition to Finnish, even though native Swedish speakers now comprise only six per cent of the population. All legislation is published simultaneously in both languages.

The common legal heritage can be seen e.g. in the introductions to the Finnish and Swedish lawbooks, both of which still contain the ethical and judicial rules for judges compiled in the 16th Century by Olaus Petri, a Swedish clergyman and legal scholar. Furthermore, certain parts of the codification of laws completed in the Kingdom of Sweden in 1734, the first of its kind in Europe, have remained in force in Finland for over 250 years.

In addition to the western neighbour, also Central Europe and especially Germany were an early influence in the development of Finnish learning. Since 1640 Finland had a University of its own in Turku, with extensive links to a number of German and French Universities.

In Sweden, the first enacted codes were compiled already in the Middle Ages, separately for the towns and for the general law of the realm. The country had also two types of general lower courts: the Town Courts, which were based on a German model and operated in connection with the Town Councils, and the Rural District Courts. In Finland, the dual court system survived until 1993, when a unified system of lower courts was set up throughout the country. These came to be called District Courts.

The establishment in the 17th Century of the Courts of Appeal, which were meant to be the supreme judicial authorities in the country, signalled the birth of the Swedish-Finnish judiciary, even if the King in Council was vested with the supreme authority until 1789. The Svea Court of Appeal, in Stockholm, was established in 1614, and the Turku Court of Appeal in 1623. The jurisdiction of the latter covered all of Finland. The Supreme Court of Sweden - and of Finland - was established in 1789.

The separation of administrative matters and general legal affairs began on the local level as early as in the 17th Century. The County Governments, which had been set up as the general administrative authorities of the State, were empowered to hear also appeals against the decisions of the local authorities. The beginning of County administration saw also the beginning of the development of the Prison Service.

The first advocates appeared in Sweden and Finland in the beginning of the 17th Century.

THE EASTERN CONNECTION

Finland's constitutional ties with Sweden were severed in 1809, when Finland in connection with the Napoleonic wars was annexed by the Russian Empire. In spite of this, Swedish laws and the underlying legal system continued to apply in Finland - a rare and exceptional situation also in a global framework.

Over a century as an autonomous Grand Duchy was for Finland the first real step towards independence. The government and administrative machinery were created, Finland got its own representative assembly and its own currency, system of education and judiciary. The supreme administrative authority of Finland, the Senate, was also the supreme judicial authority in civil and criminal cases. The financial section of the Senate acted as the Government of Finland and the legal section as the Supreme Court. The financial section heard also appeals in administrative matters.

When the Czar gave his consent to the convocation of the Finnish representative assembly, in 1863, a time of busy social and legal development in Finland could begin. That time lasted for the remainder of the century. The reforms included e.g. an extensive programme for the construction of new prisons and the establishment of the Board of Prison Administration, in 1881.

The reform work was, however, cut short by the harsher policies of the Russian regime. The last major reform took place in 1906, when the representative assembly of four Estates, which derived already from the times of Swedish rule, was superseded by a new unicameral Parliament of 200 Representatives, at the time one of the most modern in terms of organisation and breadth of representation. The suffrage was universal; Finnish women were the second in the world to receive the vote and the first in the world to have the right to run for office.

THE RULE OF LAW

The 'russification period', as it became to be known, lasted until 1917. The attempts at oppression were countered in Finland with a steadfast reliance on the law and the rule of law. Those times further intensified the spirit of the rule of law that has been the legacy of Finnish and Scandinavian legal thinking since the Middle Ages - and remains so even today. The saying "Maa on lailla rakennettava" (By law shall this country be built) crystallises one of the basic principles of Finnish history. It is there also in the Constitution, according to which "there shall be strict compliance with the law in all official functions."

The Russian revolution made the independence of Finland finally possible. In 1919 a republican Constitution was framed, with the President of the Republic as the head of state. The President is elected by popular vote; if necessary, there are two rounds of voting, so that the two candidates with the most votes in the first round stand against each other in the second. The President's term in office is six years. A person cannot be elected for more than two consecutive terms. The Parliamentary term is four years.

The Supreme Court and the Supreme Administrative Court were established in 1918. As already noted, administrative judicial proceedings have in Finland been organised in a separate hierarchy of courts. The general courts for this purpose, the County Administrative Courts, were established as sections of the County Governments in 1955; they became also formally separate and independent entities in 1989.

After World War II the development of legislation was marked by the change of Finland from an agrarian nation into an industrialised one. The 1960's were a time of intensive co-operation between the Nordic Countries; as a result there is a body of laws that are virtually identical in Finland and in Sweden.

Similar legislation has been passed also as a result of economic co-operation and integration and common goals in the European Economic Area. It can be seen that Finnish laws and Finnish legal thinking clearly have their roots in Europe. In addition, the European Human Rights Convention has been directly applicable in Finland since 1990.

In 1995 Finland acceded to the European Union. This has naturally brought new elements into the Finnish legal system, but as a Member State of the EU Finland of course is able to participate in the enactment of new European legislation. The Finnish judiciary now applies not only Finnish, but also European law.

The roots of the Finnish legal system lie in the times when the country belonged to the Kingdom of Sweden [from the 12th Century to 1809]. These 700 years of common history form the basis of the similarities between the Finnish and Swedish societies, similarities that are evident also in their legal structures. These were retained even after Finland had been ceded to Russia, as the Swedish legislation in force at the time remained in force also during Finland's 108 years as an autonomous Grand Duchy within the Empire of the Czar. As a matter of fact, some parts of the original Swedish legislation continue to be applied to this day, even though Finland has been an independent republic since 1917.

The autonomous status that Finland enjoyed during the 19th Century also allowed for legislative self-determination. Hence, virtually nothing of the legal tradition of Russia remains, while Finland continues to display the characteristics of a continental legal tradition, with influences from Scandinavia and particularly from Germany.

One lasting effect of the Swedish times is the status of the Swedish language. For centuries, it was the language of the upper classes and the administration. Finnish, on the other hand, was taken into legislative use only in the early 20th Century. Even today Finland is a bilingual country, with Finnish and Swedish enjoying the same status as official languages (detailed information on the Ministry of Justice website). All legislation and most other official publications are available in both of them. In addition, it should be noted here that the unilingually Swedish-speaking Åland Islands, which lie between Finland and Sweden, have a far-reaching autonomy, enshrined in an Act that is "constitutional by nature" even though not formally a part of the Constitution.

Finland has been a member of the United Nations since 1955, of the Council of Europe since 1989 and of the European Union since 1995.

For further information, please refer to the English-language home page of the website of the Ministry of Justice.

CONSTITUTION

The new Constitution of Finland entered into force on 1 March 2000. It superseded the four Constitutional Acts deriving from the early times of Finnish independence, incorporating the most fundamental provisions from all of them. At the same time, many provisions were relegated to the ranks of regular parliamentary legislation. *In Finland, Sovereign Power Rests with the People*, a thorough outlook in English into the background, enactment and contents of the Constitution is available online.

THE JUDICIAL SYSTEM

The Finnish Constitution guarantees everyone the right to have his case heard appropriately and without undue delay by a court or other public authority. Everyone also has the right to have a decision affecting his rights and duties reviewed by a court or other judicial body.

In addition the Constitution contains the basic provision on fair trial and good governance. The main guarantees of these are the publicity of proceedings, the right to be heard, the right to receive a decision containing the grounds, and the right to appeal against the decision.

The independence of the judiciary is constitutionally guaranteed. The courts are under the sole obligation to apply the law in force.

The professional judges must have a higher university degree in law. They are appointed by the President of the Republic. A judge cannot be dismissed except by court order, e.g. if he has been convicted for an offence. The courts of first instance also have some locally elected lay judges.

In Finland, the constitutionality of laws is examined in advance. This mainly takes place in Parliament, and especially in its Constitutional Law Committee. The goal of this parliamentary control is to prevent in advance that laws which are in conflict with the Constitution are enacted in the ordinary legislative procedure.

No constitutional court exists in Finland, but the courts and other authorities are under an obligation to interpret legislation in such a way as to adhere to the Constitution and to respect human rights. According to the Constitution, the courts should give preference to the Constitution when they decide a case if the application of an act would be in manifest conflict with the Constitution.

PUBLIC DOMAIN

All Finnish legislation, from the Constitution to regular Acts of Parliament, Presidential Decrees, Government Decrees, Ministry Decrees and various other types of subordinate regulation, is published in print in the *Suomen säädöskokoelma*, i.e. the Statute Book of Finland.

FINLEX, the data bank for the dissemination of Finnish legislation and other legal information, was established as a subscription service in the 1980s. The newest version of FINLEX was launched in 2004 and is available on the Internet free of charge. Most of the material on the website is available only in Finnish and Swedish, but there is also some material in English. FINLEX consists of five subject areas:

- *Legislative information*, containing translations of Finnish Acts and Decrees, mostly into English; consolidated and original texts of Acts and Decrees; a reference database of changes made to any Act or Decree; and all Sámi language legislation. The most recent legislation is available also as pdf files in the "Electronic Statutes of Finland".
- *Case-law* from the following courts: The Supreme Court, the Supreme Administrative Court, the Courts of Appeal, the regional Administrative Courts, the Market Court, the Labour Court and the Insurance Court. In addition, there are summaries of judgments of the European Court of Human Rights and the Court of Justice of the EC, as well as a reference database on case-law in legal literature.

- *Secondary legislation*: The decrees, decisions and regulations of Ministries and Central Agencies; the decisions of the Chancellor of Justice and of the Data Protection Board; Collective Agreements concluded by registered associations of employers and employees.

- *Treaties* concluded by Finland, including a reference database of the date of entry into force, date of ratification, parties and the reservations made by the parties. The most recent treaties are available also as pdf files in the "Electronic Treaty Series of Finland", including the texts in the original languages, e.g. English or French.

- *Government Bills* (draft legislation) are available from 1992.

COMMERCIAL LAW

A comprehensive two-volume edition of Finnish legislation, *Suomen Laki I-II*, i.e. the Laws of Finland, is published annually by a commercial enterprise, Talentum. This work is available also as an online version.

A more recent entry in the field of legal information service is Edilex, which contains a database of national legislation, a daily news service, law books, articles, journals and other material. Subscription is required for most of the services. Edilex is provided by Edita Publishing.Another similar service is WSOYPro, which is provided by WSOY, the largest publishing house in Finland.

INVESTMENT AND BUSINESS CLIMATE - STRATEGIC INFORMATION AND CONTACTS FOR STARTING BUSINESS IN FINLAND

Finland is a Nordic country located north of the Baltic States bordering Russia, Sweden, and Norway, possessing a stable and modern economy, including a world-class investment climate. It is a member of the European Union and part of the euro area. The country has a highly-skilled, educated and multilingual labor force, with strong expertise in Information Communications Technology (ICT), ship building, forestry, and renewable energy.

Key challenges for foreign investors include a rigid labor market and bureaucratic red tape in starting certain businesses, although in June 2016 the Government enacted a Competitiveness Pact that aims to reduce labor costs, increase hours worked, and introduce more flexibility into the wage bargaining system. Health, social services, and pension reforms are also being discussed.

At the end of 2016, the total stock of FDI in Finland totaled EUR 746.26 billion, of which equity accounted for EUR 60.8 billion and the value of debt capital for EUR 13.4 billion. By country, Sweden contributes the biggest stock of foreign direct investment in Finland (46 percent), followed by the Netherlands (16 percent), and Denmark (7 percent). Investments from China increased dramatically in 2016.

The GOF has taken steps to attract additional investment by cutting the corporate tax rate from 24.5 percent to 20 percent in 2014, simplifying the residence permit system for foreign experts, and creating a network called Business Finland that promotes foreign investment and the country's international image. This one-stop shop brings together the services of a variety of state-funded agencies. Both foreign and domestic companies can benefit from GOF investment incentives, research and development support, and innovation systems.

The U.S. Embassy in Helsinki, through the Foreign Commercial Service and Political/Economic Sections, is a strong partner for U.S. businesses that wish to connect to the Finnish market. Finnish companies are very active in the fields of information technology, energy, biotech, and clean technology, sectors that the government has selected – along with Arctic expertise – as priorities in their innovation policy. With excellent transportation links to the Nordic-Baltic region and Russia, Finland can be a good hub for establishing regional operations.

The Finnish MyData initiative is a relatively new human-centric system that is designed so that access to personal data would remain under the control of the individual instead of organizations (such as businesses or the government, among others). This initiative may impact foreign digital service companies, depending on how it is ultimately developed and implemented.

On January 1, 2018, Finpro, the Finnish trade promotion organization, and Tekes, the Finnish Funding Agency for Innovation, united to become Business Finland, which is now the single operator helping Finnish SMEs go international, encouraging foreign direct investment in Finland, and promoting tourism. Business Finland has around 600 staff, nearly 40 offices abroad, and operates 20 regional offices in Finland. Business Finland is part of the Team Finland network and its website is https://www.businessfinland.fi/en/do-business-with-finland/home/. Invest in Finland is the official investment promotion agency, and is part of Business Finland.

Table 1

Measure	Year	Index/Rank	Website Address
TI Corruption Perceptions Index	2017	3 of 175	http://www.transparency.org/ research/cpi/overview
World Bank's Doing Business Report "Ease of Doing Business"	2017	13 of 190	doingbusiness.org/rankings
Global Innovation Index	2017	8 of 128	https://www.globalinnovationindex.org/ analysis-indicator
U.S. FDI in Partner Country (M USD, stock positions)	2016	USD 3,395	http://www.bea.gov/ international/factsheet/
World Bank GNI per capita	2016	USD 45,050	http://data.worldbank.org/ indicator/NY.GNP.PCAP.CD

1. OPENNESS TO, AND RESTRICTIONS UPON, FOREIGN INVESTMENT

Policies Towards Foreign Direct Investment

The Finnish government is open to foreign direct investment. There are no general regulatory limitations relating to acquisitions. A mixture of domestic and EU competition rules govern mergers and acquisitions. Finland does not preclude foreign investment, but some tax policies may make it unattractive to investors. Finnish tax authorities treat the movement of ownership of shares in a Finnish company into a foreign company as a taxable event, though Finland complies with EU directives that require it to allow such transactions based in other EU member states without taxing them.

Finland does not grant foreign-owned firms any special treatment like tax holidays or other subsidies that are not available to other firms. Instead, Finland relies on policies that seek to offer both domestic and international firms better operating conditions, an educated labor force, and well-functioning infrastructure. Companies benefit from preferential trade arrangements through Finland's membership in the EU and World Trade Organization (WTO), in addition to the protection offered by Finland's bilateral investment treaties with more than sixty-five countries. The corporate income tax rate is 20 percent.

On January 1, 2018, Finpro, the Finnish trade promotion organization, and Tekes, the Finnish Funding Agency for Innovation, united to become Business Finland. Business Finland is now the single operator helping Finnish SMEs go international, encouraging foreign direct investment in Finland, and promoting tourism. Business Finland supports the Government's objectives to spread the Finnish innovation system and double SME export volumes by 2020. Business Finland has around 600 staff, nearly 40 offices abroad, and operates 20 regional offices in Finland. Business Finland is part of the Team Finland network and its website is https://www.businessfinland.fi/en/do-business-with-finland/home/. Invest in Finland is the official investment promotion agency, and is part of Business Finland.

Limits on Foreign Control and Right to Private Ownership and Establishment

The law that governs foreign investments is the Act on the Monitoring of Foreign Corporate Acquisitions in Finland. The Ministry of Employment and the Economy (TEM) monitors and confirms foreign corporate acquisitions. TEM decides whether an acquisition conflicts with "vital national interests" including securing national defense as well as safeguarding public order and security. If TEM finds that a key national interest is jeopardized, it must refer the matter to the Council of State, which may refuse to confirm the acquisition.

In the civilian sector, TEM primarily monitors transactions related to Finnish enterprises considered critical to maintaining functions fundamental to society, such as energy, communications, or food supply. Monitoring only applies to foreign owners domiciled outside the EU and European Free Trade Association (EFTA). More information is at: http://www.finlex.fi/en/laki/kaannokset/1992/en19921612.

For defense acquisitions, foreigners must apply for prior confirmation and monitoring covers all foreign owners. "Defense" includes all entities that supply or have supplied goods or services to the Finnish Ministry of Defense, the Finnish Defense Forces, the Finnish Border Guard, as well as entities dealing in dual-use goods. The substantive elements in evaluating the application are identical to those applied to other corporate acquisitions.

Right to private ownership

Private ownership is normal in Finland, and in most fields of business participation by foreign companies or individuals is unrestricted. When the government privatizes state-owned companies, both private and foreign participation is allowed except in enterprises operating in sectors related to national security.

Screening FDI

TEM is the authority responsible for monitoring and confirming corporate acquisitions. Filing an application/notification is voluntary, but the Ministry may request information connected to a foreigner's corporate acquisition. The law does not specify a time limit for filing, and a foreign owner may file either before or after the transaction. A transaction is considered approved if the Ministry does not request additional information, initiate further proceedings within six weeks, or refuse to confirm the transaction within three months. The Ministry cannot render opinions before an application is filed. It is, however, possible for investors to contact the Ministry for guidance beforehand. There is no official template for the notification, but it must include information on the monitored entity's pre-and post-transaction ownership structure and the acquiring entity's ownership structure. If known, an acquiring entity must also state its intentions relating to the monitored entity. There are no fees.

Other Investment Policy Reviews

Finland has been a member of the WTO and the EU since 1995. The WTO conducted its Trade Policy Review of the European Union (including Finland) in May 2017: https://www.wto.org/english/tratop_e/tpr_e/tp457_e.htm. The Organization for Economic Cooperation and Development (OECD) 2018 economic survey can be found here: http://www.oecd.org/eco/surveys/economic-survey-finland.htm. The Research Institute of the Finnish Economy (ETLA) regularly publishes reports that review different sectors and factors that may impact investment: https://www.etla.fi/en/publications/dp1267-en/.

Business Facilitation

All businesses in Finland must be publicly registered at the Finnish Trade Register. Businesses must also notify the Register of any changes to registration information and most must submit their financial statements (annual accounts) to the register. The website is: https://www.prh.fi/en/kaupparekisteri.html. The Business Information System BIS ("YTJ" in Finnish, https://www.prh.fi/en/kaupparekisteri/rekisterointipalvelut/ytj.html) is an online service enabling investors to start a business or organization, report changes, close down a business, or conduct searches.

Permits, licenses, and notifications required depend on whether the foreign entrepreneur originates from a Nordic country, the European Union, or elsewhere. The type of company also affects the permits required, which can include the registration of the right to residency, residence permits for an employee or self-employed person, and registration in the Finnish Population Information System. A foreigner may need a permit from the Finnish Patent and Registration Office to serve as a partner in a partnership or administrative body of a company. For more information: https://www.suomi.fi/company/responsibilities-and-obligations/permits-and-obligations. Improvements made in 2016 to the residence permit system for foreign experts, defined as those with special expertise, a university degree, and who earn at least EUR 3,000 gross per month, should help attract experts to Finland. An online permit application (https://enterfinland.fi/eServices) available since November 2016 has made it easier for family members to acquire a residence permit.

The practice of some trades in Finland requires only notification or registration with the authorities. Other trades, however, require a separate license; companies should confirm requirements with Finnish authorities. Entrepreneurs must take out pension insurance for their employees, and certain fields obligate additional insurance. All businesses have a statutory obligation to maintain financial accounts, and, with the exception of small companies, businesses must also appoint an external auditor.

Finland is the 13th best country in the world for doing business, according to the World Bank Group's 2018 Doing Business Index; it ranked 26th on "Starting a Business" (http://www.doingbusiness.org/data/exploreeconomies/finland). According to a 2016 study (FDI Attractiveness Scoreboard) by the European Commission, Finland is the most attractive EU country for FDI in terms of the political, regulatory and legal environment.

Gender inequality is low in Finland, which ranks third in the 2017 World Economic Forum Global Gender Gap Index. The employment gap between men and women aged 15-64 is the second lowest in the OECD, and women are well represented among top politicians, and increasingly on the boards of companies and among entrepreneurs. However, the gender pay gap is wide, partly because women are under-represented in well-paid jobs. The government has set targets to increase the employment of minorities in fields where they were under-represented.

Outward Investment

Business Finland, part of the Team Finland network, helps Finnish SMEs go international, encourages foreign direct investment in Finland, and promotes tourism. Business Finland has a staff of around 600 persons and nearly 40 offices abroad. It operates in 15 different regions in Finland and focuses on agrotechnology, cleantech, connectivity, ecommerce, education, ICT and digitalization, mining, and mobility as a service. While many of Business Finland's programs are export-oriented, they also seek to offer business and network opportunities. More info here: https://www.businessfinland.fi/en/do-business-with-finland/home/. In 2018, the Ministry of Education and Culture launched the Team Finland Knowledge network to enhance international education and research cooperation and the export of Finnish educational expertise. The United States will be one of the initial focus countries.

2. BILATERAL INVESTMENT AGREEMENTS AND TAXATION TREATIES

Finland does not have a bilateral investment treaty (BIT) agreement or FTA with the United States. Finland has concluded BITs with: Albania, Algeria, Argentina, Armenia, Azerbaijan, Belarus, Bosnia-Herzegovina, Bulgaria, Chile, China, Croatia, the Czech Republic, Dominican Republic, Egypt, El Salvador, Estonia, Ethiopia, Georgia, Guatemala, Hong Kong, Hungary, India, Indonesia, Iran, Jordan, Kazakhstan, Kenya, Korea, Kuwait, Kyrgyzstan, Latvia, Lebanon, Lithuania, Macedonia, Malaysia, Mauritius, Mexico, Moldova, Mongolia, Montenegro, Morocco, Mozambique, Namibia, Nepal, Nigeria, Oman, Panama, Peru, Philippines, Poland, Qatar, Romania, Russia, Serbia, Slovakia, Slovenia, South Africa, Sri Lanka, Tanzania, Thailand, Tunisia, Turkey, Ukraine, United Arab Emirates, Uruguay, Uzbekistan, and Vietnam. A full list of Finland investment agreements, including copies of the actual documents, is at: http://investmentpolicyhub.unctad.org/IIA/CountryBits/71#iiaInnerMenu.

As an EU member state, Finland is also a signatory to any treaty or agreement, including free trade agreements, signed by the European Union. Finland is a signatory to the WTO Trade Facilitation Agreement (TFA), which entered into force on 22 February 2017.

Finland and the United States signed a convention for the avoidance of double taxation and the prevention of fiscal evasion with respect to taxes on income and on capital (TIAS 12101) that entered into force on December 30, 1990. On March 5, 2014, Finland signed a Foreign Account Tax Compliance Act (FATCA). The Finnish tax administration guidance regarding FATCA is at: https://www.vero.fi/syventavat-vero-ohjeet/ohje-hakusivu/48528/verohallinnon-ohje-suomen-ja-yhdysvaltain-v%C3%A4list%C3%A4-verotietojen-vaihtoa-koskevan-fatca-sopimuksen-soveltamiseksi/?showVersionHistory=true and https://www.vero.fi/syventavat-vero-ohjeet/ohje-hakusivu/fatca_crs_ja_dac/ (available only in Finnish and Swedish).

For the full text of the FATCA agreement, see: http://www.treasury.gov/resource-center/tax-policy/treaties/Documents/FATCA-Agreement-Finland-3-5-2014.pdf.

For a list of Finland's bilateral tax agreements, see: https://www.vero.fi/en/detailed-guidance/guidance/49062/tax_treatie/.

The salary and fringe benefits paid to qualifying foreign employees living in Finland for more than six months are taxed at a flat rate of 35 percent, for a maximum assignment period of 48 months in Finland. For detailed tax guidance, see the Finnish Tax Administration's website: https://www.vero.fi/en/detailed-guidance/guidance/49113/taxation-of-employees-from-other-countries/#3.1-foreign-key-employees-(provisional-act) and the Finnish Foundation for Share Promotion's Tax Guide for Investors (2015): http://www.porssisaatio.fi/wp-content/uploads/2015/08/vero_opas_2015_eng_final_web.pdf.

3. LEGAL REGIME

Transparency of the Regulatory System

The Securities Market Act (SMA) contains regulations on corporate disclosure procedures and requirements, responsibility for flagging share ownership, insider regulations and offenses, the issuing and marketing of securities, and trading. The clearing of securities trades is subject to licensing and is supervised by the Financial Supervision Authority. The SMA is at: https://www.finlex.fi/en/laki/kaannokset/2012/en20120746_20130258.pdf.

See the Financial Supervisory Authority's overview of regulations for listed companies here: http://www.finanssivalvonta.fi/en/Listed_companies/Regulation/Pages/Default.aspx. Finland is not on www.businessfacilitation.org.

The Act on the Openness of Public Documents establishes the openness of all records in the possession of officials of the state, municipalities, registered religious communities, and corporations that perform legally mandated public duties, such as pension funds and public utilities. Exceptions can only be made by law or by an executive order for reasons such as national security. For more information see the Ministry of Justice's page on Openness: http://oikeusministerio.fi/en/act-on-the-openness-of-government-activities. The Act on the Openness of Government Activities can be found here: http://www.finlex.fi/en/laki/kaannokset/1999/en19990621.

Finland ranks third on The World Justice Project (WJP) Rule of Law Index (2017-2018) regarding constraints on government powers, absence of corruption, open government, fundamental rights, order and security, regulatory enforcement, civil justice and criminal justice. For more, see: https://worldjusticeproject.org/our-work/wjp-rule-law-index/wjp-rule-law-index-2017%E2%80%932018 . Finland ranks fifth on World Bank's Global Indicators of Regulatory Governance: http://rulemaking.worldbank.org/data/explorecountries/finland.

International Regulatory Considerations

Finland respects EU common rules and expects other Member States to do the same. The Government seeks to constructively combine national and joint European interests in Finland's EU policy, and seeks better and lighter regulation that incorporates flexibility for SMEs. The Government will not increase burdens detrimental to competitiveness during its national implementation of EU acts.

Finland, as a member of the WTO, is required under the Agreement on Technical Barriers to Trade (TBT Agreement) to report to the WTO all proposed technical regulations that could affect trade with other Member countries. In 2016, Finland submitted no notifications of technical regulations and conformity assessment procedures to the WTO, and has submitted 75 notifications since 1995. Finland is a signatory to the WTO Trade Facilitation Agreement (TFA), which entered into force on February 22, 2017.

Legal System and Judicial Independence

Finland has a civil law system. European Community (EC) law is directly applicable in Finland and takes precedence over national legislation. The Market Court is a special court for rulings in commercial law, competition, and public procurement cases, and may issue injunctions and penalties against the illegal restriction of competition. It also governs mergers and acquisitions and may overturn public procurement decisions and require compensatory payments. The Court has jurisdiction over disputes regarding whether goods or services have been marketed unfairly. The Court also hears industrial and civil IPR cases.

A working group set up to reform the Competition Act concluded in March 2017 that the Act should be further amended with regard to inspections, sanctions and information exchange between authorities, among others. For more information see the Competition Act (No. 948/2011) at: http://www.finlex.fi/fi/laki/kaannokset/2011/en20110948.pdf.

Laws and Regulations on Foreign Direct Investment

A non- European Economic Area (EEA) resident (persons or companies) operating in Finland must obtain a license or a notification when starting a business in a regulated industry. A comprehensive list of regulated industries can be found at: https://www.suomi.fi/company/responsibilities-and-obligations/permits-and-obligations.

See also the Ministry of Employment and the Economy's Regulated Trade guidelines: https://tem.fi/en/regulation-of-business-operations. The autonomously governed Aland Islands, however are an exception. Property ownership and the right to conduct business are limited to those with the right of domicile in the Aland Islands. This does not prevent people from settling in, or trading with, the Aland Islands. Immigrants who have lived in Aland for five years and have adequate Swedish may apply for domicile and the Aland Government can grant exemptions.

The Competition Act allows the government to block mergers where the result would harm market competition. The Finnish Competition and Consumer Authority (FCCA) issued guidelines in 2011: http://www.kkv.fi/en/facts-and-advice/competition-affairs/merger-control/.

EnterpriseFinland/Suomi.fi (https://www.suomi.fi/company/) is a free online service offering information and services for starting, growing and developing a company. Users may also ask for advice through the My Enterprise Finland website: https://oma.yrityssuomi.fi/en#. Finnish legislation is available in the free online databank Finlex in Finnish, where some English translations can also be found: http://www.finlex.fi/en/laki/kaannokset/.

Competition and Anti-Trust Laws

The Finnish Competition and Consumer Authority FCCA protects competition by intervening in cases regarding restrictive practices, such as cartels and abuse of dominant position, and violations of the Competition Act and the Treaty on the Functioning of the European Union (TFEU). Investigations occur on the FCCA's initiative and on the basis of complaints. Where necessary, the FCCA makes proposals to the Market Court regarding penalties. In international competition matters, the FCCA's key stakeholders are the European Commission (DG Competition), the OECD Competition Committee, the Nordic competition authorities and the International Competition Network (ICN). FCCA rulings and decisions can be found in the archive in Finnish. More information at: http://www.kkv.fi/en/facts-and-advice/competition-affairs/.

Expropriation and Compensation

Finnish law protects private property rights. Citizen property is protected by the Constitution which includes basic provisions in the event of expropriation. Private property is only expropriated for public purposes (eminent domain), in a non-discriminatory manner, with reasonable compensation, and in accordance with established international law. Expropriation is usually based on a permit given by the government or on a confirmed plan and is performed by the District Survey Office. Compensation is awarded at full market price, but may exclude the rise in value due only to planning decisions.

Besides normal expropriation according to the Expropriation Act, a municipality or the State has the right to expropriate land for planning purposes. Expropriation is mainly for acquiring land for common needs, such as street areas, parks and civic buildings. The method is rarely used: less than 1 percent of land acquired by the municipalities is expropriated. Credendo Group ranks Finland's expropriation risk as low (1), on a scale from 1 to 7: https://www.credendo.com/country_risk/finland#.

Dispute Settlement

ICSID Convention and New York Convention

In 1969, Finland became a member state to the World Bank-based International Center for Settlement of Investment Disputes (ICSID Convention). Finland is a signatory to the Convention of the Recognition and Enforcement of Foreign Arbitral Awards (1958 New York Convention).

Investor-State Dispute Settlement

The Finnish Arbitration Act (967/1992) is applied without distinction to both domestic and international arbitration. Sections 1 to 50 apply to arbitration in Finland and Sections 51 to 55 to arbitration agreements providing for arbitration abroad and the recognition and enforcement of foreign arbitral awards in Finland. Of 234 international parties in 2017, one was from the United States. There have been no reported investment disputes in Finland in recent years.

International Commercial Arbitration and Foreign Courts

Finland has a long tradition of institutional arbitration and its legal framework dates back to as early as 1928. Today, arbitration procedures are governed by the 1992 Arbitration Act (as amended), which largely mirrors the UNCITRAL Model Law on International Commercial Arbitration of 1985 (with amendments, as adopted in 2006). The UNCITRAL Model law has not yet, however, been implemented into Finnish Law. The Finland Chamber of Commerce is discussing amendments with the Ministry of Justice regarding the need to make the Act fully consistent with the Model Law, something that would increase Finland's attractiveness as a venue for international arbitration.

Finland's Act on Mediation in Civil Disputes and Certification of Settlements by Courts (394/2011) aims to facilitate alternative dispute resolution (ADR) and promote amicable settlements by encouraging mediation, and applies to settlements concluded in other EU member states: http://www.finlex.fi/en/laki/kaannokset/2011/en20110394.pdf. In June 2016, the Finland Chamber of Commerce launched its Mediation Rules under which FAI, the Institute of the Finland Chamber of Commerce, will administer mediations: http://arbitration.fi/mediation/mediation_rules/.

Any dispute in a civil or commercial matter, international or domestic, which can be settled by agreement may be referred to arbitration. Arbitration is frequently used to settle commercial disputes and is usually faster than court proceedings. An arbitral award is final and binding. FAI promotes the settlement of disputes through arbitration, commonly using the "FAI Rules": http://arbitration.fi/arbitration/rules/. In 2014, a Guide to the Finnish Arbitration FAI Rules was published: http://arbitration.fi/2015/01/15/guide-finnish-arbitration-rules-published/. The Institute appoints arbitrators both to domestic and international arbitration proceedings, and administers domestic and international arbitrations governed by its rules. It also appoints arbitrators in ad hoc cases when the arbitration agreement so provides, and acts as appointing authority under the UNCITRAL Arbitration Rules. The Finnish Arbitration Act (967/1992) states that foreign nationals can act as arbitrators. For more information see: http://arbitration.fi/arbitration/ and http://www.finlex.fi/fi/laki/kaannokset/1992/en19920967.pdf.

Finland signed the UN Convention on Transparency in Treaty-based Investor-State Arbitration ("Mauritius Convention") in March 2015. Under the new rules, all documents and hearings are open to the public, interested parties may submit statements, and protection for confidential information has been strengthened.

Bankruptcy Regulations

The Bankruptcy Act includes provisions on the prerequisites for initiating bankruptcy, bankruptcy proceedings, claims in bankruptcy, administration and the management and sales of assets: https://www.finlex.fi/en/laki/kaannokset/2004/en20040120.pdf . Companies bankrupt elsewhere may file for bankruptcy in Finland if they have Finnish assets. Finland has consistently applied its commercial and bankruptcy laws, with secured interests in property recognized and enforced.

The Reorganization of Enterprises Act (1993/47), http://www.finlex.fi/fi/laki/kaannokset/1993/en19930047, establishes a legal framework for reorganization with the aim to provide an alternative to bankruptcy proceedings. The Act excludes credit and insurance institutions and certain other financial institutions. Recognition of restructuring or insolvency processes initiated outside of the EU requires an exequatur from a Finnish court.

The bankruptcy ombudsman, http://www.konkurssiasiamies.fi/en/index.html, supervises the administration of bankruptcy estates in Finland. The Act on the Supervision of the Administration of Bankruptcy Estates dictates related Finnish law: http://www.konkurssiasiamies.fi/material/attachments/konkurssiasiamies/konkurssiasiamiehentoimistonliitteet/6JZrLGPN1/Act_on_the_Supervision_of_the_Administration_of_Bankruptcy_Estates.pdf.

Finland can be considered creditor-friendly; enforcement of liabilities through bankruptcy proceedings as well as execution outside bankruptcy proceedings are both effective. Bankruptcy proceedings are creditor-driven, with no formal powers granted to the debtor and its shareholders. The rights of a secured creditor are also quite extensive. According to the 2018 World Bank's Doing Business Report, Finland ranks second out of 190 for the ease of resolving insolvency: http://www.doingbusiness.org/data/exploretopics/resolving-insolvency.

4. INDUSTRIAL POLICIES

Investment Incentives

Foreign-owned companies are eligible for government incentives on an equal footing with Finnish-owned companies. Support is given in the form of grants, loans, tax benefits, equity participation, guarantees, and employee training. Business aid is coordinated by 15 Centers for Economic Development, Transport, and the Environment (ELY) that provide advisory, training, and expert services as well as grant funding for investment and development projects: http://www.ely-keskus.fi/en/web/ely-en/business-and-industry;jsessionid=AD25BC6992E30934024E33393E6E6BF7.

A company can use guarantees from the state-owned financing company Finnvera: https://www.finnvera.fi/eng/start/applying-for-financing/when-setting-up-a-business?source=3165. Finnvera offers services to businesses in most sectors, and is also Finland's official Export Credit Agency (ECA). Business Finland helps foreign investors set up a business in Finland. Its services are free of charge, and range from data collection and matchmaking to location management: https://www.investinfinland.fi/our-services. Support for innovative business ventures can also be obtained from the Foundation for Finnish Inventions: http://www.wipo.int/sme/en/best_practices/finland.htm.

Foreign Trade Zones/Free Ports/Trade Facilitation

The free zone area regulations have been harmonized in the EU by the Community Customs Code. The European Union Customs Code UCC, its Delegated Act and Implementing Act entered into force on May 1, 2016, and will be implemented gradually; the free zone of control type II was abolished and the operator authorizations were changed into customs warehouse authorizations on Customs' initiative. The Code also allows the processing of non-Union goods without import duties and other charges.

Performance and Data Localization Requirements

There are no performance requirements or commitments imposed on foreign investment in Finland. However, to conduct business in Finland, some residency requirements must be met. The Limited Liability Companies (LLC) Act of Finland is at: http://finlex.fi/en/laki/kaannokset/2006/en20060624?search%5Btype%5D=pika&search%5Bpika%5D=limited%20liability. A LLC must be reported for registration within three months from the signing of the memorandum of association: http://www.prh.fi/en/kaupparekisteri/yrityksen_perustaminen/osakeyhtio.html. There is no forced localization policy for foreign investments in Finland.

Finland participates actively in the development of the EU's Digital Single Market, and outside of privacy issues encourages a light regulatory approach in this area. Data transfers from Finland to non-EU countries must abide by EU Data Protection Directive 95/46/EC, which will be replaced by the General Data Protection Regulation (GDPR) on May 25, 2018.

Personal data may be transferred across borders per the Finnish Personal Data Act (PDA, at: http://finlex.fi/en/laki/kaannokset/1999/en19990523?search%5Btype%5D=pika&search%5Bpika%5D=personal%20data), which states that personal data may be transferred outside the European Union or the European Economic Area only if the country in question guarantees an adequate level of data protection. Office of the Data Protection Ombudsman legislation is at: http://www.tietosuoja.fi/en/index/rekisterinpitajalle.html.

5. PROTECTION OF PROPERTY RIGHTS

Real Property

The Finnish legal system protects property rights, and secured interest in property, both movable and real, is recognized and enforced. Finland ranked second of 127 countries in the Property

Rights Alliance 2017 International Property Rights Index (IPRI) that concentrates on the Legal and Political Environment, Physical Property Rights, and Intellectual Property Rights (IPR).

Mortgages exist in Finland, and can be applied to both owned and rented real estate. Finland ranks 27th out of 190 countries in the ease of Registering Property according to the World Bank's 2018 Doing Business Report. In Finland, real property formation, mutation, land consolidation, cadastral mapping, registration of real properties, ownership and legal rights, real property valuation, and taxation are all combined within one basic cadastral system (real estate register) maintained by the National Land Survey: http://www.maanmittauslaitos.fi/en/real-property.

Intellectual Property Rights

The Finnish legal system protects IPR, and Finland adheres to numerous related international agreements. Finland is a member of the World International Property Organization (WIPO). Finland's national IPR strategy 2014-2020 (in Finnish) is at: http://luovasuomi.fi/www.luovasuomi.fi/article/1840.html.

The Finnish Copyright Act is at: http://www.wipo.int/wipolex/en/text.jsp?file_id=397616. A set of guidelines applicable for international use, was published in 2016 and can be found at: http://www.cupore.fi/en/publications/cupore-s-publications/assessing-the-operation-of-copyright-and-related-rights-systems-141052-14122016. Trademark applicants or proprietors not domiciled in Finland are required to have a representative resident in the European Economic Area. Currently, Finland is preparing to implement the new EU Trademark Directive and amend the Finnish Trademark Act. The new Trademark Act is estimated to enter into force in early 2019. The current Trademark Act is at https://www.finlex.fi/en/laki/kaannokset/1964/en19640007_20000056.pdf.

Patent rights are consistent with international standards, and a granted patent is valid for 20 years. However, the regulatory framework regarding process patents filed before 1995, and pending in 1996, denied adequate protection to many of the top-selling U.S. pharmaceutical products currently on the Finnish market. For this reason, Finland, was placed on the 301 Watch List in 2009, but was removed from the list in 2015 given that the term for such patents has expired. U.S. industry continues to identify concerns in several EU Member States, including Finland, with respect to transparency and the opportunity to engage in policies related to pricing and reimbursement. This reportedly creates uncertainty and adversely impacts market access and incentives for further innovation. The 2017 Special 301 report can be found at: https://ustr.gov/issue-areas/intellectual-property/special-301/2017-special-301-review.

The protection of trade secrets has been ensured mainly by way of criminal legislation and proceedings, but also under the Unfair Business Practices Act subject to the jurisdiction of the Market Court: http://www.finlex.fi/fi/laki/kaannokset/1978/en19781061.pdf. The government plans to submit a bill to Parliament in spring 2018 implementing the EU Directive on the protection of undisclosed know-how and business information (2016/943). The 2015 International Association for the Protection of Intellectual Property (AIPPI) group report on Finnish legal protection of trade secrets can be found at: http://aippi.org/library/page/4/?publication_title=trade%20secrets&start_date_range&end_date_range.

Finnish customs officers have ex-officio authority to seize and destroy counterfeit goods. IPR enforcement in Finland is based on EU regulation (EU) 608/2013. Finnish authorities seized 45,900 counterfeit goods items with a value of 3.45 million USD in 2016, according to Finnish Customs statistics.

The link to WIPO's list of IPR legislation is at: http://www.wipo.int/wipolex/en/profile.jsp?code=FI. For additional information about treaty obligations and points of contact at local IP offices, please see WIPO's country profiles here: http://www.wipo.int/directory/en/details.jsp?country_code=FI.

6. FINANCIAL SECTOR

Capital Markets and Portfolio Investment

Finland is open to foreign portfolio investment and has an effective regulatory system. According to the Bank of Finland, in March 2018 Finland had EUR 8.6 billion worth of official reserve assets, mainly in foreign currency reserves and securities. Credit is allocated on market terms and is made available to foreign investors in a non-discriminatory manner, and private sector companies have access to a variety of credit instruments. Legal, regulatory, and accounting systems are transparent and consistent with international norms.

The Helsinki Stock Exchange has since 2003 been part of OMX, referred to as NASDAQ OMX Helsinki (OMXH). NASDAQ OMX Helsinki is part of the NASDAQ OMX Nordic division, together with the Stockholm, Copenhagen, Iceland, and Baltic (Tallinn, Riga, and Vilnius) stock exchanges.

Finland accepts the obligations under IMF Article VIII, Sections 2(a), 3, and 4 of the Fund's Articles of Agreement. It maintains an exchange system free of restrictions on payments and transfers for current international transactions, except for those measures imposed for security reasons in accordance with Regulations of the Council of the European Union.

Money and Banking System

Banking is open to foreign competition. At the end of 2016, there were 274 credit institutions operating in Finland and total assets of the domestic banking groups and branches of foreign banks operating in Finland amounted to 526 billion USD. For more information see: www.finanssiala.fi/en/material/FFI-Finnish-Banking-2016.pdf.

Foreign nationals can in principle open bank accounts in the same manner as Finns. However, banks must identify customers and this may prove more difficult for foreign nationals. In addition to personal and address data, the bank often needs to know the person's identifier code (i.e. social security number), and a number of banks require a work permit, a certificate of studies, or a letter of recommendation from a trustworthy bank, and details regarding the nature of transactions to be made with the account. All authorized deposit-taking banks are members of the Deposit Guarantee Fund, which guarantees customers' deposits to a maximum of EUR 100,000 per depositor.

Obtained capital and accumulated profit strengthened the banking sector's capital adequacy in 2016. At the end of the year, the overall capital adequacy ratio was 23.9 percent, one of the strongest in Europe. Measured in Core Tier 1 Capital, the ratio was 21.7 percent. The average CET1 ratio in the EU banking sector was 14.2 percent at the end of 2016. Return on equity (ROE) was 8.2 percent, and the cost ratio (costs divided by profits) also improved, reaching 54 percent in 2016. Standard & Poor's announced in September 2017 that it was retaining Finland's AA+ credit rating, while Fitch kept Finland's credit rating at AA+ in February 2018. Moody's lowered its triple-A rating to Aa1 in June 2016, keeping it there in October 2017.

Nordea, which has the leading market position among household and corporate customers in Finland, became a member of the "we.trade" consortium in November 2017. The consortium is building a platform aiming to make domestic and cross-border commerce easier for European companies by harnessing the power of distributed ledger and block chain technology. The Finnish State Treasury released cryptocurrency guidelines in February 2018: http://www.valtiokonttori.fi/download/noname/%7B8A176917-BFD9-4851-B1E1-37A651E44B8C%7D/95443.

Foreign Exchange and Remittances

Foreign Exchange Policies

Finland adopted the Euro as its official currency in January 1999. Finland maintains an exchange system free of restrictions on the making of payments and transfers for international transactions, except for those measures imposed for security reasons.

Remittance Policies

There are no legal obstacles to direct foreign investment in Finnish securities or exchange controls regarding payments into and out of Finland. Banks must identify their customers and report suspected cases of money laundering or the financing of terrorism. Banks and credit institutions must also report single payments or transfers of EUR 15,000 or more. If the origin of funds is suspect, banks must immediately inform the National Bureau of Investigation. There are no restrictions on current transfers or repatriation of profits. Residents and non-residents may hold foreign exchange accounts. There is no limit on dividend distributions as long as they correspond to a company's official earnings records.

Travelers carrying more than EUR 10,000 must make a declaration upon entering or leaving the EU. As a Financial Action Task Force (FATF) member, Finland observes most of FATF's 49 standards. FATF has praised Finland for improving its anti-money laundering legal framework: http://www.fatf-gafi.org/media/fatf/documents/reports/mer/Finland_FUR_2013.pdf.

Sovereign Wealth Funds

Solidium is an investment company that is fully owned by the State of Finland. Although it is not explicitly a sovereign wealth fund, Solidium's mission is to manage and increase the long-term value of the listed shareholdings of the Finnish State. Solidium is a minority owner in twelve listed companies; the market value of Solidium's equity holdings is approximately EUR 8.3 billion (March 2018, https://www.solidium.fi/en/holdings/holdings/).

7. STATE-OWNED ENTERPRISES

State Owned Enterprises (SOEs) in Finland are active in chemicals, petrochemicals, plastics and composites; energy and mining; environmental technologies; food processing and packaging; industrial equipment and supplies; marine technology; media and entertainment; metal manufacturing and products; services; and travel. The Ownership Steering Act (1368/2007) regulates the administration of state-owned companies: http://www.finlex.fi/en/laki/kaannokset/2007/en20071368?search%5Btype%5D=pika&search%5Bpika%5D=ownership%20steering. In general, SOEs are open to competition except where they have a monopoly position, namely in alcohol retail and gambling. The Ownership Steering Department in the Prime Minister's Office has ownership steering responsibility for Finnish SOEs, and is responsible for Solidium.

The GOF, directly or through Solidium, is a significant owner in 16 companies listed on the Helsinki stock exchange. The market value of all State shareholdings was approximately EUR 24.2 billion as of April 2018. More info can be found here: http://vnk.fi/en/value-of-state-shareholdings. As of March 2016, the GOF has majority ownership of shares in two listed companies (Finnair and Fortum) and owns shares in 35 commercial companies: http://vnk.fi/en/state-shareholdings-and-parliamentary-authorisations (March 2018). The business development company Vake was established in 2016 and should be fully operational in 2018. Vake's role is to manage the State shareholdings under its control and to create conditions for reform.

Finnish state ownership steering complies with the OECD Principles of Corporate Governance.

The Parliamentary Advisory Council in the Prime Minister's Office serves in an advisory capacity regarding SOE policy; it does not make recommendations regarding the actual business in which the individual companies are engaged. The government has proposed changing its ownership levels in several companies and increasing the number of companies steered by the Prime Minister's Office. The Government also proposed to lower the limit for retaining a strategic interest to 33.4 percent.

Finland opened domestic rail freight to competition in early 2007, and in July 2016, Fenniarail Oy, the first private rail operator on the Finnish market, began operations. Passenger rail transport services will be opened to competition in stages, starting with local rail services in southern Finland. The ensuing transport systems are scheduled to be operational by 2026. Three wholly state-owned companies will be separated from Finnish State Railways (VR) to create a level playing field for all operators: a rolling stock company, a maintenance company, and a real estate company. The Finnish Ministry of Transport and Communications and VR have negotiated a rail traffic service purchase agreement covering long-distance services as well as commuter services outside the Helsinki Region. The agreement is valid until December 31, 2019, and affords the VR Group exclusive rights for passenger rail services.

Cross-border transportation between Finland and Russia was opened to competition in December 2016. Trains to and from Russia can be operated by any railroad with permission to operate in the EU. This was earlier VR's exclusive domain. Fenniarail Oy has an agreement with VR regarding information exchange between authorities in Finland and Russia, approvals of rail wagons on the Finnish rail network and the safety of rail wagons. The agreement was signed in January 2017 for an initial trial period.

Privatization Program

Parliament makes all decisions identifying the companies in which the State may relinquish sole ownership (100 percent of the votes) or control (minimum of 50.1 percent of the votes), while the Government decides on the actual sale. The State has privatized companies by selling shares to Finnish and foreign institutional investors, through both public offerings and directly to employees. Sales of direct holdings of the State totaled EUR 412 million from 2010 to 2016. Solidium's share sales totaled some EUR 4.4 billion from June 2009 – January 2018. Proceeds are primarily used for repayment of central government debt, with a smaller proportion to strengthen the economy and promote growth. The Government issued a new resolution on state-ownership policy in May 2016, seeking to ensure that corporate assets held by the State are put to more efficient use to boost economic growth and employment.

8. RESPONSIBLE BUSINESS CONDUCT

The Government promotes Corporate Social Responsibility (CSR) through the Ministry of Employment and the Economy CSR Guidelines (http://tem.fi/en/key-guidelines-on-csr). The Committee on Corporate Social Responsibility acts as the Finnish National Contact Point (NCP) for the effective implementation of the OECD Guidelines for Multinational Enterprises (MNEs) together with the Ministry of Economic Affairs and Employment: https://mneguidelines.oecd.org/ncps/finland.htm.

The government's SOE policy establishes CSR as a core value at SOEs. Finnish companies perceive that the central component of responsible business conduct or corporate responsibility is to conduct due diligence to ensure compliance with law and regulations. There are no national codes for CSR in Finland; rather, Finnish companies and public authorities have promoted global CSR codes, such as the OECD Guidelines for Multinational Enterprises; the UN Global Compact for Business and Human Rights; ILO principles; EMAS; ISO standards; and the Global Reporting Initiative (GRI).

The Directive of the European Parliament and the Council on the disclosure of non-financial information has been implemented via amendments to the Finnish Accounting Act, requiring affected organizations make the first report in 2018. The obligation to report non-financial information and corporate responsibility reports will apply to large public interest entities with more than 500 employees. There are 150 Finnish companies that publish annual CSR reports that were not previously obligated to do so. Finland is committed to the implementation of the OECD Guidelines for Multinational Enterprises, the ILO Declaration on Fundamental Principles and Rights at Work, and the tripartite declaration of principles concerning multinational enterprises and social policy by the ILO. Finland has joined the Extractive Industries Transparency Initiative (EITI), which supports improved governance in resource-rich countries.

Labor and environmental laws and regulations are not waived to attract or retain investments and the Government published a guide to socially responsible public procurement in November 2017: http://julkaisut.valtioneuvosto.fi/handle/10024/160318.

The Corporate Responsibility Network (FiBS) is the leading corporate responsibility network in Finland and has 314 members: http://www.fibsry.fi/fi/english/home. The Human Rights Center (HRC), administratively linked to the Office of the Parliamentary Ombudsman, encourages foreign and local enterprises to follow the most important international norms: http://www.ihmisoikeuskeskus.fi/in-english/what-we-do/monitoring-of-the-implementation/.

The Securities Market Association, http://cgfinland.fi/en/, developed and updated (2015) the Finnish Corporate Governance Code (http://cgfinland.fi/files/2015/10/hallinnointikoodi-2015eng.pdf) for companies listed on the Helsinki Stock Exchange: http://business.nasdaq.com/list/Rules-and-Regulations/European-rules/nasdaq-helsinki/index.html.

9. CORRUPTION

The Internal Security Program of 2017 does not list corruption as a risk in Finland and there is no dedicated national anti-corruption strategy. Over the past decade, Finland has placed first or second on Transparency International's (TI) Corruption Perceptions Index (CPI). In 2017, TI ranked Finland third, saying that Finland still faces issues related to "old-boys' networks" and because of several conflict of interest scandals in 2017 that involved issues concerning blurred lines between public and private interests, and public office holders who had not recused themselves from decisions affecting them. In January 2017, Helsinki announced plans for a new service to anonymously inform authorities about suspected corruption. At the beginning of 2017, a new Public Procurement Act based on the new EU directives on public procurement entered into force. Under the new law, a foreign bribery conviction remains a mandatory ground for exclusion from public contracts.

Corruption in Finland is covered by the Criminal Code and sanctions range from fines to imprisonment of up to four years. Both giving and accepting a bribe is considered criminal and Finland has statutory tax rules concerning non-deductibility of bribes. Finland does not have an authority specifically charged to prevent corruption. The Ministry of Justice coordinates anti-corruption matters, but Finland's EU anti-corruption contact is the Ministry of the Interior. The National Bureau of Investigation also follows corruption, while the tax administration has guidelines obliging tax officials to report suspected offences, including foreign bribery, and the Ministry of Finance has guidelines on hospitality, benefits, and gifts. The Ministry of Justice describes its anti-corruption efforts at: http://oikeusministerio.fi/en/anti-corruption-activities.

The Act on a Candidate's Election Funding (273/2009) delineates election funding and disclosure rules. The Act requires presidential candidates, Members of Parliament, and Deputy Members to declare total campaign financing, the financial value of each contribution, and donor names for donations exceeding EUR 1,500: http://www.finlex.fi/en/laki/kaannokset/2009/en20090273.pdf. The Act on Political Parties (10/1969) concerning the funding of political parties is at: http://www.finlex.fi/fi/laki/kaannokset/1969/en19690010.pdf. The National Audit Office of Finland keeps a register containing election funding disclosures at: http://www.vaalirahoitusvalvonta.fi (available in Finnish and Swedish). Election funding disclosures must be filed with the National Audit Office of Finland within two months of election results being confirmed.

Finland does not regulate lobbying; there is no requirement for lobbyists to register or report contact with public officials. The ethical Guidelines of the Finnish Prosecution Service were published in December 2016: http://www.vksv.fi/en/index/julkaisutjaohjeet/theethicalguidelinesofthefinnishprosecutionservice.html.

The following are ratified or in force in Finland: the Convention on Laundering, Search, Seizure and Confiscation of the Proceeds from Crime; the Council of Europe Civil Law Convention on Corruption; the Criminal Law Convention on Corruption; the UN Convention against Transnational Organized Crime; and, the UN Anticorruption Convention. Finland is a member of the European Partners against Corruption (EPAC). Finland is a signatory to the OECD Convention on Anti-Bribery, and a TI progress report released in August 2015 rated Finland's enforcement as moderate: http://www.transparency.org/exporting_corruption/Finland.

In March 2017, the OECD Working Group on Bribery noted Finland has been active in enforcing its foreign bribery laws. However, all of the cases that progressed to prosecution resulted in acquittal, and the OECD recommended assigning cases to courts or judges with specialized experience and that Finland provide detailed training to law enforcement and the judiciary: http://www.oecd.org/newsroom/high-acquittal-rate-jeopardises-finland-efforts-to-combat-foreign-bribery.htm?src=ilaw. In March 2018, the Council of Europe's anticorruption body GRECO (Group of States against Corruption) issued recommendations to Finland for preventing corruption among ministers, senior government officials and members of law enforcement agencies (the police and the Border Guard). The report recommended that Finland adopt and implement a national anticorruption strategy and pay special attention to the risks related to privatization in the forthcoming health, social services and regional government reform.

The National Bureau of Investigation is responsible for the investigation of organized and international crimes, including economic crime and corruption, and operates an anti-corruption unit to detect economic offences. The Ministry of Justice has set up a specialist network which meets a few times a year to discuss and exchange information.

Resources to Report Corruption

Contact at government agency or agencies are responsible for combating corruption:

Contact at government agency:

Markku Ranta-Aho
Head of Financial Crime Division
National Board of Investigation
P.O. Box 285, 01310 Vantaa, Finland
markku.ranta-aho@poliisi.fi

Contact at "watchdog" organization Contact at watchdog organization:

Jaakko Korhonen, Chairperson , Chairperson
Transparency Finland
info@transparency.fi

10. POLITICAL AND SECURITY ENVIRONMENT

There are no instances of political violence in Finland. Some isolated anti-immigration incidents, including the September 2016 death of a Finnish citizen after an altercation with the neo-Nazi Nordic Resistance Movement, sparked large anti-racism rallies. There have been some subsequent demonstrations calling for a stop to deportations of asylum seekers and counter-protests to these demonstrations in central Helsinki, but they have been rare and relatively small. In August 2017, a stabbing attack took place in central Turku in southwest Finland in which two pedestrians were killed and eight injured. Finnish authorities considered the attack a terrorist act, making it the first of its kind since the end of World War II.

The Fund for Peace (FFP) ranked Finland as the most stable country in the world again in 2017 based on political, social, and economic indicators including public services, income distribution, human rights, and the rule of law. According to BMI Research, Finland will remain one of the most politically stable countries globally over the 10-year forecast period (2016-25) because of the well-established and functioning state bureaucracy, effective rule of law, personal freedoms and civil liberties, and some of the world's most progressive gender equality legislation.

11. LABOR POLICIES AND PRACTICES

Finland has a long tradition of trade unions. The country has a unionization rate of 75 percent, and approximately 90 percent of employees in Finland participate in the collective bargaining system. Extensive tripartite cooperation between the government, employer's groups, and trade unions characterize the country's labor market system. Any trade union and employers' association may make collective agreements, and the Ministry decides on the validity of the agreement. The Act on Employment Contracts regulates employment relationships regarding working hours, annual leave, and safety conditions, although minimum wages, actual working hours, and working conditions are determined to a large extent through collective agreements instead of parliamentary legislation. Collective bargaining and collective labor agreements are generally binding. In recent years, local labor market partners have been given more flexibility to enforce the collective agreements.

Finland adheres to most ILO conventions; enforcement of worker rights is effective. Freedom of association and collective bargaining are guaranteed by law, which provides for the right to form and join independent unions, conduct legal strikes, and bargain collectively. The law prohibits anti-union discrimination and any obstruction of these rights. The National Conciliator under the Ministry of Employment and the Economy assists negotiating partners with labor disputes. The arbitration system is based on the Act on Mediation in Labor Disputes and the Labor Court is the highest body for settlement. The ILO's Finland Country profile can be found here: http://www.ilo.org/dyn/normlex/en/f?p=1000:11110:0::NO:11110:P11110_COUNTRY_ID:102625.

The Ministry of Employment and the Economy is responsible for drafting labor legislation and the Ministry of Social Affairs and Health is responsible for enforcing labor laws and regulations. Finnish authorities adequately enforce contract, wage, and overtime laws. New legislation concerning the hiring of foreign workers in Finland entered into force on June 18, 2016. Its objective is to intensify monitoring and to ensure improved compliance with the terms of employment in Finland. Finland allows the free movement of EU citizen workers. During 2016, there were a total of 69 strikes in Finland, compared to 163 in 2015

In 2016, Statistics Finland estimated that the working age population would shrink by well over 100,000 persons by 2030. With the robust economic growth in 2016 and 2017, labor shortages are starting to appear in the social, health, and construction sectors.

The government reformed social protection and unemployment security to encourage people to accept job offers, shorten unemployment periods, reduce structural unemployment and save public resources. The unemployed are granted a labor market subsidy which, if linked to earnings as is the case for about 60 percent of the unemployed, guarantees moderate income for a period up to 400 working days. Those without jobs after the 400-day period need to demonstrate that they are actively pursuing employment to continue receiving benefits. The period of eligibility was shortened from 500 days to 400 days starting on January 1, 2017, except for those with a work history shorter than three years (reduced to 300 days), and for those aged over 58 (remains 500 days).

On January 1, 2017, Finnish authorities started a two-year, universal basic income trial. The goal is to determine whether a basic income, received without conditions, incentivizes recipients to seek paid work. Separately, new legislation that entered into force on January 1, 2018, stipulated that unemployed persons will forfeit 4.65 percent of benefits unless, during a three-month period, they either: a) find employment for 18 hours, b) receive at least 241 euro in income from entrepreneurial activity, c) participate in a five-day training course, or d) be available for other services offered by an employment office, such as attend training courses. The aim is to get an estimated 8,000 long-term unemployed people back to work by making unemployment less attractive. Unions opposed the action vigorously.

12. OPIC AND OTHER INVESTMENT INSURANCE PROGRAMS

The U.S. Overseas Private Investment Corporation (OPIC) and Finnvera (the former Finnish Guarantee Board) share an agreement to encourage joint U.S.-Finnish private investments in Russia and the Baltic States. For more information see: https://www.finnvera.fi/eng/Export/Export-Credit-Guarantee-operations/Export-Credit-Guarantee-operations. Finland is a member of the Multilateral Investment Guarantee Agency (MIGA).

13. FOREIGN DIRECT INVESTMENT AND FOREIGN PORTFOLIO INVESTMENT STATISTICS

Table 2: Key Macroeconomic Data, U.S. FDI in Host Country/Economy

	Host Country	USG or	USG or International Source of Data:

	Statistical Source		International Statistical Source		BEA; IMF; Eurostat; UNCTAD, Other
Economic Data	Year	Amount	Year	Amount	
Host Country Gross Domestic Product (GDP) (M USD)	2016	USD 278,000	2016	USD 239,000	www.worldbank.org/en/country
Foreign Direct Investment	Host Country Statistical Source		USG or International Statistical Source		USG or International Source of Data: BEA; IMF; Eurostat; UNCTAD, Other
U.S. FDI in Partner Country (M USD, stock positions)	2016	USD 1,670	2016	USD 3,395	BEA data available at http://bea.gov/international/direct_investment_multinational_companies_comprehensive_data.htm
Host Country's FDI in the United States (M USD, stock positions)	2016	USD 8,300	2016	USD 9,587	BEA data available at http://bea.gov/international/direct_investment_multinational_companies_comprehensive_data.htm
Total Inbound Stock of FDI as % host GDP	2016	0.6%	2016	1.4%	N/A

Table 3: Sources and Destination of FDI

Direct Investment from/in Counterpart Economy Data					
From Top Five Sources/To Top Five Destinations (US Dollars, Millions)					
Inward Direct Investment			Outward Direct Investment		
Total Inward	80,734	100%	Total Outward	111,110	100%
Sweden	37,198	46.1%	Sweden	29,775	26.8%
Netherlands	12,561	15.6%	Netherlands	19,256	17.3%
Luxembourg	8,300	10.3%	France	14,710	13.2%
Denmark	5,743	7.1%	United States	7,052	6.3%
Germany	3,481	4.3%	Belgium	3,351	3.0%
"0" reflects amounts rounded to +/- USD 500,000.					

Table 4: Sources of Portfolio Investment

Portfolio Investment Assets
Top Five Partners (Millions, US Dollars)

Total			Equity Securities			Total Debt Securities		
All Countries	340,642	100%	All Countries	189,387	100%	All Countries	151,255	100%
United States	57,415	16.9%	Ireland	41,683	22.0%	United States	20,230	13.4%
Ireland	46,094	13.5%	United States	37,186	19.6%	Sweden	19,203	12.7%
Luxembourg	37,248	10.9%	Luxembourg	33,172	17.5%	Germany	17,753	11.7%
Sweden	34,089	10.0%	Sweden	14,887	7.9%	France	14,686	9.7%
Germany	23,220	6.8%	Cayman Islands	13,645	7.2%	Netherlands	11,402	7.5%

14. CONTACT FOR MORE INFORMATION

U.S. Embassy Helsinki
HelsinkiPolEconAll@state.gov

COMPANY FORMATION IN FINLAND: STRATEGIC AND PRACTICAL INFORMATION

Business can be conducted as a private entrepreneur, as a partnership or limited liability company formed of one or more individuals or legal entities, or a co-operative. A foreign entrepreneur may also establish a branch in Finland. In certain circumstances, those not resident/domiciled in the EEA need a permit from the National Board of Patents and Registration.

Enterprises must submit a basic declaration to the trade register using the start-up notification, with which they may also apply for registration in the trade register, employer register, prepayment register and/or VAT register.

Finland's economic stability and high-tech industrial base has made it a key target for international investors considering company formation Finland. Anyone can set up business in Finland, irrespective of nationality, so long as one of the company's founding members is resident in the European Economic Area. If the founder is a legal person, its domicile should be in an EEA country (the EEA compromises all the EU countries plus Iceland, Liechtenstein, Norway and Switzerland). If you want to know more about Finnish incorporation please contact us or read on.

The two most popular forms of Finland incorporation are:

- public limited company - osakeyhtiö Oyj
- private limited company – osakeyhtiö Oy

The minimum share capital for a public limited company is €80,000.

- a minimum of three board directors plus a chief executive
- it is usual to be listed in the Helsinki Stock Exchange
- there is a statutory requirement for audited accounts
- flat corporate tax rate of 26%

The minimum share capital for a private limited company is €2,500.

- at least one board director and a deputy
- there is a statutory requirement for audited accounts only if the company has a turnover of more than €200,000, balance sheet total of more than €100,000 and 3 or more employees
- a local serviced office is advisable, click here for details
- flat corporate tax rate of 26%

Set up business in Finland general or limited partnership

- small private company, usually sole trader
- branch of a foreign company

PRINCIPAL CORPORATE LEGISLATION

The Oy/Ab and Oyj/Abp are both governed by the Finnish Private Companies Act (Osakeyhtiölaki).

New Companies Act (624/2006).

FINLAND COMPANY INFORMATION

Type of company for international Trade and Investment

Oy/Ab - Private Limited Company or LTD

Oyj/Abp - Public Limited Company or PLC

Procedure to Incorporate

The promoter of the company will draw up and sign the Memorandum and Articles of Association. This together with evidence of the minimum share capital payment is then submitted to the Companies Registry for registration. A statutory general meeting of shareholder must also be held for the purposes of adopting the Articles of Association, electing the board of directors or director and the auditors.

Restrictions on Trading

Yes, specified groups, which include for example, banking, insurance and financial services.

Powers of Company

A Company incorporated in Finland has the same powers as a natural person.

Language of Legislation and Corporate Documents

Finnish or Swedish.

Shelf Companies Available

Yes.

Time to Incorporate

Three to four weeks.

Name Restrictions

A name that is similar to or identical to an existing company. A well-known name that is known to exist elsewhere.

Language of Name

The name of the company can be expressed in any language using the Latin alphabet. The Registrar may request a Finnish or Swedish translation to ensure that the proposed name does not contravene name restrictions.

Names Requiring Consent or Licence

Bank, building society, savings, loans, insurance, assurance, reinsurance, fund management, investment fund, trust, trustees, Chamber of Commerce, co-operation, council, municipal or their foreign language equivalents or any name in English or a foreign language that may suggest association with the banking or Insurance industries.

Registered Office Required

Yes, must be maintained in Finland.

Suffixes to Denote Limited Liability

Osakeyhtiö (Oy) in Finnish language or Aktiebolag (Ab) in Swedish language for private limited company and Julkinen osakeyhtiö (Oyj) in Finnish language or Publikt aktiebolag (Abp) for public limited company or the relevant abbreviations. .

Disclosure of Beneficial Ownership to Authorities

No.

FINLAND COMPLIANCE

Authorised and Issued Share Capital

Private Company - The minimum share capital is EURO 2,500 and must be issued and fully paid.

Public Company - The minimum authorised share capital for a public company is EURO 80,000 and must be paid up.

Classes of Shares Permitted

Ordinary shares, preference shares, deferred shares, redeemable shares and shares with full or with limited voting rights.

Taxation

Tax is paid by companies in Finland based upon annual accounts, which are submitted to the Finnish tax authorities at the end of the company's financial year. A company is free to choose its own year-end. The current tax rate is 26%.

Double Taxation Agreements

Finland is party to more than 60 double tax treaties.

Licence Fee

None.

Financial Statements Required

The introduction of new rules concerning the statutory auditing have recently been introduced.

A Finnish company only needs to appoint a Certified Auditor if two or more of below conditions are met during the accounting period and the preceeding accounting period:

- if the Balance Sheet (total assets or liabilities) exceeds €100,000
- if Turnover exceeds €200,000
- if the average number of employees exceeds three (3)

Otherwise the Board of Directors self-certify the annual accounts/report.

However if OCRA provide officers to a Finnish client company, we require that the Company be audited by an external Certified Auditor even if the statutory requirements above are not met. This is in both our and the client's interest.

Directors

Private Companies - One member of the board and one alternate member. They must be natural persons. A member may be of any nationality and need not reside in Finland, however at least half of the members of the board must reside within European Economic Area.

Public Companies - There is a two-tier management structure required for public companies and large private companies. This consists of a minimum of three board members who must appoint a CEO.

Company Secretary

N/A.

Shareholders

The minimum number of shareholders is one. A company must maintain a public record of its shareholders.

DIFFERENT FORMS OF BUSINESS

Factors such as the number of founders, the required capital and its availability affect any decision on form of business. There are no set rules determining which form of business should be chosen. The most suitable and appropriate form of business must be determined individually in each situation. The following information is useful to know when selecting the form of business:

Number of founders

An individual engaged in business without a partner may do so in the form of a single-member company or as a private entrepreneur. Partnerships (general partnership and limited partnership) always require a minimum of two partners. When there are several founders, the alternative forms of business are a limited liability company and a cooperative. A limited liability company may also be a single-member company, or there can be several partners. The minimum number of founders for a cooperative is three.

Required capital and its availability upon establishing an enterprise

The amount of capital required for business activities depends on the type and scope of the activities. Acting as a private entrepreneur (so-called private business name) is usually appropriate if the amount of required capital is relatively small.

A general partnership can be established without monetary investments. Work contribution by the partners is sufficient.

In a limited partnership a monetary investment is required of the silent partner, while work contribution is sufficient for general partners.

Limited liability companies are the most common form of business in areas requiring large amounts of capital. The minimum share capital required of a limited liability company is prescribed in the Companies Act as EUR 2,500. The share capital must be paid to the company's account in full before the company can be entered in the trade register maintained by the National Board of Patents and Registration. For legal purposes, a limited liability company is established when it is entered in the trade register.

There are no minimum requirements concerning the capital of cooperatives. The type and scope of the cooperative's activities determine the required capital.

Division of responsibilities in an enterprise

A private entrepreneur is responsible for any liabilities of the business with his/her personal property. The partners in a general partnership and the general partners in a limited partnership have a similar personal responsibility. The partners in a general partnership and the general partners in a limited partnership may make commitments on behalf of the partnership. Thus it is particularly important to select the right partner in this type of business. The responsibility of shareholder in a limited liability company, and of a member of a cooperative, is limited to the capital they have invested in the enterprise. In practice, especially in the early stages of the business, the property of shareholders or members or guarantees by the shareholders and members may be required as surety for the enterprise's debts.

Flexibility of operations

A private entrepreneur makes all decisions himself/herself and is responsible for the activities with his/her personal property. The partners in a general partnership and the general partners in a limited partnership make decisions either solely or jointly. Limited liability companies and cooperatives are represented by their Boards of Directors.

In a limited liability company there is a certain amount of statutory paperwork to take care of. One Ordinary General Meeting must be held in each accounting period, unless otherwise stipulated in the Articles of Association.

In a cooperative decision-making is characterised by the requirement for democracy. Each member has one vote, irrespective of the amount of their investment.

Partnerships, limited liability companies and cooperatives may elect a Managing Director to see to the day-to-day management of the business.

Continuity of operations

A private entrepreneur's business operations are the most vulnerable on the death of the entrepreneur. In a partnership the share of the partner may be transferred to another person with the agreement of the other partners, if this has been agreed in the partnership agreement. In a limited liability company changes in the shareholders do not affect the existence of the company. While membership in a cooperative cannot be sold, the cooperative itself may be sold if the members reach a sufficient level of unanimity.

Profit distribution and loss coverage

A private entrepreneur retains any profits himself/herself, but is also responsible for the losses incurred by the business. In a general partnership profits and losses are distributed among the partners as decreed by law (Partnerships Act, 389/1988) or in the partnership agreement.

In a limited partnership a silent partner is first paid a share of the profits on his investment as at the beginning of the accounting period, as decreed in the partnership agreement. The remaining part of the profit will be distributed among the general partners in accordance with the partnership agreement. Silent partners do not contribute to the coverage of losses.

A limited liability company pays its shareholders a dividend. Only the profit of the previous accounting period and unrestricted shareholder's equity may be used for dividends. If the results for the accounting period were negative or the company has made losses in previous accounting periods, these must first be subtracted from the above-mentioned items. The company's restricted equity may not be distributed as dividends. In a limited liability company profits are distributed as dividends paid to the shares of the shareholders.

In a limited liability company a shareholder's losses will only amount to the investment, unless he/she has pledged a personal guarantee for the company's debts.

Instead of obtaining a profit for its members, the purpose of a cooperative is to offer services for its members. Only a limited consideration on capital invested in the cooperative is paid from the profits. The profits, or the surplus, may be distributed to the members as extra wages, interest on cooperative capital or return of the surplus according to the use of the cooperative?s services by the members, or as otherwise stipulated in the rules. Work cooperatives may pay extra wages to the members. Cooperatives are subject to a reserve requirement; part of the surplus must be transferred to the reserve fund, after the losses shown by the balance sheet have been subtracted.

Taxation

Tax treatment varies depending on the form of business. Direct taxation in particular may affect the choice of enterprise formation. The major direct taxes are the state income tax and wealth tax payable to the State and the municipal income tax payable to the appropriate Municipality. When determining the tax burdens falling on different forms of business, attention must also be paid to the tax burden of the entrepreneur. The joint effect only determines which form of business is the most profitable in terms of taxation.

PRIVATE ENTREPRENEUR

An European Economic Area (EEA) resident may act as a private entrepreneur. Non-EEA residents need a permit from the National Board of Patents and Registration. With regard to the establishment of a business, citizenship is not of importance. The decisive factor is the individual's permanent place of residence.

Auditors

There are no statutory provisions concerning the audit of a private entrepreneur's accounts.

Establishment of a private entrepreneur for legal purposes

A private entrepreneur's business is established when the entrepreneur starts his/her activities.

Establishment documents

A private entrepreneur need not draw up a separate Charter of Foundation when setting up a business.

Concluding legal acts on behalf of the enterprise

The private entrepreneur himself/herself acts on behalf of the company, represents the business and writes the business name. See Administration and organs

Holder of procuration
An entrepreneur who has been entered in the trade register may authorise another person as a holder of procuration by granting him/her a power of attorney, which is defined as procuration in the text, or by showing other proof of the matter. There are no statutory requirements concerning the citizenship or place of residence of the holder of procuration. The holder of procuration may be entered in the trade register.

Representative
If neither the private entrepreneur nor the person entered in the trade register as a holder of procuration are Finnish residents, the entrepreneur must appoint a representative domiciled in Finland. The representative is to be entered in the trade register.

Administration and organs

The private entrepreneur himself/herself acts on behalf of the company.

Capital required at start-up

There are no statutory provisions concerning the minimum capital of a private entrepreneur.

GENERAL PARTNERSHIP

There must be at least two partners (founders) in a general partnership. At least one of the partners in a general partnership must have a permanent place of residence, or, if the founder is a legal entity, be domiciled in the European Econmic Area (EEA). If none of the partners in a general partnership has a place of residence/domicile in the EEA, all partners from outside the EEA need a permit from the National Board of Patents and Registration.

No legally incompetent person, bankrupt person or anyone banned from engaging in business may act as a founder.

Auditors

The Auditing Act specifies the circumstances when an auditor must be used.The new Auditing Act entered into force at the beginning of July 2007.

If the Partnership Agreement of the general partnership allows partnerships that meet no more than one of the following conditions in both the closing accounting period and in the accounting period preceding it may neglect the appointment of an auditor:

1) the balance sheet total exceeds EUR 100,000;

2) net sales or corresponding earning exceed EUR 200,000; or

3) there are more than three employees on average.

The obligation to appoint an auditor also applies to a general partnership launching operations if the general partnership already has business operations that meet the conditions for auditing obligation in the launching stage.

If the Partnership Agreement does not contain any regulations on auditors, and no more than one of the conditions mentioned above are met, the partnership has not an obligation to appoint an auditor.

HTM and KHT are titles for authorised auditors. HTM refers to an auditor authorised by a local Chamber of Commerce, and KHT refers to an auditor authorised by the Central Chamber of Commerce. The new enterprises (partnerships, companies and cooperatives) must appoint a KHT or HTM auditor or a KHT or HTM corporation (lay auditors are no longer used).

The partnership agreement may, however, stipulate that the partnership shall have one or more than one auditor. The partners participating in the election of the auditor may also elect one or more deputy auditors. In a general partnership the auditor is elected by the partners with a unanimous decision, unless otherwise agreed.

The auditor must be separately elected for each accounting period, unless the term of office has been stipulated in the partnership agreement. The auditor's term of office ends after the delivery of an auditor's report for the last accounting period during his/her term of office. If an auditor has been appointed until further notice, the term of office ends when a new auditor is appointed.

Establishment of a general partnership for legal purposes

A general partnership is established through a partnership agreement between the partners. A written agreement is required for the trade register.

Establishment documents

When a general partnership is entered in the trade register, a written partnership agreement is required as an attachment to the notification form. For legal purposes, an oral agreement is also possible.

Basic declaration to the trade register: general partnershipEstablishment documents: general partnershipStart-up notification to the tax administration.

Concluding legal acts on behalf of the enterprise

Each partner in a general partnership is entitled to represent the partnership and sign for the partnership in matters related to the partnership?s line of business. This right may be restricted through an agreement between the partners by removing the right of one or more partners to represent the partnership or by stipulating that two or more partners together have the right to represent the partnership. This restriction must be submitted for registration in the trade register. The restriction is valid concerning a third party of the promulgation from the date of registration in the trade register. See also Administration and organs.

Holder of procuration

In a general partnership partners may together authorise a designated person as their holder of procuration by granting him/her a procuration. The power of attorney granting the procuration authorises the holder of procuration to act for the company in all matters related to its business.

In a general partnership procurations may be given by all the partners together. It is possible to stipulate that the holder of procuration may only sign for the partnership jointly with one or more partners. Unless otherwise agreed, procurations may be cancelled by any partner, who, alone or together with another partner, is entitled to act for the partnership.

There are no statutory requirements concerning the citizenship or place of residence of the holder of procuration. The holder of procuration may be entered in the trade register.

Representative

A general partnership must have a representative who is domiciled in Finland. The representative is entered in the trade register. If the partnership has a partner, Managing Director or holder of procuration who has been entered in the trade register and who is domiciled in Finland, a separate representative is not required.

Administration and organs

A general partnership does not have any statutory organs. A general partnership may have a Managing Director, a Board of Directors and a meeting of partners, if these have been agreed on. The Managing Director, if any, must be submitted for registration in the trade register. The Managing Director of a general partnership is entitled to represent the partnership in matters relating to its day-to-day management. The Board of Directors and the meeting of partners are not entered in the trade register.

Capital required at start-up

No monetary investment is required of the partners in a general partnership. Work contribution is sufficient.

LIMITED PARTNERSHIP

There must be at least two partners (founders) in a limited partnership, at least one of whom must be a general partner.

At least one of the general partners in a limited partnership must have a permanent place of residence, or, if the founder is a legal entity, be domiciled in the European Econimic Area (EEA). Otherwise, a permit is required from the NBPR for all general partners that are not from the EEA. This requirement does not apply to the silent partners.

Auditors

The Auditing Act specifies the circumstances when an auditor must be used. The new Auditing Act entered into force at the beginning of July 2007.

If the Partnership Agreement of the limited partnership allows partnerships that meet no more than one of the following conditions in both the closing accounting period and in the accounting period preceding it may neglect the appointment of an auditor:

1) the balance sheet total exceeds EUR 100,000;

2) net sales or corresponding earning exceed EUR 200,000; or

3) there are more than three employees on average.

The obligation to appoint an auditor also applies to a limited partnership launching operations if the limited partnership already has business operations that meet the conditions for auditing obligation in the launching stage.

If the Partnership Agreement does not contain any regulations on auditors, and no more than one of the conditions mentioned above are met, the partnership has not an obligation to appoint an auditor.

With the new law, lay auditors are no longer used. Partnerships founded after the law has entered into force (1 July 2007) may not elect lay auditors (other than KHT or HTM auditors) any more.

The partnership agreement may, however, stipulate that the partnership shall have one or more than one auditor. The partners participating in the election of the auditor may also elect one or more deputy auditors. In a limited partnership the auditor is elected by the general partnerspartners with a unanimous decision, unless otherwise agreed.

The auditor must be separately elected for each accounting period, unless the term of office has been stipulated in the partnership agreement. The auditor's term of office ends after the delivery of an auditor's report for the last accounting period during his/her term of office. If an auditor has been appointed until further notice, the term of office ends when a new auditor is appointed.

Establishment of a limited partnership for legal purposes

A limited partnership is established through a partnership agreement between the partners. A written agreement is required for the trade register.

Establishment documents

When a limited partnership is entered in the trade register, a written partnership agreement is required as an attachment to the notification form. For legal purposes, an oral agreement is also possible.

Basic notification of a limited partnership

Limited partnerships use the start-up notification form Y2. The start-up notification is delivered as original. The partnership agreement is attached to the notification as original.

In case of a licenced trade a copy of the trade licence is attached to the trade register notification. If a licence has not yet been granted, the applicant may file the basic notification with the trade register and deliver a copy of the licence to the trade register once it has been granted.

In a limited partnership the general partners are responsible for filing a start-up notification form for the partnership. The notification must be signed by a person responsible for the notification or someone authorised by such person. If the notification is signed by a person authorised to do so, the original power of attorney must be attached to the notification. See Start-up notification of a limited partnership, p. 2.

Start-up notifications are available on the Business Information System (BIS) website at www.ytj.fi.

Limited partnership

The partnership agreement of a limited partnership may be made orally or in writing. However, the agreement should always be made in writing since the original written agreement is required as an attachment to the start-up notification. A written agreement is also advisable in case of disagreements between the partners.

The content of the partnership agreement should be determined case by case on the basis of the partnership's line of business and the scope of its operations. In the agreement, the partners agree on the foundation of the partnership and other relevant matters regarding its activities.

The trade register requires that at least the following matters are defined in the agreement:

1. business name

2. the municipality from which the operations are managed

3. line of business (type of activities)

4. the partners, and which of the partners are general partners and which silent partners

5. the monetary investment of a silent partner

6. the accounting period of the partnership

In addition, the following issues may be settled in the agreement:

- the division of responsibilities between the general partners

- signing for the partnership

- Managing Director (if to be elected)

- the accounting period and auditing of the accounts of the partnership and the number of auditors (if any auditor)

- provisions stipulating how the silent partner's share in the profits is calculated

- whether the silent partner has the right to transfer his partnership share to another person without the consent of general partners

- dismissal of partners

- continuing with the business after the death of a partner

If the partnership agreement does not contain any provisions on the above-mentioned issues, the provisions of the Partnerships Act will be applied.

The partnership agreement is dated and signed by all the partners.

If none of the general partners of a limited partnership is resident/domiciled (legal entity) in the EEA, all general partners with a permanent residence/domicile outside the EEAneed permit from the National Board of Patents and Registration to serve as general partners.

Start-up notification to the tax administration

A new company must submit a start-up notification to the tax administration registers and the Trade Register using the same form. If the company already has a business ID, it should use the amendment notification form.

The tax administration registers referred to here include the prepayment register, employer register and VAT register.

Concluding legal acts on behalf of the enterprise

A general partner has the same rights to represent the partnership as partners in a limited partnership. A silent partner does not have the right to represent the company or act on its behalf without a separate agreement.

A limited partnership does not have statutory organs. A limited partnership may have a Managing Director, a Board of Directors and a meeting of partners, if these have been agreed on. The Managing Director, if any, must be submitted for registration in the trade register. The Managing Director of a limited partnership is entitled to represent the partnership in matters relating to its day-to-day management. The Board of Directors and the meeting of partners are not entered in the trade register.

Holder of procuration

In a limited partnership partners may together authorise a designated person as their holder of procuration by granting him/her a procuration. This authorises the holder of procuration to act for the company in all matters related to its business. It is possible to stipulate that the holder of procuration may only sign for the partnership jointly with one or more partners.

The procuration may be entered in the trade register.

Representative

A limited partnership must have a representative who is domiciled in Finland. The representative is entered in the trade register. If the partnership has a general partner, Managing Director or holder of procuration who has been entered in the trade register and who is domiciled in Finland, a separate representative is not required.

Administration and organs

A limited partnership does not have any statutory organs. A limited partnership may have a Managing Director, a Board of Directors and a meeting of partners, if these have been agreed on. The Managing Director, if any, must be submitted for registration in the trade register. The Managing Director of a limited partnership is entitled to represent the partnership in matters relating to its day-to-day management.

Capital required at start-up

A silent partner must make a capital investment in the partnership, while work contribution is sufficient for general partners.

LIMITED LIABILITY COMPANY

There must be one or more founders in a limited liability company.

The new Companies Act does not any restrictions for the place of residence or domicile for share subscribers (even if the question is about a single-member company).

It must also be noticed that if a limited liability company is a single-member company, that is, the company has only one shareholder and he/she is the only member of the Board, the Board must then have at least one deputy member.

Auditors

The Auditing Act specifies the circumstances when an auditor must be used. The new Auditing Act entered into force at the beginning of July 2007.

If the Articles of Association allow, companies that meet no more than one of the following conditions in both the closing accounting period and in the accounting period preceding it may neglect the appointment of an auditor:

1) the balance sheet total exceeds EUR 100,000;

2) net sales or corresponding earning exceed EUR 200,000; or

3) there are more than three employees on average.

The obligation to appoint an auditor also applies to a limited liability company launching operations if the limited liability company already has business operations that meet the conditions for auditing obligation in the launching stage.

If the Articles of Association for a limited liability company do not contain any regulations on auditors, and no more than one of the conditions mentioned above are met, the company has not an obligation to appoint an auditor. A limited liability company with regulations concerning auditors included in the Articles of Association must change the document before they can stop appointing auditors. Changes in the Articles of Association must be reported to the trade register.

If there are no regulations concerning auditors in the Articles of Association, no changes are required in order to stop appointing auditors. However, the company must report to the register the general meeting decision by which they renounce auditors. Based on this decision, the information regarding an auditor is removed from the company's register entry.

HTM and KHT are titles for authorised auditors. HTM refers to an auditor authorised by a local Chamber of Commerce, and KHT refers to an auditor authorised by the Central Chamber of Commerce. The new enterprises (partnerships, companies and cooperatives) must appoint a KHT or HTM auditor or a KHT or HTM corporation (lay auditors are no longer used).

If the organisation is subject to public trading or if at least two of the following conditions are met in the most recent accounting period, at least one of the auditors must be a KHT auditor or a KHT corporation:

1) the balance sheet total exceeds EUR 25 million;

2) net sales or corresponding earnings exceed EUR 50 million; or

3) there have been more than 300 employees on average in the organisation. In these organisations, other possible auditors must be authorised auditors (HTM or KHT).

At least one of the parent company's auditors must be included in the auditors of a subsidiary.

If an authorised auditor corporation has been appointed as the auditor, they must inform the company to be audited which of their auditors has the main responsibility for the auditing. The authorisation of the auditor with the main responsibility must be at least equal to that of the corporation.

The auditor cannot resign during the term of office, but he can be removed from office during the term if a justifiable reason exists.

An auditor who is a natural person must not be legally incompetent, bankrupt or banned from engaging in business, or have restricted competency. If one or more natural persons have been appointed as auditors, at least one of them must have a residence within the EEA.

The general meeting of shareholders may elect one or more deputy auditors. If only one auditor has been appointed, and if the auditor is not an HTM or KHT corporation, at least one deputy auditor must be elected. The provisions of the Auditing Act and other laws concerning auditors apply to the deputy auditor.

If a deputy auditor is appointed, the auditor's term of office will continue in a private limited liability company until further notice. In a public limited company the term of office terminates when the ordinary general meeting of shareholders following the election ends. The term of office can be determined otherwise in the Articles of Association.

The auditors and deputy auditors must be registered in the Trade Register

Establishment of an enterprise for legal purposes

For legal purposes, a limited liability company is established when it is entered in the trade register maintained by the National Board of Patents and Registration. A limited liability company must file a notification for registration in the trade register within three months of the signing of the Foundation Contract.

Establishment documents

The establishment documents of a limited liability company are

Basic notification of a limited liability company
A limited liability company must file a notification for registration within three months of the signing of the Memorandum of Association. In other cases the foundation will become void. The amount payable for the shares must be in the possession and control of the company before it files an application for registration. A limited liability company is established when it is entered in the trade register.

Limited liability companies use the start-up notification form Y1. They must also complete the attachment form 1 for the trade register. The start-up notification form and the attachment form are delivered as original. The following documents are to be attached:

- Memorandun of Association as original

- Receipt of the handling fee must be attached to the form.

Required attachments to a start-up notification concerning a limited liability company:
- Original Foundation Contract
- Articles of Association (can be a part of the Memorandum of Association or its separate attachment) and when necessary
- The minutes of the Board meeting (for example, about procuration holders, auxiliary business names, etc.)

Additional clarification for foreigners:
- For a foreign person (By foreign person it is meant a person who does not have a Finnish social security number.): a copy of the person's passport or other reliable clarification of identity
- For a foreign company which is a shareholder: an extract from the register of the company's home country.

In case of a licenced trade, a copy of the trade licence is attached to the trade register notification. If a licence has not yet been granted, the applicant may file the basic notification with the trade register and deliver a copy of the licence to the trade register once it has been granted.

In a limited liability company the members of the Board of Directors are responsible for filing the start-up notification. The notification must be signed by a person responsible for the notification or someone authorised by such person. If the representative signs the start-up notification, the notification must be attached with the original power of attorney or individual power of attorney as a verified copy. See Start-up notification of a limited liability company Y1, p. 2.

Using the attachment form I to the start-up notification form Y1 for limited liability companies, all the members of the Board of Directors and the Managing Director affirm that the provisions of the Companies Act have been observed when founding the limited liability company, that the shares have been paid in full and that the company is in possession and control of the amount paid for the shares. See Start-up notification of a limited liability company Y1, p. 1.

The limited company formation package includes all the documents you need to form a limited company and notify it to the Trade Register: Memorandum of Association, Articles of Association, Start-up Notification Form Y1 and the Trade Register´s Appendix Form 1.

Limited liability company
The establishment of a limited liability company includes the following stages:

1. Preparing a written Memorandum of Association.
2. The Articles of Association must be included or attached to the Memorandum of Association.
3. Share subscription will take place through the signing of the Memorandum of Association.
4. Paying the share capital to a company's deposit bank in Finland or into the account of a foreign credit institution's branch office or corresponding account abroad.
5. The company is signed up for registration in the Trade Register. The registration should take place within three months from the date when the Memorandum of Association was signed.
6. The limited liability company is legally created through registration.

Basic notification of a limited liability company
A limited liability company must file a notification for registration within three months of the signing of the Memorandum of Association. In other cases the foundation will become void. The amount payable for the shares must be in the possession and control of the company before it files an

application for registration. A limited liability company is established when it is entered in the trade register.

Limited liability companies use the start-up notification form Y1. They must also complete the attachment form 1 for the trade register. The start-up notification form and the attachment form are delivered as original. The following documents are to be attached:

Memorandun of Association as original
Receipt of the handling fee must be attached to the form.
Required attachments to a start-up notification concerning a limited liability company:
- Original Foundation Contract
- Articles of Association (can be a part of the Memorandum of Association or its separate attachment) and when necessary
- The minutes of the Board meeting (for example, about procuration holders, auxiliary business names, etc.)

Additional clarification for foreigners:
- For a foreign person (By foreign person it is meant a person who does not have a Finnish social security number.): a copy of the person's passport or other reliable clarification of identity
- For a foreign company which is a shareholder: an extract from the register of the company's home country.

In case of a licenced trade, a copy of the trade licence is attached to the trade register notification. If a licence has not yet been granted, the applicant may file the basic notification with the trade register and deliver a copy of the licence to the trade register once it has been granted.

In a limited liability company the members of the Board of Directors are responsible for filing the start-up notification. The notification must be signed by a person responsible for the notification or someone authorised by such person. If the representative signs the start-up notification, the notification must be attached with the original power of attorney or individual power of attorney as a verified copy. See Start-up notification of a limited liability company Y1, p. 2.

Using the attachment form I to the start-up notification form Y1 for limited liability companies, all the members of the Board of Directors and the Managing Director affirm that the provisions of the Companies Act have been observed when founding the limited liability company, that the shares have been paid in full and that the company is in possession and control of the amount paid for the shares. See Start-up notification of a limited liability company Y1, p. 1.

The limited company formation package includes all the documents you need to form a limited company and notify it to the Trade Register: Memorandum of Association, Articles of Association, Start-up Notification Form Y1 and the Trade Register´s Appendix Form 1.

Start-up notification to the tax administration
A new company must submit a start-up notification to the tax administration registers and the Trade Register using the same form. If the company already has a business ID, it should use the amendment notification form.

The tax administration registers referred to here include the prepayment register, employer register and VAT register.

Appointing the Chairman of the Board of Directors and the Managing Director

Managing Director

A limited liability company must have a Managing Director, if so decreed in the Articles of Association. According to the Companies Act, a Managing Director must always be appointed for limited liability companies with a minimum share capital of EUR 80,000.

The Managing Director is (generally) appointed by the Board of Directors. The written consent of the Managing Director and Deputy Managing for the task shall be obtained prior to the appointment. The consent may be given as a separate document or on the attachment form 1 of the start-up notification. The consent must be dated and signed.

Board of Directors

The company must have a Board of Directors, with a minimum of three members. If the share capital is less than EUR 80,000, the board may nevertheless consist of fewer than three members. At least one deputy must then be appointed.

If the Board of Directors consists of at least two ordinary members, a Chairman must be elected for the Board. The Chairman is elected by the Board of Directors, unless otherwise decreed in the Articles of association or at the time the Board was elected.

In a company with a minimum share capital of EUR 80,000 the Managing Director may serve as the Board of Directors only when the company has a Supervisory Board.

A written consent for the task shall be obtained from the Members of the Board of Directors and Deputy Members prior to the appointment. The consent may be given as a separate document or on the attachment form 1 of the start-up notification. The consent must be dated and signed.

The model establishment documents may be used by a limited liability company whose minimum capital is less than EUR 80,000 and whose share capital is paid in cash.

Subscribing and paying for shares

The share capital need not be divided into several shares. One share is sufficient. When signing the Memorandum of Association, a shareholder subscribes for the number of shares mentioned in the contract.

The subscription price is registered as share capital, if the Memorandum of Association or the Articles of Association do not order it to be marked partly in the fund of the unrestricted shareholders' equity.

The amount payable for the shares must be in the possession and control of the limited liability company before it files an application for registration. The limited liability company must be submitted for registration to the trade register notification within three months from the signing of the Memorandum of Association. Otherwise the foundation will become void.

The amounts paid in cash must be paid to the company's account in a Finnish deposit bank or a branch of a foreign credit institution in Finland entitled to accept deposits, or to a corresponding account located abroad.

- the Memorandum of Association

Memorandum of Association

When founding a limited liability company, you must make a Memorandum of Association that must be signed by all shareholders. When signing the Memorandum of Association, a shareholder subscribes for the number of shares mentioned in the Memorandum of Assiciation. The subscription cannot be cancelled after all shares have been subscribed for, unless otherwise agreed.

The term of office and the responsibilities of management members and auditors start from the signing of the Memorandum of Association.

In the Memorandum of Association you must always mention:
1. The date of the contract
2. All shareholders and the number of shares for which they have subscribed
3. Amount payable to the company for each share (subscription price)
4. The period during which the shares must be paid
5. The ordinary members of the Board
6. Auditors.

The Articles of Association must be included or attached to the Memorandum of Association. The accounting period must be determined in the Memorandum of Association or in the Articles of Association. If necessary, Managing Director and members of Supervisory Board should be mentioned in the Memorandum of Association. The Chairman of Board and Chairman of Supervisory Board can also be named in the Memorandum of Association.

Apport Property

If the subscription price is, instead of money, paid totally or partially with other property (apport property), it should be assigned in the Memorandum of Association.The apport property's financial value to the company must be at least as large as the payment at the moment of handover. Obligation to perform work or services cannot be apport property.

In addition, the Memorandum of Association must include an explanation that itemises the apport property and the payment from it, clarifies the matters affecting the property assessment, and the methods followed in the property assessment.

If a share has been paid with apport property, the statement of an authorised author on the abovementioned assessment and the clarification, if the property has had the value for the company corresponding to the payment, must be attached to the notification to register.

Formation package of a limited companies

To help you to fill in the documents needed for the formation and registration of a limited company, National Board of Patents and Registration of Finland has prepared a formation package for limited companies in English.

The package contains formation instructions and document templates and notification forms you need to establish a limited company. The English document templates and notification forms can however only be used as models and cannot therefore be submitted to the Trade Register. The formation documents of a limited company as well as other corporate forms shall be submitted either in Finnish or in Swedish.

- the Articles of Association

Articles of Association

The Memorandum of Association should include or be attached with the Articles of Association. The New Companies Act makes it possible to use a very short Articles of Association.

The Articles of Association must always include the following:
1. business name
2. the Finnish domicile municipality of the company
3. the line of business.

The accounting period must be determined in the Memorandum of Association or in the Articles of Association.

If the limited liability company uses its business name in two or more languages, each indication of the business name must be mentioned in the Articles of Association.

The new Companies Act also includes assumption regulations that can be applied unless otherwise stated in the Articles of Association. The same sections of law include regulations according to which the enactment of a certain arrangement requires an indication of the arrangement in the Articles of Association.

Formation package of a limited companies

To help you to fill in the documents needed for the formation and registration of a limited company, National Board of Patents and Registration of Finland has prepared a formation package for limited companies in English.

The package contains formation instructions and document templates and notification forms you need to establish a limited company. The English document templates and notification forms can however only be used as models and cannot therefore be submitted to the Trade Register. The formation documents of a limited company as well as other corporate forms shall be submitted either in Finnish or in Swedish.

Concluding legal acts on behalf of the enterprise

The Board of Directors represents the company.

The Managing Director can represent the limited liability company in a matter that, according to legislation, belongs to his/her duties, that is, handles the company's everyday management according to the guidelines and orders of the Board of Directors (general authority to render decisions). The managing Director is responsible for ensuring that the company's accounting is legal and the financial administration is arranged reliably.

The managing Director is allowed, taking into consideration the extent and quality of operation, to start unusual and large-scale operations only if the Board has given him/her authority for it or it is not possible to wait for the Board's decision without causing a remarkable disadvantage to the company's operation.

It may be stipulated in the Articles of Association that a member of the Board of Directors or the Managing Director is entitled to represent the company, or that the Board of Directors may grant this right to one of its members, the Managing Director or another named person. The Board of Directors may at any time revoke the right to represent the company.

It is possible to enter in the trade register only one restriction for the right to represent the company. According to the restriction the right can be used only for two or more persons together.

The rule for the line of business in the Articles of Association restricts the authority of the representative.

Holder of procuration
Procuration refers to a special commercial power of representation. The procuration holder may act on behalf of the principal in all matters related to the principal's business and sign for the principal. However, without a specific authorisation, the holder of procuration does not have the right to surrender the principal's immoveable property or tenancy rights or to seek a mortgage thereon. In a limited liability company procurations may be granted by the Board of Directors. In a limited liability company it is possible to stipulate that the holder of the procuration may only sign for the company jointly with a member of the Board of Directors, the Managing Director or another person authorised to sign for the company. The holder of procuration may be entered in the trade register. There are no statutory requirements concerning the citizenship or place of residence of the holder of procuration.

Representative
A limited liability company must have a representative who is domiciled in Finland. The representative is entered in the trade register. If the company has a member of the Board of Directors, Managing Director or holder of procuration who has been entered in the trade register and who is domiciled in Finland, a separate representative is not required.

Administration and organs

The highest decisive organ is the shareholders' meeting, in which shareholders use their power of decision.

The limited liability company must have a Board of Directors that includes from one to five members, unless otherwise stated in the Articles of Association. If there are fewer than three members on the Board, it must then have at least one deputy member.

A limited liability company can also have a Managing Director and a Supervisory Board.

Board of Directors
The only obligatory organ of a limited liability company is the Board of Directors. The Board must include from one to five members, unless otherwise stated in the Articles of Association. If there are fewer than three members on the Board, it must the have at least one deputy member If there are several members in the Board, a Chairman must be elected for the Board. The Chairman is elected by the Board, unless otherwise decided when the Board was elected or otherwise stated in the Articles of Association.

The members of the Board are elected by the General Meeting of Shareholders, unless it has been stated in the Articles of Association that the task belongs to the Supervisory Board. The Articles of Association may also stipulate that less than half of the members of the Board of Directors are to be appointed in a different order.

A member of the Board of Directors cannot be a legal entity or a person whose interests are supervised by another person, whose competence to act has not been restricted, or who has declared bankruptcy or been banned from engaging in business.

At least one of the Board members and deputy members must be resident in the European Economic Area, unless the National Board of Patents and Registration grants the company an exemption.

The opinion of the majority of the Board will be the decision of the Board, unless the Articles of Association requires a qualified majority. If there is a tie, the vote of the Chairman is decisive. In the event of a tie in the election of the Chairman, and if it has not been stated otherwise when calling the Board or in the Articles of Association, the election is decided by drawing lots. The Board of Directors shall have a quorum when more than half of the members are present, unless a larger number is required in the Articles of Association. The number is calculated from the nominated members of the Board.

A Board member's term of office continues until further notice in a private limited liability company, unless otherwise stated in the Articles of Association. The term of office ends and the term of a new member starts at the end of the Ordinary General Meeting in which the new member is elected, unless otherwise stated in the Articles of Association or when electing the new member.

The members and deputy members of the Board must be notified for registration in the trade register.

Chairman of the Board of Directors
If there are several members in the Board of a limited liability company, a Chairman must be elected for the Board. The Chairman is elected by the Board, unless otherwise decided when the Board was elected or otherwise stated in the Articles of Association.

Managing Director
It is possible to elect a Managing Director for a limited liability company. The Board of Directors elects the Managing Director.

The Managing Director and the possible deputy Managing Director shall have a place of residence in the EEA, unless the National Board of Patents and Registration grants the company an exemption.

The Managing Director and his/her deputy must be notified for registration in the trade register.

Supervisory Board
The Articles of Association may stipulate that the limited liability company shall have a Supervisory Board. The Supervisory Board supervises the management of the company under the responsibility of the Board and the Managing Director.

The Supervisory Board shall have a minimum of three members. The Managing Director or a member of the Board of Directors may not be a member of the Supervisory Board. The Supervisory Board shall elect a Chairman for the Supervisory Board, unless otherwise stated in the Articles of Association or when electing the Supervisory Board.

At least one of the Supervisory Board members and deputy member must be resident in the European Economic Area, unless the National Board of Patents and Registration grants the company an exemption.

The term of office for a member of the Supervisory Board continues until further notice in a private limited liability company, unless otherwise stated in the Articles of Association.

The members and deputy members of the Supervisory Board must be notified for registration in the trade register.

General Meeting of Shareholders
Shareholders use their power of decision in the General Meeting of Shareholders. The decisions are made according to a majority of votes, unless otherwise stated in the Companies Act or in the Articles of Association.

The General Meeting of Shareholders decides on the matters mentioned in the Companies Act. The Articles of Association can determine that the General Meeting of Shareholders can decide over matters belonging to the Managing Director's and Board's general authority to render decisions.

The Ordinary General Meeting of Shareholders must be held within six months of the end of the accounting period. The meeting shall decide on:

- Confirmation of the financial statements (the parent company also confirms consolidated financial statements)

- How the profit shown by the balance sheet is used

- Release from liability for the members of the Board of Directors, the members of the Supervisory Board and the Managing Director

- The election of the members of the Board of Directors and the Supervisory Board and the auditor, unless otherwise stated in the Articles of Association about the term of office or election

- Other matters to be handled in the General Meeting of Shareholders according to the Articles of Association.

An extraordinary general meeting must be held, if:

- It is determined in the Articles of Association.

- The Board of Directors finds one necessary.

- A shareholder or auditor finds one necessary.

The Supervisory Board finds one necessary and it has the right, according to the Articles of Association, to decide on the holding of an extraordinary general meeting.

An extraordinary general meeting must be held if the auditor of shareholders having in total one tenth of the company's shares, or a smaller share defined in the Articles of Association, demand in writing the meeting to be held for the handling of a certain matter.

Unanimous decision by the shareholders without holding a General Meeting of Shareholders

Shareholders may unanimously decide an issue belonging to the General Meeting of Shareholders without holding a General Meeting of Shareholders. This kind of decision shall be recorded, dated, numbered and signed. If the company has more than one shareholder, at least two of them shall sign the decision.

Capital required at start-up

The share capital of a private limited liability company must be at least EUR 2,500, and the share capital of a public limited liability company must be at least EUR 80,000.

The shares of public limited liability companies only may be subject to trade as referred to in the Securities Market Act.

COOPERATIVE

A cooperative may be established by no fewer than three founders. The founders may be private individuals or corporations, or foundations of other legal entities. A founder must become a member of the cooperative.

The founder's place of residence or citizenship is not a decisive factor for the cooperative; foreigners may also act as founders. Non-EEA residents or those domiciled outside the EEA may also act as founders. No legally incompetent or bankrupt person may act as a founder. A founder must become a member of the cooperative.

Auditors

The Auditing Act specifies the circumstances when an auditor must be used.The new Auditing Act entered into force at the beginning of July 2007.

If the Rules of the Cooperative allow, cooperatives that meet no more than one of the following conditions in both the closing accounting period and in the accounting period preceding it may neglect the appointment of an auditor:

1) the balance sheet total exceeds EUR 100,000;

2) net sales or corresponding earning exceed EUR 200,000; or

3) there are more than three employees on average.

The obligation to appoint an auditor also applies to a cooperative launching operations if the cooperative already has business operations that meet the conditions for auditing obligation in the launching stage.

HTM and KHT are titles for authorised auditors. HTM refers to an auditor authorised by a local Chamber of Commerce, and KHT refers to an auditor authorised by the Central Chamber of Commerce. The new enterprises (partnerships, companies and cooperatives) must appoint a KHT or HTM auditor or a KHT or HTM corporation (lay auditors are no longer used).

If the organisation is subject to public trading or if at least two of the following conditions are met in the most recent accounting period, at least one of the auditors must be a KHT auditor or a KHT corporation:

1) the balance sheet total exceeds EUR 25 million;

2) net sales or corresponding earnings exceed EUR 50 million; or

3) there have been more than 300 employees on average in the organisation. In these organisations, other possible auditors must be authorised auditors (HTM or KHT).

A dated and signed consent for the task shall be obtained from the auditor and deputy auditor of a cooperative.

The consent may be given in the start-up or amendment notification to be delivered to the Trade Register or Register of Foundations, or as a separate document.

The auditors and deputy auditors must be submitted for registration in the trade register.

Establishment of a cooperative for legal purposes

For legal purposes, a cooperative is established when it is entered in the trade register maintained by the National Board of Patents and Registration. A cooperative must always submit a declaration for registration within six months of signing the Charter of Foundation; otherwise the foundation will become void.

Liability for an obligation resulting from an act undertaken on behalf of the cooperative prior to its registration shall, jointly and severally, lie with the persons who have participated in, or decided on, the said act.

Establishment documents

The establishment documents of a cooperative are

- the Instrument of incorporation

- rules

- the Minutes of the meeting of the Board of Directors, if a chairman of the Board and a Managing Director are appointed

Concluding legal acts on behalf of the enterprise

The Board of Directors represents the cooperative and signs for the cooperative. If the cooperative has a Managing Director, he/she has the right to represent the cooperative in matters related to the day-to-day management of the cooperative.

Those authorised to sign for the cooperative

It may be stipulated in the rules that a member of the Board of Directors or the Managing Director is entitled to sign for the cooperative, or that the Board of Directors (or Supervisory Board) may grant this right to its members, the Managing Director or another person.

The right to sign for the cooperative may also be restricted by stipulating that two or more persons shall jointly have the right to sign for the cooperative. Restrictions other than the above must not be entered in the trade register.

The Board of Directors may at any time revoke a right to sign for the cooperative.

Holder of procuration

In a cooperative procurations are granted by the Board of Directors, unless it is stipulated in the rules that procurations are granted by the Supervisory Board. In a cooperative it is possible to stipulate that the holder of the procuration may only sign for the cooperative jointly with a member of the Board of Directors or another person authorised to sign for the cooperative. There are no statutory requirements concerning the citizenship or place of residence of the holder of procuration of a cooperative. The holder of procuration may be entered in the trade register.

Representative

A cooperative must have a representative who is domiciled in Finland. The representative is entered in the trade register. If the cooperative has a member of the Board of Directors, Managing Director or holder of procuration who has been entered in the trade register and who is domiciled in Finland, a separate representative is not required.

Administration and management

A cooperative must have a Board of Directors with a minimum of one and a maximum of seven members. If there is more than one member, one of the members must act as chairman.

A cooperative may have a Managing Director, if so stipulated in the rules or decided by the Board of Directors. The rules may stipulate that the cooperative shall have a Supervisory Board. The Supervisory Board shall have a minimum of three members.

The members exercise their power of decision in matters related to the cooperative in general meeting of the cooperative.

Board of Directors

A cooperative must have a Board of Directors with a minimum of one and a maximum of seven members. An exception to the above is possible through a provision included in the rules. If there are fewer than three members, the Board must have at least one deputy member. When the Board of Directors has more than one member, one of them must act as chairman.

At least one of the members and deputy members must have a place of residence in the EEA, unless the National Board of Patents and Registration grants the company an exemption.

Licence application to the Board of Patents and Registration from outside the EEA

A general meeting of the cooperative elects the members of the Board of Directors. The rules may stipulate that the Supervisory Board elects the members of the Board of Directors. The rules may also stipulate that less than half of the members of the Board of Directors are to be appointed in a different order. A dated and signed consent for the task shall be obtained from the members and deputy members of the Board of Directors.

A member of the Board of Directors is elected until further notice, unless there is a stipulation on a fixed term of office in the rules.

The Board of Directors shall have a quorum when more than half of the members are present, unless a larger number is stipulated in the rules. Unless a qualified majority is required in the rules, the decision of the Board shall be the opinion receiving the support of over half the directors present, or, if there is a tie, the opinion receiving the support of the chairman.

Chairman of the Board of Directors

If the Board of Directors has more than one member, one of the members must act as chairman. The chairman is elected by the Board of Directors, unless otherwise stipulated in the rules or at the time when the Board was elected. In the event of a tie, the election is decided by drawing lots.

Managing Director

A cooperative may have a Managing Director, if so stipulated in the rules or decided by the Board of Directors.

The Managing Director is appointed by the Board of Directors, or, if so stipulated in the rules, the Supervisory Board or the general meeting of the cooperative.

The Managing Director (and the deputy Managing Director, if any) shall have a place of residence in the EEA, unless the National Board of Patents and Registration grants the company an exemption.

A signed and dated consent for the task shall be obtained from the Managing Director and the deputy Managing Director in writing.

Supervisory Board

The rules of a cooperative may stipulate that the cooperative shall have a Supervisory Board. The Supervisory Board shall have a minimum of three members. The Managing Director or a member of the Board of Directors may not be a member of the Supervisory Board. At least one of the members and deputy members must have a place of residence in the EEA, unless the National Board of Patents and Registration grants the company an exemption.

The number or the minimum and maximum numbers of the members and the deputy members of the Supervisory Board must be stipulated in the rules.

A dated and signed consent for the task shall be obtained from the members and deputy members of the Supervisory Board.

Licence application to the Board of Patents and Registration from outside the EEA

General meeting of the cooperative and delegates

The members exercise their power of decision in matters related to the cooperative in a general meeting. A member may exercise the right in person or through a representative. One member has one vote in all matters to be considered by the general meeting, unless otherwise stipulated in the rules.

The ordinary general meeting of the cooperative must be held within six months of the end of the accounting period, unless an earlier date has been stipulated in the rules.

It may be stipulated in the rules that, instead of the general meeting of the cooperative, the members' power of decision is to be exercised by delegates elected by the members.

Capital required at start-up

The amount of the participation share is decided by the founders and included in the rules. Participation shares must be of equal value. The accumulated participation shares form the cooperative capital.

BRANCH OF A FOREIGN ENTERPRISE

The branch of a foreign entrepreneur refers to the part of a foreign corporation or foundation that engages in continuous business or trade activities in Finland from a permanent establishment in Finland in the name of the foreign corporation or foundation.

If the corporation or foundation is from outside the EEA, it must apply for a permit from the National Board of Patents and Registration for the establishment of the branch.

The branch must submit a basic declaration to the trade register maintained by the National Board of Patents and Registration.

Basic notification for a branch of a foreign entrepreneur

Before starting operations the branch of a foreign entrepreneur must submit a basic notification using the start-up notification Y1 and the Trade Register attachment form 3. The forms are available here or by order from the National Board of Patents and Registration. Forms are also available at city administrative courts, Employment and Economic Development Centres and Tax Administration offices.

The start-up notification form is signed by a person authorised to write the business name or appointed as a representative of the branch or someone authorised by such person. If the notification is signed by a person authorised to do so, the original power of attorney granted to the authorised person must be delivered to the trade register authority.

The following information must be included in the basic notification of a branch of a foreign entrepreneur

- the business name and domicile of the branch

- the postal address of the branch

- the accounting period

- the business name and legal form of the entrepreneur, as well as the business name of the branch (the business name of the branch must include the business name of the foreign entrepreneur and an addition indicating it is a question of a branch, such as 'sivuliike Suomessa' ('branch in Finland').

- the register in which the entrepreneur establishing a branch has been entered in its home country and the entrepreneur's registration number in the register

- the personal details of a representative referred to in Section 6(3) of the Act on the Right to Carry on a Trade. The representative is a person who is entitled to receive summons and other notifications on behalf of the trader. If the trader is a foreign corporate body or foundation that is founded under the legislation of a country belonging to the EEA and has its domicile (designated in the statutes), its central administration or head office in a country belonging to the EEA, the representative must be resident in the EEA. In other cases, the representative must be domiciled in Finland

- personal data of each person authorised to write the business name of the branch and how the business name must be signed

- persons authorised to represent the business as a statutory organ or a member of such an organ and their personal information ('statutory organ' often refers to the Board of Directors of the foreign enterprise. Each situation must be interpreted in accordance with the legislation of the home country of the foreign corporation or foundation.)

If the statutory domicile, central administration or main place of business of a foreign entrepreneur is located outside the European Economic Area, the State whose legislation the entrepreneur establishing a branch is subject to must be indicated on the basic notification, as well as the statutory domicile, central administration or main place of business of the entrepreneur. If a foreign entrepreneur not domiciled in the EEA is a limited liability company, or a comparable company, its share capital or comparable capital must also be noted in the basic notification, unless this information is shown in the Charter of Foundation, the Articles of Association or another comparable document.

The following documents are to be attached:

- an account of the establishment of a branch (for example, minutes of the meeting of a Board of Directors)

- an account of appointing a representative as defined in Section 6, Paragraph 3 of the Act on the Right to Carry on a Business (for example, minutes of the meeting of a Board of Directors)

- an account of the people representing the business as a statutory organ or a member of such an organ, and of the granting of the right to write the business name and of how the business name must be signed

- an extract from the register in which the foreign entrepreneur has been entered in its home country, or another account of the existence of the entrepreneur

- a copy in Finnish or Swedish, or a legally valid translation into one of these languages, of the entrepreneur's Charter of Foundation, the Articles of Association, rules or other corresponding documents

- if the corporation of foundation establishing a branch is located outside the EEA, an account is required of a permit granted for the establishment of a branch. See permits for foreigners.

- if a person to be registered does not have a Finnish personal identity number and has not been included in the register extract concerning the foreign corporation or foundation, an account of the existence of the person in question, such as a certified copy of the person's passport, is required as an attachment.

A copy of the minutes of the meeting of the Board of Directors of the foreign company is often used as an account of the establishment of a branch, appointment of a representative and the granting of rights to write the business name of the branch. However, the legislation of the home country determines the organ authorised to decide on these matters. Organs representing the company by virtue of law are often shown by the trade register extract issued by the authorities in the company's home country.

If the notification is accompanied by a document in a foreign language, a translation thereof into Finnish or Swedish must also be attached to the application.

Start-up notifications (in Finnish and in Swedish) are available on the Business Information System (BIS) website at www.ytj.fi.

Audit

A branch is not a separate legal entity. Auditors are elected in accordance with the type of office of the foreign entrepreneur and the appropriate regulations. The obligation to audit the accounts is based on the Auditing Act. In practice the auditors of a branch are probably elected by the entrepreneur's representatives in Finland.

Concluding legal acts on behalf of a branch of a foreign entrepreneur

The branch of a foreign entrepreneur must have a representative domiciled in Finland. No legally incompetent or bankrupt person may act as a representative. The representative must be submitted for registration in the trade register maintained by the National Board of Patents and Registration.

ACQUISITION OF A BUSINESS

You do not need to found a business yourself; you can also acquire an enterprise or its business operations, or become a partner in an existing enterprise. The object of acquisition may be, for example, a private undertaking, shares in a general or limited partnership, the entire stock of a limited liability company or a majority of the shares. You can become a member of an existing cooperative by paying the participation share. One way of starting your own business is to become involved in a ready-made, proven concept of operation – that is, become a franchisee.

Finnish law does not impose any restrictions on foreign ownership; foreigners may also acquire Finnish enterprises. More information on the right of non-EEA residents to found an enterprise or be involved in the administration of a Finnish enterprise can be found on the section "Permits from the National Board of Patents and Registration for non-EEA residents".

A large number of transfers of businesses to younger generations are expected in Finland in the next few years. According to different estimates, between 60,000 and 80,000 enterprises are going to change hands in the next few years. If no new owner can be found within the family, an alternative is to sell the business to a third party.

FRANCHISING OPERATIONS

Franchising is a form of cooperation between two businesses by which one, the franchisor, grants the other, the franchisee, the right to use a business idea and operating model it has developed and tested, against the payment of a fee. The franchisee can use the franchisor's know-how and trademarks and gain benefits from chain purchases and common marketing. Such a cooperation network is called a franchising chain.

Franchising chains operating in Finland include, among others, R-kioski, Kotipizza and Café Picnic. There are about 200 franchising chains in Finland. Most of these operate in the service industries and retail trade.

Characteristics of franchising chains include:

• Franchising refers to long-term contractual cooperation between two independent enterprises, the franchisor and the franchisee. The franchisor does not normally finance the franchisee or own any shares in it. However, the franchisor usually operates some outlets of its own in the chain.

• The cooperation is based on a concept developed by the franchisor and licensed to the franchisee; all members of the chain operate in the market in accordance with the same concept. The members of the chain also operate under a common brand and with a uniform appearance.

• The franchisor transfers the concept and the related know-how to the franchisee by means of training and manuals. The manuals document all the most essential issues and instructions that the entrepreneur must know in his or her operations. The franchisee commits to compliance with these instructions and guidelines in its business and undertakes to fulfil the quality requirements of the concept. The franchisor provides and arranges continuous commercial and technical support for the franchisees in the chain. When the entrepreneur starts his or her business, the franchisee provides him or her with training and assistance in issues related to starting the business, such as acquiring and equipping the premises, purchasing agreements, arranging an opening celebration, etc. The franchisee continuously develops the competitive ability and operations of the chain members through marketing actions, training, monitoring and planning systems, advice, internal communication of information and exchange of experiences.

• The operations are fee-based for the entrepreneur - he or she pays the franchisor one-time and/or recurring fees for the right to use the concept, membership of the chain and the benefits and services received (recurring fees include cooperation and/or marketing fees, generally 0–10 % of net sales).

• The franchisor manages the cooperation chain and controls the operations of the franchisee. The rights and obligations of the parties, and the rules of cooperation, as well as termination of the cooperation and its consequences, are always specified in a written agreement.

More information is available on the website of the Finnish Franchising Association.

ACQUIRING AN ENTERPRISE OR ITS BUSINESS OPERATIONS

You do not need to found a business yourself; you may acquire

• the entire business operations or a business unit
• the entire enterprise engaging in business
• a share of the company's stock or a share in a partnership.

The object of a business acquisition usually includes the fixed assets and inventories (machinery, equipment and inventories), the business name and goodwill. The premises may be transferred to the new owner by means of a transfer of lease. Goodwill is formed on the basis of the business organisation, its client base and brands. The advantages of acquiring the business operations include that the acquisition applies to specific asset items and the customer base, for example, but all old tax liabilities and other hidden risks remain with the selling enterprise.

When acquiring the entire stock of a limited liability company, the company is transferred to the new owner with its liabilities and assets. The buyer should carefully study the financial position of the company before the acquisition. The analysis requires financial statements for at least 2 to 3 years and recent intermediate financial statements. Expert advice should be sought for determining the financial value of the acquisition. The buyer often assumes responsibility for the seller's debts. This saves the need for new credit negotiations. The buyer must investigate all the seller's liabilities, such as any pending additional taxes. The sales contract shall indicate the date until which the seller is liable for taxes.

You can also become a partner in an existing enterprise. It is possible to purchase a share in a general or limited partnership or part of the stock in a limited liability company. You can join a cooperative by paying the participation share.

When acquiring stock in a limited liability company or shares in a general or limited partnership, the company or partnership continues its operations as before. The buyer should investigate the state of the enterprise by studying the financial statements before the acquisition. It should be kept in mind that if more than one-half of the stock of a limited liability company or shares in a partnership changes hands, old losses are no longer deductible. The partners in a general partnership and general partners in a limited partnership are liable for the partnership's taxes for the entire tax year in which the sale is executed. The shareholders of a limited liability company are not liable for the company's taxes.

The following should be investigated before the acquisition:

• Are the operations profitable?
• How much debt does the enterprise have (in a general partnership or as a general partner in a limited partnership, you are responsible for the partnership's liabilities with your entire personal property)?
• What is the volume of orders in hand?
• What is the future outlook for the enterprise and the sector?
• How is your partner as a person; can you trust him or her, do you get along with each other?

The assistance of an outside expert is required for the investigations in order to avoid any surprises in the future.

Determining the Value of an Enterprise

The buyer?s first problem is how to assess the enterprise that is to be acquired: is the asking price correct and what are the enterprise's possibilities for success in the future.

There are two principal methods for determining the value of an enterprise: the substance or asset value and the productive value.

In addition, the discontinuation value can also be calculated. This indicates the amount of cash left in the company if the operations are discontinued, all assets are sold and all liabilities are paid off. The discontinuation value is the lower limit for the sale price, particularly from the seller's point of view. It can often be negative as well.

Information about enterprises and business operations for sale is available from the Yrityspörssi Web site of the Federation of Finnish Enterprises and the Chamberbusiness Web site of the Central Chamber of Commerce.

The Invention Market of the Foundation for Finnish Inventions offers product and business ideas for entrepreneurs, funded by the Foundation. The information can be found below Invention Market on the Foundation's website.

Determining the Value of an Enterprise
The buyer´s first problem is how to assess the enterprise that is to be acquired: is the asking price correct and what are the enterprise's possibilities for success in the future.

There are two principal methods for determining the value of an enterprise: the substance or asset value and the productive value.

In addition, the discontinuation value can also be calculated. This indicates the amount of cash left in the company if the operations are discontinued, all assets are sold and all liabilities are paid off. The discontinuation value is the lower limit for the sale price, particularly from the seller's point of view. It can often be negative as well.

Information about enterprises and business operations for sale is available from the Yrityspörssi Web site of the Federation of Finnish Enterprises and the Chamberbusiness Web site of the Central Chamber of Commerce.

The Invention Market of the Foundation for Finnish Inventions offers product and business ideas for entrepreneurs, funded by the Foundation. The information can be found below Invention Market on the Foundation's Web site.

SELECTING A BUSINESS NAME

Before the establishment documents have been completed and the enterprise has applied for entry in the trade register, a business name must be selected for the enterprise. The business name must identify the business and be distinct from the business names already in the register.

The enterprise may use an auxiliary business name to carry on a part of its activities. The business name may have parallel business names in different languages, which are translations of the business name in Finnish or Swedish. The expressions in different languages must be similar in content. Both the actual business name and the auxiliary business names may have parallel business names.

The business name may be, for example, a combination of the name of the entrepreneur or the area and the business activities. It may also be an invented word, although it is recommended that the spelling rules of the Finnish language are followed.

Registered business names, names pending registration and auxiliary business names can be investigated in the Business Information System available over the Internet (www.ytj.fi). The system also includes information on new businesses whose names have not yet been registered.

The business name must not be such that it can be confused with a protected business name, a secondary symbol or trademark. Anything that may be interpreted as another person's last name or professional name, or the name of a protected literary or artistic work, may not be used as part of the business name without the appropriate consent. Protected national or international appellations or abbreviations of names may not be used as part of the business name without consent; and the business name may not be contrary to good practice or public order, or misleading to the public.

Business names are registered in Finnish or Swedish in the trade register maintained by the National Board of Patents and Registration.

Although the validity of a business name cannot be examined in advance, it is possible to verify that an identical business name has not already been registered or that its registration is not pending. The name will only be investigated and its validity approved after the notification has been filed with the trade register. The exclusive right to use the business name is effective as of the date the notification is filed with the public authority stipulated in section 10 of the Business Information Act, provided the business name is registered in its presented form.

It is useful to make data base searches of business names and trademarks before choosing a name. To get help with the searches. More information on the National Board of Patent and Registration of Finland web site.

ESTABLISHMENT DOCUMENTS

While the establishment of a partnership (general and limited partnerships) does not require adherence to the proper form, a written agreement should be made for the trade register.

For legal purposes, limited liability companies and cooperatives are only established when they have been entered in the trade register maintained by the National Board of Patents and Registration.

The basic declaration to the trade register is made using the start-up notification form, with which the enterprise may also apply for registration in the tax administration registers.

BUSINESS LICENCES AND NOTIFICATIONS

In accordance with the principle of industrial freedom, the following are entitle to carry on a legal trade in Finland in accordance with good practice without a licence from the authorities:

- individuals resident in the EEA,

- Finnish corporations and foundations, and

- foreign corporations and foundations that have a registered branch in Finland, have been established under the law of a State included in the EEA and have their statutory domicile, central administration or main place of business in an EEA State.

The National Board of Patents and Registration may also grant licences to applicants other than the above-mentioned groups.

The acts and decrees governing licenced trades stipulate the licencing authorities. In some cases a licence is not required, but the individual/corporation must deliver a written notification to the appropriate authorities. Licences are usually granted by the Regional State Administrative Agency of the area in which the business is established.

A copy of the trade licence granted is attached to the trade register notification. If a licence has not yet been granted, the applicant may file the basic declaration with the trade register and deliver a copy of the licence to the trade register once the licence has been granted.

LICENCED TRADES

Licenced trades are governed by acts and decrees, which stipulate the licencing authorities, for example. In some cases a licence is not required, but the individual/corporation must deliver a written notification to the appropriate authorities. Licences are usually granted by the State Provincial Office of the area in which the business is established.

A copy of the licence granted is attached to the trade register notification. If a licence has not yet been granted, the applicant may file the basic declaration with the trade register and deliver a copy of the licence to the trade register once the licence has been granted.

Licenced trades include (the licencing authority is given in brackets)

• inspection of motor vehicles (Finnish Transport Safety Agency Trafi)

• production, import, export, wholesale, special sale and usage subjected to the licencing of alcoholic beverages and spirits, as well as production, import, wholesale and usage subjected to licence (The National Supervisory Authority for Welfare and Health (Valvira)

• production, import, distribution and selling, as well as other types of release to consumption, of medicines, and pharmaceutical companies, pharmaceutical wholesalers and pharmacies engaged in the aforementioned activities. Hospital pharmacies and medicine centres in health centres and hospitals engaged in the production and distribution of medicines. Selling of pharmaceutical, veterinary and drug preparations. (The Finnish Medicines Agency Fimea)

• production and import of precious metal products (with the exception of gold or platinum products weighing less than 1g and silver products weighing less than 10g); a written application for a stamped signature, or registered stamped signatures, will be entered in the registry of stamped signatures (Finnish Safety and Chemicals Agency Tukes)

• mining operations and prospecting: applications for mining claims and patents (The Ministry of Employment and the Economy), reservation notifications (the local register office in which the reservation area is located)

• production of synthetic fertilizers and manufactured feeds and trade in seeds (Finnish Food Safety Authority Evira)

• commercial airline operations (scheduled and charter airline traffic): air operator certificates and operating licences (Finnish Transport Safety Agency Trafi): In addition to the above, airline companies in EU Member States: a company commencing scheduled and charter airline traffic to and from Finland or within Finland must file a notification to the Flight Safety Authority at the Civil Aviation Administration. Airline companies in non-EU Member States: regular scheduled traffic to and from Finland is based on bilateral flight operations agreements between Finland the respective countries. Once the country in question has appointed an airline company or airline companies to operate on the route specified in the agreement, the Flight Safety Authority will grant the company permission to start the agreed traffic. Charter airline traffic operated by companies in non-EU Member States is subject to a charter operator certificate granted by the Finnish Transport Safety Agency Trafi (Finnish Transport Safety Agency Trafi).

• credit institutions, pawnbroking institutions, investment service companies, mutual fund companies and custodians (The Financial Supervisory Authority)

• collection of debts on behalf of others (alla licences granted by Regional State Administrative Agency for Southern Finland)

• postal services (postal matters with an address, weighing less than 2kg). Courier services as well as distribution and delivery operations concerning minor postal matters do not require a licence (Postal Services Act 313/2001) (Government).

• stock exchanges, central securities depositories, option institutions, clearing houses (Ministry of Finance)

• electrical contracting (electrician activities, repair of electrical appliances): the person responsible for the service must be a director of electricians' work with appropriate qualifications. The qualification is indicated by a qualification certificate issued by the relevant qualification institution (Henkilö- ja Yritysarviointi SETI Oy). Notification of operations before starting the operations (Finnish Safety and Chemicals Agency Tukes). The aforementioned also applies to the installation and maintenance of lifts.

• design, construction, manufacture, repairing, servicing and using of electrical appliances, production and transport of electricity for other than personal use (Finnish Safety and Chemicals Agency Tukes and Henkilö- ja Yritysarviointi SETI Oy)

• telecommunications activities (The Finnish Communications Regulatory Authority, FICORA)

• handling and storage of chemicals hazardous to health and the environment (Finnish Safety and Chemicals Agency Tukes)

• large-scale handling (Finnish Safety and Chemicals Agency Tukes)

• small-scale handling (local chief fire officer or chemicals control authority)

• insurance brokering (the Financial Supervisory Authority)

• insurance agencies (the Financial Supervisory Authority)

• package tour agencies (Consumer Agency)

• security companies (the National Police Board).

START-UP NOTIFICATION TO THE TAX ADMINISTRATION

A new company must submit a start-up notification to the tax administration registers and the Trade Register using the same form. If the company already has a business ID, it should use the amendment notification form.

The tax administration registers referred to here include the prepayment register, employer register and VAT register.

COMMERCIAL PREMISES

Most enterprises start their operations in rented premises. The issue of purchasing business premises or commercial real estate may arise with the expansion of business.

Before purchasing or renting any commercial property the entrepreneur should determine whether it is suitable for the intended operations. Is it possible to make the required alterations; are the alterations technically viable, allowed by written plan regulations or other building regulations? Alterations made to a building or premises usually require a building licence granted by the local building supervision authority. The owner or proprietor of the site may apply for the licence. An entrepreneur with a lease on a commercial property may apply for the licence if granted a power of attorney by the owner or proprietor of the site.

LEASE OF BUSINESS PREMISES

The lease of business premises is prescribed by the Act on the Lease of Business Premises (LHVL 482/95).

It is always advisable to sign a lease in writing. If there is no written lease, the lease is considered to be valid until further notice. A fixed-term lease must always be made in writing. Fixed-term leases are usually made for 3–5 years.

The lease should always contain at least the following information:

1. Name, business ID (or personal identity number), address, telephone number and bank connection of the lessor

2. Business ID (or personal identity number), address and telephone number of the tenant

3. The premises to be leased and their intended use

4. The lease period: in the case of a fixed-term lease, the length of the lease period (start date and end date); in the case of a lease valid until further notice, the start date of the lease, period of notice and the first possible date of giving notice of termination

5. The rent (possibly specified as absolute net rent and maintenance rent) and other payments: the period of payment of rent, the amount of rent, the due date and the interest for delay, separate charges payable by the tenant such as water, electricity, etc.

6. Deposits, if any, payable for one or more periods

7. Guarantee and its value (for example, a bank deposit)

8. Rent increases: the rent is tied to an index (cost-of-living index, building cost index, or cost index for real estate maintenance), other basis

9. Date of transfer of the proprietary right to the premises if the tenant cannot occupy the premises immediately

10. Other clauses: alterations to the premises (who pays), use of common premises, etc.

11. Date and the lessor's and tenant's signatures.

Index clause

When a lease is agreed to continue until further notice or for at least three years, it is possible to tie the adjustment of the rent to an index.

In this event the following information is to be noted in the lease: the relevant index, the publication month and year of the basic index, as well as the index value known at the time of signing the lease, and the adjustment date. The indices used are the cost-of-living index, building cost index and the cost index for real estate maintenance.

The cost-of-living index will be published on the 14th day of each month for the previous month, or the working day closest to this date. Information on the value of the cost-of-living index is available on +358 (0)9 1734 3476 and (0)9 1734 3559 or on the Statistics Finland website.

The building cost index will be published on the 12 day of each month for the previous month. If the 12th day falls on a Saturday or Sunday, the statistics will be published on the previous working day. The values are published by Statistics Finland. Information on the value of the building cost index is available from +358 (0)9 1734 2231 and (0)9 1734 2551 or on the Statistics Finland website.

The cost index for real estate maintenance describes the price development of real estate management and is a suitable basis for rent adjustment. The index is published by Statistics Finland 4 times each year in May, August, November and February.

Information on the value of the cost index for real estate maintenance is available from Statistics Finland on +358 (0)9 1734 2231 and (0)9 1734 2551.

Notice of termination

A fixed-term lease ends on the agreed date without notice. The parties may provide for the continued validity of the lease at the time of signing the lease.

A lease valid until further notice ends on the expiry of the agreed period of notice. The period of notice is calculated from the last day of the calendar month during which the notice was given, unless otherwise agreed.

The period of notice is three months from the lessor's side and one month from the tenant's side, unless otherwise agreed. Where the tenancy concerns business premises, the lessor and tenant may freely agree on the period of notice.

When the lessor wishes to give notice of termination of the lease, the notice must be delivered to the tenant in writing in a verifiable way. The termination date and the grounds for the notice of termination must be stated on the notice. A summons for tenant eviction, including a claim for the termination of the tenancy, is acceptable as a notice of termination.

When the tenant wishes to give notice of termination of the lease, the notice must be delivered to the lessor in writing in a verifiable way. The reason for termination of the tenancy only needs to be stated if the Act on the Lease of Business Premises or another act or decree requires special grounds for the notice of termination. Thus the tenant is not normally required to state the grounds for giving notice of termination of a lease valid until further notice.

Notice of termination of subtenancy of business premises

The tenant is entitled to sublet or otherwise convey to another no more than 50 % of the premises without the consent of the lessor, unless this causes significant inconvenience or disturbance to the lessor. In the case of subtenancy, the period of notice on the sublessor's side is one month.

If the sublessor has given notice of termination of the subtenancy without justifiable grounds, the subtenant is entitled to reasonable compensation for removal costs and costs incurred by the acquisition of a new tenancy.

In the case of subtenancy, the period of notice on the subtenant's side is 14 days. However, if the parties have agreed on another period of notice, or if the tenancy has been agreed to end on a certain date without notice, this agreement must be observed.

Grounds for notice of termination

If notice of termination is given by the lessor, the grounds for the notice must always be stated.

If notice of termination is given by the tenant, the grounds for the notice only need to be stated in the following situations:

• the tenant has been granted a permit to give notice of termination of a fixed-term lease by a court of law
• the death estate of the tenant gives notice of termination of a fixed-term lease
• the notice of termination is based on the termination of an employment relationship and the lessor wishes to have the tenancy terminated simultaneously with the employment relationship.

The day of removal is the first weekday after the termination of the lease.

Payment of rent

The rent must be paid on the second day of the period of payment of rent at the latest, unless otherwise agreed. The period of payment of rent corresponds to a calendar month or another period agreed on. The lessor and tenant may agree to make rent payable in advance for one or more months.

Lease forms for business premises are available on the Kiinteistöalan Kustannus Oy website under the section Internetlomakkeet. The forms can be completed on the Internet, paid for (through Solo Payment, Kultaraha or Sampo Bank's WebBank service) and printed. The price is 2.5 Euro per form. When you begin to fill in the form on the Internet, it is advisable you take note of the reference number given by the service. Should the connection be terminated for some reason, you can use the reference number to retrieve the form.

OPENING A BANK ACCOUNT

Bank accounts in Finland may be opened by anyone who can present an adequate statement of the person opening the account, the holder of the account, and the necessity for and purpose of the account. The bank must ultimately determine what constitutes an adequate statement for the establishment of a customer relationship in each case.

A bank account must be opened for a new business during the establishment process. In the case of a limited liability company, a bank account must be opened before the company is entered in the trade register. The share capital of the company must be paid to the company's account in a Finnish deposit bank before filing the trade register notification and its entry in the register. It is only possible to make payments from the account after a certificate of arrival concerning the delivery of the start-up notice issued to the trade register and showing the business ID of the company has been delivered to the bank.

The person opening an account for a limited liability company or cooperative must present a decision (either minutes of the meeting or an extract of the minutes) by the decision-making body (usually the Board of Directors) on the opening of the account and the persons authorised to use the account, as well as the required services (electronic funds transfer, Internet service, debit card, etc.). The right of the person in question to open the account on behalf of the corporation, or the authorisation granted him/her, must also be shown in the statement.

A person opening a bank account for a partnership (general partnership and limited partnership) must present the partnership agreement showing the names of the partners. Partners (in a limited partnership, the general partners) not present when the account is opened must grant a separate power of attorney for the opening of the account.

With regard to the establishment of customer relationships and the opening of accounts, banks have a statutory obligation to carefully identify both the person opening the account and the holder of the account, if the account is opened by a person other than the holder. This applies to situations where the holder is a legal entity, for example. If the person opening an account on behalf of a corporation does not have a personal identity number, he/she must present a passport issued by authorities in his/her home country; otherwise, identification is made on the basis of a Finnish passport or another valid personal identification document issued by the police. Banks recommend that individuals moving to Finland make application to the local register office for a personal identity number. If the identification documents of the person opening an account on behalf of a legal entity are not adequate for reliable identification, the person cannot open a bank account.

The bank may, at its discretion, require a letter of recommendation concerning the holder of the account from a correspondent bank or another bank it considers reliable. Banks are obligated by law to request a statement on the type of the customer's operations, the purpose of the account and the type and extent of the intended payment transfers, etc.). If necessary, the bank may request a statement on the origin of the money deposited in the account from the customer. In the case of a foreign legal entity, the bank may also request a statement on its owners.

INDUSTRIES REQUIRING A BUSINESS LICENCE OR NOTIFICATION

Finland has freedom of trade, which means that you may engage in business operations that are lawful and in accordance with good practice without requiring a business licence from the authorities. However, in certain industries, a business licence is required in order to protect the community, the environment and consumer safety. In other fields, notifying the authorities is sufficient and an official business licence is not required.

Before commencing operations, it is always important to check whether a special business licence or declaration is needed and what other requirements apply in your chosen field. To acquire a business licence, the applicant must generally be professionally competent, qualified to enter into legal contracts and possess a good reputation. The applicant's financial situation will also have an impact on whether s/he can obtain a business licence. Business licences are granted by local authorities (municipalities and cities) and regional administration offices along with government departments, local environmental protection authorities and other licensing authorities.

A business licence is generally granted for a fixed period, and it can be revoked if the person does not comply with the provisions of the licence. Application for a business licence is usually subject to a charge. In some cases, a business licence is needed from many different authorities. For example, in the catering industry, hygiene certification and licences to serve food and alcohol are required, and declarations must be made to the health inspector, the rescue services and local building supervision authorities, amongst other things.

INDUSTRY	LICENCE/NOTIFICATION/ REGISTRATION	ORGANIZATION/ AUTHORITY
Retail sales of alcoholic beverages	Retail trade licence	Regional State Administrative Agencies (www.avi.fi)
Pharmacies, pharmaceutical industry, pharmaceutical wholesalers	Pharmacy and subsidiary pharmacy licences/medicinal product manufacturer's licence and pharmaceutical wholesale licence	Finnish Medicines Agency Fimea (www.fimea.fi)
Garage operations	www.trafi >Road> Liceces and approvals > Garages	Trafi (www.trafi.fi)
Driving schools	Driving school licence	Trafi (www.trafi.fi)
Food establishments (grocery stores, restaurants, kiosks)	Notification of a food establishment	Municipal food control authority (www.kunnat.net)
Lifts and lift installations	Notification of electrical work (SL1)	Finnish Safety and Chemicals Agency, Tukes (www.tukes.fi)
Manufacturers and sellers of precious metals	Application for responsibility mark	Tukes (www.tukes.fi)
Public transport	Public transport licence / Community	South Ostrobothnia Centre

services in Finland and the EU	licence for passenger transport	for Economic Development, Transport and the Environment (www.ely-keskus.fi)
Professional waste carriage and brokerage	Application for approval of activity in a waste management register	Centres for Economic Development, Transport and the Environment (www.ely-keskus.fi)
Mining	Reservation notification, mining permit, mining safety permit, Environmental permit	Tukes (www.tukes.fi) Regional State Administrative Agencies (www.avi.fi)
Beauty parlours, hairdresser-barbershops	Notification pursuant to section 13 of the Health Protection Act	Municipal health protection authority (www.kunnat.net)
Manufacture and import of chemicals	Chemical notification Environmental permit	Tukes (www.tukes.fi) Municipal environmental protection authority (www.kunnat.net)
Industrial handling and storage of (dangerous) chemicals	Licence for plants dealing in large-scale industrial handling and storage	Tukes (www.tukes.fi)

Brokerage of real estate	Notification of the commencement of brokerage of real estate	Regional State Administrative Agencies (www.avi.fi)
Gold panning	Gold panning permit	Tukes (www.tukes.fi/en)
Refrigeration and fire extinguisher operators	Notification of operations	Tukes (www.tukes.fi)
Laboratories	Laboratory approval	Finnish Food Safety Authority Evira (www.evira.fi)
Land extraction	Land extraction permit, notification on the hearing of neighbours, notification pursuant to section 23 a of the Land Extraction Act	The municipal authority in charge (www.kunnat.net)
Exploration	Reservation notification, exploration permit, gold panning permit	Tukes (www.tukes.fi)
Tour operators and retailers	Registration of a travel agency	Finnish Competition and Consumer Authority (www.kkv.fi)
Opinion polls and market surveys	Notification of operations	Data Protection Ombudsman (www.tietosuoja.fi)
Sales along the roads	Permit for sales as well as signposts for the seasonal sales operations	Centres for Economic Development, Transport and the Environment (www.ely-keskus.fi)
Trust and company services, foreign exchange transactions	Registration application of trust and company services, register application for foreign exchange transactions	Regional State Administrative Agency of Southern Finland (www.avi.fi)

Operation of debt collection (on behalf of another)	Licence for a collection business, notification of operations	Regional State Administrative Agency of Southern Finland (www.avi.fi), Data Protection Ombudsman (www.tietosuoja.fi)
Grocery stores	Notification of a food establishment, retail trade licence for alcohol, retail trade licence for nicotine products	Municipal food control authority (www. kunnat. net), Regional State Administrative Agencies (www.avi.fi), municipal authority (www.kunnat.net)

Retail sales of alcoholic beverages	Retail trade licence	Regional State Administrative Agencies (www.avi.fi)
Pharmacies, pharmaceutical industry, pharmaceutical wholesalers	Pharmacy and subsidiary pharmacy licences/medicinal product manufacturer's licence and pharmaceutical wholesale licence	Finnish Medicines Agency Fimea (www.fimea.fi)
Garage operations	www.trafi >Road> Liceces and approvals > Garages	Trafi (www.trafi.fi)
Driving schools	Driving school licence	Trafi (www.trafi.fi)
Food establishments (grocery stores, restaurants, kiosks)	Notification of a food establishment	Municipal food control authority (www.kunnat.net)
Lifts and lift installations	Notification of electrical work (SL1)	Finnish Safety and Chemicals Agency, Tukes (www.tukes.fi)
Manufacturers and sellers of precious metals	Application for responsibility mark	Tukes (www.tukes.fi)
Public transport services in Finland and the EU	Public transport licence / Community licence for passenger transport	South Ostrobothnia Centre for Economic Development, Transport and the Environment (www.ely-keskus.fi)
Professional waste carriage and brokerage	Application for approval of activity in a waste management register	Centres for Economic Development, Transport and the Environment (www.ely-keskus.fi)
Mining	Reservation notification, mining permit, mining safety permit, Environmental permit	Tukes (www.tukes.fi) Regional State Administrative Agencies (www.avi.fi)
Beauty parlours, hairdresser-barbershops	Notification pursuant to section 13 of the Health Protection Act	Municipal health protection authority (www.kunnat.net)
Manufacture and import of chemicals	Chemical notification Environmental permit	Tukes (www.tukes.fi) Municipal environmental protection authority (www.kunnat.net)

Industrial handling and storage of (dangerous) chemicals	Licence for plants dealing in large-scale industrial handling and storage	Tukes (www.tukes.fi)

Electrical works (electrical installations and repair of electrical appliances)	Notification of electrical work (form SL1)	Tukes (www.tukes.fi)
Operation of taxi services	Taxi licence, notification of commencement of taxi services	Centres for Economic Development, Transport and the Environment (www.ely-keskus.fi)
Goods transport (domestic goods transport and goods transport within the EU economic area)	Domestic goods transport licence / Community licence	South Ostrobothnia Centre for Economic Development, Transport and the Environment (www.ely-keskus.fi)
Telecommunications, programmes, videoon-demand and pay TV services	Telecommunications notification / Program broadcasting notification / VOD notification / Pay TV service notification	Finnish Communications Regulatory Authority (www.viestintavirasto.fi)
Slaughterhouses and facilities connected thereto as well as game processing facilities	Approval of a food establishment as a facility	Evira (www.evira.fi), reindeer slaughter facilities: Regional State Administrative Agencies (www.avi.fi)
Insurance agents and brokers	Registration as an agent / registration as an insurance broker	Financial Supervisory Authority (www.finanssivalvonta.fi)
Private security services	Private security company license, approval as a key person	National Police Board, supervision of the security sector (www.poliisi.fi)
Undertakings engaged in web server renting	Notification of operations	Data Protection Ombudsman (www.tietosuoja.fi)
Brokerage of rental apartments	Notification of the commencement of brokerage of rental apartments	Regional State Administrative Agencies (www.avi.fi)
Private social welfare services (round-the-clock)	Licence to provide round-theclock social welfare services	Regional State Administrative Agencies (www.avi.fi)

LICENCE/NOTIFICATION/ ORGANIZATION/ INDUSTRY REGISTRATION AUTHORITY

Private social welfare services (other than round-the-clock)	Notification of the provision of social welfare services	The municipality where the service is provided (www.kunnat.net)
Private health care services	Application for licence to provide private health care services	Operations within the region of one AVI Agency: Regional State Administrative Agencies (www.avi.fi), operations within the region of two or more AVI Agencies: Valvira (www.valvira.fi)

PROFESSIONAL APPROVALS AND QUALIFICATIONS		
PERSON(S)	APPROVAL/ QUALIFICATION	ORGANIZATION/ AUTHORITY
Person acting as the responsible manager or his/her substitute in licensed premises	Licence to serve alcohol (alcohol passport)	Educational establishments offering the alcohol passport examination (www.valvira.fi)
Persons who handle unpackaged perishable foodstuffs in their work	Food Hygiene Proficiency Certificate (Hygiene passport)	Proficiency examiners (www.evira.fi)
Property valuers (AKA and KHK)	AKA and KHK examination	Property Valuation Board of Finland Chamber of Commerce (www.kauppakamari.fi)
Real estate agents (LKV)	LKV examination	Board of Examiners for Real Estate Agents (www.kauppakamari.fi)
Driving instructors	Driving instructor permit	Trafi (www.trafi.fi). Service provider Ajovarma Oy (www.ajovarma.fi)
Professionals in Building, HVAC and Real Estate sector	Qualification of Professionals in Building, HVAC and Real Estate sector	FISE Qualification of Professionals in Building, HVAC and Real Estate sector
PERSON(S)	APPROVAL/ QUALIFICATION	ORGANIZATION/ AUTHORITY
Supervisors of electrical work and lift work	Certificate of electrical and lift qualification	Henkilö- ja yritysarviointi SETI Oy
Taxi drivers	Taxi driver licence	Applications to Ajovarma Oy (www.ajovarma.fi), licences Trafi (www.trafi.fi/en)
Goods inspectors (HTT)	HTT examination	Goods Inspection Board of Finland Chamber of Commerce (www.kauppakamari.fi)
Health care professionals	Application to practice as a licenced professional/use a protected occupational title	Valvira (www.valvira.fi)
Private health care service providers	Notification of private health care service provision	Regional State Administrative Agencies (www.avi.fi)
Accountants	HT examination as well as KHT and JHT qualification examinations	Accounting supervision (www.prh.fi)
Hot work professionals	Hot work card	Finnish National Rescue Association SPEK (www.spek.fi)
(Private) persons working in the (private) security sector	Approval as a security guard (security guard licence) / approval as a security officer (security officer licence) / approval as a security steward (security steward licence)	Municipal police department (www.poliisi.fi)
Transport of dangerous goods	ADR licence	ADR training organisations (www.trafi.fi)
Letting agents (LVV)	LVV examination	Board of Examiners for Real Estate Agents (www.kauppakamari.fi)

Persons working in joint work sites	Occupational safety card	The Centre for Occupational Safety (www.ttk.fi/en)
OTHER PERMITS AND NOTIFICATIONS		
APPROVAL/ QUALIFICATION		ORGANIZATION/ AUTHORITY
Abnormal transport	Abnormal transport permit	Pirkanmaa Centre for Economic Development, Transport and the Environment (www.ely-keskus.fi)
Work carried out in road areas	Permit for work carried out in road areas	Centres for Economic Development, Transport and the Environment (www. ely-keskus.fi)

The Finnish Trade Register is the official public register for information about enterprises. As a rule, all businesses must be enrolled in the register. Enrolment is achieved via a notification and is subject to charge. As the Trade Register, which is maintained by the Finnish Patent and Registration Office (PRH), has a joint notification procedure and information service with the Finnish Tax Administration, a business will only need to submit one notification to be enrolled in the trade, prepayment, employer and VAT registers and there is no separate charge.

The line of business of an enterprise is always declared when the enterprise is registered with the Finnish Trade Register and the Finnish Tax Administration. It is also possible to register so-called "general commercial activities" with the Finnish Trade Register, meaning that the business may engage in all types of lawful business activities that are accordant with good practices. However, it is advisable to state the line of business explicitly, so that the nature of the business's operations is clear.

The Finnish Tax Administration requires that you declare your main line of business. The enterprise may have only one main line of business and it must be clearly described along with the form of the operations. A main line of business that is too general will not be accepted into the register.

As a general rule, starting up business operations requires that the business is enrolled in the prepayment register maintained by the Finnish Tax Administration. You can enrol in the prepayment register using the same form that is used for notifying the Finnish Trade Register of your new business. For more information and details about the prepayment register, please view the chapter on taxation.

EMPLOYER REGISTER

The employer register is maintained by the Finnish Tax Administration. A business must enrol in the employer register when it starts regular salary payments if it has: 1) at least two permanent employees during the calendar year or 2) at least six temporary employees at one time. If the payment of salaries and wages is temporary, or they are paid to only one employee, the business does not need to enrol in the employer register.

VAT REGISTER

Businesses that are subject to value added tax (VAT) enrol in the Finnish Tax Administration's register via their declaration of foundation. At registration, they need to state the date of commencement of the operations that are subject to VAT. For more information and details about the VAT register, please view the chapter on taxation.

NOTE that VAT registration is needed for international trade.

The necessary registration forms are available at: www.ytj.fi

Estimated processing time for notifications is between three to five working days. This is only an estimate, not a guarantee that the matter will be processed within the time indicated.

SETTING UP A BUSINESS THROUGH ACQUISITION

One option to start business operations in Finland is the acquisition of a working enterprise. This offers a simple way to get started and the possibility to commence business operations immediately, as the company is already officially registered, has a business ID, and customers and turnover already exist.

The same requirements for board of directors and managing director – as described in the previous chapter – still abide.

To contact a Finnish lawyer to help with the transaction. Lawyers who advise on and assist in legal matters can be divided into two categories: members of the Finnish Bar Association (attorneys-at-law) and non-members of the Bar (jurists). You will find contact information for all Bar association members by using the search engine on the Finnish Bar Association website: www.asianajajaliitto.fi/en

Restrictions on the purchase of Finnish companies may be imposed when required by the national interests of Finland (for example national defence, security of supply and functions fundamental to society). In such cases, foreign buyers are obliged to request permission from the Ministry of Economic Affairs and Employment. Further information: www.tem.fi/acquisitions.

There are many enterprises in Finland with owners willing to sell them. Some enterprises are actively and openly for sale, but most owners are looking for a buyer silently. Regional players like development companies and ELY Centres can provide expertise to help you find such companies.

To find basic information on all registered enterprises in Finland from the business information system, YTJ (www.ytj.fi), where a search can be run by the name or business ID of a company. More advanced information about the financial status of a company etc. can be found in Finnish or Swedish by using web services such as www.asiakastieto.fi or tietopalvelut.kauppalehti.fi.

More information:

Invest in Finland: www.investinfinland.fi
Local Regional Development Companies:
see chapter "Finnish enterprise agencies and business funding"
ELY Centre: www.ely-keskus.fi
More information about companies for sale:
Finnish Company Acquisition Ltd: www.yrityskaupat.net
Search service of the Federation of Finnish Enterprises: www.yritysporssi.fi
Enterprise Finland: www.yrityssuomi.fi/en/omistajanvaihdos

LEGAL OBLIGATIONS FOR AN EMPLOYER

• Pay wages during the sick leave of an employee (the collective agreement may obligate for the payment of wages also during a maternity leave and during a short-term absence to care for a sick child)

• Arrange preventive occupational healthcare for employees
• Take out employment pension insurance (TyEL)
• Take out group life insurance (in connection with the statutory workers' compensation insurance through a non-life insurance company)
• Pay unemployment insurance contributions, which are withheld from an employee's wages
• Insure employees against occupational injuries and occupational diseases
Indirect staff costs in addition to wage:
• Employees' pension insurance
• Employer's health insurance contribution
• Unemployment insurance contribution
• Accident insurance premiums
• Group life insurance premiums

BUSINESS FINANCING

Loans granted by a bank or Finnvera are common sources of financing for entrepreneurs. Finnvera is a specialised financing company owned by the State of Finland. It provides financing for the start, growth, and internationalisation of enterprises and guarantees against risks arising from exports. Businesses, that meet the prerequisites to maintain profitable operations but do not have the down payment or collateral required by banks, may be granted a loan or a security by Finnvera. Contact your local Finnvera office for more information about different financing options for your company and its needs.

Finnvera: www.finnvera.fi

ELY Centres (The Centres for Economic Development, Transport and the Environment) are responsible for the regional implementation and development tasks of the central government. ELY Centres support the establishment, growth and development of small and medium-sized enterprises by providing advisory, training and expert services. ELY Centre experts assist entrepreneurs in matters concerning inventions and intellectual property rights and grant funding for investment and development projects.

ELY Centres: www.ely-keskus.fi

Tekes (the Finnish Funding Agency for Innovation) is the main government financing and expert organisation for research and technological development in Finland. Tekes provides targeted financing for innovative and risk-intensive projects and offers R&D funding for enterprises to develop products or services, production methods, and business models. It can also provide funding for companies that are looking to enter export markets or expand their international business. Tekes funding is available for companies registered in Finland.

TEKES: www.tekes.fi

Free business advice is available to everyone in Finland. Advice, assistance, and support for company establishment processes are offered in almost every city in Finland. Finnish enterprise agencies, regional development companies, and, in some cities, business development functions provide guidance for people planning to start a business. Experts at these agencies can help, for example, with business plans, market research, profitability calculations, financing, and finding suitable premises.

Finnish enterprise agencies: www.uusyrityskeskus.fi/in-english/

• Alajärvi, Soini and Vimpeli region – Järvi-Pohjanmaan Yrityspalvelut Oy JPYP: www.jpyp.fi
• Espoo Innovation Garden: www.espooinnovationgarden.fi
• Forssa region – Forssan yrityskehitys Oy: www.fskk.fi
• Helsinki region – Helsinki Business Hub: www.helsinkibusinesshub.fi
• Hämeenlinna region – Hämeenlinnan, Linnan Kehitys Oy: www.linnan.fi
• Imatra region – Imatran seudun kehitysyhtiö Kehy Oy: www.kehy.vlu.fi
• Inari region – Inarin elinkeinot & kehitys Nordica: www.nordicainari.fi
• Joensuu region – Joensuun seudun kehittämisyhtiö Josek Oy: www.josek.fi
• Joensuun tiedepuisto: www.tiedepuisto.fi
• Jämsä region – Jämsän seudun kehittämisyhtiö Jämsek Oy: www.jämsek.fi
• Kaarina region – Kaarinan kehitys Oy: www.kaarina.fi
• Kainuu region – Kainuun Etu Oy: www.kainuunetu.fi
• Kankaanpää region – Pohjoisen Satakunnan Kehittämiskeskus Oy: www.pskk.fi
• Karstula region – Kehittämisyhtiö Karstulanseutu Oy: www.karstulanseutu.fi
• Kaustinen region – Kaustisen seutukunta: www.kase.fi
• Keitele region – Kehitysyhtiö Savogrow Oy: www.savogrow.fi
• Kemi region – Kemin Digipolis Oy: www.digipolis.fi
• Kerava, Järvenpää, Tuusula region – Keski-Uudenmaan Kehittämiskeskus Oy KEUKE: www.keuke.fi
• Keuruu region – Kehittämisyhtiö Keulink Oy: www.keulink.fi
• Kitee region – Keski-Karjalan kehitysyhtiö Oy KETI: www.keti.fi
• Kokkola region – Kokkolanseudun Kehitys Oy KOSEK: www.kosek.fi
• Kotka & Hamina region – Kotkan ja Haminan seudun kehittämisyhtiö Cursor Oy: www.cursor.fi
• Kouvola region – Kouvola Innovation Oy Kinno: www.kinno.fi
• Kuusamo region – Koillis-Suomen kehittämisyhtiö Naturpolis Oy: www.naturpolis.fi
• Lahti region – Lahden Seudun Kehitys LADEC: www.ladec.fi
• Lappeenranta region – Wirma Lappeenranta Oy: www.wirma.fi
• Lieksa region – Lieksan teollisuuskylä: www.lieksada.fi
• Lohja region Länsi-Uudenmaan NOVAGO yrityskehitys Oy: www.novago.fi
• Mikkeli region – Mikkelin kehitysyhtiö Miksei Oy: www.mikseimikkeli.fi
• Mäntsälä region - Mäntsälän Yrityskehitys Oy www.yrityskehitys.net/
• Mänttä-Vilppula region – Mänttä-Vilppulan, MW-kehitys Oy: www.manttavilppula.fi
• Nivala-Haapajärvi region – Nivala-Haapajärven seutu NIHAK ry: www.nihak.fi
• Oulu region – Business Oulu: www.businessoulu.fi
• Pielinen region – Pielisen Karjalan Kehittämiskeskus Oy PIKES: www.pikes.fi
• Pietarsaari region – Pietarsaaren seudun kehittämisyhtiö Concordia Oy: www.concordia.jakobstad.fi
• Pori region – Satakunnan elinkeinoyhtiö Prizztech Oy: www.prizz.fi
• Porvoo region – Itä-Uudenmaan kehitysyhtiö Posintra Oy: www.posintra.fi
• Raahe region – Raahen seudun yrityspalvelut: www.raahenseutukunta.fi
• Rovaniemi region – Rovaniemen Kehitys Oy: www.rovaniemenkehitys.fi
• Saarijärvi region – Saarijärven kehitysyhtiö SSYP Oy: www.ssypkehitys.fi
• Salo region – YritysSalo: www.yrityssalo.fi
• Savonlinna region – Savonlinnan Yrityspalvelut SYKE: www.savonlinnanyrityspalvelut.fi
• Seinäjoki region – Into Seinäjoki Oy: www.intoseinajoki.fi
• Suupohja region – Suupohjan Elinkeinotoimen kuntayhtymä: www.suupohja.fi
• Tampere region – Tredea, Tampereen kaupunkiseudun elinkeino- ja kehitysyhtiö: www.tredea.fi
• Turku region – Turku Science Park Oy: www.turkusciencepark.com
• Vaasa region – Vaasanseudun Kehitys Oy VASEK: www.vasek.fi and Vaasa Parks www.vaasaparks.fi/
• Varkaus region – Navitas Kehitys Oy, Varkauden seutu: www.navitas.fi
• Viitasaari region – Kehittämisyhtiö Witas Oy: www.witas.fi
• Ääneseutu region – Ääneseudun Kehitys Oy: www.aaneseudunkehitys.fi

BUSINESS ADVICE

REGIONAL DEVELOPMENT COMPANIES
SOURCES AND FURTHER INFORMATION:
Enterprise Finland: www.yrityssuomi.fi
Finnish Enterprise Agencies: www.uusyrityskeskus.fi
Finnvera: www.finnvera.fi
ELY Centre: www.ely-keskus.fi
TEKES: www.tekes.fi
Invest in Finland website: www.investinfinland.fi

PRACTICAL AND LEGAL INFORMATION FOR BUSINESS AND TRADE

STARTING BUSINESS IN FINLAND

No.	Procedures	Time to Complete	Associated Costs
1	Deposit the paid-in share capital in a bank; pay the registration fee and get a receipt Agency : Bank According to the Companies Act, the paid-in share capital must be paid in full into the company's bank account. To open a bank account, the company must provide at least a copy of memorandum of association. Normally also following materials need to be provided to the bank when opening an account: - The minutes of the meeting of the Board of Directors including a resolution of opening an account and identifying persons authorized to use the bank account to be opened, - A brief description of the nature of company's future banking transactions, - A description of the company's field of business, - Sufficient information regarding the shareholders and the directors of the company, - Copies of the passports regarding the persons authorized to use the bank account The subscription price may be paid to a bank account outside of Finland. However, the bank account should correspond to a bank account of a Finnish depository bank or a branch of a foreign credit institute in Finland. The receipt of the bank regarding the payment of the share capital is sufficient in order to register the company. However, if an auditor is elected in accordance with applicable law, the auditor shall provide a statement confirming the payment of the share capital.	1 day	no charge
2	Submit a single start-up notification form to the National Board of Patents and Registration (PRH) and the Tax Administration as well as VAT registration. Agency : NBPR and the Tax Administration A basic declaration to the Trade Register must be filed (in either Finnish or Swedish) as the National Board of Patents and Registration specifies. For each type of business association, a separate basic declaration form	16 days (1 day for company registration and 15 days for tax requirements)	EUR 380 (start-up notification in paper form) and EUR 330 (online start-up notification of a limited liability company)

No.	Procedures	Time to Complete	Associated Costs
	must be used. The forms are available on the National Board of Patents and Registration, regional tax offices, local tax offices, Centers for Economic Development, Transport and the Environment ("ELY" Centers), local register offices, and Chamber of Commerce and Enterprise Agencies. All registrations to the Trade Register and to the Tax Administration are performed with the same basic declaration. Moreover, since December 2012, it has been possible to file a start-up notification online for EUR 330. In order to be able to use the online system, it is necessary to obtain an ID with the National Board of Patents and Registration of Finland. If the company has employees, the company must be entered into the Employer Register, according to Section 31 of the Preliminary Taxation Act, which happens at the same time as the registration to the administration. Registration to the Tax administration includes registration for the Value Added Tax. When the basic declaration is submitted, a certificate of the company's business identification number may be obtained at a fee of EUR 7. This certificate allows companies to use their bank accounts before registration has been completed. The online registration is possible only when the following conditions are met: - The standard Article of Association is sufficient. - The shares are paid in euros to the bank account of the company to be established. - The subscription price is entered in share capital entirely. - All subscribers of shares and the Members of the Board of Directors shall have a Finnish social security number and a personal code for online banking system or an identity card with chip (HST-card). This applies also to possible CEO and a possible auditor who is a natural person. - The possible procuration holders and those who are entitled to represent the company have a Finnish social security number.		

No.	Procedures	Time to Complete	Associated Costs
	According to the Finnish Limited Liability Companies Act (624/2006) chapter 2, section 8(1), the company shall be notified for registration within three months of the signing of the Memorandum of Association. If failing this, the incorporation of the company shall lapse. If the company shall carry on business, farming or any other income deriving activity, it shall be registered in the prepayment register.		
⇉3	File at a private insurer for pension insurance, accident insurance, and medical insurance of employees Agency : Private Insurer Under the statutory pension insurance scheme, an employer must subscribe its employees for pension insurance with a pension provider handling earnings-related pensions. Supplemental pension insurance is optional. The employer also pays the pension institution statutory employee earnings-related contributions, such as: accident insurance, unemployment insurance, and group life assurance premium. A social security contribution is also payable to the Regional Tax Office. The employer must insure its employees against accidents and occupational diseases, according to Section 3 of the Occupational Accidents, Injuries and Diseases Act, which has been in force as of 1 January 2017. In addition, certain collective labor agreements require that employers provide their employees with group life insurance. No proof of insurance is needed to start operations. The accident insurance is paid to the insurance company and must be obtained before the work for the company starts. The group life insurance is also paid to the insurance company. The group life insurance is compulsory only if the applicable collective labor agreement requires the employer to take the group life insurance. Unemployment insurance is paid to The Unemployment Insurance Fund.	1 day (simultaneous with previous procedure)	no charge

⇉ Takes place simultaneously with previous procedure.

TYPES OF COMPANIES IN FINLAND

A company who's willing to **start a business in Finland** must first check the types of Finnish companies, in order to choose the one that best suits the type of business it's covering it.

Private Person Carrying on Trade (yksityinen elinkeinonharjoittaja), or a private trader, is an entrepreneur member of EEA who establish a company in Finland. It's responsible for paying the taxes and it's free to withhold profit.

A **Partnership (avoin yhtiö-Ay) in Finland is** composed by at least two members (one of them must be a EEA resident).The profits are divided among the partners according to the number of shares they have (except the case when the partnership agreement dispose something else).There is no originally share capital required.

The **Limited Partnership (kommandiittiyhtiö,-Ky) in Finland,** must have at least 2 partners, one of them must be the general partner and one the silent partner. The general one has the right to contribute to the management's decisions and ask for profit, unlike the limited one. The silent one has no decisional power but doesn't absorb the losses.

The **Limited Company (osakeyhtiö-Oy) in Finland has** the following attributes: the minimum share capital is 2500 euros (cash or property) a person is sufficient to set up the company and the management is provided by the management board. It must be recorded at the Trade Register before the beginning of activity.

A **Public Limited Company (julkinen osakeyhtiö-Oyj) in Finland** is founded after registration in the Trade Register. It must have a share capital of minimum 80000 euros (cash or property). At least one statutory person establishes the company. If the company has the share capital above 80000 euro, the management board must have more than 3 members (more than 50% of them must be EEA residents) and a managing director. An Oyj must also provide semi-annuals reports and can be listed on the Helsinki Stock Exchange.

The basic difference between a Limited and a Public company is that only the Public Limited Company can trade or transfer the shares. They are both governed by the Companies Act (Osakeyhtiölaki, 21.7.2006/624).

A **Branch of a Foreign Company (sivuliike)** it's a society that operates in Finland even though it has it's headquarters in another country. The branch representative must have a Finnish domicile and if it's not an EEA member a special permission must be granted by NBPR.

FORM AN OY (LIMITED LIABILITY COMPANY) IN FINLAND

A **Limited Liability Company in Finland** is also known as osakeyhtiö(Oy), and it's the most usual form a small or medium company can take.

In **Finland setting up an Oy** is covered by the Companies Act, fully reformed in 2006.

There's a minimal share capital of 2,500 euro (cash or property) that has to be deposited into a bank before the company registration.

To **establish an Oy in Finland**, a Memorandum of Association must be developed and signed. This Memorandum includes: the date of the Memorandum, information regarding the Management Board, the auditors, the shareholders, the shares, the price of the shares, the payment term of the shares.

Also next to the Memorandum of Association the entrepreneur must enclose: the name of the company, the domicile and the type of business. These are all included in the Articles of Association.

Within three months after signing the Memorandum, the company must be enrolled at the Trade Register; otherwise the setting up the company expires.

A **Limited Liability Company in Finland** can be formed by one or more legal persons.

All the shareholders have equal rights in the company except the case when the difference it's clearly stipulated in the Memorandum of Association.

An Oy in Finland must have a Board of Directors (according to the Companies Act), elected by the General Meeting of Shareholders.

The Board of Directors must include one or two common members and at least one adjunct. It is responsible for the administration and the suitable disposal of the operations as well as for the proper monitoring of the accountancy and the check of the financial issues of the company.

Also a managing director, named by the Board of Directors must be invested. In the matters which belong to his tasks he has the right to represent the Company. Furthermore, it is the duty of the Managing Director to see if the accountancy and that the financial issues are being handled reliably.

Extended or unusual acts (considering the scope and the kind of the company's transactions) may be taken by the Managing Director only when he's authorized by the Board of Directors.

Also an external audit can be requested by a shareholder, at Ordinary General Meeting or at a General Meeting where the matter is according to the notice to be approached. The special auditor can be an individual or an audit firm.

It is not mandatory for a **Finnish LTD company** to name an internal auditor unless certain conditions are met: the staff is composed by more than three employees, the balance sheet total overcome 100.000 euro; net sales or appropriate gains overcome 200.000 euro.

As a special requirement in setting up an Oy, at least half of the Board of the Directors must be EU residents. Also a Finnish headquarters is requested for a **Limited Liability Company in Finland.**

LIMITED LIABILITY COMPANIES ACT IN FINLAND

The act that governs all the Finnish organization and function of all types of **limited liability companies is the Companies Act**, also known as osakeyhtiölaki (first posted in 1978 and reformed in its entirety in September 2006). It applies to the public and private companies as well.

This act governs all the concerns regarding the Limited Liability Companies in Finland, in matters such as: the company operations and the applications of this, incorporation of a limited liability company, shares, administration and financial statements(the general meeting, management and representation of the company, audit and special audit, equity, financial statements, annual report and group),finance(share issue, increase of the share capital, capital loan),distribution of the company assets, changes in company structure and the dissolution of the company, sanctions and remedies.

Establishment and articles of association of an OY:

The first step in setting up a limited liability company in Finland is the preparation of the Memorandum of Association, signed by the shareholders. This has to be registered at the Trade Register within three months from signing it. Also the articles of association (containing the company name, the headquarters and the type of business) must be included in the registration.

The minimum share capital for a Finnish limited liability company is 2500 euro and 80000 euro if it's a public one.

Leadership and representatives of the Finnish company:

A Finnish limited liability company must have a Board of Directors, responsible for the proper control of the company accounts and finances.

It may also have a Managing Director and a Supervisory Board, if the dimension of it requires it.

The Managing Director must make sure that the accounts of the company are in accordance with the law and that its financial affairs have been arranged in a reliable manner .

The Supervisory Board supervises the administration of the company (the responsibility of the Board of Directors and the Managing Director).

Shares:

Is not compulsory for the shares to have a nominal value, (in certain cases it may have in the future but this should be specified in the articles of association)

Changes in the company structure and the dissolution of the company:

An Oy can merge in another limited liability company, the assets and liabilities of the merging company are transferred to the buying company (also it may transfer cash, further assets and future enterprises). The shareholders of the merging company receive shares in the acquiring company.

A limited liability company can be changed in a public one if it meets the demands of a public company. In this case it must amend the Articles of Association within a month from the General Meeting decision and register it at the Trade Register, if not, the changing decision fails.

The decision of liquidation can only be taken by the General Meeting, and it's made for paying the company's debts(by changing the needed amount of assets into cash).After this, the surplus is returned to the shareholders or others, as specified in the Articles of Association.

COMPANY REGISTRATION IN FINLAND

The **company registration in Finland** requires only a few straightforward steps. The laws are very encouraging to the investors (as an exemple in the north where local authorities have special interests to attract foreign investments or domestic, some facilities are granted).

The company registration in Finland is governed by the Foundations Act nr. 734 from 1930 and The Finnish Companies Act from 1978 (the last one has been reformed in its entirety on 2006 and it is now modern and comprehensible).

To **register a company in Finland** first of all the entrepreneur must deposit the paid-in share capital in a bank (2500 eur if it's a limited liability company, 80000 eur if it's a Public Liability Company) and pay the registration fee and obtain a receipt. This process usually takes approximately one day.

There are six forms of business ventures: Limited Company (Oy), Public Limited Company (Oyj), Limited Partnership(Ky), Partnership (Ay), Private Person Carrying on Trade, Branch of a Foreign Company (sivuliike).

All the companies must be registered at the National Board of Patents and Registration. The application must include the Memorandum of Association (containing information on the members of the Board of Directors and the auditors of the Company, all the shareholders and the shares they have subscribed, the subscription price of the shares, the term of payment of the shares), the minute of the founding meeting and Board meeting, the receipt certifying that the minimum capital was deposited into a bank account.

A Limited Company must be announced for registration at the Trade Register within three months from the signing of the Memorandum of the Association, or the forming of the company shall expire. The registration is regulated in Trade Register Act (Kaupparekisterilaki, 129/1979)

The process of registration can take from two weeks to eight weeks (according to the type of company). Meanwhile, the company may start trading before registration but with limited liability.

The last step (if the company will hire employees) is to file with a private insurer for a list of employee insurances (eg. pension, accident, medical etc.)

If a company wants to **establish a branch in Finland** must submit a statutory notice concerning its branch to the Trade Register before the branch commences its operations. If the foreign investor setting up the branch is from a country located outside the European Economic area, it will also need a special approval from the Finnish Trade Register for the setup of the branch on the country's territory.

The branch, which is a part of a foreign company, must have a representative, whose domicile must be in Finland. The representative must be named in the special notification.

For an entrepreneur who wants to open a subsidiary in Finland and has his main organization outside the European Economic Area(EEA), the Start-up Notification registered at NBPR must also mention the state whose laws govern it, the place of legal residence and the central government. Also if the foreign trader is from a country outside the EEA is a limited liability company, the notification must also mention the share capital (except the case it's already given in the memorandum of association, the articles of association or in a affiliated document.)

Company formation in Finland is preferred because it offers an industrialized economic environment, extremely competitive in manufacturing, engineering, telecommunications and electronics industries. Finland also excels in high-tech exports such as mobile phones.

Finland is well-known as one of the world's leading wood producers and provider of raw materials for the wood-processing industries (2/3 of the Finland surface is covered with woods)

Also the communication network is highly developed, especially in the waterway transport (90% foreign trade is carried by sea).

DOING BUSINESS IN FINLAND BASICS

MARKET OVERVIEW

Finland, a member of the European Union (EU) since 1995, has been on a remarkable journey, redefining itself from a quiet agricultural based economy to a trend setting, global center for technology. Local company Nokia is often cast as the country's flagship illustration of Finland's penchant for technology oriented businesses. Finland has commercial clout far in excess of its modest 5.3 million population. Finland routinely ranks at the very top in international surveys of research and development funding, competitiveness, transparency, literacy, and education.

Helsinki, a modest sized metropolis, was recently designated the Design Capital for 2012, underscoring the global influence of Finnish design and innovation. In Finland, nature reigns supreme and it is no surprise that Helsinki was the site of the first LEED certified building in the Nordics. Finland, along with all its Nordic neighbors, has a focused interest in green build and energy efficient products, services and technologies.

Contrary to popular misconception, Finland is not a part of Scandinavia. It does share with Russia a 900-mile long border, the longest contiguous land border in the EU. Interestingly, some 40 percent of the EU's overland transshipments into Russia go through Finland underscoring Finland's role as a regional business hub complemented by its logistical capabilities. Russia is Finland's largest trading partner and a variety of Finnish companies are successful in Russia, a challenging marketplace. We believe that there are opportunities for certain U.S. exporters to exploit this existing business by providing U.S. goods via the Finnish corridor. Finland is striving to capitalize upon its unique position as the center of a rapidly developing marketplace formed by northwestern Russia, the Scandinavian countries, and the Baltic States, with more than 80 million prospective consumers.

Two-way trade between the U.S. and Finland was about $8.8 billion in 2008, chiefly in the electronics, paper, medical equipment, and telecommunications industries. The U.S. remains an important trading partner for Finland outside of Europe. With Finnish imports of U.S. goods and services in 2008 valued at around $2.7 billion, the United States was Finland's ninth largest supplier after Russia, Germany, Sweden, China, the Netherlands, United Kingdom, France and Italy. In 2008, the U.S. was Finland's fourth largest customer after Russia, Sweden, and Germany, with Finnish exports of goods and services to the United States valued at about $6.1 billion.

Finland is the only Nordic country to replace its national currency, the Finnish mark, with the euro. Finland has a largely homogeneous population. There are about 5,000 Americans resident in Finland and some 50,000 visit the country each year. Per capita income was about $46,300 in 2008.

MARKET CHALLENGES

Finland's import climate is open and receptive to U.S. products and investments. While the domestic market is small, Finland can effectively serve as a base for business operations in the Nordic, Baltic, and/or Western Russian markets. There is one specific trade barrier that starkly contrasts with an otherwise remarkable transparent and predictable business environment. In 2008, the Finnish government approved a pharmaceutical reference pricing system. The new law casts products protected by process patents to the reference pricing restrictions applicable to generic products and deprives pharmaceutical process patent holders in Finland appropriate compensation for the value of the intellectual property they created in the original products.

MARKET ENTRY STRATEGY

Finnish businesspeople and consumers are sophisticated and conscious of quality and value. Prices in Finland, as well as throughout the Nordics, are high. Flexibility in consumer behavior and in Finland's distribution channels allows for a variety of market entry strategies. Representatives and distributors are common methods employed for initial market entry.

LEADING SECTORS FOR U.S. EXPORT AND INVESTMENT

COMPUTERS AND PERIPHERALS (CPT)

Unit: USD thousands

	2010	2011	2012	2017 (estimated)
Total Market Size	1803	1805	1805	1800
Total Local Production	83	80	80	80
Total Exports *	605	600	600	460
Total Imports	2325	2325	2325	1630
Imports from the U.S.	105	105	105	105

Finland's population of 5.4 million people comprises a highly sophisticated market for computer hardware and software. This is illustrated by the fact that Finland has one of the highest numbers of computers per capita connected to the Internet. Presently, the majority of Finnish homes have computers as well as access to the Internet either at home, at work, or through a local institution, such as a library.

Finland offers one of the world's most sophisticated Information and Communications Technology (ICT) infrastructure and application environments. This environment provides cutting-edge, high efficiency settings for all kinds of businesses. In 2011, the total turnover for ICT-manufacturers in Finland was approximately 31.4 billion USD. The respective shares of telecommunications and software/consulting etc. were 5.1 billion USD and 3.1 billion USD respectively, the rest constituting of ICT hardware manufacturing.

The United States is Finland's leading external source of computers and peripherals. In 2012, computer imports alone were worth approximately 40.5 million USD. There are about 4,200 local computer-related companies in Finland. About 3,700 companies have less than five employees, and the five largest companies cover about 60 percent of the industry sector's sales volume.

The year 2011 saw some growth, with an increase in hardware sales. The consumer interest in tablet PCs and smart phones is expected to reduce the demand for traditional and mini laptops as well as desktops.

Finland's import climate is very open and receptive to U.S. products. Because Finland is a member of the European Union (EU), products manufactured in the EU are not subject to import duty if manufactured within the common market. However, since the beginning of 1999, computer hardware imported to Finland from third countries, such as the United States, has also entered Finland duty-free. Regardless of the origin of production, Finland applies a value-added tax of 24 percent to all imported goods. For more information on Finland's ICT markets, please visit

http://www.ficora.fi/attachments/68jZSgWFY/Viestintavirasto_vuosi2011_englanti_2706.pdf

SUB-SECTOR BEST PROSPECTS

Products on the cutting edge of technology dominate the Finnish hardware market. Modest growth is expected for 2013, as companies increase their ICT investments. Smart phones and tablet PCs are expected to increase in demand.

On the consumer electronics market, HDTV sales continue their growing trend, followed by digital high-tech electronic products. Demand remains high for home-IT equipment. The demand for affordable, light and fast mini laptops is expected to remain high.

Best future prospects are likely to come from innovation and advances in existing technology.

OPPORTUNITIES

Please see the Supplement to the European Union Official Journal http://ted.europa.eu .

WEB RESOURCES

Helsinki Fair Center www.messukeskus.com
Ministry of Transport and Communications www.mintc.fi
Finnish Federation for Communications and Teleinformatics www.ficom.fi
Invest-in-Finland - http://www.investinfinland.fi/industries/ict/en_GB/ict/
katie.janhunen@trade.gov (local contact)

COMPUTER SOFTWARE (CSF)

The software industry is one of Finland's most prominent industry sectors. The industry - along with software entrepreneurship - has grown rapidly since the early 1990s.

The Finnish software industry consists of about 1,100 software companies. The companies are mainly owned by their founders and their family members, with only minor foreign and external ownership. Their business ranges from infrastructure software and data security solutions to various Internet and wireless applications, with strong technology forming the basis for innovative products. An increasing number of Finnish software companies seek to expand their operations to global markets and welcome contacts from U.S. companies.

The United States is the number one supplier of standard, non-customized application software. Competition for new-to-market computer software companies is strong and comes from previously established U.S. companies, such as Microsoft, Novell etc.

Despite the challenging economic situation, Finnish software product companies have been able to adjust to the weakened economic conditions. As companies are rather small, their capacity to modify business operations in the short-term in order to keep the business running is relatively good. As the downturn of the economy makes growth intentions more difficult, it also forces companies to improve their processes and efficiency.

The Finnish software industry is characterized by the following trends:

* Greater degrees of both productivity and internationalization, i.e. from custom software developed for local markets towards mass-market software intended for international distribution.

* In 2012, Finnish software companies placed heavier emphasis on cloud computing platforms over mobile – as many as 47% of all firms included in a national survey said they were utilizing a cloud computing platform at least in some form when developing new software.

* Three operating systems dominated the mobile software subsector in 2012 – The respective market shares were Android for 20%, iOS for 19% and the Windows

Phone for 15%. As expected, the interest in Symbian continued to fall and was at 5%.

* Developing server software and software for the Windows (desktop) operating system were the two most common cases among Finnish software companies in 2011, and apparently also in 2012.

* According to local sources, many students today are interested in software as a service instead of packaged software products, which used to be the norm. There is "huge interest" in software development.

* Finnish software companies have increasingly sought international revenue. In 2012, more than half of Finnish companies had international revenue streams and the trend has been towards international expansion.

More than two out of three Finnish software companies develop and produce traditional ICT software. International software vendors have, however, rapidly increased their shares in the Finnish market. Finland's most common exporting countries are Sweden, the United States, and Germany.

The software sector has coped relatively well throughout the recession. The (software and IT-services) sector grew by 5.8% in 2012 – the growth was spurred on particularly by small and medium sized software companies. The industry growth outlook for 2017 is conservative but expected to continue the trend of steady increase.

SUB-SECTOR BEST PROSPECTS

The software market is expected to grow, and growth in the IT spending of companies is expected to offer opportunities for software companies. Quality products in Business Intelligence, offering clear value to the customer, are expected to do well in the market, as are security software, and CRM software. The Finnish market is small, and large companies are few in number - they tend to have established software systems. Therefore, software market opportunities for U.S. companies are mostly within the small and medium-sized enterprises (SME) market.

Finland has expertise in developing computer software products and is looking for U.S. partners that can provide financial resources.

OPPORTUNITIES

Please see the Supplement to the European Union Official Journal http://ted.europa.eu . See also www.e-finland.fi (E-business projects).

Due to changes in recent years in Russia and the Baltic countries, Finland serves as an excellent gateway to these emerging markets.

WEB RESOURCES

Helsinki Fair Center – www.messukeskus.com
Ministry of Transport and Communications - www.mintc.fi
Finnish Federation for Communications and Teleinformatics - www.ficom.fi
The Finnish Software Entrepreneurs Association - http://www.ohjelmistoyrittajat.fi/english
Software Industry Survey - http://softwareindustrysurvey.org/index.html
katie.janhunen@trade.gov (local contact)

ENERGY (ELP)

Total Energy Consumption by Energy Source	
Oil	23%
Wood fuels	24%
Nuclear Energy	18%
Coal	11%
Natural Gas	8%
Peat	4%
Hydro and Wind Power	4%
Net Imports of Energy	4%
Others	4%
Total Energy Consumption:	1,341 PJ (Source: Statistics Finland

Energy Consumption by Sector	
Industry	46%
Space Heating	25%
Transport	16%
Others	12%

Source: Statistics Finland

A Nordic country, Finland shares a long border with Russia. Finland is the world's northern-most industrialized nation and energy consumption per capita is high. In terms of land area, Finland is the seventh largest country in Europe, but has a population of only 5.4 million, mostly concentrated in urban areas. Finland's energy needs are high due to its energy-intensive industry, cold climate, high standard of living and long distances. Finland does not have its own fossil fuels – coal, oil or natural gas – but does have biofuels, rich reserves of peat, and extensive wood resources. Also, as indigenous fuel, peat has considerable effect on regional policy. It increases employment and security of the energy supply.

According to Statistics Finland's data, total consumption of energy was 1,341 petajoule (PJ) in 2013. Finland's energy consumption has increased more than 50 percent since the early 1970s. During the same period, industrial output and the total volume of construction have more than doubled. On an international scale, energy production and usage in Finland are quite efficient, due to resource availability, production infrastructure and geographical location.

Energy-intensive industries play a large role in the Finnish economy, which has spurred the development of efficient energy systems. The pulp and paper industry supplies over two-fifths of heat and electricity needs by utilizing solid and liquid wood residues.

Finland has presently four existing nuclear plants, two in Olkiluoto and two plants in Loviisa. The Loviisa plants were built by Soviet Atomenergoexport but fitted with western instrumentation and control system. They started electricity production in 1977 and 1980. New licenses were granted to Fortum to operate the units until 2027 and 2030 conditional on safety reviews before 2015 and 2023.

Finland's fifth nuclear power plant is currently under construction in Olkiluoto (OL3). OL3 is being implemented on a turnkey basis by the French-German consortium formed by Areva NP and Siemens AG. According to original timetable, OL3 was to start generating electricity at the end of 2009. Areva's OL3 project is now nearly three billion euros over the original price and six years behind the original schedule. A Finnish nuclear power company Teollisuuden Voima Oyj (TVO), expects to have the station ready in 2016.

The Government of Finland is endorsing the applications of two companies for the construction of two new nuclear reactors. Olkiluoto is to be the location of TVO's http://www.tvo.fi/Home next nuclear reactor as well. Fennovoima, http://www.fennovoima.fi/en is a newcomer to the nuclear energy game. Fennovoima decided in 2011 to build its nuclear power plant in Pyhajoki, located in North Ostrobothnia.

If two new reactors will be built, large amounts of electricity will be flowing abroad from Finland, and exports may reach 5 to 9 TWH of electricity. This is up to three-quarters of the annual output of one of the plants. However, by 2030, the capacity available for export will fall because of acceleration in domestic demand and coal-fired condensing power plants closing down. Finland will eliminate coal-fired plants due to stringent environmental regulations no later than 2023.

Finland participates in the energy-related work of the Council of the Baltic Sea States and Barents Council and supports the strengthening of the European Union's (EU's) Northern Dimension in the energy sector. Finland is also active in OECD (Organization for Economic Cooperation and Development), IEA (International Energy Agency), and NEA (Nuclear Energy Agency) energy discussions. Among the UN agencies, the IAEA (International Atomic Energy Agency) and the Sustainable Energy Committee of UNECE (UN Economic Commission for Europe) are important forums for cooperation in the energy field. Finland participates in these forums and also cooperates on energy and environment with several countries outside of Europe (http://www.tem.fi/index.phtml?l=en&s=415)

Renewable energy – Please see section Renewable Energy & Energy Efficiency RE&EE below.

SUB-SECTOR BEST PROSPECTS

U.S. companies have possibilities to bid as subcontractors in TVO's Olkiluoto and Fennovoima's Pyhajoki nuclear power plant projects, as well as Finland's future nuclear power plant projects.

See also RE&EE sector below on best prospects for U.S. companies.

OPPORTUNITIES

Finnish energy companies use open tenders according to European Union (EU) regulations. The development of renewable energy in Finland is expected to offer opportunities for U.S. companies in introduction of innovative renewable energy source equipment technology. Finland's Ministry of Employment and the Economy has bilateral cooperation on energy and environment with several countries. U.S. companies can also participate in cooperation with Finnish companies in TEKES (Finnish Funding Agency for Technology and Innovation) funded projects (http://www.tekes.fi/).

WEB RESOURCES

Finnish Energy Industries www.energia.fi

Invest in Finland Bureau www.investinfinland.fi

Ministry of Employment and Economy, www.tem.fi

Finnish Funding Agency for Technology and Innovation www.tekes.fi

Statistics Finland http://www.stat.fi/index_en.html

http://www.easyfairs.com/events_216/saehkoe-puhtaus-ekorakennus2013_35311/saehkoe-2013_35312/exhibitors_35326/welcome_35340/ mia.maki@trade.gov (local contact)

RENEWABLE ENERGY & ENERGY EFFICIENCY (RE&EE)

Renewable Energy

One of the world's leading countries in clean energy utilization, especially biomass, Finland has been active in expanding the role of renewable energy in energy production, in accordance with the Long-term Climate and Energy Strategy, launched by the Ministry of Employment and the Economy (the former Ministry of Trade and Industry) in 2008. The goal for Finland is to increase the share of renewable energy to 38 percent by 2020. EU statistics show that currently 34.3% of energy in Finland comes from renewable resources.

In 2013, 46% of electricity and heat consumption was from renewable sources, a growth of 5% from 2012. The most important renewable sources of energy in Finland include bio energy – wood and wood-based fuels in particular – as well as hydropower, wind power and ground-source heat. Peat has also been defined as slowly renewing biomass

fuel. It has a substantial share, about seven percent, of Finland's energy balance. As indigenous fuel, peat has considerable effect on regional policy.

To implement the national objective for utilization of renewable energy set by the European Union, a new feed-in tariff scheme was established in 2011. The purpose is to promote the production of electricity based on wind power, biogas and wood-based fuel. The feed-in tariff scheme seeks to increase electricity production based on wind power up to six terawatt hours, and electricity and heat production based on forest chips utilized as fuel up to 22 terawatt hours.

In addition, the biofuel distribution obligation will increase from the current four to six percent for 2011-2014, followed by a phased increase to 20 percent by 2020. In 2013, 23% of energy consumption in Finland was from oil.

The production of wind energy currently accounts for only 0.9 percent of Finnish electricity consumption and the combined production capacity of current wind parks is 447 megawatts, double the capacity level of 2012. The goal is to increase the capacity of wind energy up to 2000 megawatts by the year 2020, once the seven wind parks that are currently under construction are completed, plus the first land-based wind park that has been planned for the Lapland community of Tervola,

Energy Efficiency

Traditional Finnish energy efficiency strengths are in the areas of energy intensive industrial processes, power electronics, combustion and gasification technologies, combined heat and power production, and biomass based fuels. Additional growth comes from smaller firms operating in the areas of new materials, smart grids, recycling, and measurement technologies. Surprisingly, a new area to watch includes power electronics used in automotive manufacturing.

To promote energy efficiency, Finland has employed a voluntary agreement scheme from as early as the 1990s. The practical measures boosted by the agreements, such as energy audits and analyses subsidized by the Government, have provided companies and communities with an excellent means of ascertaining their own energy usage and the scope of improving it, as well as integrating improvements in energy efficiency in their daily operations.

The latest energy efficiency agreements for industries, municipal and oil sectors were signed for the period 2008-2016. Additional agreements have been applied for goods transportation and logistics, public transportation and housing sectors. These agreements are under the governance of the related Ministries and have a central role in the national implementation of the EU Energy Services Directive applied to companies that are not part of the emissions trading scheme.

Finland has been involved in the development of low-energy and eco-efficient construction alternatives since the late 1980s. The basic principles of energy efficiency in buildings include:

• Controlled ventilation and efficient heat recovery

• Improved thermal insulation of building skin

• Careful design and construction

• Using building structures as heat and cool storage units

• Improved indoor climate quality

• Innovative home automation systems.

Driven by a continuous challenge to decrease the energy use and to meet new energy savings within the built-environment, the Finnish building industry is moving towards developing and searching for new high-performance building solutions and technologies.

Sub-Sector Best Prospects

- Effective insulation materials

- HRV-systems

- Heating and cooling pumps

- Pellet furnaces and technology used for pellet production

- Low energy construction building concepts

- Recycled building materials

- Heating and cooling systems using alternative energy sources, such as solar, geothermal and small-scale wind

- Heat exchangers and heat meters

- Technology used in agricultural biomass

- Controls, pumps, piping

- Indoor and outdoor lighting solutions.

Opportunities

For public procurement tenders, please see the online version of the Supplement to the European Union Official Journal http://ted.europa.eu .

Public/private research programs: http://www.cleen.fi/en/

Web Resources

Finnish Energy Industries http://www.energia.fi

The Finnish Wind Power Association http://www.tuulivoimayhdistys.fi/

Motiva Oy http://www.motiva.fi/en/

Finland's Environmental Administration http://www.ymparisto.fi/

FINBIO – The Bio Energy Association of Finland, http://www.finbioenergy.fi/ mia.maki@trade.gov (local contact)

ENVIRONMENTAL TECHNOLOGIES (ENV)

Unit: USD millions

	2011	2012	2017	2014 (estimated)
Total Market Size	4705	4487	4731 (est)	4888
Total Local Production	6892	6489	6618 (est)	6751
Total Exports	5514	5191	5008	5108
Total Imports	3327	3190	3121	3245
Imports from the U.S.	168	160	217	223

Exchange Rate: $1= 0.75€ (year 2017 average)

Source: National Board of Customs

Traditionally, the metals and the pulp and paper industry have been the two major investors in environmental technology. The primary technology investments for these industries have been air pollution and water protection technologies. In recent years, the Finnish environmental technology and services sector has evolved into a dynamic area where production of new innovative technologies and services has expanded and also gained international prominence.

In Finland, the necessity for utilizing the best available technology is included in the Water Act, Air Pollution Control Act, Waste Act and Sea Protection Act. In addition, the producer responsibility principle in waste management has increased reuse and recycling, offering new business opportunities. It is estimated that the share of waste management and handling represents one third of the environmental technologies sector, followed by recycling.

On 13 June 2013, the Finnish Government adopted a resolution concerning the promotion of new and sustainable environmental and energy solutions in public procurement. The objective is for the public sector to procure new cleantech solutions with at least EUR 300 million every year. This equates to approximately one per cent of total public procurement expenditure and would double current public research, development and innovation spending on cleantech solutions. Following sectors have particular importance; waste management, electricity, property development, transport, energy-related products, services for which ecolabel criteria have been established, as well as food and catering.

The key competitive factors in selling environmental technology in Finland are quality and level of technology, price being a secondary factor. Finding a Finnish partner or using a distributor / importer is highly recommended as they have direct distribution channels to the end users, strong relations with various industry representatives, and direct access to the municipalities.

On May 14th 2014, The Council of State approved the national Cleantech strategy, which points the way for Finland to develop into one of the world's leading countries in clean technology. Cleantech is a field that is forecast to grow dramatically over the next few years. The Ministry of Employment and the Economy aims to increase the turnover of

the industry to 50 billion euros by 2020, and to create 40,000 new jobs. It is estimated that there are about 3,000 environmental technology companies in Finland, operating in different segments of the market, including cleantech. The number of companies operating in the more traditional segments of environmental technology such as waste management and handling, recycling, and remediation is close to 800. About 20 percent of the companies have operations abroad and exports account for nearly 80 percent of local production. The majority of the companies are small-to-medium size companies but there a few big global players as well.

To support Finnish environment technologies know-how in the field, Tekes, the Finnish Funding Agency for Technology and Innovation and VTT (Technical Research Center of Finland) support and enhance R&D in environmental technologies. As a result of a national environmental business development program in 2007, the Cleantech Finland concept was launched with an objective to make Finland the leading country in the environmental business, thus creating a market with increased local competition. According to a survey by Cleantech Finland, the annual growth of the cleantech sector in 2012 was 15 percent and rapid growth is predicted also for the year 2013. In 2013, the Finnish cleantech sector had a combined turnover of 25.8 billion euros and was growing annually by 5 percent.

Sub-Sector Best Prospects

- Waste management: Equipment to improve waste management processes, in particular closed systems for lumber companies and for the prevention of phosphorous discharges.

- Municipal waste recycling and recovery: New technical advances for the entire recycling logistics chain, including sensors, separators, monitoring, optic handling device for metal recycling, crushers, and bio waste separation equipment.

- Air and water pollution: Monitoring, measuring and sampling instruments for detection of air and water pollution.

- Small particles and dust reduction equipment: Products such as dynamic and electrostatic precipitators; fabric filters; centrifugal fans and blowers.

- Environmental geotechnics: New process and product innovations for contaminated soil remediation.

Opportunities

Please see the Supplement to the Official Journal of the European Union http://ted.europa.eu/

Environment Technology Exhibitions: Environment & Municipal engineering, Water & Wastewater, Waste & Recycling, 1-3 October 2014, Helsinki Exhibition & Convention Centre http://www.messukeskus.com/Sites3/EnviroExpo/en/Pages/default.aspx

Web Resources

Finland's Environmental Administration, http://www.environment.fi/en-US/Consumption_and_production/Public_procurement

Finnish Society of Indoor Air Quality and Climate, http://www.sisailmayhdistys.fi/

Good News from Finland, http://www.goodnewsfinland.com/archive/news/40-000-new-jobs-expected-for-finnish-cleantech-sector/

Supplement to the Official Journal of the European Union, http://ted.europa.eu/

Tekes, the Finnish Funding Agency for Technology and Innovation, http://www.tekes.fi

VTT, Technical Research Center of Finland, http://www.vtt.fi

Cleantech Finland, http://www.cleantechfinland.com/ tiina.ketela@trade.gov (local contact)

FRANCHISING (FRA)

Note: Official statistics not available.

Franchising continues to develop successfully even at times of economic downturn. According to local sources, franchise concepts seem to be better equipped to tackle the difficult financial times than their non-franchised competition, thanks to the structured franchise models. The total market for franchising in Finland is estimated to be over $6 billion and the annual growth rate in terms of revenue is expected to continue at a steady 5 percent for 2014 and 14 percent for the number of units. The number of franchising systems operating in Finland is close to 300 and the number of units is over 7,000.

The growth potential for franchising businesses continues to be good in Finland. Population density in urban areas, changes in economic and social factors, and the continuously active field of franchising indicate that franchising will continue expanding into new business areas. Growing demand in the services sector along with increased interest in self-employment will foster many new franchising opportunities.

Domestic franchises dominate the market. Just over one-quarter of the franchising systems are foreign. The neighboring Nordic countries have a good share of the foreign presence. U.S. franchise companies in Finland are mostly fast food restaurants and automotive service businesses. U.S. franchises tend to have high brand recognition among the general public.

There is no special legislation covering franchising. The most important of the statutory regulations are Contracts Act, the Unfair Business Practices Act, the Trademarks Act and the Competition Restrictions Act. The Finnish Franchising Association's Code of Ethics also sets a good framework for franchise agreements.

SUB-SECTOR BEST PROSPECTS

Franchising opportunities exist in all market sectors – retail, restaurant and services. The services sector, which includes consumer and Business-to-Business services, is the fastest growing and offers the best market potential for new franchise businesses.

U.S. franchise companies in Finland are concentrated in automotive services (car rental) and fast food. Most of these companies have strong brand recognition and are considered old-timers in the market. The U.S. companies currently in the market include: Avis, Budget, Hertz, National, McDonald's, Subway, Pizza Hut, Novus (car windshield repair), RE/MAX real estate, TOYS"R"US, and Home Instead Senior Care. The newest additions, Starbuck's opened its first coffee shop in Finland at the Helsinki-Vantaa airport in April 2012, and has since expanded, Hard Rock Café Helsinki had its Grand Opening in April of 2013, and Burger King opened its first restaurant in December 2017 followed by another in the spring of 2014.

Opportunities

The best opportunities for new franchises are in the areas of Business-to-Business (B2B) and consumer services. B2B services, such as personnel, building repair/maintenance, training, and Information Technology (IT) offer great opportunities for U.S. companies. Demand is also increasing for consumer services such as cleaning services, nursing, interior design, and other personal welfare services such as senior care, beauty, health/exercise, children's activities, and general well-being.

The retail sector offers new franchising opportunities in the field of consumer electronics, consumer durables, and giftware. Apparel, food, and personal care products continue to be good prospects for U.S. franchises.

The franchise-based restaurant sector is currently made up of mostly coffee shops and quick service restaurants. The "casual dining" concept offers potential for U.S. restaurant chains.

Web Resources

The Finnish Franchising Association, http://www.franchising.fi mia.maki@trade.gov (local contact)

MEDICAL EQUIPMENT (MED) AND HEALTHCARE TECHNOLOGIES

Unit: USD millions

	2010	2011	2012	2017 (estimated)
Total Market Size	860	848	930	967
Total Local Production	1465	1534	1550	1612
Total Exports	1290	1278	1345	1570
Total Imports	685	592	634	725
Imports from the U.S.	190	195	205	213

Exchange Rate: $1= €0.75 (year 2017 average)

Sources: The Finnish Healthcare Technology Association, National Board of Customs Finland, and local sources.

In Finland, the total market for medical equipment is estimated at $940 million in 2012 by the Finnish Healthcare Technology Association. The operating costs of Finnish hospitals have been reduced, and major hospital procurement is mainly replacing older equipment and buying some new. However, investments in new medical equipment within the private health care sector are expected to increase.

After a pause in growth in 2011, Finnish health technology exports rocketed 23% higher to $2.2 billion in 2012. Health technology now represents nearly 40% of Finland's total high-tech industry; second to the electronics and telecommunications-sector exports. Finns can be satisfied that in health technology trade, the country has achieved long-term growth, employment and generated a significant cumulative trade surplus of over $6 billion.

Over 80 percent of the medical equipment imported to Finland comes either from or through the European Union. Direct imports from the United States account for 8 percent; however, the total market share is 28 percent. Other important external supplier countries are Germany, the United Kingdom, France, Japan, and China. High quality and technically sophisticated medical equipment has the best market potential in Finland, especially equipment that increases efficiency and reduces occupancy rates in hospitals. Products, such as the following, have the best sales potential in Finland:

- Electronic Medical Records (EMR's)
- Patient monitoring systems
- Mini invasive surgery (MIS)
- Day surgery equipment
- Magnetic resonance imaging (MRI) equipment
- Video endoscopes
- Digital image processing
- Picture archiving

Additional statistics:
http://www.finnishhealthtech.fi/images/stories/industry/reports/0219_fihta_eng_healthtrade_a4_paino.pdf

Finland joined the European Union (EU) in 1995. As a member of the EU, Finland's local legislation concerning medical devices complies with EU directives. Please see www.valvira.fi/en/licensing/medical_devices (National Supervisory Authority for Welfare and Health Valvira) and ec.europa.eu/health/medical-devices/index_en.htm (European Commission, DG Health & Consumers, Public Health, Medical Devices) for further information.

Medical trade is duty-free within the European Union. Import duties are collected from production coming from non-EU countries. The amount of duty for medical equipment exported from the United States fluctuates according to a specific product, ranging from 5-12 percent.

Local production is estimated at close to $2 billion in 2012, consisting mainly of electro-medical equipment, dental equipment, and specialized x-ray and IVD equipment. Local production and imports do not overlap, as they do not compete with each other.

Sub-Sector Best Prospects

Products such as patient monitoring systems, mini invasive surgery (MIS), day surgery equipment, magnetic resonance imaging (MRI) equipment, video endoscopes, digital image processing, and picture archiving.

Opportunities

Please see the Supplement to the Official Journal of the European Union: http://ted.europa.eu

Finnish Dental Congress and Exhibition 2014 (Finland's largest event for dentistry professionals): www.messukeskus.com

The Finnish Medical Convention and Exhibition 2015 (Finland's largest medical exhibition): www.messukeskus.com

WEB RESOURCES

Association of Laboratory and Health Care Products Suppliers – SAI-LAB, www.sailab.fi
European Commission, DG Health & Consumers, Public Health, Medical Devices-
ec.europa.eu/health/medical-devices/index_en.htm
The Finnish Healthcare Technology Association- www.teknologiateollisuus.fi/fi/ryhmat-ja-yhdistykset/terveysteknologian-liitto-ry.html
Finnish Medicines Agency Fimea- www.fimea.fi
Helsinki Fair Center- www.messukeskus.com
Ministry of Social Affairs and Health- www.stm.fi
National Board of Customs- www.tulli.fi
National Supervisory Authority for Welfare and Health Valvira- www.valvira.fi
VTT Industrial Systems, Medical Device Technology Group- www.vtt.fi
katie.janhunen@trade.gov (local contact)

EHEALTH/ HEALTH IT

Overall social protection expenditure in Finland amounted to 30.4 percent of GDP, or USD 73.8 billion, in 2010 (THL 2012a), while healthcare accounted for nine percent, or USD 21.8 billion (2010), of GDP in Finland (THL 2012b). Universal coverage is accessible for all citizens and permanent residents in the country, with a range of comprehensive health services delivered primarily by publicly owned and operated providers. Approximately 75 percent of services and programs within the system are funded through public expenditure.

The Ministry of Social Affairs and Health (STM) manages the preparation and implementation of Finland's social welfare and healthcare policy. Additionally, they mandate and organize programs and reforms regarding eHealth provisions, while the Finnish Office for Health Technology Assessment (FinOHTA), operating under the National Institute for Health and Welfare (THL), is the agency responsible for providing assessments and analyses related to Health IT. The Finnish Electronic Patient Record system (KanTa) allows every citizen to access his or her medical records, as well as prescription services. Physicians also utilize this database not only to view patient records, but also to gain access to the Picture Archiving and Communications System (PACS), from which they can see and send relevant information to other entities within the healthcare system.

The 336 municipalities are legally obligated to provide healthcare services for their residents (i.e. primary, secondary and tertiary healthcare), as well as to collect taxes for the financing of services provided. They accomplish this through local municipal healthcare centers, or by regional healthcare districts, all containing a central hospital, of which there are 20. These districts provide secondary care specialists, who are only available through a referral from a primary provider. The population of hospital districts varies between about 60,000 and 1,500,000 inhabitants.

Today, municipalities contract a small proportion of primary care to private providers; however, that proportion is expected to increase. There are about 40 private hospitals which provide approximately five percent of hospital care in Finland. Private healthcare, excluding occupational services, accounts for about six percent of total healthcare expenditure. In these districts, university hospitals in the major cities of Finland form the basis of tertiary care, and contain the most technologically advanced facilities and medical equipment in the nation. All of the levels of healthcare are funded by the municipalities, but the national government covers the cost of medical training and participates in financing by providing a general, non-earmarked, subsidy to the municipalities.

Finland is very advanced in its use of IT systems within the healthcare industry, relative to other European nations. According to the European Commission, Finland ranks 5th in terms of the deployment of Health IT within the EU. Individuals within the healthcare system have widespread, simple access to convenient ePrescription and eArchive services via KanTa. In 2010, the use of electronic patient records among the primary health centers and secondary care hospital districts was at 100 percent.

The Finnish government has recognized that there is a need for a more stable synergy in regards to Health IT communications and EPR sharing between municipalities, regional districts, and private care providers (outlined in the eHealth Strategy and Action Plan for Finland in a European Context). In a 2010 poll conducted by the Finnish Medical Journal on doctors' opinions of the patient data system, 75 percent of doctors are not

satisfied with the time it takes to receive patient data from another organization. This may be due to the fact that patient data exchange between organizations is carried out electronically at 90 percent of hospital districts and at 68 percent of municipal healthcare centers. Furthermore, the development of health IT at the national government level began in an uncoordinated manner, primarily due to the decentralized healthcare system. As a result, several non-interoperable IT systems are often used even within a single healthcare organization, which inhibits information exchange within and across provider organizations. This calls for an improvement in communications between all healthcare-related groups, both public and private.

Sub-Sector Best Prospects

Finland's most populous city of Helsinki is currently moving forward with its Apotti project, which is a cooperative effort to invest in and develop a regional information structure for health and social services for 1-2 million people in the Helsinki-Uusimaa hospital district. The Apotti program is being followed closely by other health districts, and is the first of its kind in Finland to blanket such a massive number of individuals.

Opportunities

Finland has long been a Health IT forerunner with a history of user satisfaction and ease of accessibility to information. The country is continually developing and improving its nationwide electronic archive of patients' health information (KanTa), and health-related services, such as the Electronic Prescription program. In addition, innovative and ambitious projects are in the works at the municipal, regional, and national levels, all of which are viable entry points for U.S. products and services.

Health IT and telemedicine in Finland are expected to gain an even more visible presence in the near future, as far-reaching goals that the sector has been allotted in recent years show continued promise in improving the healthcare system. The sector demands new innovations and fresh ideas, in order to increase efficiency and productivity, which will make up for the constantly decreasing amount of available clinicians.

The Finnish workforce is aging at a rapid pace. This widespread change of patient demographics will affect the availability of clinicians. The coming wave of retiring healthcare professionals will occur at a critical time during which there will be a greater need for these specialists. However, this presents a useful opportunity for new innovations in health IT to bridge the gap created by the lack of clinicians, albeit temporary.

eHealth 2015 Trade Event, January 7-9, 2015 (Helsinki Fair Center) : http://www.easyfairs.com/en/events_216/terveysteknologia-2015_55989/ehealth-2015_59288/

Web Resources

Finnish Office for Health Technology Assessment (FinOHTA)
Ministry of Social Affairs and Health (STM) – www.stm.fi/en
The National Institute for Health and Welfare (THL) – www.thl.fi
The Finnish Electronic Patient Record system (KanTa) – www.kanta.fi/en
eHealth Strategy and Action Plan for Finland in a European Context
katie.janhunen@trade.gov (local contact)

Safety and Security (SEC)

Note: Official statistics not available.

The safety and security market is estimated to be over $2.5 billion in 2012 (estimated). Turnover in the security business grew by 25.6 percent in 2012. The market has grown quite continuously for the last ten years and it is expected to continue its steady growth over the next years. Information technology as an instrument to criminal acts has increased significantly. Systematic crime against property from outside Finnish borders continues to grow.

General interest in private security products and services, public funding cutbacks in law enforcement resources and outsourcing of safety and security related services by private and public entities have increased the market demand.

The safety and security sector is very scattered with over 400 companies in the market, mostly ranging from small to middle-size companies. Characteristic for the market is that the largest security companies, which represent a minority in the market, employ close to 80 percent of the industry's personnel, and generate most of the sector's turnover. The private safety and security sector employed over 15,000 employees in 2014.

Information security products and services, guarding services, structural security products are the largest sub-sectors, but new emerging business areas are security of logistics, home security, environmental and infrastructural security solutions, information security and work security. The largest industries contracting security services are the manufacturing industry, real estate and construction, and trade in general. U.S. made safety and security products have a good reputation and are considered to be of high quality. On the downside, some products are also seen as expensive and not necessarily up to EU product standards.

The EU Commission has proposed a new directive, which is intended to ensure that confidential information is adequately protected throughout the entire European Union. The proposal is supposed to be a harmonizing measure, which means that it would most probably require the removal of national protection that goes beyond what is provided by the Directive. Europan Parliament will vote on it in 2014, but when it will come into force is not known. This new act will be applied to all companies working in the EU area.

Sub-Sector Best Prospects

Information security products and services, electronic security systems such as camera surveillance, lock systems and door automation, home security and personal safety accessories such as burglar alarm systems and fire detection equipment are considered best prospects in the Finnish safety and security market.

The public government sector, especially on municipal level, along with private residences are becoming more and more interested in safety and security solutions available in the market.

OPPORTUNITIES

There are no trade barriers for safety and security equipment. The customs duties vary between two to five percent. Products that are imported or exported within the EU must have CE marking and in some cases, must meet EU product standards.

The annual security industry trade fair "Safety and Security" in the city of Tampere has been replaced by "EuroSafety", which is a contemporary event with a strong international focus, and it provides exhibitors with improved opportunities for extensive networking and new contacts. The bi-annual FinnSec in Helsinki will be held next time in November 2015. Both fairs attract a large number of decision makers responsible for safety and security at companies and other organizations and offer a good forum to present products and services in the field.

WEB RESOURCES

Finnsecurity RY http://www.finnsecurity.fi
Europan Commission, http://ec.europa.eu/justice/data-protection/index_en.htm
Laurea University of Applied Sciences
http://www.laurea.fi/fi/tutkimus_ja_kehitys/julkaisut/laurea_julkaisut/Documents/23.%20Manninen%20Merist%C3%B6%20Laitinen%20Tulevaisuus%20turvassa.pdf
Ammattinetti,
http://www.ammattinetti.fi/ammattialat/detail/13/31_ammattiala;jsessionid=65482BFF8CC31C03EB0953FACC16A041
EuroSafety in Tampere, November 5-7, 2014,
http://www.eurosafety.fi/eurosafety/index.tmpl?sivu_id=3232
FinnSec trade fair in Helsinki, November 18-20, 2015, www.finnsec.fi tiina.ketela@trade.gov (local contact)

TELECOMMUNICATIONS SERVICES AND EQUIPMENT (TEL, TES)

Note: Please visit Ficora – Finnish Communications Regulatory Authority for most recent communications market statistics and surveys - https://www.viestintavirasto.fi/attachments/Toimialakatsaus_2012_EN.pdf

Finland is known as a world leader in ICT innovation, information society development and high quality ICT products. It is one of the most advanced information societies in

the world. As a percentage of GDP, Finnish R&D investments are the third largest in the world. Also the number of patents per capita, especially in the ICT field, is among the highest of the world, well known technologies and services originating from Finland include Linux, the SMS, ring tones and Internet banking services. Finland is also renowned as a pioneer in mobile telecommunications services and applications. Finland is the home of many niche leaders in related fields such as mobile commerce, wireless equipment and data security.

In the spring of 2013, Finland placed first in an international study where countries were ranked based among other factors on their technical infrastructure and possibilities and prevalence of use of ICT. According to recent study by Statistics Finland, the share of Internet users among the whole population aged 16 to 74 is 90% and as many as 49% of the same group has a smart phone in use.

Although with only 5.4 million people the Finnish market is small, Finnish consumers and companies have proven to be quick to adopt new technologies. Finland is seen as a pioneering adapter and an important research center for new technology: in a 2012 survey up to 49% of all mobile phones used in Finland were smart phones. The trend is also set to continue – in the first quarter of 2013, 71% of mobile phones sold to the public were smart phones

International companies (e.g., ICL, IBM, Siemens, Hewlett-Packard and Ericsson) have set up research units in Finland, increased their cooperation with Finnish firms, or acquired small companies in the sector. Many companies and researchers have found that Finland makes an ideal environment for developing and testing new types of communications and IT products, and this has no doubt helped drive the sector generally.

According to Ficora, the amount of mobile data transferred in Finland grew 20-fold between 2008 and 2012. Eurostat places Finland among the top countries in the European Union in terms of the number of mobile data connections, partly owing to a strongly grown interest in smart phones and tablet computers.

The telecommunications market in Finland is fully liberalized. No licenses are needed, except for digital television and mobile networks. Finland's Ministry of Transport and Communications is responsible for licensing. Finland was also the first country in the world to grant operating licenses for the third-generation (3G) mobile communications market in March 1999.

As of July 1, 2010, 1 Mbit Internet connection has been defined as a universal service. This means that telecom operators defined as universal service providers must be able to provide every permanent residence and business office with access to a reasonably priced and high-quality connection with a downstream rate of at least 1 Mbit/s.

In 2009, the Finnish Communications Regulatory Authority determined which telecom operators required to offer universal service programs. This requirement is expected to improve the quality and availability of connections in Finland's sparsely populated areas and to promote the economic vitality of rural areas, provide a good environment for businesses, and further enable electronic communications. Some variation will be allowed in the universal service connection speed to enable services also in mobile networks.

The number of online shoppers is growing. In 2012, two-thirds of Finnish residents bought or ordered something via the web. One half of Finnish residents followed some social network service on the Internet.

The typical Finnish online store is a small company that focuses on a narrow specialist field. It is estimated that the larger online stores will start acquiring the smaller ones that have a well-functioning concept. The fastest growing customer segment for e-commerce in Finland consists of people over 50 years old.

Product information and prices are better in the online stores, which can also direct personal offers to the customers. The major e-commerce trends in Finland include the introduction of social media in e-commerce, standalone e-commerce applications for mobile devices, and online stores becoming cloud services.

See e-commerce trends in Finland: https://www.maksuturva.fi/en/suomen-maksuturva-oy/news/e-commerce-and-online-payment-trends-in-finland/

SUB-SECTOR BEST PROSPECTS

Although highly competitive, the telecommunications sector also offers promise, with high demand for Internet and mobile services and content. Mobile phone sales seem to be recovering from the downturn, and the interest in smart phones is expected to increase, though price competition is also high. With the popularity of mobile Internet, and the increasing numbers of broadband Internet connections, e-commerce is expected to benefit.

OPPORTUNITIES

Due to high technical standards and the liberalized telecommunications market, Finland serves as an excellent test base for new technologies for U.S. Information technology (IT) companies. U.S. IT companies wishing to enter the Baltic markets and Russia (especially St. Petersburg) should view Finland as a natural gateway and Finnish companies as experienced partners in any such effort.

Please see the Supplement to the European Union Official Journal http://ted.europa.eu .
See also www.e-finland.fi (e-business projects).

WEB RESOURCES

Helsinki Fair Center – www.messukeskus.com
Ministry of Transport and Communications - www.mintc.fi
Finnish Federation for Communications and Teleinformatics- www.ficom.fi
Finnish Communications Regulatory Authority http://www.ficora.fi/en/
katie.janhunen@trade.gov (local contact)

TRAVEL AND TOURISM SERVICES (TRA)

Unit: USD millions

	2010	2011	2012	2017
Total Travel	4750	4780	5020	5261
Domestic Travel	6100	6200	6510	6835
Incoming Travel	2920	3060	3210	3370
Foreign Travel	4270	4480	4700	4935
Travel to the USA	240	252	265	278

Exchange Rate: $1= €0.75 (year 2017 average)

Sources: The Association of the Finnish Travel Agents, Statistics Finland, Balance of Payments, The U.S. Department of Commerce's Office of Travel and Tourism, and local sources.

The United States is one of the main long-haul destinations for Finns with 127,978 Finnish arrivals in 2017 (Jan-Dec). Florida, New York and California continue to be the best prospects for the U.S. travel industry. First time travelers, families with children, and senior citizens favor Florida, whereas younger people and experienced travelers favor New York and the West Coast.

A growing interest in travel has increased the number of Finns traveling abroad. Finns favor long-haul travel and Mediterranean destinations. Majority of Finns traveling abroad favor "sun and sand" followed by city destinations. However, a growing number of travelers are looking for activity holidays. Local culture, golf, fishing, diving, sailing, skiing and many other activities have become important for Finns when traveling abroad. Therefore, Finns have shown interest in other destinations such as Alaska, Arizona, Hawaii, Nevada, and New Mexico.

In 2012, the share of business travel was 18.8 percent, while Finns made 81,000 business trips to the United States (a 2.1 percent increase from 2012). This number is expected to increase in the future. New York City, Chicago, Boston, Los Angeles, Atlanta, and Las Vegas are the most important destinations for Finnish business people.

Finnair, the national air carrier is currently the only airline based in and operating flights from Finland to the United States. During the high season, Finnair has daily non-stop flight service to New York. American Airlines will start seasonal daily non-stop operations from Chicago to Helsinki, Finland on June 12, 2014, ending August 18, 2014. Delta Air Lines is represented by AIR FRANCE KLM and United Airlines code shares with Lufthansa German Airlines. U.S. Airways is represented through its sales offices in Sweden.

There are no restrictions on the Finnish foreign travel. Since October 1, 1991, Finland has been included in the visa waiver program for visits up to 90 days in length. Machine-readable passports were introduced in Finland in 1987 and biometric passports in August 2006.

Sub-Sector Best Prospects

Florida, New York, and California continue to be the best sales prospects for the U.S. travel industry. Chicago, Boston, Los Angeles, Atlanta, Las Vegas, and New York City are the most popular destinations for Finnish business travelers.

Opportunities

Matka Nordic Travel Fair 2015 (the largest travel fair in Northern Europe):
www.messukeskus.com

Discover America Committee Finland: www.discoveramerica.fi

Web Resources

Association of Finnish Travel Agents- www.smal.fi
Discover America Committee Finland- www.discoveramerica.fi
Finnish Business Travel Association- www.fbta.net
Finnish Tourist Board/Visit Finland- www.mek.fi
Helsinki Fair Center- www.messukeskus.com
League of Finnish American Societies- www.sayl.fi
Statistics Finland- www.stat.fi
katie.janhunen@trade.gov (local contact)

AGRICULTURAL SECTORS

Due to the severe Nordic winters and relatively short growing season, Finland relies heavily on imported food and agricultural products. Finland's geographical proximity and long-established connections to the Baltic States and Russia offers an ideal business base in Northern Europe.

Increased demand for consumer goods, agribusiness opportunities, food industry investments and tourism in the region has been generated by structural reforms and development of market economies in the Baltic countries and Russia.

BEST PRODUCTS/SERVICES

Best prospects: wine, beer, healthy snacks, dried fruits and nuts, ethnic foods, organic foods, health and diet foods, convenience foods, frozen juices, TexMex items, sauces/seasonings, rice, seafood, pet food, canned fruits and vegetables, and fresh fruits: apples, pears, grape fruits, grapes, cherries.

OPPORTUNITIES

Finland is a sophisticated market with a high standard of living, a well-educated workforce and growing incomes. The Finnish consumer has a high acceptance of new products and concepts. U.S. products are considered high quality and trendy. There is growing consumer demand for value-added products, convenience foods and functional foods as well as a proliferation of "healthy" and "greener" foods.

RESOURCES

The Agricultural Service at the American Embassy in The Hague represents the interests of the USDA's Foreign Agricultural Service (FAS) in the Benelux and the Nordic countries. These responsibilities are principally accomplished via reporting commodity and trade developments to the USDA, coordinating policy issues with host government officials and promoting the sale of U.S. food, agricultural, forestry and fishery products. The office provides trade services for local importing companies seeking U.S. products and U.S. companies wishing to develop markets in the region of responsibility.

Contact: Ms. Mary Ellen Smith, Agricultural Counselor

Office of Agricultural Affairs Embassy of the United States of America Lange Voorhout 102 2514 EJ The Hague, Netherlands Tel: +31 70 310 2299, Fax: +31 70 365 7681 E-mail: agthehague@fas.usda.gov

SELLING U.S. PRODUCTS AND SERVICES

USING AN AGENT OR DISTRIBUTOR

One exclusive agent/distributor is usually appointed to cover commercial activities throughout Finland, mainly due to the relatively small size of the country's market. Finnish importers often represent many different product lines. In selecting a representative, the exporter should ascertain whether that company handles competing products. Consumer goods and similar merchandise requiring maintenance of stock are often imported through wholesalers or trading houses. Such products may also be sold directly to retail chains, department stores, and other retail outlets.

Contacting local trade associations for a list of importers is a good way of finding a distributor in Finland. Finnish importers attend major trade fairs in Europe and in the United States in order to find new products and ideas, but also to find new representation. The Commercial Section of the American Embassy also assists in finding agents/distributors for U.S. exporters through an

International Partner Search (IPS), a matching Gold Key Service (GKS), or other networking activity.

ESTABLISHING AN OFFICE

Please visit http://www.investinfinland.fi/services/setting-up-a-business/en_GB/setting-up-a-business/ for information on establishing an office in Finland.

FRANCHISING

The Finnish franchising market is estimated to be over $6 billion in 2009. There are over 200 franchising systems in Finland operating over 6,000 units around the country. Characteristic for the Finnish franchising market is the local origin of concepts, only one-quarter of the franchising systems are foreign-owned.

There are no specific statutes regulating franchises, but as with distribution agreements, a number of statutes impact on them indirectly. For more information on franchising see Chapter 4: Leading Sectors for U.S. Export and Investment.

DIRECT MARKETING

Direct Mail (including telemarketing, mobile marketing and brochures) comprised 24 percent of the total marketing communication investments in 2008, representing an increase of 3.4 percent compared to the previous year. The share of Unaddressed Bulk Mail increased by 8.7 percent while Addressed Delivery decreased by 2.9 percent.

Direct marketing campaigns are becoming more diversified and the size of consignments is becoming smaller. Advertising is being more precisely segmented and special media is used to reach new target groups. The use of electronic messaging for marketing purposes is also growing briskly. The direct marketing channels most commonly used in Finland are:

- Direct mail (Unaddressed Bulk Mail and Addressed Delivery)
- Telemarketing
- Face-to-face selling
- Internet marketing
- Direct-response advertising
- Catalogs/brochures

JOINT VENTURES/LICENSING

Joint ventures serve as an option for setting up a business in Finland. Issues that need to be addressed include possible tax implications, local legal systems, accounting principles, special permits and registration procedures. Invest in Finland Bureau, a government agency promoting foreign investments to Finland is a good source of providing information and services on market entry strategies, including joint ventures and licensing.

Several U.S. companies have established themselves in the Finnish market with subsidiaries or joint ventures, with an interest in access to Finnish-Russian joint ventures. Due to its physical proximity and Finland's network of railroad and air connections, there are many strong selling features regarding access to Russia. In addition to unique access, Finland possesses profound expertise about the Russian market.

Product Licensing agreements are quite common in Finland because of the good quality of Finnish manufacturing, the small size of the market and the relatively high cost of transporting goods to the country. Royalties and licensing fees may be freely transferred out of Finland.

SELLING TO THE GOVERNMENT

The annual total amount of public procurement is estimated at around $31 (€22.5) billion, approximately 15% of Finland's GDP.

Finnish procurement agencies follow the procurement procedures of the EU and the World Trade Organization (WTO). The EU rules of procurement and the WTO's GPA agreement only apply to procurements above the threshold value. National legislation requires procurement units to submit competitive tenders for procurements that fall below the threshold value. This is done by sending requests for tenders to a number of potential suppliers or by publishing an announcement. For more information on Government tenders, please see Ministry of Employment and the Economy http://www.tem.fi , Public Procurement Advisory Unit http://www.hankinnat.fi , and TED - Tenders Electronic Daily: http://ted.europa.eu/

DISTRIBUTION AND SALES CHANNELS

Distribution channels in Finland are similar to those in the United States. Goods may be sold through an agent, distributor, established wholesaler, or selling directly to retail organizations. Most of the larger importers, wholesalers, and trading houses are members of the Federation of Finnish Commerce (www.kauppa.fi), which is a central organization of 10,000 companies as well as trade associations covering the bulk of foreign goods sold to Finnish trade and industry.

The Finnish Foreign Trade Agents' Federation (www.agenttiliitto.fi) is an association of commercial agents, distributors, and importers. It has 18 divisions for different products. Its members are relatively small, private companies, most of them operating in sectors such as textiles, apparel, furnishings, and raw materials.

SELLING FACTORS/TECHNIQUES

Selling factors and techniques are very similar in Finland to those in the United States. Terms generally applied to international trade with industrialized countries apply to selling in Finland. When selling to the Finnish market, it is recommended that a local agent/distributor that has a sales network covering the whole of Finland be appointed. Only one local distributor is needed to cover the whole country, as Finland's market is small; but, because distances are long, a distributor with a countrywide network is most desirable. Consumer goods and similar merchandise requiring maintenance of stock are often imported through wholesalers or trading houses. These products can also be sold directly to retail chains, department stores, and other retail outlets. U.S. suppliers should provide the local distributor with English language product literature and export prices. Strong promotion efforts are very important to introduce new products into the Finnish market.

ELECTRONIC COMMERCE

Online shopping in Finland is increasing rapidly. According to an online shopping index published by Gagar Oy that includes a third of all active on-line shopping sites in Finland, online shopping has increased almost sevenfold in the last three years. The growth has slightly slowed, but is still rapid.

According to Statistics Finland's data collected in spring 2008, 83% of 16-74 year-old Finns had used the Internet during the three months preceding the interview. The Internet is most commonly used for e-mail (90% of the respondents), for finding information on goods and services (86%), for using online bank services (84%), for finding information on travel and accommodation services (71%), and for reading online magazines and newspapers (63%). The use of online bank services, online shopping, and travel service browsing have increased significantly. In spring 2008, the survey also included questions on the use of instant messaging (Skype, Messenger). 37% of the respondents had used instant messaging service during the three months prior to the survey.

Also, gender differences in on-line shopping have disappeared, with women constituting approximately 50% of all Internet users and of those who had bought commodities via the Internet.

In July 2003, the EU started applying Value Added Tax (VAT) to sales by non-EU based companies of Electronically Supplied Services (ESS) to EU based non-business customers. U.S. companies that are covered by the rule must collect and submit VAT to EU tax authorities. European Council Directive 2002/38/EC further developed the EU rules for charging Value Added Tax. These rules were indefinitely extended following adoption of directive 2008/8/EC.

Key Link: http://ec.europa.eu/taxation_customs/taxation/vat/how_vat_works/e-services/index_en.htm

TRADE PROMOTION AND ADVERTISING

General Legislation

Laws against misleading advertisements differ widely from Member State to Member State within the European Union (EU). To respond to this imperfection in the Internal Market, the Commission adopted a Directive, in force since October 1986, to establish minimum and objective criteria regarding truth in advertising. The Directive was amended in October 1997 to include comparative advertising. Under the Directive, misleading advertising is defined as any "advertising which in any way, including its presentation, deceives or is likely to deceive the persons to whom it is addressed or whom it reaches and which, by reason of its deceptive nature, is likely to affect their economic behavior or which for those reasons, injures or is likely to injure a competitor." Member States can authorize even more extensive protection under their national laws.

Comparative advertising, subject to certain conditions, is defined as "advertising which explicitly or by implication identifies a competitor or goods or services by a competitor." Member States can, and in some cases have, restricted misleading or comparative advertising.

The EU's Audiovisual Media Services Directive lays down legislation on broadcasting activities allowed within the EU. From 2009 the rules allow for US-style product placement on television and the three-hour/day maximum of advertising will be lifted. However, a 12-minute/hour maximum will remain. Child programming will be subject to a code of conduct that will include a limit of junk food advertising to children.

Following the adoption of the 1999 Council Directive on the Sale of Consumer Goods and Associated Guarantees, product specifications, as laid down in advertising, are now considered as legally binding on the seller. (For additional information on Council Directive 1999/44/EC on the Sale of Consumer Goods and Associated Guarantees, see the legal warranties and after-sales service section below.)

The EU adopted Directive 2005/29/EC concerning fair business practices in a further attempt to tighten up consumer protection rules. These rules outlaw several aggressive or deceptive marketing practices such as pyramid schemes, "liquidation sales" when a shop is not closing down, and artificially high prices as the basis for discounts in addition to other potentially misleading advertising practices. Certain rules on advertising to children are also set out.

Medicine

The advertising of medicinal products for human use is regulated by Council Directive

2001/83/EC. Generally speaking, the advertising of medicinal products is forbidden if market authorization has not yet been granted or if the product in question is a prescription drug. Mentioning therapeutic indications where self-medication is not suitable is not permitted, nor is the distribution of free samples to the general public. The text of the advertisement should be compatible with the characteristics listed on the product label, and should encourage rational use of the product. The advertising of medicinal products destined for professionals should contain essential characteristics of the product as well as its classification. Inducements to prescribe or supply a particular medicinal product are prohibited and the supply of free samples is restricted.

The Commission presented a new framework for information to patients on medicines in 2008. The framework would allow industry to produce non-promotional information about their medicines while complying with strictly defined rules and would be subject to an effective system of control and quality assurance.

Nutrition & Health Claims

On July 1, 2007, a new regulation on nutrition and health claims entered into force. Regulation 1924/2006 sets EU-wide conditions for the use of nutrition claims such as “low fat” or “high in vitamin C” and health claims such as “helps lower cholesterol”. The regulation applies to any food or drink product produced for human consumption that is marketed on the EU market. Only foods that fit a certain nutrient profile (below certain salt, sugar and/or fat levels) will be allowed to carry claims. Nutrition and health claims will only be allowed on food labels if they are included in one of the EU positive lists. Food products carrying claims must comply with the provisions of nutritional labeling directive 90/496/EC . From 2010, only nutrition clams in the Annex will be allowed.

The development of nutrient profiles, originally scheduled for January 2009, is being delayed due to the 2009 Parliamentary elections and the appointment of a new Commission. Once they have been set, there will be another two-year period before the nutrient profiles begin to apply to allow food operators time to comply with the new rules. Nutrition claims can fail one criterion, i.e. if only one nutrient (salt, sugar or fat) exceeds the limit of the profile, a claim can still be made provided the high level of that particular nutrient is clearly marked on the label. For example, a yogurt can make a low-fat claim even if it has high sugar content but only if the label clearly states “high sugar content”. Health claims cannot fail any criteria.

The deadline of January 31, 2010, for compiling a list of well-established health function claims such as ‘calcium is good for your bones’ will not be met due to the vast amount of applications that have to be screened by EFSA. Disease risk reduction claims and claims referring to the health and development of children will require an authorization on a case-by-case basis, following the submission of a scientific dossier to EFSA. A simplified authorization procedure has been established for health claims based on new scientific data. GAIN Report E48055 describes how application dossiers for authorization of health claims should be prepared and presented. A guidance document on how companies can apply for health claim authorizations can be downloaded from EFSA's website at:

Food Supplements

Regulation 1925/2006, applicable as of July 1, 2007, harmonizes rules on the addition of vitamins and minerals to foods. The regulation lists the vitamins and minerals that may be added to foods. This list was most recently revised in November 2009. A positive list of substances other than vitamins and minerals has not been established yet, although it is being developed. Until then, Member State laws will govern the use these substances.

Tobacco

The EU Tobacco Advertising Directive bans tobacco advertising in printed media, radio, and internet as well as the sponsorship of cross-border events or activities. Advertising in cinemas and on billboards or merchandising is allowed though these are banned in many Member States. Tobacco advertising on television has been banned in the EU since the early 1990s and is governed by the TV without Frontiers Directive.

Local Fair Authorities:

The Finnish Fair Corporation/Helsinki Fair Center, www.finnexpo.fi
Helsinki Fair Ltd./Wanha Satama, www.wanhasatama.com
Jyvaskyla Congress Center Ltd, Jyvaskyla Fair Ltd, and the Keskimaa Group/Jyvaskyla Paviljonki, www.jklfairs.fi
The Turku Fair and Congress Center Ltd., www.turunmessukeskus.fi
Lahti Fair Ltd., www.lahdenmessut.fi
Tampere Trade Fairs Ltd., www.tampereenmessut.fi
Local Newspapers:
Helsingin Sanomat, www.hs.fi
Hufvudstadsbladet (Swedish daily), www.hbl.fi
Aamulehti, www.aamulehti.fi
Iltalehti, www.iltalehti.fi
Iltasanomat, www.iltasanomat.fi
Kaleva, www.kaleva.fi
Keskisuomalainen, www.ksml.fi
Savon Sanomat, www.savonsanomat.fi
Turun Sanomat, www.ts.fi
Business Magazines/Journals:
Kauppalehti (Business daily), www.kauppalehti.fi
Talouselama (Business weekly), www.talouselama.fi
Tekniikka & Talous (Business weekly), www.tekniikkatalous.fi
Tietoviikko TIVI (Business weekly), www.tietoviikko.fi

Radio/TV:

Metroradio Finland Oy (Groove FM, www.groovefm.fi , MetroFM, www.metrofm.fi , SuomiPOP, www.radiosuomipop.fi)

MTV Media Radio Group (Radio Nova, www.radionova.fi)

SBS Finland Oy (Iskelma-ketju, www.iskelma.fi , Radio 957, www.radio957.fi , Radio Sata, www.sata.fi , Radio Jyvaskyla, www.radiojkl.fi , Radio Mega, www.radiomega.fi , and Voice, www.voice.fi)

Sanoma Corporation (Radio Helsinki, www.radiohelsinki.fi)

Finnish Broadcasting Company YLE Radio (YLE Radio 1, YLEX, YLE Radio Suomi, YLE Radio Peili, Radio Extrem, Radio Vega), and TV (YLE TV1, TV2, Teema, Swedish Language Television FST5) Center, www.yle.fi

MTV OY (Commercial TV www.mtv3.fi , and SubTV www.sub.fi)

NELONEN (Channel Four Finland, JimTV, LivTV, SportProTV, KinoTV, Radio Rock, Radio Aalto), www.nelonen.fi

WELHO (SW Television OY / Welho), www.welho.fi

U.S. Commercial Service Helsinki services: Business Service Providers (BSP), Featured U.S. Exporters (FUSE), and Single Company Promotion (SCP), www.buyusa.gov/finland/en

PRICING

All goods and services are subject to a value-added tax (VAT), which ranges from 8 percent on books, drugs, pharmaceuticals, cinema tickets, passenger transportation, accommodation services, cultural and entertainment events and TV licenses; 12 percent on foodstuffs and animal feed, to 22 percent on industrial goods. Excise taxes are levied on alcohol and alcoholic drinks, beer, tobacco, liquid fuels, electricity and certain fuels and soft drinks. Waste tax and oil discharges and also subject to excise taxes.

Finland is an EU country. Imports from the other EU countries enter Finland duty-free and without customs formalities. The EU also has free trade agreements with a large number of non-EU countries (e.g., countries that belong to the Pan-European Cumulation and the European Free Trade Association, or EFTA). Imports from these countries, with some exceptions, enter Finland duty-free if the products have been manufactured in one of these countries. However, import duties are levied on imports from countries such as the United States, Australia, Japan, and Canada, depending on specific product lines.

SALES SERVICE/CUSTOMER SUPPORT

As a rule, one exclusive agent/distributor is appointed to cover the entire country. Finnish importers often represent several different product lines. Importers may serve large customers themselves, while dealers work with smaller customers, often located outside the Helsinki metropolitan area. Dealers are often specialized in supplying a specific industry area. Training, usually organized and carried out by dealers, is an important aspect. Service points should cover the whole country rather than just the southern parts.

Conscious of the discrepancies among European Union Member States in product labeling, language use, legal guarantee, and liability, the redress of which inevitably frustrates consumers in cross-border shopping, the EU institutions have launched a number of initiatives aimed at harmonizing national legislation. Suppliers within and outside the EU should be aware of existing and upcoming legislation affecting sales, service, and customer support.

Product Liability

Under the 1985 Directive on liability of defective products, amended in 1999, the producer is liable for damage caused by a defect in his product. The victim must prove the existence of the defect and a causal link between defect and injury (bodily as well as material). A reduction of liability of the manufacturer is granted in cases of negligence on the part of the victim.

Product Safety

The 1992 General Product Safety Directive introduces a general safety requirement at the EU level to ensure that manufacturers only place safe products on the market. It was revised in 2001 to include an obligation on the producer and distributor to notify the Commission in case of a problem with a given product, provisions for its recall, the creation of a European Product Safety Network, and a ban on exports of products to third countries that are not deemed safe in the EU.

Legal Warranties and After-sales Service

Under the 1999 Directive on the Sale of Consumer Goods and Associated Guarantees, professional sellers are required to provide a minimum two-year warranty on all consumer goods sold to consumers (natural persons acting for purposes outside their trade, businesses or professions), as defined by the Directive. The remedies available to consumers in case of non-compliance are:

- Repair of the good(s);
- Replacement of the good(s);
- A price reduction; or
- Rescission of the sales contract.

Key link: http://ec.europa.eu/comm/consumers/cons_int/safe_shop/guarantees/index_en.htm

Other issues pertaining to consumers' rights and protection, such as the New Approach Directives, CE marking, quality control and data protection are dealt with in Chapter 5 of this report.

PROTECTING YOUR INTELLECTUAL PROPERTY

Several general principles are important for effective management of intellectual property rights in the European Union (EU). First, it is important to have an overall strategy to protect IPR. Second, IPR is protected differently in the EU than in the U.S. Third, rights must be registered and enforced *in* the EU under local laws. Companies may wish to seek advice from local attorneys or IP consultants.

It is vital that companies understand that intellectual property is primarily a private right and that the US government generally cannot enforce rights for private individuals in the EU. It is the responsibility of the rights' holders to register, protect, and enforce their rights where relevant, retaining their own counsel and advisors. While the U.S. Government is willing to assist, there is little it can do if the rights holders have not taken these fundamental steps necessary to securing and enforcing their IPR in a timely fashion. Moreover, in many countries, rights holders who delay enforcing their rights on a mistaken belief that the USG can provide a political resolution to a legal problem may find that their rights have been eroded or abrogated due to doctrines such as statutes of limitations, laches, estoppel, or unreasonable delay in prosecuting a law suit. In no instance should USG advice be seen as a substitute for the obligation of a rights holder to promptly pursue its case.

It is always advisable to conduct due diligence on partners. Negotiate from the position of your partner and give your partner clear incentives to honor the contract. A good partner is an important ally in protecting IP rights. Keep an eye on your cost structure and reduce the margins (and the incentive) of would-be bad actors. Projects and sales in the EU require constant attention. Work with legal counsel familiar with local laws to create a solid contract that includes non-compete clauses, and confidentiality/non-disclosure provisions.

It is also recommended that small and medium-size companies understand the importance of working together with trade associations and organizations to support efforts to protect IPR and stop counterfeiting. There are a number of these organizations, both EU- and U.S.-based. These include:

A wealth of information on protecting IPR is freely available to U.S. rights holders. Some excellent resources for companies regarding intellectual property include the following:

Copyright

The EU's legislative framework for copyright protection consists of a series of Directives covering areas such as the legal protection of computer programs, the duration of protection of authors' rights and neighboring rights, and the legal protection of databases. Almost all Member States have fully implemented the rules into national law; and the Commission is now focusing on ensuring that the framework is enforced accurately and consistently across the EU.

Key Link: http://ec.europa.eu/internal_market/copyright/documents/documents_en.htm

The on-line copyright Directive (2001/29/EC) addresses the problem of protecting rights holders in the online environment while protecting the interests of users, ISPs and hardware manufacturers. It guarantees authors' exclusive reproduction rights with a single mandatory exception for technical copies (to allow caching), and an exhaustive list of other exceptions that individual Member States can select and include in national legislation. This list is meant to reflect different cultural and legal traditions, and includes private copying "on condition right holders receive fair compensation."

Patents

EU countries have a "first to file" approach to patent applications, as compared to the "first to invent" system currently followed in the United States. This makes early filing a top priority for innovative companies. Unfortunately, it is not yet possible to file for a single EU-wide patent that would be administered and enforced like the Community Trademark though negotiations are progressing (see below). For the moment, the most effective way for a company to secure a patent across a range of EU national markets is to use the services of the European Patent Office (EPO) in Munich. It offers a one-stop-shop that enables rights holders to get a bundle of national patents using a single application. However, these national patents still have to be validated, maintained and litigated separately in each Member State.

Trademarks

The EU-wide Community Trademark (CTM) can be obtained via a single language application to the Office of Harmonization in the Internal Market (OHIM) in Alicante, Spain. It lasts ten years and is renewable indefinitely. For companies looking to protect trademarks in three or more EU countries the CTM is a more cost effective option than registering separate national trademarks.

On October 1, 2004, the European Commission (EC) acceded to the World Intellectual Property Organization (WIPO) Madrid Protocol. The accession of the EC to the Madrid Protocol establishes a link between the Madrid Protocol system, administered by WIPO, and the Community Trademark system, administered by OHIM. As of October 1, 2004, Community Trademark applicants and holders are allowed to apply for international protection of their trademarks through the filing of an international application under the Madrid Protocol. Conversely, holders of international registrations under the Madrid Protocol will be entitled to apply for protection of their trademarks under the Community Trademark system.

Designs

The EU adopted a Regulation introducing a single Community system for the protection of designs in December 2001. The Regulation provides for two types of design protection, directly applicable in each EU Member State: the registered Community design and the unregistered Community design. Under the registered Community design system, holders of eligible designs can use an inexpensive procedure to register them with the EU's Office for Harmonization in the Internal Market (OHIM), based in Alicante, Spain. They will then be granted exclusive rights to use the designs anywhere in the EU for up to twenty-five years. Unregistered Community designs that meet the Regulation's requirements are automatically protected for three years from the date of disclosure of the design to the public.

Trademark Exhaustion

Within the EU, the rights conferred on trademark holders are subject to the principle of "exhaustion." Exhaustion means that once trademark holders have placed their product on the market in one Member State, they lose the right to prevent the resale of that product in another EU country. This has led to an increase in the practice of so called "parallel importing" whereby goods bought in one Member State are sold in another by third parties unaffiliated to the manufacturer. Parallel trade is particularly problematic for the research-based pharmaceutical industry where drug prices vary from country to country due to national price Regulation.

Community wide exhaustion is spelled out in the Directive on harmonizing trademark laws. In a paper published in 2003, the Commission indicated that it had no plans to propose changes to existing legal provisions.

IPR Climate in Finland

See Investment Climate Statement.

The Finnish legal system protects property rights, including intellectual property, and Finland adheres to numerous international agreements concerning intellectual property. Finland has joined the most important copyright agreements. For further information, please see http://www.prh.fi (National Board of Patents and Registration of Finland Industrial Property Office), and http://www.minedu.fi (Ministry of Education and Culture Copyright Office).

DUE DILIGENCE

Dun & Bradstreet Finland Oy and Suomen Asiakastieto Oy offer a variety of business and credit information services. For further information, please contact:

Dun & Bradstreet Finland Oy

Kumpulantie 3
FI-00520 Helsinki, Finland
Tel: +358-9-2534 4400,
E-mail: asiakaspalvelu@dnbnordic.com
http://dbfinland.dnb.com/English/default.htm

One can also contact any Dun & Bradstreet office in the United States.
Suomen Asiakastieto Oy
Työpajankatu 10 A
FI-00580 Helsinki, Finland
Tel: +358-10 270 7000, Fax: +358-10 270 7338
E-mail: international@asiakastieto.fi
http://www.asiakastieto.fi/en/index.shtml

U.S. Commercial Service Finland offers U.S. Companies International Company Profile (ICP) reports. The ICPs are designed to help U.S. companies enter international business relationships with confidence. ICPs provide background checks on overseas companies that provide U.S. firms with information to help assess foreign firms as business partners. For further information please visit http://www.buyusa.gov/finland/en

LOCAL PROFESSIONAL SERVICES

Please visit U.S. Commercial Service Finland's website - Local Business Service Providers: http://www.buyusa.gov/finland/en/bsn.html

WEB RESOURCES

The Finnish Franchising Association: http://www.franchising.fi
The Finnish Direct Marketing Association (Finnish DMA): http://www.asml.fi
Invest in Finland Bureau: http://www.investinfinland.fi
Local government authorities:
Ministry of Employment and the Economy: http://www.tem.fi
Public Procurement Advisory Unit: http://www.hankinnat.fi
Tenders Electronic Daily: http://ted.europa.eu/
The Federation of Finnish Commerce, www.kauppa.fi
The Finnish Foreign Trade Agents' Federation www.agenttiliitto.fi
Trade Promotion and Advertising (EU):
General Legislation,
http://ec.europa.eu/comm/consumers/cons_int/safe_shop/fair_bus_pract/index_en.htm
http://ec.europa.eu/avpolicy/reg/avms/index_en.htm

Nutrition & Health Claims, http://www.efsa.europa.eu/EFSA/efsa_locale-1178620753812_1178620835814.htm

Food Supplements, http://useu.usmission.gov/agri/foodsupplements.html
Tobacco, http://ec.europa.eu/health/ph_determinants/life_style/Tobacco/tobacco_en.htm
Local Fair Authorities:
The Finnish Fair Corporation/Helsinki Fair Center, www.finnexpo.fi
Helsinki Fair Ltd., www.wanhasatama.com
Jyvaskyla Fair Ltd., www.jklfairs.fi
The Turku Fair and Congress Center Ltd., www.turunmessukeskus.fi
Lahti Fair Ltd., www.lahdenmessut.fi
Tampere Trade Fairs Ltd., www.tampereenmessut.fi
Local Newspapers:

Helsingin Sanomat, www.hs.fi
Hufvudstadsbladet (Swedish daily), www.hbl.fi
Aamulehti, www.aamulehti.fi
Iltalehti, www.iltalehti.fi
Iltasanomat, www.iltasanomat.fi
Kaleva, www.kaleva.fi
Keskisuomalainen, www.ksml.fi
Savon Sanomat, savonsanomat.fi
Turun Sanomat, www.ts.fi
Business Magazines/Journals:
Kauppalehti (Business daily), www.kauppalehti.fi
Talouselama (Business weekly), www.talouselama.fi
Tekniikka & Talous (Business weekly), www.tekniikkatalous.fi
Tietoviikko TIVI (Business weekly), www.tietoviikko.fi

Radio/TV:

Metroradio Finland Oy (Classic Radio Oy, www.classicradio.fi , Groove FM, www.groovefm.fi , MetroFM, www.metrofm.fi , SuomiPOP, www.radiosuomipop.fi)

MTV Media Radio Group (Radio Nova, www.radionova.fi)

SBS Finland Oy (Iskelma-ketju, www.iskelma.fi , Radio 957, www.radio957.fi , Radio Sata, www.sata.fi , Radio Jyvaskyla, www.radiojkl.fi , Radio Mega, www.radiomega.fi , and Voice, www.voice.fi)

Sanoma Corporation (Radio Helsinki, www.radiohelsinki.fi)

Finnish Broadcasting Company YLE Radio (YLE Radio 1, YLEX, YLE Radio Suomi, YLE Radio Peili, Radio Extrem, Radio Vega), and TV (YLE TV1, TV2, Teema, Swedish Language Television FST5) Center, www.yle.fi

MTV OY (Commercial TV www.mtv3.fi , and SubTV www.sub.fi)

NELONEN (Channel Four Finland), www.nelonen.fi

WELHO (SW Television OY / Welho), www.welho.fi

U.S. Commercial Service Helsinki services: Business Service Providers (BSP), Featured U.S.

Exporters (FUSE), and Single Company Promotion (SCP), www.buyusa.gov/finland/en

Product Safety, http://ec.europa.eu/consumers/safety/prod_legis/index_en.htm

Protecting Your Intellectual Property (EU):

Copyright, http://ec.europa.eu/internal_market/copyright/documents/documents_en.htm

Patents, http://ec.europa.eu/internal_market/indprop/patent/index_en.htm

http://www.european-patent-office.org

Trademarks, http://oami.europa.eu/ , http://www.wipo.int/madrid/en

Designs, http://oami.europa.eu/

Trademark Exhaustion, http://ec.europa.eu/internal_market/indprop/tm/index_en.htm

IPR in Finland:

National Board of Patents and Registration of Finland Industrial Property Office, http://www.prh.fi

Ministry of Education and Culture Copyright Office, http://www.minedu.fi

TRADE REGULATIONS AND STANDARDS

IMPORT TARIFFS

Duties and other import taxes are levied on the customs value of the goods at the point of importation. The customs value is based on the transaction value of the goods imported. In practice, the C.I.F. (cost, insurance, freight) value is commonly used as the customs value. To assess customs value, the place of importation must be indicated. In the case of sea and air cargo, the place of importation is the unloading location. In surface transportation, it is the Customs Office at the frontier. The customs value is determined according to the GATT Valuation Agreement and the Community Customs Code (Council regulation 2913/92), and the Regulation Laying Down Provisions for Implementation of the Customs Code (Commission regulation 2454/93). Depending on the product and excluding the foodstuff, the import tariff ranges from 0-17%.

For further information, please visit www.tulli.fi (Finnish Customs).

TRADE BARRIERS

Finland's adoption of European Union's (EU) internal market practices in 1995 defines Finland's trade relations both inside the EU and with non-EU countries.

Finland replaced its turnover tax with a value-added tax (VAT) in 1994. The government has kept the standard VAT rate at 22 percent, the same level as the old turnover tax. In July 2010, the VAT will increase by one percentage point to 23 percent. Food products are taxed at 12 percent. Sport facilities usage, medicines, books, cinemas, passenger transport services, hotel and other accommodation, entertainment performances, sporting events, zoos, museums, and other such events or institutions are taxed at 8 percent. Other services, including health care, education, insurance, newspaper & periodical subscriptions and rentals are not subject to VAT. Agricultural and forestry products continue to be subject to different forms of taxation outside the VAT.

In March 1997 EU commitments required the establishment of a tax border between the autonomously governed, but territorially Finnish, Aland Islands and the rest of Finland. As a result, the trade of goods and services between the rest of Finland and Aland Islands is now treated as if it were trade with a non-EU area. Even though the Aland Islands are part of the EU, just as Finland is, Aland does not belong to the Union's tax area. This exception was drafted in order to protect the important shipping traffic and the tax-free sales when EU countries abandoned duty-free sales. The trade effect of this treatment is minimal since the Aland Islands are part of the EFTA tariff area.

For further information on existing trade barriers, please see the 2009 National Trade Estimate Report on Foreign Trade Barriers, published by USTR and available through the following link: http://www.ustr.gov/about-us/press-office/reports-and-publications/2009/2009-national-trade-estimate-report-foreign-trad

IMPORT REQUIREMENTS AND DOCUMENTATION

Certain import/export items need to meet with special requirements and certifications set by the European Union or national standards. These are mostly articles that might damage health, welfare or country's economy, or result in the spread of animal and plant diseases.

The following items, among others, are subject to restrictions:

Foodstuffs, fodder and fertilizers, alcoholic beverages and other products containing alcohol, pharmaceuticals, narcotics and dangerous drugs, some chemicals, nuclear and radioactive substances, explosives, blade knives, firearms and ammunition, obscene publications, and pressure vessels.

For further information, please visit www.tulli.fi (Finnish Customs).

The Integrated Tariff of the Community, referred to as TARIC (Tarif Intégré de la Communauté), is designed to show various rules applying to specific products being imported into the customs territory of the European Union or, in some cases, when exported from it. To determine if a license is required for a particular product, check the TARIC.

The TARIC can be searched by country of origin, Harmonized System (HS) Code, and product description on the interactive website of the Directorate-General for Taxation and the Customs Union. The online TARIC is updated daily.

Many EU Member States maintain their own list of goods subject to import licensing.

For example, Germany's "Import List" (Einfuhrliste) includes goods for which licenses are required, their code numbers, any applicable restrictions, and the agency that will issue the relevant license. The Import List also indicates whether the license is required under German or EU law. For information relevant to Member State import licenses, please consult the relevant Member State Country Commercial Guide: EU Member States' Country Commercial Guides or conduct a search on the Commerce Department's Market Research Library, available from: http://www.export.gov/mrktresearch/index.asp .

Import Documentation

Non-agricultural Documentation

The official model for written declarations to customs is the Single Administrative Document (SAD). European Free Trade Association (EFTA) countries including Norway, Iceland, Switzerland, and Liechtenstein also use the SAD. However, other forms may be used for this purpose. Information on import/export forms is contained in Title VII, of Council Regulation (EEC) No. 2454/93, which lays down provisions for the implementation of Council Regulation (EEC) No. 2913/92 establishing the Community Customs Code (Articles 205 through 221). Articles 222 through 224 provide for computerized customs declarations and Articles 225 through 229 provide for oral declarations.

Additional information on import/export documentation can be found in Title III, of Council Regulation (EEC) No. 2913/92 of October 12, 1992, establishing the Community Customs Code (Articles 37 through 57). Goods brought into the customs territory of the Community are, from the time of their entry, subject to customs supervision until customs formalities are completed.

Goods presented to customs are covered by a summary declaration, which is lodged once the goods have been presented to customs. The customs authorities may, however, allow a period for lodging the declaration, which cannot be extended beyond the first working day following the day on which the goods are presented to customs. The summary declaration can be made on a form corresponding to the model prescribed by the customs authorities. However, the customs authorities may permit the use, as a summary declaration, of any commercial or official document that contains the particulars necessary for identification of the goods. It is encouraged that the summary declaration be made in computerized form.

The summary declaration is to be lodged by:

Non-EU goods presented to customs must be assigned a customs-approved treatment or use authorized for such non-Community goods. Where goods are covered by a summary declaration, the formalities for them to be assigned a customs-approved treatment or use must be carried out:

Where circumstances so warrant, the customs authorities may set a shorter period or authorize an extension of the period.

The Modernized Customs Code (MCC) of the European Union is expected to be fully put into place by 2017 although there are concerns that this deadline may be missed due to the complexity of the project. Some facets of the MCC implementation have already been put into place such as Economic Operators Registration and Idendification (EORI) numbers. The MCC will replace the existing Regulation 2913/92 and simplify various procedures such as introducing a paperless environment, centralized clearance, and more. Check the EU's Customs website periodically for updates: http://ec.europa.eu/taxation_customs/customs/procedural_aspects/general/community_code/index_en.htm .

Batteries

EU battery rules changed in September 2006 following the publication of the Directive on batteries and accumulators and waste batteries and accumulators (Directive 2006/66). This Directive replaces the original Battery Directive of 1991 (Directive 91/157). The updated Directive applies to all batteries and accumulators put on the EU market including automotive, industrial and portable batteries. It aims to protect the environment by restricting the sale of batteries and accumulators that contain mercury or cadmium (with an exemption for emergency and alarm systems, medical equipment and cordless power tools) and by promoting a high level of collection and recycling. It places the responsibility on producers to finance the costs associated with the collection, treatment, and recycling of used batteries and accumulators. The Directive also includes provisions on the labeling of batteries and their removability from equipment. For more information, see our market research report: http://www.buyusainfo.net/docs/x_8086174.pdf or visit the CS EU website Batteries Direct page at: http://www.buyusa.gov/europeanunion/batteries.html

REACH

REACH is a major reform of EU chemicals policy that was adopted in December 2006 and became national law in the 27 EU Member States in June 2007 (Regulation 1907/2006). Virtually every industrial sector, from automobiles to textiles, is affected by the new policy. REACH stands for the "Registration, Evaluation and Authorization and Restriction of Chemicals." Since June 1 2008, REACH requires chemicals produced or imported into the EU in volumes above 1 ton per year per to be registered with a central European Chemicals Agency (ECHA), including information on their properties, uses and safe ways of handling them. Chemicals pre-registered before December 1 2008, benefit from extended registration deadlines, from three to eleven years depending on the volume of the substance and its hazard properties. U.S. companies without a presence in Europe cannot register directly and must have their chemicals registered through their importer or EU-based 'Only Representative of non-EU manufacturer'. A list of Only Representatives can be found on the website of the U.S. Mission to the EU: http://www.buyusa.gov/europeanunion/reach.html .

U.S. exporters to the EU should carefully consider the REACH 'Candidate List' of substances of very high concern. Substances on that list are subject to communication requirements and may at a later stage require Authorization for the EU market. For more information, see the ECHA website: http://echa.europa.eu/chem_data/authorisation_process/candidate_list_table_en.asp

WEEE & RoHS

EU rules on waste electrical and electronic equipment (WEEE), while not requiring specific customs or import paperwork, may entail a financial obligation for U.S. exporters. They require U.S. exporters to register the products with a national WEEE authority, or arrange for this to be done by a local partner. Similarly, related rules for EEE restricting the use of the hazardous substances (RoHS) lead, cadmium, mercury, hexavalent chromium, PBBs, and PBDEs, do not entail customs or importation paperwork. However, U.S. exporters may be asked by a European RoHS enforcement authority or by a customer to provide evidence of due diligence in compliance with the substance bans on a case-by-case basis. The WEEE and RoHS Directives are currently being revised to enlarge the scope and add substances to be banned in electrical and electronic equipment; the new rules could take effect as early as 2011. U.S. exporters seeking more information on WEEE and RoHS regulations should visit: http://www.buyusa.gov/europeanunion/weee.html

Agricultural Documentation

Phytosanitary Certificates: Phytosanitary certificates are required for most fresh fruits, vegetables, and other plant materials.

Sanitary Certificates: For commodities composed of animal products or by-products, EU countries require that shipments be accompanied by a certificate issued by the competent authority of the exporting country. This applies regardless of whether the product is for human consumption, for pharmaceutical use, or strictly for non-human use (e.g., veterinary biologicals, animal feeds, fertilizers, research). The vast majority of these certificates are uniform throughout the EU, but the harmonization process is not complete. During this transition period, certain Member State import requirements continue to apply. In addition to the legally required EU health certificates, a number of other certificates are used in international trade. These certificates, which may also be harmonized in EU legislation, certify origin for customs purposes and certain quality attributes. Up-to-date information on harmonized import requirements can be found at the following website: http://www.fas.usda.gov/posthome/useu/certificates-overview.html

Sanitary Certificates (Fisheries): In April 2006, the European Union declared the U.S. seafood inspection system as equivalent to the European one. Consequently, a specific public health certificate must accompany U.S. seafood shipments. Commission Decision 2006/199/EC places specific conditions on imports of fishery products from the U.S. Sanitary certificates for live shellfish are covered by Commission Regulation (EC) 1664/2006 and must be used for gastropods, bivalve mollusks, tunicates and echinoderms. The two competent Authorities for issuing sanitary certificates are the FDA and the U.S. Department of Commerce, National Marine Fisheries Service (NMFS/NOAA/USDC).

Since May 1, 2007, with the implementation of the second Hygiene Package, aquaculture products coming from the United States must be accompanied by a public health certificate according to Commission Decision 2006/199/EC and the animal health attestation included in the new fishery products certificate covered by Regulation (EC) 1664/2006. This animal health attestation is not required in the case of live bivalve mollusks intended for immediate human consumption (retail).

For detailed information on import documentation for seafood, please contact the NOAA Fisheries office at the U.S. Mission to the EU (stephane.vrignaud@mail.doc.gov) or visit the following FDA dedicated web site: http://www.cfsan.fda.gov/ .

U.S. EXPORT CONTROLS

A booklet on Finland's export controls is available from the Ministry for Foreign Affairs, Export Controls Unit http://formin.finland.fi - E-mail: heikki.yrjola@formin.fi

TEMPORARY ENTRY

Temporary exemption from duty can be granted, for instance, to the following:

- Goods intended for public displays at exhibitions and fairs

- Commercial samples

- Professional tools and equipment

If the goods are put to unauthorized use or are not exported within the prescribed time they must go through normal customs clearance, and become liable for relevant duties and taxes.

In Finland, the ATA-Carnet, the international customs documentation for temporary duty-free admission, is issued by the Chamber of Commerce. The ATA-Carnets are frequently used for temporary imports, e.g. samples, exhibition materials, and professional equipment (laptop computers, software), and are valid for one year.

LABELING AND MARKING REQUIREMENTS

Labeling and marking requirements in Finland are based on the Act on Product Safety, which was enacted in accordance with the EU directive on general product safety. Mandatory information must be provided in Finnish and Swedish. The following information should be included in a retail packaging, or otherwise marked on the product (a sticker, label, etc.):

-The name and purpose of the product (for example hair color).

- The name of the manufacturer or importer, which the consumer or authority can contact if necessary.

When applicable, the following information should be provided to secure safe use of a consumer product:

- Product contents and size of contents.

- Patch number identifying the consignment.

- Instructions for assembly and information if the assembly requires specific qualifications for safe assembly.

- Instructions for use and storage.

- Warning labels and instructions for the use of necessary personal safety device.

- Washing, cleaning and care instructions.

- Instructions for disposal of the product and information on hazards for using the product and disposal of product.

Finland has precise labeling requirements for foodstuff. The general provisions are prescribed in the ***Decree of the Ministry of Trade and Industry on the Labeling of Foodstuffs*** (1084/2004, 888/2005, 1224/2007).

For more information on labeling and marking requirements, please visit the Finnish Consumer Agency www.kuluttajavirasto.fi and www.evira.fi (Finnish Food Safety Authority).

PROHIBITED AND RESTRICTED IMPORTS

Finnish Customs keeps an updated handbook on prohibited and restricted imports. The following items are included in the listing:

- PCB and PCT chemicals used in transformers and condensers causing problem waste products

- CFC, HBFC, HCFC chemicals

- Whale meat (CITES – Convention on International Trade in Endangered Species of Wild Flora and Fauna)

For further information on other prohibited and restricted imports, please see http://www.tulli.fi

CUSTOMS REGULATIONS AND CONTACT INFORMATION

Finnish Customs is a part of the customs system of the European Union (EU). In addition to customs regulations information, it offers customs statistics service. Finnish Customs: http://www.tulli.fi

STANDARDS

The central body for standardization in Finland is the Finnish Standards Association - SFS (www.sfs.fi). SFS and its standards writing bodies, SESKO (Electrotechnical Standardization in Finland - www.sesko.fi) and Finnish Communications Regulatory Authority (www.ficora.fi) are members of the European standards organizations CEN, CENELEC and ETSI.

National SFS Standards are sold in Finland only by SFS. National ISO member bodies abroad handle distribution of SFS standards. SFS and SESKO are the Finnish sources for all international standards and drafts of the International Organization for Standardization (ISO), for

European standards and drafts of CEN and for publications of ISO member bodies. SFS also distributes other foreign standards and technical regulations.

Products tested and certified in the United States to American standards are likely to have to be retested and re-certified to EU requirements as a result of the EU's different approach to the protection of the health and safety of consumers and the environment. Where products are not regulated by specific EU technical legislation, they are always subject to the EU's General Product Safety Directive as well as to possible additional national requirements.

European Union standards created under the New Approach are harmonized across the 27 EU Member States and European Economic Area countries to allow for the free flow of goods. A feature of the New Approach is CE marking. For a list of new approach legislation, go to http://ec.europa.eu/enterprise/policies/european-standards/documents/harmonised-standards-legislation/list-references/index_en.htm

While harmonization of EU legislation can facilitate access to the EU Single Market, manufacturers should be aware that regulations and technical standards might also function as barriers to trade if U.S. standards are different from those of the European Union.

Agricultural Standards

The establishment of harmonized EU rules and standards in the food sector has been ongoing for several decades, but it took until January 2002 for the publication of a general food law establishing the general principles of EU food law. This Regulation introduced mandatory traceability throughout the feed and food chain as of Jan 1, 2005. For specific information on agricultural standards, please refer to the Foreign Agricultural Service's website at: http://www.fas.usda.gov/posthome/useu/

There are also export guides to import regulations and standards available on the Foreign Agricultural Service's website: http://www.fas.usda.gov/posthome/useu/

STANDARDS ORGANIZATIONS

EU standards setting is a process based on consensus initiated by industry or mandated by the European Commission and carried out by independent standards bodies, acting at the national, European or international level. There is strong encouragement for non-governmental organizations, such as environmental and consumer groups, to actively participate in European standardization.

Many standards in the EU are adopted from international standards bodies such as the International Standards Organization (ISO). The drafting of specific EU standards is handled by three European standards organizations:

CENELEC, European Committee for Electrotechnical Standardization

(http://www.cenelec.eu/Cenelec/Homepage.htm)

ETSI, European Telecommunications Standards Institute (http://www.etsi.org/)

CEN, European Committee for Standardization, handling all other standards

(http://www.cen.eu/cenorm/homepage.htm)

The only organization that develops standards in Finland is the Finnish Standards Association (http://www.sfs.fi/en/).

To know what CEN and CENELEC have in the pipeline for future standardization, it is best to visit their websites. CEN's "sectors" page provides an overview by sector and/or technical committee whereas CENELEC offers the possibility to search its database. ETSI's portal (http://portal.etsi.org/Portal_Common/home.asp) leads to ongoing activities.

With the need to adapt more quickly to market needs, European standards organizations have been looking for "new deliverables" which are standard-like products delivered in a shorter timeframe. While few of these "new deliverables" have been linked to EU Regulations, expectations are that they will eventually serve as the basis for EU-wide standards.

CONFORMITY ASSESSMENT

Conformity Assessment is a mandatory step for the manufacturer in the process of complying with specific EU legislation. The purpose of conformity assessment is to ensure consistency of compliance during all stages of the production process to facilitate acceptance of the final product. EU product legislation gives manufacturers some choice with regard to conformity assessment, depending on the level of risk involved in the use of their product. These range from self-certification, type examination and production quality control system, to full quality assurance system. You can find conformity assessment bodies in individual Member State country in this list by the European Commission.

To promote market acceptance of the final product, there are a number of voluntary conformity assessment programs. CEN's certification systems are the Keymark, the CENCER mark, and CEN workshop agreements (CWA) Certification Rules. CENELEC has its own initiative. ETSI does not offer conformity assessment services.

PRODUCT CERTIFICATION

Product certification is voluntary in Finland.

To sell products on the EU market of 27 Member States as well as Norway, Liechtenstein and Iceland, U.S. exporters are required to apply CE marking whenever their product is covered by specific product legislation. CE marking product legislation offers manufacturers a number of choices and requires decisions to determine which safety/health concerns need to be addressed, which conformity assessment module is best suited to the manufacturing process, and whether or not to use EU-wide harmonized standards.

Products manufactured to standards adopted by CEN, CENELEC and ETSI, and published in the Official Journal as harmonized standards, are presumed to conform to the requirements of EU Directives. The manufacturer then applies the CE marking and issues a declaration of conformity. With these, the product will be allowed to circulate freely within the EU. A manufacturer can choose not to use the harmonized EU standards, but then must demonstrate that the product meets the essential safety and performance requirements. Trade barriers occur when design, rather than performance, standards are developed by the relevant European standardization organization, and when U.S. companies do not have access to the standardization process through a European presence.

The CE marking addresses itself primarily to the national control authorities of the Member States, and its use simplifies the task of essential market surveillance of regulated products. Although CE marking is intended primarily for inspection purposes by Member State inspectors, the consumer may well perceive it as a quality mark.

The CE marking is not intended to include detailed technical information on the product, but there must be enough information to enable the inspector to trace the product back to the manufacturer or the authorized representative established in the EU. This detailed information should not appear next to the CE marking, but rather on the declaration of conformity (which the manufacturer or authorized agent must be able to provide at any time, together with the product's technical file), or the documents accompanying the product.

ACCREDITATION

Independent certification bodies, known as notified bodies, have been officially accredited by competent national authorities to test and certify to EU requirements. However, under U.S.-EU Mutual Recognition Agreements (MRAs), notified bodies based in the United States and referred to as conformity assessment bodies, are allowed to test in the United States to EU specifications, and vice versa. The costs are significantly lower which results in U.S. products becoming more competitive. At this time, the U.S.-EU MRAs cover the following sectors: EMC (in force), RTTE (in force), medical devices (in transition), pharmaceutical (on hold), recreational craft (in force) and marine equipment (in force). The U.S. Department of Commerce, National Institute of Standards and Technology (NIST), has a link on its website to American and European Conformity Assessment bodies operating under a mutual recognition agreement.

Accreditation is handled at Member State level. "European Accreditation" (http://www.european-accreditation.org/content/home/home.htm) is an organization representing nationally recognized accreditation bodies. Membership is open to nationally recognized accreditation bodies in countries in the European geographical area that can demonstrate that they operate an accreditation system compatible with EN45003 or ISO/IEC Guide 58.

Please contact the Finnish Accreditation Service (FINAS) for further information (see http://www.mikes.fi/frameset.aspx?url=finas.aspx%3FpageID=0%26categoryID=2&langID=uk)

PUBLICATION OF TECHNICAL REGULATIONS

The Official Journal is the official gazette of the European Union. It is published daily on the internet and consists of two series covering draft and adopted legislation as well as case law, studies by committees, and more (http://eur-lex.europa.eu/JOIndex.do)It lists the standards reference numbers linked to legislation (http://ec.europa.eu/enterprise/policies/european-standards/documents/harmonised-standards-legislation/list-references/index_en.htm). National technical Regulations are published on the Commission's website http://ec.europa.eu/enterprise/tris/index_en.htm to allow other countries and interested parties to comment.

Member countries of the World Trade Organization (WTO) are required under the Agreement on Technical Barriers to Trade (TBT) Agreement to report to the WTO all proposed technical regulations that could affect trade with other member countries.

Notify U.S. is a free, web-based e-mail subscription service that offers an opportunity to review and comment on proposed foreign technical regulations that can affect access to international markets. Register online at Internet URL: http://tsapps.nist.gov/notifyus/data/index/index.cfm

LABELING AND MARKING

Manufacturers should be mindful that, in addition to the EU's mandatory and voluntary schemes, national voluntary labeling schemes might still apply. These schemes may be highly appreciated by consumers, and thus, become unavoidable for marketing purposes.

Manufacturers are advised to take note that all labels require metric units although dual labeling is also acceptable. The use of language on labels has been the subject of a Commission Communication, which encourages multilingual information, while preserving the right of Member States to require the use of language of the country of consumption.

The EU has mandated that certain products be sold in standardized quantities. Council Directive 2007/45/EC, , harmonizes packaging of wine and spirits throughout the EU. Existing national sizes will be abolished with a few exceptions for domestic producers.

The Eco-label

The EU eco-label is a voluntary label which US exporters can display on products that meet high standards of environmental awareness. The eco-label is intended to be a marketing tool to encourage consumers to purchase environmentally-friendly products. The criteria for displaying the eco-label are strict, covering the entire lifespan of the product from manufacture, to use, to disposal. These criteria are reviewed every three to five years to take into account advances in manufacturing procedures. There are currently twenty-three different product groups, and approximately 250 licenses have been awarded for several hundred products.

Applications to display the eco-label should be directed to the competency body of the member state in which the product is sold. The application fee will be somewhere between €300 and €1300 depending on the tests required to verify if the product is eligible. The eco-label also carries an annual fee equal to 0.15% of the annual volume of sales of the product range within the European community. However, the minimum annual fee is currently set at €500 and maximum €25,000.

There are plans to significantly reform the eco-label in the near future, reducing the application and annual fees and expanding the product ranges significantly. It is also possible that future eligibility criteria may take into account carbon emissions.

The Swan Label

Besides the CE Mark, which is required across the European Union, the Swan Label is a neutral and reliable Nordic Environmental Label. It directs products, their production and consumption into a more environmentally friendly direction. The Swan Label indicates that the products burden the environment less than other corresponding products - without compromising performance characteristics.

TRADE AGREEMENTS

Membership in Free Trade Arrangements

Finland joined the European Union on January 1, 1995, which means that Finland complies with trade agreements that the EU has made with third countries. Finland is also a member of the European Free Trade Association, and the European Economic Area.

Bilateral Investment Agreements

Finland has concluded bilateral investment agreements with the following 62 countries: Azerbaijan, Albania, Algeria, Argentina, Armenia, Belarus, Bosnia-Herzegovina, Bulgaria, Chile, China, Croatia , the Czech Republic, the Dominican Republic, Egypt, El Salvador, Estonia, Ecuador, Ethiopia, Georgia, Guatemala, Hungary, India, Indonesia, Iran, Jordan, Kazakhstan, Kirghizia, , Kuwait, Latvia, Lithuania, Macedonia, Malaysia, Mauritius, Mongolia, Morocco, Mozambique, Mexico, Namibia, Nigeria, Oman, Oriental Republic of Uruguay, Peru, Philippines, Poland, Qatar, Republic of Korea, Republic of Lebanon, Republic of Moldova, Republic of Slovenia, Romania, Russia, Slovakia, South Africa, Sri Lanka, Tanzania, Thailand, Tunisia, Turkey, Ukraine, United Arab Emirates, Uzbekistan, and Vietnam.

In September 1989, Finland and the U.S. signed a convention (TIAS 12101) for the avoidance of double taxation and the prevention of fiscal evasion with respect to taxes on income and on capital. The convention entered into force December 30, 1990. The tax convention was amended on 31 May 2006 under a protocol signed in Helsinki.

For a list of trade agreements with the EU and its Member States, as well as concise explanations, please see http://tcc.export.gov/Trade_Agreements/index.asp .

WEB RESOURCES

National Board of Customs, http://www.tulli.fi/en/index.jsp
The Finnish Consumer Agency & Ombudsman, http://www.kuluttajavirasto.fi
Finnish Food Safety Authority, http://www.evira.fi
USTR Reports, Document library; reports & publications, http://www.ustr.gov
National Supervisory Authority for Welfare and Health, http://www.valvira.fi
Environmental Administration, http://www.ymparisto.fi/default.asp?node=4032&lan=en
Finnish Customs, www.tulli.fi
EU websites:
EU's Customs website:
http://ec.europa.eu/taxation_customs/customs/index_en.htm
Online customs tariff database (TARIC):
http://ec.europa.eu/taxation_customs/common/databases/taric/index_en.htm
The Latest on REACH: http://www.buyusa.gov/europeanunion/reach.html .
WEEE and RoHS in the EU: http://www.buyusa.gov/europeanunion/weee.html
Agricultural Trade Barriers:
http://www.fas.usda.gov/posthome/useu/
Taxation and Customs Union: http://ec.europa.eu/taxation_customs/customs/index_en.htm
Legislation related to the Electronic Customs Initiative:
http://ec.europa.eu/taxation_customs/customs/policy_issues/electronic_customs_initiative/electronic_customs_legislation/index_en.htm

U.S. websites:

National Trade Estimate Report on Foreign Trade Barriers:
http://www.ustr.gov/about-us/press-office/reports-and-publications/2009/2009-national-trade-estimate-report-foreign-trad
Trade Compliance Center: http://www.trade.gov/tcc
U.S. Mission to the European Union: http://www.buyusa.gov/europeanunion
Overview of EU Certificates:
http://useu.usmission.gov/agri/certificates-overview.html
Center for Food Safety and Applied Nutrition: http://www.cfsan.fda.gov/
Trade Agreements: http://tcc.export.gov/Trade_Agreements/index.asp

USEFUL INFORMATION FOR CONDUCTING BUSINESS IN FINLAND

DIRECT SALES

The most important exporters to Finland were (in this order) Germany, Sweden and the Commonwealth of Independent States. Together they accounted for 34,47% of the imports to Finland. Altogether 58,9% of the imports to Finland originated from the countries of the European Union and 5,5% from the European Free Trade Area ("EFTA").

Most products are freely importable to Finland. However, there are exceptions concerning, e.g., certain agricultural products, live animals, chemicals, arms, etc., the imports of which require a license or a special permission from the authorities.

When importing commodities to Finland, VAT as well as customs duties (depending on the nature of the commodity) has to be paid. More information regarding customs and imports is available at the website of the Finnish National Board of Customs at www.tulli.fi, where a leaflet called Customs Today has been published.

There are no particular Finnish regulations concerning bills of lading and other shipping documentation, insurance or letters of credit.

Goods cannot be imported to Finland by a foreign exporter without a local agent in Finland who technically qualifies as the importer.

Direct sales to Finland are not taxable in Finland. The presence of a representative in Finland may sometimes constitute a permanent establishment in the country, which pursuant to the Finnish tax laws and most tax treaties results in the taxability of such sales in Finland. When considering whether a foreign company has a permanent establishment in Finland, the independence of the agent is taken into account.

As already pointed out above, Finland is a member of the European union. In addition, Finland has entered into several separate bilateral free trade agreements and other agreements and conventions (with GATT, OECD and the USA, among others). For more information on agreements and conventions entered into by Finland, please contact the Council of State/Ministry of Foreign Affairs, at www.vn.fi.

The trade relations between the United States and Finland have traditionally been very good. Neither country has ever taken any actual actions against the other country. Finland or Finnish companies have occasionally been claimed to have violated the anti-dumping provisions of the United States, but these claims have never led to any actual import restrictions concerning Finnish products.

Finland's trade relations with other countries have been mostly good and there have been few trade disputes. For instance, Finnish authorities have rarely had to implement measures to prevent the import of goods subject to dumping or for which subsidies are granted in a foreign country.

EXPORTS FROM FINLAND

Finland exports to numerous countries of the world. Approximately 43% of exports consist of metal and engineering products. Paper products account for approximately 23% of exports, and 7,3% of exports consist of wood products. Chemical products account for 9,8% of exports. Finland further exports, e.g., high technology products (incl. especially telecommunications) and clothing.

Exports from Finland are exempt from VAT. In addition, the goods used for manufacturing of export products are on certain conditions exempt from customs duty. The exporting companies can also on certain conditions make use of state export guarantees in case they do not receive payment for their exports.

Finland is a signatory to the General Agreement on Tariffs and Trade (GATT) of 1947 and grants the other signatories most favored nation (MFN) treatment. Pursuant to GATT's MFN clause, every signatory may enjoy the privileges concerning customs duties or other provisions on imports and exports accorded by any signatory to another country, however, with the exception that the signatories have a possibility of forming privileged customs unions and free trade areas.

Since Finland is a member of the EU, there are few import restrictions applicable to the trade between Finland and other EU member states.

REPRESENTATIVES - DISTRIBUTORS - FRANCHISERS

The general use of agents in Finland does not differ very much from other Western countries. An agent is usually appointed in order to promote sales of certain products for the account of the principal, which may be done by obtaining purchase offers for the principal or concluding sales agreements in the name of the principal. The Act on Sales Representatives and Salesmen (417/1992, "Agency Act") brought the Finnish legislation in line with the EC Directive concerning sales representatives (86/653/EEC). Most of the provisions of the Agency Act are optional and non-mandatory and, thus, the parties' freedom to agree on the terms of the agency has largely been preserved. However, the Agency Act contains some essential non-optional and mandatory rules concerning termination of the agreement and the compensation payable in connection therewith, restrictions of competition and the agent's right to information from the principal.

Pursuant to the Agency Act, a notice period provided for in the Act shall be observed when terminating an agency agreement. If the agency agreement has been in force for less than a year, the notice period is one month. After the first year, the notice period is prolonged by one month at a time at the beginning of each new year, however, the longest notice period being six months. The parties to the agreement cannot effectively agree on a shorter notice period than the notice period provided for in the Agency Act, with the exception that the parties may agree that the agent's notice period shall not become longer than three months.

The principal and the agent may cancel the agreement to end immediately in the event that the other party neglects his obligations or otherwise acts in such a way that it would be unreasonable to demand the contractual relationship to be continued. The parties may also in other cases cause the agreement to expire prematurely, but the party thus terminating the agreement is liable to compensate the damages suffered by the other party for such premature termination.

After the expiration of the agency agreement, the agent is entitled to compensation provided that he has acquired new customers for the principal or significantly increased trade with the principal's old customers. The maximum compensation equals the agent's average remuneration for one year. In case the agent has caused the expiration of the agreement, he is not entitled to compensation. The agent cannot, prior to the expiration of the agency agreement, effectively waive his right to compensation as stipulated in the Agency Act.

If a salesman is an employee of the principal, the labor laws are also applicable to the contractual relationship. The Finnish labor legislation contains numerous mandatory and non-optional provisions, which restrict the right of the employer to terminate the employment agreement (see Section XV). The Agency Act in its turn stipulates that a salesman shall be entitled to a special compensation for his travel, mail and other similar expenses and a daily allowance for travelling.

The foreign company is subject to income tax on sales in case its activities in Finland can be deemed to constitute a permanent establishment in Finland pursuant to Finnish tax laws and the applicable tax treaty. The presence of an agent may under certain circumstances constitute a permanent establishment in Finland.

There are no administrative regulations governing the relationships between the principal and the agent.

The Finnish legislation partly supersedes the terms and conditions of agency agreements, e.g., the agent cannot, prior to the expiration of the agency agreement, effectively waive his right to compensation. The agency agreement may, under Finnish law, be made subject to the laws of another country than those of Finland, and Finnish courts and generally give effect to such choice of law. However, pursuant to the Agency Act, the mandatory provisions of the Act aiming at protecting the agent shall supersede any conflicting provisions of applicable foreign law in case the Act would otherwise apply to the agreement. As a rule, the Agency Act is applicable to an agency agreement in case the place of business of the agent is in Finland.

Commission rates are not regulated in Finland.

The Finnish competition laws are applicable to an agency agreement provided, as a rule, that the agreement may be deemed to restrict competition in Finland. Certain provisions in agency agreements may, e.g., constitute abuse of a dominant market position, which is prohibited per se pursuant to the Act on Restrictive Business Practices (480/1992 as amended). With the main exception of vertical price fixing that is also prohibited per se pursuant to said Act, harmful effects of restrictions of competition included in agency agreements are, in the first instance, to be eliminated by negotiations between the competition authorities and the parties to the agreement.

Finnish law contains no specific rules relative to distributorships. However, due to the similarity of distributorship as compared to an agent relationship, it is possible in certain situations that the Agency Act or the principles of the same by way of application would also be applied to distributorships if so claimed in a Finnish court. The termination rights of a distributor should thus be assessed in light of those of an agent (see Section VII.). The question, as a matter of law and application, has to be considered somewhat unclear.

In Finland, there are no special laws on franchising. However, various other laws, i.e., laws concerning intellectual property, of course, have to be taken into consideration in connection with franchising. Furthermore, like any other contractual stipulations, a provision of a franchising agreement may be mitigated or set aside by a court of law in case the provision is deemed to be unreasonable per se or be or if the application of the provision would be unreasonable. Franchising agreements must comply with Finnish competition laws with respect of which the prohibitions regarding the abuse of a dominant market position and vertical price fixing should be taken into account (see Section VII.).

In case the franchiser hires premises for his own account and allows the franchisee to use them, this would be clearly stipulated in the franchising agreement so that at the termination of the agreement, the franchise would not be tempted to try to misuse the remedies of a tenant provided for in the Tenancy Act. Also, the position of the franchisee should be described thoroughly in the agreement so that at the termination of the agreement, he could not be regarded as an employee or agent of the franchiser.

INTELLECTUAL PROPERTY - LICENSING

Exclusive rights to a trademark can be obtained either by registration, or also without registration if the trademark has become established. The exclusive rights can be maintained ten years from registration, and the registration can be renewed indefinitely for like periods. The application for trademark can be submitted only through a Finnish agent.

A person who has created literary or artistic work has the copyright therein. With certain limitations, a copyright includes the exclusive right to control a work by producing copies thereof and by making it available to the public. The period of protection is, as a rule, for the remainder of the life of the author and for 70 years thereafter.

A patent can be obtained for an invention that can be exploited commercially provided that the invention is new and not obvious in the light of prior art and knowledge. Foreigners wishing to submit a patent application must have an agent in Finland. Patents are normally granted within one to five years from the application date. A granted patent may be maintained for 20 years from the date of filing the patent application. A patent term extension of a maximum of five years can be obtained for medical products and plant protection products in accordance with the European Union Regulations 1768/92 and 1610/96.

Rights to an industrial design (e.g., the shape or ornament of an object) can be obtained by registration. The right to a registered design may be maintained for 5 to 15 years from the day on the application was filed.

It is also possible to apply for utility model rights to technical solutions that can be used industrially. The technical solutions protected by utility model rights comprise, e.g., the shape or construction of an object or a combination of them. A utility model right may be maintained for four to ten years from the day on which the utility model application was filed.

There is no specific legislation on the protection of know-how, but the provisions of the Act on Unfair Business Practices (1061/1978) concerning business secrets may in some cases be applied also to know-how. Pursuant to the Act, no one may, without justification, obtain or attempt to obtain information regarding a business secret or use or disclose information thus obtained. Furthermore, employees are, during the duration of the employment agreement, prohibited from using, without justification, business secrets, which have come to their knowledge during the employment relationship. Employees may also not disclose such business secrets in order to benefit therefrom or to harm another. Violation of the provisions concerning business secrets may lead to fines or a maximum imprisonment of two years.

Finland is a party to the following treaties: Convention Establishing the World Intellectual Property Organisation 1967, Paris Convention for the Protection of Industrial Property 1883-1967, Berne Convention for the Protection of Literary and Artistic Works 1886-1971, Universal Copyright Convention 1952-1971, International Convention for the Protection of Performers, Producers of Phonograms and Broadcasting Organisations (Rome Convention) 1961, Convention for the Protection of Producers of Phonograms Against Unauthorized Duplication of Their Phonograms (Geneva Phonograms Convention) 1971, Nice Agreement Concerning the International Classification of Goods and Services for the Purposes of the Registration of Marks 1957-1977, Protocol Relating to the Madrid Agreement Concerning the International Registration of Marks 1989, Locarno Agreement Establishing an International Classification for Industrial Designs 1968, International Convention for the Protection of New Varieties of Plants (UPOV)1961, Strasbourg

Agreement Concerning the International Patent Classification 1967, Patent Cooperation Treaty 1970, Budapest Treaty on the International Recognition of the Deposit of Microorganisms for the Purposes of Patent Procedure 1977, European Patent Convention 1977 and the Agreement on Trade-Related Aspects of Intellectual Property Rights (TRIPs) 1995.

There are no prior approvals by national investment boards regarding licensing in Finland.

Licensing of patents, trademarks and designs may be reported for registration with the Trade Register. Only thus can a bona fide third party that is unaware of previous licensing be prohibited from registering the latter licensing in his name.

There are no regulatory guidelines regarding the contents of license agreements.

There are no specific exceptions or requirements relating to the licensing of certain types of products.

Royalties from licenses are for taxation purposes deemed to be excessive in a group of companies if they are higher than they would be between any other arbitrary companies at arm's-length. In this case, provisions on concealed distribution of dividends would be applicable.

The Finnish competition laws are applicable to restrictions of competition included in license agreements unless such restrictions only have effects outside Finland and Finnish customers are not affected by such restrictions.

Foreign corporations usually enter into the following agreements with their wholly owned subsidiaries in Finland: license/royalty agreements, management and service/trading agreements.

DIRECT INVESTMENT

In Finland, business, trade or professional activities in general may be carried out by either sole proprietorships or corporate entities. The principle of free enterprise has been manifested in the Freedom of Trade Act (122/1919, as amended). Accordingly, natural persons domiciled in a state within the European Economic Area (the "EEA"), Finnish associations and foundations, and duly registered branches of EEA associations and foundations are, as a general rule, entitled to carry on a legitimate trade or business without prior permission from the government. Unless Finland's international obligations provide otherwise, other natural and legal persons are entitled to carry on a trade or business in Finland only if they are granted a permit by the Ministry of Trade and Industry and fulfil certain requirements set forth in specific legislation. Often such permits are mere formalities.

It should be noted, however, that due to strong public interests certain types of trade and business, whether carried out by Finnish or non-Finnish persons or entities, are subject to permit requirements. Often the sole purpose of such permit requirements is to ensure that persons engaged in the trade or business concerned are competent and sufficiently committed.

With certain exceptions specified by law, the form of carrying out a trade or business in Finland may be freely elected. Presently, Finnish law recognizes the following forms of doing business:

- Sole Proprietorships;
- General partnerships (avoin yhtiö, öppet bolag);
- Limited partnerships (kommandiittiyhtiö, kommanditbolag);

- Public limited companies (julkinen osakeyhtiö (oyj), publikt aktiebolag (abp));
- Private limited companies (yksityinen osakeyhtiö (oy), privat aktiebolag (ab));
- Co-operatives (osuuskunta, andelslag); and
- European Economic Interest Groupings (eurooppalainen taloudellinen etuyhtymä (ETEY), europeisk ekonomisk intressegruppering (EEIG)).

Choosing the appropriate form of doing business is singularly important since such matters as tax treatment, exposure to liability, efficiency and methods of administration vary significantly between these forms. If the owner wishes to limit his personal liability, the limited company is a natural choice, whereas the partnership provides far-reaching opportunities to withdraw invested property from the company at any given time. The most popular form of doing business in Finland is, by far, the limited company and also foreign investment in Finland usually takes the form of a limited company, which is governed by the Companies Act (734/1978, as amended). The Companies Act provides regulation on private as well as public limited companies.

By purchasing the stock or assets of an existing company, the foreign enterprise may reach its investment goal sooner than by, e.g., creating a subsidiary, but it may also take some time to adopt the existing company to the needs of the foreign enterprise (registration of amendments to Articles of Association, etc.). A subsidiary can be created to the exact needs of the foreign enterprise.

A Limited Partnership company has two different types of partners -- partners with unlimited liability and silent partners with limited liability, whereas a General Partnership consists of a partnership with two or more partners all of whom are jointly and severally responsible for the liabilities of the partnership.

A foreign corporate body or trader may establish a branch office in Finland. To this date, only a small number of foreign branch offices have been established in Finland, which may be due to the fact that the operations of a branch are not governed by any specific rules applicable to corporations in general. A branch is not considered an independent legal entity, wherefore its foreign "parent" is fully responsible for its liabilities. A branch, which shall be registered with the Trade Register, is, however, separately subject to taxation and may act as plaintiff and defendant before a court of law. A branch office, unlike a limited company, does not need to observe any particular equity ratio rules that would limit its possibilities to transfer funds to its foreign parent company.

By participating in a joint-venture company or partnership with a Finnish partner, the foreign investor may be the advantage of local know-how and expertise.

In addition to the above listed forms of doing business, there are a few other associations that may, to a limited extent, engage in business activities. Housing Associations, which are organized by private apartment and homeowners for the administration of their common affairs, are governed by the 1991 Housing Associations Act. Foundations, which are governed by the 1930 Foundations Act, may also engage in business activities, often in the form of holding companies. Unincorporated associations, too, are encountered in the business world, but often their economic activities are restricted by their bylaws or to such enterprises that are directly related to the aims of the association.

All of the above mentioned company types must be reported for registration with the Trade Register. Fees for registration with the Trade Register of the National Board of Patents and Registrations are FIM 1,500 for a limited company and a branch and FIM 700 for a limited partnership and a general partnership. The registration procedure requires approximately one to three months from reporting the company for registration with the Trade Register.

Limited companies should be reported for registration within six months from the signing of the Memorandum of Association of the company.

A limited company might not, before it has been registered, acquire rights or assume liabilities, nor may the company sue or bring or defend actions in a court of law or before other authorities. The Board of Directors may, however, plead in actions concerning the formation of the company and may otherwise take action for the payment of subscribed shares.

If liabilities arise through measures taken in the name of the company before the company has been registered, the persons who have taken part in said measures or in the decisions thereon will be jointly and severally responsible therefor. When the company is registered, the liability is transferred to the company if it has arisen from the Memorandum of Association or otherwise after the Constitutory Shareholders' Meeting.

It is thus possible that the persons acting on behalf of the company enter into government contracts, hire local labor, open a bank account, import equipment, obtain work permits and import and export materials before the company is registered.

Failure to register with the Trade Register can result in fines.

There no major financing restrictions imposed on foreign owned companies. However, the rules regarding so-called thin capitalization are applicable, i.e., the company cannot deduct from its taxable funds the part of the debt that is to be considered as investment of capital to the company. Also, thin capitalization may also cause piercing of the corporate veil and thus result in parent liability for subsidiary obligations.

Intercompany agreements of different types are permitted if they are entered into on general terms and cannot be considered to differ essentially from agreements that other companies at arm's-length would be entering into between each other.

PURCHASE BY FOREIGN CORPORATION OF BUSINESS IN FINLAND

The restrictions on foreign ownership of shares in Finnish limited companies were generally abolished as of January 1, 1993. Shares in Finnish companies can, in principle, be acquired by foreign investors without the approval of the authorities. Finnish law contains no general requirement that a certain percentage of Finnish companies be held by Finnish citizens or legal entities held by Finnish citizens.

The Act on the Control of Acquisition by Foreigners of Finnish Companies (1612/1992, the "Control Act") provides certain governmental control possibilities for purposes of protecting essential national interests. The provisions of the Control Act, apart from those that regard acquisition of companies within the defense industry, do not, however, apply to legal and natural persons from the EEA member states or member states of the OECD.

The Finnish Act on Restrictions on Competition ("the Competition Act, 480/1992, as amended) covers the following practices:

(i) vertical price-fixing and collusive arrangements in connection with competitive bidding;

(ii) horizontal agreements or concerted practices between traders operating at the same level of production or distribution, which determine or recommend prices, restrict production, or share markets or sources of supply;

(iii) abuse of a dominant position; and

(iv) other restrictive business practices.

Practices or agreements covered by the first three categories are prohibited as such, whereas harmful effects on competition resulting from the fourth category, "other restrictive business practices", are to be eliminated in the first place by negotiation between the Competition Office and the party or parties concerned. If no agreement is reached, the practices may be prohibited by the Competition Council. Such prohibition is, in practice, not always needed, as traders often amend their conduct if required to do so by the Competition Office.

The Competition Act applies to goods and services, which are collectively termed "commodities". The agricultural sector also falls within the scope of the Competition Act, except for those arrangements concerning the primary production of agricultural products which promote: (i) the productivity of agriculture; (ii) the operation of the market; (iii) the availability of food supplies; and (iv) the achievement of reasonable consumer prices and a lower price level. If these agreements, to a significant extent, hinder sound and effective competition on the relevant market, or lead to an abuse of a dominant position, the Competition Act shall, however, apply.

The Competition Act applies to all activities by traders. It shall not apply, however, to agreements or practices, which concern the labor market, nor to restrictions on competition outside Finland insofar as they are not directed against Finnish customers.

The relevant legislation on the subject of merger control in Finland is also the Competition Act. Currently the Competition Act does not contain any provisions on merger control that would empower the competition authorities to prohibit a merger, nor does the Competition Act set forth any general duty for a company to submit a notification on mergers or acquisitions. However, in April 1998 the Finnish Parliament enacted considerable amendments, including national merger control provisions, to the Competition Act. Said amendments, which will be presented below, will enter into force on October 1, 1998.

According to the enacted amendments to the Competition Act, concentrations where the combined aggregate turnover of the parties concerned exceeds FIM 2 billion and where the aggregate turnover of at least two of the parties exceeds FIM 150 billion will have to be notified to the Competition Office. The merger control regulations are applicable when at least one of the parties to such concentration is engaged in business activities in Finland. The Competition Council has the power to prohibit a concentration if it creates or strengthens a dominant position as a result of which competition within the field concerned is significantly impeded in the Finnish market or a substantial part of it.

The purchase of real estate, the transfer of land lease agreements under certain circumstances and the transfer of securities are subject to asset transfer tax (see Section XIV.) The practice in Finland is for the asset transfer tax or stamp duty to be borne wholly by the buyer.

BRANCH OFFICES

A foreign company establishing a business in Finland without choosing to incorporate a subsidiary may conduct its business through a branch office. In Finland, the operations of a branch office are not regulated by any specific laws and the general principles of civil law shall therefore apply. Consequently, a branch office is not considered to be an independent legal entity, but merely an extension of the foreign parent company. The parent company is therefore considered to be fully responsible for the liabilities of its branch office. Nevertheless, a branch office is separately subject to taxation in Finland and is also entitled to act as plaintiff and defendant before the Finnish courts.

Establishment of a branch office in Finland has, by virtue of the implementation of the Agreement on the European Economic Area (the "EEA Agreement") and particularly since Finland joined the European Union, become substantially easier and less time consuming. After the conclusion and ratification of the EEA Agreement the statutory formalities have included only a duty to file a notice of registration with the Trade Register and a requirement that the foreign parent company shall have a representative of the branch residing in Finland.

The branch office must be registered with the Trade Register kept by the National Board of Patents and Registration. For the purposes of registration, a basic notice must be filed with the registration authorities before the branch office commences its business operations in Finland. This notice shall contain basic information on the foreign enterprise, on the branch office to be established and on the trade in which the branch will be engaged. The Trade Register notice has to be accompanied by certified copies of the documentation on the establishment of the branch office and the appointment of the individual, citizen of and resident in Finland, who is authorized and entitled to represent the branch office and to sue and defend on its behalf. Documentation proving that the foreign parent body carries on trade in its home country and Register extracts or certificates of the foreign parent body and its statutes, as well as their translations into Finnish or Swedish also have to be submitted.

Foreign entities from non-EEA countries need, in addition to the obligation to register with the Trade Register, permission by the Ministry of Trade and Industry to conduct a business in Finland.

The Finnish tax status of a branch office will be determined on the basis of the status of the foreign parent body. A branch office of a foreign limited company will be taxed in Finland pursuant to the rules relative to the taxation of Finnish limited companies. Assuming this to be the case, there are few differences in the taxation of a Finnish subsidiary limited company and a Finnish branch office of a foreign company.

There are no additional withholding taxes on branch offices.

No further prior approvals than the above mentioned are required.

INCORPORATION

A limited company is by far the most frequently used type of business by foreign investors in Finland. If a limited company is formed according to the provisions in law, the shareholders' responsibility for the company's liabilities is limited to the share capital. In a limited partnership, there are two types of partners: those jointly and severally responsible towards third parties for the liabilities of the partnership and those whose responsibility is limited only to the funds they have invested in the partnership (silent partners). In a general partnership, all of the partners are responsible for the liabilities of the partnership.

All Finnish limited companies are subject to the provisions of the Act on limited companies (the "Companies Act", 734/1978, as amended). As a general rule, the Finnish Companies Act applies to all limited companies, private as well as state owned, family enterprises as well as enterprises the shares of which are subject to public trading. Banks and insurance companies limited by shares are regulated by specific legislation. Provisions of such specific legislation usually supersede the provisions of the Companies Act.

Under the Finnish Companies Act, limited companies are divided into public limited companies and private limited companies. The name of a private limited company must include the term "osakeyhtiö" in Finnish or "aktiebolag" in Swedish or the respective abbreviations "Oy" or "Ab", whereas the name of a public limited company must include the words "julkinen osakeyhtiö" in Finnish or "publikt aktiebolag" in Swedish, the respective abbreviations of which are "Oyj" and "Abp". The minimum share capital requirement for a private limited company is FIM 50.000 and for a public limited company FIM 500.000.

A limited company may be established by one or more natural or legal persons, who are the founders. The domicile of at least half of the founders has to be in a state within the European Economic Area ("EEA"), unless the Ministry of Trade and Industry grants an exemption from this rule. A legal person is considered to have its domicile within the EEA when it has been established in accordance with the rules and regulations applicable in a member state and when its registered office, central administration or head office is located in a EEA member state. A person who is legally incompetent or declared bankrupt may not act as the founder of a limited company.

There are no specific requirements regarding the minimum number of shareholders nor on the number of shares. Accordingly, all shares issued may be held by one or more shareholders. As a general rule, the shareholders are not subject to any requirements regarding nationality or domicile.

For the formation of a limited company, the following is required:

(i) a Memorandum of Association;
(ii) a subscription of the shares of the company;
(iii) a constitutory shareholders' meeting;
(iv) a board meeting; and
(v) a notice to be filed with the Trade Register in Finland.

Not until the limited company has been registered with the Trade Register may it, in the capacity of independent legal entity, acquire rights or undertake obligations. Persons who have undertaken or participated in actions or decisions taken on behalf of the company prior to its registration are jointly and severally liable for any obligations incurred on the basis of such actions or decisions. Once the company has been registered, the liability for these obligations is transferred to the company, provided that the obligation either arises from the Memorandum of Association or the action or decision, as applicable, has been taken after the constitutory shareholders' meeting. The share capital of a limited company must be paid in full prior to the registration of the company.

It should be noted that the incorporation of a limited company becomes final only when the company is registered with the Trade Register.

A limited partnership, as well as a general partnership, is formed by a deed of partnership in which the partners regulate their reciprocal rights and obligations and which should contain all the conditions agreed upon relating to the partnership. An absolute requirement that will have to be fulfilled in order for a partnership to be able to engage in business or trade operations, is that the partnership is registered with the Trade Register. The registration has no constitutive effect, however, since the partnership legally exists from the moment of concluding the partnership agreement.

Finnish law contains no general requirement that a certain percentage of a Finnish company be held by Finnish citizens or legal entities owned by Finns.

The management of a limited company is vested with the Board of Directors and, where applicable, with the Managing Director and the Supervisory Board.

The Board of Directors shall consist of at least three members, unless the share capital is less than FIM 500,000 in which case the board may consist of one or two ordinary members and at least one deputy member. The members of the Board of Directors are normally elected by the General Meeting of Shareholders or by the Supervisory Board. Less than half of the board members may be appointed otherwise, if so stipulated in the Articles of Association. At least one half of the board members must be residents of an EEA member state unless an exemption is granted to this end by the Ministry of Trade and Industry. Persons legally incompetent or bankrupt may not act as members of the Board of Directors of the company.

There are no specific regulations as to where the meetings of the Board of Directors have to take place. The Board may also take unanimous resolutions without convening. The General Meeting of Shareholders shall be held in the company's domicile unless it is stated in the Articles of Association that they can be held somewhere else in Finland. For especially important reasons, the General Meeting of Shareholders may also be held elsewhere.

No specific incentives for direct foreign investment exist. The Government encourages investments in business in a number of different ways, such ways basically being: i) tax incentives, and ii) direct subsidies. All Finnish companies have access to assistance from the government. Due to the membership in the European Union, EU funding has become an important part of government assistance.

In some areas classified as development areas, companies are entitled to accelerated tax depreciations on certain qualifying investments in machinery and industrial buildings.

Accelerated depreciations are accepted upon the request of the taxpayer in the tax return, in case the requirements relating to the location and the type of investment are met. The taxpayer will have to show that the same accelerated depreciations are also applied in the accounts of the company and that the machinery and the buildings to which the accelerated depreciations are to be applied are sufficiently specified in the accounts of the company. A report stating the type and the time of the investment will also have to be attached to the tax return.

EXCHANGE CONTROLS

Finland has abolished most of the currency regulation system previously in force, as a result of which the Bank of Finland, which is the central bank, no longer regulates foreign movements of capital. The only remaining provisions are related to the risk control of the financial institutions and to the supply of information for balance of payment statistics. Financial institutions, such as deposit banks, mortgage banks and credit institutions, must seek authorization to obtain and arrange foreign credit or to make foreign investments. Consequently, exchange restrictions do not apply, *inter alia*, to the following transactions carried out by entities other than financial institutions:

(i) payments of imports or exports;
(ii) currency account transactions;
(iii) outbound/inbound direct investments;
(iv) purchases or sales of portfolio investments; and
(v) repayment of capital, interest, dividends etc.

Under the regulation currently in force, residents of Finland are for statistical purposes required to report their foreign-currency transactions exceeding FIM 50.000 to the Bank of Finland. If the foreign payment is made through an authorized financial institution, the institution will automatically supply the required information to the Bank of Finland. In case the payment is made otherwise, it must be reported to the Bank of Finland personally by the resident in question. However, this reporting requirement will be abolished on January 1, 1999.

The convertability of the Finnish markka is unrestricted.

Earnings from direct investment (including the surplus of a branch office) may be transferred to non-resident shareholders abroad through an authorized bank.

There are no limitations on the purchase of foreign exchange.

Dividends and royalties paid by a Finnish company to foreign recipients are, as a rule, subject to Finnish withholding tax at a rate of 28 %. However, these withholding taxes are often reduced to 0 - 15 % in Finnish tax treaties.

Interest paid to foreign creditors on assets deposited in a credit institution in Finland, bonds, mass debt instruments and loans, which shall not be considered equity of the debtor, is according to Finnish internal legislation exempted from Finnish withholding tax.

There are no special taxes on income repatriation.

No foreign exchange limitations are related to capital remittances when operations are wound down or dissolved.

According to Finnish labor legislation, payments of salaries to employees shall be made in local currency. Additional benefits may, however, be agreed between the employer and the employee.

TAXATION

In the 1980s Finland implemented a tax reform aiming at a broader tax base and lower rates. This was, in the beginning of the 1990s, followed by the adoption of the newly created Nordic model of income taxation, which involved a still more fundamental structural change in the income tax system. The Nordic model is based on the following three elements:

(i) a clear distinction between capital income and earned income;
(ii) a relatively low proportional tax on capital income; and
(iii) a progressive tax on earned income.

Income tax laws based on this model entered into force in 1993. The main sources of tax law are the Income Tax Act (1535/1992, as amended) and the Business Income Tax Act (360/1968, as amended), which govern, among other things, the taxability of income and the deductibility of expenses as well as the computing of income tax.

National income tax, municipal income tax and net wealth tax are the principal direct taxes in Finland. As stated above, earned income of individuals is taxed progressively by the state. Earned income is also subject to church tax and municipal income tax, which are imposed at flat rates. Income earned by corporations and the capital income received by individuals are subject to national income tax at a flat rate of 28 %.

Apart from income tax, individuals and corporations are charged inheritance and gift tax, real estate tax and asset transfer tax.

The principal indirect taxes are value added tax, which is charged on sales and imports, and excise tax, which are charged on certain products and energy.

A resident individual is subject to Finnish national income tax and municipality income tax in the municipality or the city in which he or she has a domicile. Individuals are subject to tax on their global income only to the extent that they are deemed to be resident in Finland during the tax year. An individual is deemed to be resident if he resides in Finland for a continuous period of 6 months or more or if he has a permanent abode in Finland. Non-residents are subject to tax on the income they have derived from Finland.

A Finnish company is liable to Finnish income tax on its global income at a flat tax rate of 28 %. Since a Finnish subsidiary of a foreign corporation is established in accordance with Finnish law, the subsidiary is for Finnish tax purposes resident in Finland and liable to pay Finnish income tax on its global income. A foreign company with a permanent establishment in Finland is taxed at the same income tax rate of 28 % on the income from the permanent establishment.

The question whether a foreign company has a permanent establishment in Finland is normally resolved in accordance with the provisions of the applicable tax treaty. Income tax payable by the Finnish permanent establishment of a foreign corporation is computed according to the same rules applicable to resident corporations. A Finnish branch of a foreign company usually constitutes a permanent establishment and is thus taxed on the profits attributable to the branch.

Sole proprietorships and general and limited partnerships are not treated as separately taxable entities.

Sole proprietorships are generally used by individuals for entrepreneurial businesses. The business income of a sole proprietor is calculated according to the rules of the Business Income Tax Act but is thereafter for tax computation purposes divided into elements of earned income and capital income according to specific provisions laid down in the Income Tax Act. The net income earned by a partnership is computed in accordance with the rules of the Business Income Tax Act. No income tax is, however, levied on partnerships since partnerships are not treated as independent entities for tax purposes. Once computed, the income of the partnership is for tax purposes considered divided between the partners in proportion to their holdings in the partnership, unless otherwise agreed among the partners. If a partner liable to pay tax for his share of the income of the partnership is a natural person, the income allocated on him shall be divided into elements of capital income and earned income in accordance with specific rules in the Income Tax Act.

A company is, in its capacity as employer, obliged to withhold preliminary taxes on salaries paid to persons liable to tax in Finland if the salaries are paid in Finland. The obligation to pay employer's social security charge in Finland is linked to the obligation to withhold preliminary taxes. Consequently, if such an obligation exists, the employer is also obliged to pay the employer's social security charge. The social security charge payable by an employer equals 4-6.5 % of the gross salary.

According to the Act on Employment Pensions, each employer shall provide for and defray the costs of a pension cover for each of his employees whose employment relationship has continued for at least one month. The pension insurance premium is in 1998 approximately 21.5 % of the salaries paid. The employer's contribution is 16.8 % and the employee's 4.7 %. The employer deducts the employee's contribution from the employee's salary before payment. The contributions are paid to domestic pension insurance companies offering such insurances.

Individuals generally liable to pay taxes in Finland are subject to Finnish net wealth tax on their global net wealth, if its value exceeds FIM 1,100,000. The term net wealth may generally be defined as the market value of the assets less the liabilities of the individual. Finnish limited companies and co-operatives are exempted from wealth tax.

Non-residents are liable to pay net wealth tax on their Finnish assets. In case the non-resident is a corporation, net wealth tax is assessed at the rate of 1 % of net assets (assets less liabilities). Non-resident individuals are, on the other hand, liable to pay wealth tax in case the value of their net wealth exceeds FIM 800,000. Wealth tax equals in this case to 0.9 % of the net wealth in excess of FIM 800,000. Non-residents are, however, not liable to pay wealth tax on certain debt instruments, on funds deposited in financial institutions or on receivables accruing from foreign trade.

In addition to value added tax (VAT) being charged on domestic supply of goods and services in Finland, VAT is also imposed on the importation of goods. VAT is levied on the total amount payable, excluding VAT.

VAT is levied on the sale of goods and the supply of services in the form of business operations in Finland. VAT is levied even if the seller is a foreign taxable person and the sale or supply is not conducted from a permanent establishment in Finland. When the seller is a foreign taxable person without a permanent establishment in Finland, the buyer is, as a rule, liable to pay VAT for goods and services sold in Finland. If the foreign entity has a permanent establishment in Finland, as is the situation if the company issuing the invoices to clients in Finland establishes a branch in Finland, the branch is entered into the VAT register as Finnish taxable entity and the rights, obligations and other regulations pertaining to Finnish taxable entities apply to it as well.

Certain types of goods and services are excluded from the value added taxation. Exemptions apply, *inter alia*, to the conveyances of real property, education, health care, social welfare and financial and insurance services.

The general VAT tax rate tax for the time being is 22%.

The purchase of real estate, the transfer of land lease agreements under certain circumstances and the transfer of securities are subject to asset transfer tax. The asset transfer tax on the purchase of real estate and on transfers of land lease agreements is levied at a rate of 4 % of the purchase price. Asset transfer tax on the transfer of securities is levied at the rate of 1.6 % of the purchase price. Share transfers on the Helsinki Exchanges are, however, exempted from asset transfer tax.

The Council of State has during the spring of 1998 submitted a bill to Parliament proposing that the stamp duty currently levied at a rate of 1.5 % on loan agreements and mortgages would be abolished. Honorary titles and certain types of licenses would, however, still be subject to stamp duty.

Finland has entered into quite an extensive number of double taxation treaties affecting the taxation of income and net wealth. The treaties are (with few exceptions) closely based on the OECD Model Tax Convention. The older Finnish treaties were based on the exemption method (with progression clause), but since 1975 Finland has used the credit method in its treaties. Finland has a double taxation treaty with Argentina, Australia, Austria, Barbados, Belgium, Brazil, Bulgaria, Canada, China, Croatia (the tax treaty between Finland and former Yugoslavia), Czech Republic, Denmark (incl. The Faroe Islands), Egypt, Estonia, France, Germany, Greece, Hungary, Iceland, India, Indonesia, Ireland, Israel, Italy, Japan, the Republic of Korea, Latvia, Lithuania, Luxembourg, Malaysia, Malta, Morocco, the Netherlands, New Zealand, Norway, the Philippines, Poland, Portugal, Republic of Pakistan, the Philippines, Poland, Portugal, Rumania, Russia (the tax treaty between Finland and former Soviet Union), Singapore, Slovakia (the tax treaty between Finland and former Czechoslovakia), Slovenie (the tax treaty between Finland and former Yugoslavia), South Africa, Spain, Sri Lanka, Sweden, Switzerland, Tanzania, Thailand, Turkey, the Ukraine, the United Arab Emirates, the United Kingdom, the United States of America and Zambia.

Foreign expenses actually incurred by a Finnish company for the purposes of obtaining income are, as a rule, deductible. However, arm's-length prices must be applied in transactions between affiliated companies.

Outside management fees, technical assistance, licensing fees and lease payments to parent or related companies are, as a rule, deductible where such expenses have actually been incurred for the purposes of obtaining income for the Finnish company concerned. However, the principle of arm's-length pricing is applied by the tax authorities when considering the deductibility of a transaction between related companies.

The principal restriction on intercompany transactions is that the principle of arm's-length pricing shall be applied when considering their acceptability from the fiscal point of view.

According to a specific Act on Group Contributions, companies within the same group may, provided that certain strict requirements are met, pay group contributions as a means of setting off losses against profits between different companies within the group. Group contributions are only allowed when made between Finnish limited companies conducting business activities and belonging to the same group. The other requirements for group contributions between such companies are:

(i) one of the companies must hold, directly or indirectly, at least 90 % of the share capital of the other company, or they must both be under common control of one or more companies holding at least 90 % of both companies;

(ii) the above mentioned ownership relationship must have existed throughout the entire fiscal year of both companies;

(iii) the fiscal year of both companies must end simultaneously, unless the Accounting Board has granted an exemption from this requirement; and

(iv) neither the payer nor the payee of the group contribution may be a bank, credit, pension or insurance institution.

The group contribution is a deductible expense of the payer and taxable income of the receiver. The group contribution may not exceed the net income of the business activities of the payer before the deduction of the group contribution.

LABOR

In the Finnish labor legislation, the concept of "employment relationship" is of considerable importance. According to the Finnish Act on Employment Agreements, the employment relationship is a contractual relationship in which the employee has agreed to work for another party, the employer, under the direction and supervision of the latter for salary or other remuneration. When the existence of employment relationship can be established, the labor laws are applicable to the relationship.

The most important sources of regulations regarding the employment relationship are the Finnish labor legislation and the collective agreements entered into between various labor unions and the employers' associations. The purpose of the collective agreements is to establish a certain minimum level of working conditions in the employment contracts. The employer shall observe the conditions of a general nationwide collective agreement established in the field concerned for the relevant work or work closely comparable therewith, regardless of the fact that the employer and the employee would not be members of respective labor or employers' unions.

A foreign business is not, as such, under any obligation to employ Finnish nationals and, consequently, the percentage of payrolls paid to local employees is free of regulation. However, the foreign business may need to employ local nationals due to the rules concerning, for example, managing director, board members in limited companies and partners in partnerships (see Section XII. above).

The issue of residence and work permits for aliens is regulated in the Act on Foreigners (378/1991, as amended). The regulation naturally differs depending on whether the alien in question is a citizen of an EEA member state or not. Traditionally, Finland has conducted a fairly restricted policy regarding the possibilities of foreigners to establish themselves in Finland, which is illustrated by the low number of alien residents in our country.

The regulation in the Act on Foreigners regarding EU-nationals is equivalently applicable on citizens of EEA member states. A foreigner who is a citizen of an EU member state shall be granted a residence permit for a period of time limited to five years. An EU-national entering Finland for other reasons than tourism but without a residence permit, shall, according to the provisions of the Act on Foreigners, be granted such permit. An EU-national is not required to obtain a residence permit if his or her stay in another EU member state is limited to three months. For purposes of finding a job, an EU-national may also be entitled to stay in the country for a longer period than three months, provided that the possibilities to find a job are realistic.

In accordance with relevant EC regulations, the Act on Foreigners sets forth that an EU-national is not obliged to apply for a work permit in order to be able to engage in gainful employment in Finland. The same regulation is applicable on the employee's spouse and their children to the age of 21 years or until they are no longer economically dependent. According to specific provisions in treaties between the Nordic countries, a national of Iceland, Norway, Sweden or Denmark may reside and engage in gainful employment in Finland without a residence or a work permit.

Whereas EU-nationals are, as a general rule, automatically granted a residence permit for five years, non-EU-nationals are granted residence permits in accordance with their respective needs and under the specific requirements set forth in the Act on Foreigners. Whereas EU-nationals may be granted residence permits without specific requirements being fulfilled even if they have entered Finland without such permit, there are certain requirements that have to be fulfilled with respect to non-EU-nationals.

As a general rule, a foreigner, who only has a residence permit for a limited period of time, is obliged to obtain a work permit from the relevant authorities, in order to be able to conclude an employment contract in Finland. The residence permit is a pre-requisite for obtaining a work permit. The foreigner should obtain said permit before entering Finland, but may also under certain conditions apply for the permit once he has entered.

The work permit, if applied for before entry into the country, should be applied for from and is granted by the Finnish diplomatic, trade or consular representation in the individual's home country. If the permit is applied for after entry into the country, it should be applied for from, and is granted by the Immigration Office of the Ministry of Interior. The work permit may be granted for a specified field of employment.

Minimum wages and salaries are stipulated in the collective agreements of the relevant branch of business.

Finnish labor legislation contains restrictions on the weekly and daily working hours of an employee, in addition to which there are stipulations on the compensations payable for supplementary hours as well in labor legislation as in the collective agreements of the relevant branch of business.

Employees are entitled to sick leave, maternity and paternity leave or parent leave, leave for the treatment of their sick children and other similar benefits are from time to time provided by law and the relevant applicable collective agreements. In most situations, the benefits are largely provided for by the state and on a limited basis only by the employer. Employees are entitled to an annual paid vacation of 24 weekdays and, in case the employment has continued for at least one year, of 30 weekdays. Weekdays are considered to be all days except Sundays and certain public holidays. Furthermore, the employee is, under certain conditions, entitled to a holiday premium payable by the employer partly at the start of the vacation and partly at the return from the vacation. The premium in most fields equals 50% of the employee's statutory vacation salary.

The social security system of Finland is a complex mixture of subsystems consisting of national pension law, health insurance, accident insurance, traffic insurance and unemployment funds. The social security system is financed by the social security charges paid by the employers and the employees along with the payment of taxes deducted from the employees' wages and salaries.

The Finnish social security system consists of national pension, employment pension and additional voluntary pensions. All residents of Finland over the age of 16 are covered by the national pensions scheme for retirement (generally at the age 65), disability and unemployment. The national pension contribution consists of a flat basic amount and a supplementing amount, which depends on income, marital status and the place of residence.

The Employment Pensions Scheme supplements the basic security provided by the National Pensions Scheme and covers all employees at the age of 14 - 64. The employment pension provides employees with security for retirement, disability, unemployment and certain other situations. The amount of employment pension contributions depends on the salary received in the person's employment relationships and the number of years the employee has been employed. (See Section XIV.)

The Finnish regulations concerning the employment agreements are usually applicable to the foreign employees also, if the employer is a Finnish company (i.e., a company established according to the Finnish law.

Foreign personnel working in Finland have the same rights to social benefits as Finnish citizens as long as they are resident in Finland. After leaving Finland, the citizens of the Member States of the EEA and EU, as well as citizens of Switzerland, Canada, Quebec, Estonia and the USA maintain their right to pension from Finland. Citizens of other countries may receive pension from Finland if they are granted such right by the Finnish Pension Security Centre.

A written employment contract is not necessary in order to establish an employment relationship (see Section XV. above).

The employee may always terminate his employment agreement with the employer, whereas the employer may terminate the employment agreement only provided that specific grave reasons exist. These reasons have not been specified in law but are considered separately in each case. However, certain matters have been enumerated in the Act on Employment Agreements as not constituting specific grave reasons. Such unacceptable reasons are temporary decrease of work, illness or pregnancy, participation in strikes and other lawful industrial conflicts, political, religious and other similar convictions and memberships in lawful associations.

Unlawful termination of the employment agreement by the employer will entail an obligation on the employer to compensate the employee for the damage suffered. Such damages shall equal a minimum three months' and a maximum twenty-four months' salary depending on (besides general circumstances of both the employee and the employer), in particular, the employer's manner of proceeding in terminating then employment, the cause given by the employee for the termination, the employee's estimated loss of salary, age and possibilities in the future to get work commensurate with his profession or education and other comparable matters.

The 1978 Act on Cooperation within Enterprises sets out procedural rules concerning, *inter alia*, terminations of employment and lay-offs caused by financial, productional or other equivalent reasons. The Act provides that Finnish companies employing at least 30 employees regularly, or at least 20 employees when the employer is considering the termination of at least 10 employments, are obliged to discuss the reasons for the planned lay-offs or terminations, their effects and possible alternatives with the employees concerned before any decisions are made. The Act only requires that the stipulated negotiation procedures are observed, while the employer still maintains the exclusive right to decide on lay-offs and terminations.

DISSOLUTION

If the Board of Directors, when preparing the annual accounts or otherwise establishes that the equity of the company does not amount to at least one-half of the share capital, the Board shall without delay prepare an interim balance sheet in order to determine the financial position of the company and have the balance sheet audited. The Board shall, within two months from the preparation of the balance sheet, convene the General Meeting of Shareholders to consider the entering of the company into liquidation. If, at the following General Meeting of Shareholders, held within twelve months from the first mentioned General Meeting of Shareholders, it is not established when adopting the balance sheet that the equity of the company amounts to at least one-half of the share capital, the company shall be entered into liquidation. These rules apply also to foreign-owned companies.

A private person who is insolvent can be adjudged bankrupt either by his own petition or by a creditor's petition. A company entered into liquidation shall be entered into bankruptcy proceedings if the assets of the company are not sufficient for settling its debts. The bankruptcy petition shall be filed by the liquidator, but the creditors are also entitled to file the bankruptcy petition during liquidation proceedings.

Further, a company may also without preceding liquidation procedure, either by its own petition or by the petition of its creditors, be entered into bankruptcy proceedings. In the first mentioned case, the competent court of law declares the debtor bankrupt. In case a creditor has filed a petition for bankruptcy, the court of law summons the debtor to a hearing of the debtor, in which hearing the court of law shall decide whether the petition of the creditor is justified, and if this is the case and the debtor cannot immediately satisfy the creditors, the court shall declare the debtor bankrupt. After the debtor has been declared bankrupt, a hearing of the creditors will take place. Approximately two to four months later, the securing of claims will take place, and within three to four weeks from the bar date regarding the securing of claims, creditors may file objections against the claims filed by other creditors. The judgement in bankruptcy is then adjudged within two months.

Foreign-owned Finnish limited companies are not required to deposit any security with regard to the possibility of insolvency. Branch offices of non-Finnish companies are, however, required to deposit security for three years' state and municipal taxes and public dues when applying for a permission to do business in Finland.

The Act on Reorganization of Companies (25.1.1993/47, as amended) is to a large extent based on the Chapter 11 procedure applied in the United States.

INTERNATIONAL RELATIONSHIPS

Finland has not been involved in many international trade disputes. Also, the trade disputes to which Finland has been a party can be characterized as quite occasional. It has not usually taken a particularly long time to settle the disputes, and an amicable settlement has generally been reached.

Finland has entered into several bilateral and multilateral agreements with the United States and other countries. Some of the agreements with the United States can be mentioned: Agreement regarding Arbitration of 1928, Convention for the Avoidance of Double Taxation and the Prevention of Fiscal Evasion with respect to Taxes on Estates and Inheritances of 1952 and the Treaty regarding Visa Requirements of 1958. Among multilateral agreements can be mentioned conventions on OECD of 1960 and the Agreement on Technical Barriers to Trade (regarding GATT) of 1979.

DISPUTE RESOLUTION

Most commercial and other private law matters which may be compromised by agreement are arbitrable under Finnish law. The question of damages in connection with a criminal suit may also be submitted to arbitration. The condition that the subject matter be compromisable by agreement excludes arbitration in settlement of many family law matters and certain commercial matters, such as patents, trademarks and anti-trust matters, partly or wholly. There are no requirements with respect to the parties particular to arbitration.

The parties, and failing them the arbitrators, may, as a general rule, decide on the rules applicable to the proceedings. Such rules may be a national law of procedure or any other rules that the parties may agree on (however not contrary to fundamental legal principles of due process such as audiatur et altera pars). If the parties have not agreed on the applicable rules, an arbitral tribunal seated in Finland is likely to apply the rules laid down in the Finnish Arbitration Act. Such procedural rules are not very numerous but some of them are mandatory.

In order to initiate the proceedings, according to the Arbitration Act, the claimant must give the respondent a written notice of arbitration, setting forth the questions with respect to which an arbitral award is requested.

The parties are free to arrange for the choice or appointment of any number of arbitrators. Failing a decision by the parties in this respect, the Act provides for three arbitrators, one chosen by each party and a chairman chosen by such two arbitrators.

The proceedings normally begin with an exchange of the parties' written pleadings. A general rule is that the parties are given full and equal opportunity to present their case. The arbitrators are free to decide on the evidence that they admit.

The arbitrators will apply the law chosen by the parties to the merits of the dispute; otherwise, the arbitrators of Finnish nationality would be likely to apply the law most closely connected with the matter in dispute. Arbitrators seated in Finland are under no obligation to apply Finnish substantive law or the Finnish rules governing conflict of laws. If arbitrators are more than one and they cannot reach a unanimous decision, the decisions are taken by majority vote.

In order to be valid, the award must be in writing and signed by all of the arbitrators. It is no longer required to file the award with the competent court. Finally, the parties may not reserve themselves the right to appeal to a court. Judicial review of the award on its merits is thus excluded.

The judicial power in Finland is exercised by independent and permanent courts of law. The court system and jurisdiction is based on the division of courts into the general courts of law, administrative courts and special courts.

General legal procedure comprises three instances, with the exception of administrative and special court proceedings that usually comprise only two instances.

The general courts of law are the courts of first instance, the courts of appeal and the Supreme Court. Appeals to the Supreme Court are only permitted if the Court grants leave to appeal. The Supreme Court handles normally only cases with value as precedents and it is not obliged to follow its earlier decisions. Under the jurisdiction of the general courts of law fall all the matters that have not by law expressly been submitted to the special courts or administrative courts. A major part of the matters handled in the general courts of law are civil law or criminal law cases. Aside from the general and administrative courts, there are several special courts with specifically defined jurisdictions. Such special courts are the Land Courts, the Insurance Court, the Labor Court, the Water Rights Court, the Housing Courts and the Market Court. The Supreme Administrative Court is the highest authority in matters involving administrative law. The matters subject to the jurisdiction of administrative courts concern mostly taxation, although almost all administrative decisions made by the authorities can be examined in these courts.

The judges in Finnish courts have a legal education, and although in the courts of first instance lay members quite commonly appear, the chairman is always a professional lawyer. Some members of the special courts are often specialists without legal training, in the matters subject to jurisdiction of that court.

The personal presence of the parties in the court is not usually required and the parties are often represented by advocates or attorneys-at-law. A party appealing in the court need not to be represented or assisted by a professional lawyer, but he may appear without counsel or be represented or assisted by a layman. In practice, legal proceedings are usually handled by professional lawyers. The members of the Finnish Bar Association are called "advocates" or "attorneys-at-law" and the competence of the members and their practice is supervised by the association. An advocate has to have a degree in law and several years practical experience in the field.

Civil proceedings are characterized by pre-trial preparation, oral hearings and a concentrated process. The procedure of the court of appeals has recently been reformed by introducing oral testimony and cross examinations. In the Supreme Court, oral hearings may be held, but in practice this is very seldom the case.

FINLAND CUSTOMS SYSTEM: IMPORTANT INFORMATION

MARKET ACCESS PROCEDURES

INTERNATIONAL CONVENTIONS

Member of World Trade Organisation
Member of OECD
Party to the Kyoto protocol
Party to the Washington convention on International trade in endangered species of wild fauna and flora
Party to the Basel convention on the Control of Transboundary Movements of Hazardous Wastes and their disposal
Party to the Montreal protocol on Substances that deplete the Ozone Layer
Wassenaar arrangement on export controls for conventional arms and dual-use goods and technologies
Party of the International coffee agreement 2001

MAIN INTERNATIONAL ECONOMIC COOPERATION

Finland is a member of European Union and European Monetary Union. The EU is firmly committed to the promotion of open and fair trade with all its trading partners and has multilateral agreements and bilateral agreements trade agreements with several countries.

NON TARIFF BARRIERS

In accordance with its European Union membership, Finland applies the EU rules that are in force in all European Union countries. While the EU has a rather liberal foreign trade policy, there is a certain number of restrictions, especially on farm products, following the implementation of the CAP (Common Agricultural Policy): the application of compensations on import and export of farm products, aimed at favoring the development of agriculture within the EU, implies a certain number of control and regulation systems for the goods entering the EU territory. Restrictions apply to certain items such as products containing alcohol, pharmaceuticals, narcotics and dangerous drugs, explosives, etc. Beef cattle bred on hormones is forbidden to import. The BSE crisis (often called the "mad cow disease") urged the European Authorities to strengthen phytosanitary measures to make sure of the quality of meats entering and circulating in the EU territory. The principle of precaution is now widespread: in case of doubt, the import is prohibited until proof is made of the non-harmfulness of products.

CUSTOMS DUTIES AND TAXES ON IMPORTS

The duties for non-European countries are relatively low, especially for manufactured goods 2.61% or 4.17%. However, textile and clothing items still have high duties and quotas. Click here to access the European Online Customs Tariff Database (TARIC).

CUSTOMS CLASSIFICATION

Finland, like most member states of the European Community, bases its Harmonized Tariff Schedule on the TARIC (Integrated Tariff of the European Community) which is issued by the Commission and the Member States for the purpose of applying Community measures relating to import and exports, and when necessary to trade between member states. The TARIC also serves as a basis for the working tariffs and tariff file of Finland and other Member States.

IMPORT PROCEDURES

A customs declaration for imported goods is submitted on the SAD form (Single administrative document), for VAT levy. It will become mandatory to submit summary declarations electronically within the entire EU territory as of 1 July 2009.

IMPORTING SAMPLES

May qualify for duty free entry if:
- They are of negligible value (EUR 6 or less);
- They are for solicitation of orders for the goods of the kind represented by the sample;
- There is not more than one sample of each style or quality in a consignment;
- The goods are supplied directly from abroad;
- They will be consumed or destroyed during demonstration and are packaged and properly marked in a manner which precludes their being used as other than samples, examples: foodstuffs, non alcoholic beverages, perfumes and chemical products.

STATES AND TERRITORIES INCLUDED IN THE CUSTOMS AND/OR FISCAL TERRITORIES OF THE EU

EU countries and their territories	included in the customs territory of the EU	included in the fiscal territory of the EU
The Netherlands (the territories in Europe)	yes	yes
Belgium	yes	yes
Bulgaria	yes	yes
Spain	yes	yes
-- The Canary Islands	yes	no
-- Ceuta and Melilla	no	no
Irland	yes	yes
Italy	yes	yes
-- Livigno and Campione d'Italia	no	no
-- the Italian waters of Lake Lugano	no	no
Austria	yes	yes
Greece	yes	yes
-- Agia Óros	yes	no
Cyprus	yes	yes
-- Northern Cyprus	no	no
Latvia	yes	yes
Lithuania	yes	yes
Luxembourg	yes	yes
Malta	yes	yes
Portugal	yes	yes
Poland	yes	yes
France	yes	yes

-- overseas departments		
Guadaloupe, French Guyana, Martinique, Reunion	yes	no
-- other overseas departments and territories Mayotte and St.Pierre-et-Miquelon, New Caledonia, Wallis and Futuna, French Polynesia, the French territories in Australasia and on the Antarctic continent	no	no
Romania	yes	yes
Sweden	yes	yes
Germany	yes	yes
-- Helgoland and Büssingen	no	no
Slovakia	yes	yes
Slovenia	yes	yes
Finland	yes	yes
-- The Åland Islands	yes	no
Denmark	yes	yes
Czeck Republic	yes	yes
Hungary	yes	yes
Estonia	yes	yes
The United Kingdom and Northern Irland	yes	yes
-- Gibraltar	no	no

States and territories outside the EU	included in the customs territory of the EU	included in the fiscal territory of the EU
Andorra *)	yes (concerning headings 25-97)	no
The Faeroe Islands	no	no
Greenland	no	no
The Channel Islands	yes	no
The Isle of Man	yes	See ***) and ****)
Monaco	yes	See ***) and ****)
San Marino **)	yes (except headings 72 and 73)	included in the excise territory ****), not included in the VAT territory
The Vatican State	no	no

The customs territory of the Community is defined in Article 3 of the Community Customs Code.

*) In 1990, **the EC and Andorra** established a customs union concerning the trade of goods belonging to chapters 25-97 of the Harmonized System (HS). The Community customs transit procedure was extended to the trade of these goods in 1996. The export and import of goods belonging to chapters 1-24 of the HS is still comparable with the export and import by countries outside the Community.

) In 1992, **the EC and San Marino signed a temporary agreement on trade and on a customs union. The customs union concerns goods in chapters 1-97 of the common customs tariff, except for goods in chapters 72 and 73 of the HS, which are subject to the treaty establishing the European Coal and Steel Community (so called ECSC products). Regulations applied on goods transports between the Community and San Marino were agreed on in the EEC-San Marino Cooperation Committee in 1992.

***) According to Article 7(1) of the Council Directive 2006/112/EC (VAT Directive), in view of the conventions and treaties concluded with France, the United Kingdom and Cyprus respectively, the Principality of Monaco, the Isle of Man and the United Kingdom Sovereign Base Areas of Akrotiri and Dhekelia shall not be regarded, for the purposes of the application of this Directive,

as third countries. According to Article 7(2), however, Member States shall take the measures necessary to ensure that transactions originating in or intended for the Principality of Monaco are treated as transactions originating in or intended for France, that transactions originating in or intended for the Isle of Man are treated as transactions originating in or intended for the United Kingdom, and that transactions originating in or intended for the United Kingdom Sovereign Base Areas of Akrotiri and Dhekelia are treated as transactions originating in or intended for Cyprus.
****) According to Article 2(4) of the Directive 92/12/EEC (System Directive), the Member States shall take the necessary measures to ensure that transactions originating in or intended for:
- the Principality of Monaco are treated as transactions originating in or intended for the French Republic,
- Jungholz and Mittelberg (Kleines Walsertal) are treated as transactions originating in or intended for the Federal Republic of Germany,
- the Isle of Man are treated as transactions originating in or intended for the United Kingdom of Great Britain and Northern Ireland,
- San Marino are treated as transactions originating in or intended for the Italian Republic.

CUSTOMS BASICS FOR TRAVELERS

CUSTOMS RULES

IMPORT REGULATIONS::

Free import for passengers arriving with goods purchased within the E.U. which are for personal use only:
a there is no limit on the quantity of purchases made, inclusive of tax, in the shops of an E.U. country and brought to Finland, provided that these goods are for the travellers own or their families consumption or brought in as a non commercial gift.
b. there is also no limit on the following food items, provided brought in for the travellers own consumption: meat, meat-products, fish, fish-products, milk, milk-products and egg-products from an E.U. country;
Free import to passengers arriving from non-E.U. countries (including the Aland Islands, Canary Islands and similar territories):
1. tobacco products (for passengers aged 17 years of age and over):
- 200 cigarettes; or
- 100 cheroots; or
- 50 cigars; or
- 250g of tobacco; or
- a proportional mix of these products;

2. alcoholic beverages (passengers aged 20 years of age and older may import all of the below; those passengers aged over 18 years of age are allowed to carry only alcoholic beverages with max. 22% vol.):
- 1 litre of spirits over 22% volume, or non-denatured ethyl alcohol with more than 80% volume; or
- 2 litres of spirits or aperitifs made of wine or similar beverages less than 22% volume, or sparkling wines or liqueur wines; or
- a proportional mix of these products; and in addition
- 4 litres still wine; and
- 16 litres of beer;

3. cut flowers, except for chrysanthemums and carnations (from countries outside Europe) and orchids from Thailand;
4. other goods (for air travellers) up to a total value of EUR 430.- per traveller.

Prohibited:
Products of animal origin, not originating from an EU member state, Andorra, Liechtenstein, Norway, San Marino or Switzerland, are not permitted to be imported into an EU Member state,

with the exception of limited amounts from Andorra, Croatia, the Faeroe Islands, Greenland, Iceland and small amounts of specific products from other countries.
For full details, please see or refer to the website of the European Union, http://europa.eu/.
For full details please see Terms & Definitions, section 5. Customs, or refer to the website of the European Union, http://europa.eu/.

ARMS AND AMMUNITION REGULATIONS::

Transfer and importation for private purposes of firearms, parts of firearms and cartridges suitable for use in firearms, requires a permit indicating that the person is authorised to possess the firearm concerned, issued by the police authority at the importer's home municipality or place of residence. The transfer and importation of especially dangerous cartridges or dangerous edged weapons is prohibited.
For more information contact the Police Department of the Finnish Ministry of Interior, tel.: +358-9-1601.

ADDITIONAL INFORMATION ON REGULATIONS::

Import of narcotic drugs is only allowed with special permission from authorities of Finland.

EXPORT REGULATIONS::

Free export:
tobacco products: no restrictions;
alcoholic beverages: passengers of 20 years of age or more up to 12 litres of strong beer and up to 5 litres of other alcoholic beverages (18 years of age only mild ones).

PETS::

Cats and dogs are subject to special regulations (EC) No. 998/2003 of the European Parliament and of the Council. For more information contact the Ministry of Agriculture and Forestry, Department of Food and Health, tel: +358-9-160 53387, fax: +358-9-160 53338. Pets may enter as passengers' checked baggage or as cargo. Birds as pets: import of birds requires an Import License, to be obtained from the Finnish Ministry of Agriculture and Forestry.

BAGGAGE CLEARANCE REGULATIONS::

Baggage is cleared at the airport of final destination in Finland. However, if passenger has goods to declare, he shall notify the customs authorities at the first entry point in Finland:
baggage of passengers who embarked in another E.U. country are exempt;

AIRPORT EMBARKATION TAX

No airport tax is levied on passengers upon embarkation at the airport.

CURRENCY RULES

CURRENCY IMPORT REGULATIONS:

Local currency (Euro-EUR) and foreign currencies: same regulations as for Export apply (see: Export).

CURRENCY EXPORT REGULATIONS:

Local currency (Euro - EUR) and foreign currencies: no restrictions if arriving from or traveling to another E.U. country. If arriving directly from or traveling to a country outside the E.U.: amounts exceeding EUR 10,000.- or more or the equivalent in another currency (incl. banker's draft and cheques of any kind) must be declared.

CUSTOMS SERVICE IN FINLAND

Finnish Customs is a part of the customs system of the European Union. Customs is central state agency supervised by the Ministry of Finance through management by results. Finnish Customs cooperates with the trade community as well as with domestic and foreign authorities.Finnish Customs has approximately 2 400 employees.

CENTRAL ADMINISTRATION, FIVE CUSTOMS DISTRICTS AND THE CUSTOMS LABORATORY

Finnish Customs is subordinate to the Ministry of Finance. The National Board of Customs is the central administration for Finnish Customs. The Director General (since 1998) is Mr Tapani Erling.

The regional administration comprises five customs districts

- Southern Customs District, Director Mr Leo Nissinen (Helsinki)
- Western Customs District, Director Mr Arto Honka (Turku)
- Northern Customs District, Director Mr Juha Heikkilä (Tornio)
- Eastern Customs District, Director Mr Tommi Kivilaakso (Lappeenranta)
- Åland Customs District, Director Christina Ehrnström (Mariehamn)

The **Customs Laboratory** is also part of Finnish Customs, and its operating range covers the whole country. The customs districts and the Customs Laboratory are subordinate to the National Board of Customs.

NATIONAL BOARD OF CUSTOMS

PO Box 512, 00101 Helsinki
Erottajankatu 2
tel. +358 (0)9 6141 (switchboard), Monday to Friday 8 - 16.15
telefax +358 (0)20 492 2852
e-mail: kirmo(at)tulli.fi (to the registry) or firstname.lastname@tulli.fi
From 1 June to 31 August, the registry office is at your service from 9 a.m. to 3 p.m.

Customs Information Service
tel. +358 (0)20 690 600
telefax +358 (0)20 492 1812
You can also contact the Customs Information Service by e-mail using >> Enquiry form

Statistics Service
tel. +358 (0)20 690 603
telefax +358 (0)20 492 1812
e-mail: statistics(at)tulli.fi
Statistics Service's enquiry and order form »
Intrastat
tel. +358 (0)20 690 614

Communications
Director of Communications, Ms Hannele Ahokas, mobile +358 (0)40 332 1870
Head of Communications, Ms Sallamaari Repo, mobile +358 (0)40 332 1869

FINNISH CUSTOMS LABORATORY

Tekniikantie 13, PO Box 53
02151 Espoo
tel. +358 (0)9 6141
telefax +358 (0)9 463 383

DISTRICT CUSTOMS OFFICES

Southern District Office
District Director's Office
Vilhonvuorenkatu 12 B, PO Box 62
00501 Helsinki
tel. +358 (0)9 6141
telefax +358 (0)20 492 1042

Eastern District Office
District Director's Office
Terminaalinkatu 5, PO Box 66
53501 Lappeenranta
tel. +358 (0)9 6141
telefax +358 (0)20 492 5077

Western District Office
District Director's Office
Satamakatu 22, PO Box 386
20101 Turku
tel. +358 (0)9 6141
telefax +358 (0)20 492 4244

Northern District Office
District Director's Office
Hallituskatu 1, PO Box 47
95401 Tornio
tel. +358 (0)9 6141
telefax +358 (0)20 492 8082
Customer service at Kemi Customs Office is closed from 1 January 2010 and moved to Tornio Etelätulli, Tullipuistonkatu 6, Tornio. Opening times: Monday to Friday 8 - 22, Saturday 8 - 19 and Sunday 12 - 20.

Åland Islands District Office
District Director's Office
Torggatan 16, Ämbetshus, PO Box 40
22101 Mariehamn
tel. +358 (0)9 6141
telefax +358 (0)20 492 6077

TRADE REGULATIONS, CUSTOMS AND STANDARDS

MEMBERSHIP IN FREE TRADE ARRANGEMENTS

Finland joined the EU on January 1, 1995. The customs union membership means that Finland complies with trade agreements that the EU has made with third countries. Finland is also a member of the European Free Trade Association and the European Economic Area.

TARIFF AND NON-TARIFF BARRIERS

Finland's adoption of EU internal market practices in 1995 defines Finland's trade relations both inside the EU and with non-EU countries.

Finland's import trade was not greatly affected by EU membership. Changes dealt with border protection procedures related to non-EU countries. Most of these restrictions concern import of certain types of steel, in particular from the NIS, as well as import of certain articles from China. The restrictions are in the form of quotas, licensing and other control measures. The quotas are

EU-wide. Access to quotas may depend on whether the importer is an established traditional supplier or a newcomer.

Finland is now covered by EU antidumping legislation. Finland has also adopted the Generalized System of Preferences (GSP) of the EU. Furthermore, Finland applies import taxes imposed by the EU.

Finland replaced its turnover tax with a value-added tax in June 1994. While the change has had little effect on overall revenues, several areas not previously taxed or taxed at a lower rate, including many corporate and consumer services and construction, are now subject to the new VAT in conformity with EU practices. The government has kept the basic VAT rate at the same level as the old turnover tax, which is 22 percent. Foodstuffs are taxed at 17 percent. Sport facilities usage, medicines, books, cinemas, passenger transport services, hotel and other accommodation, entertainment performances, sporting events, zoos, museums, and other such events or institutions are taxed at 8 percent. Other services, including health care, education, insurance, newspaper & periodical subscriptions and rentals are not subject to VAT. Agricultural and forestry products continue to be subject to different forms of taxation outside the VAT. A uniform tax rate of 28 percent on capital gains took effect in 1996, which includes dividends, rental income, insurance, savings, forestry income, and corporate profits. The sole exception was bank interest, where the tax rate was increased from 20 to 25 percent at the beginning of 1994.

In March 1997, EU Commitments required the establishment of a tax border between the autonomously governed, but territorially Finnish, Aland Islands and the rest of Finland. As a result, the trade of goods and services between the rest of Finland and Aland Islands is now treated as if it were trade with a non-EU area. Even though, the Aland islands are part of the EU, just as Finland is, Aland does not belong to the Unions tax area. This exception was drafted in order to protect the important shipping traffic and the tax-free sales when EU countries abandoned duty-free sales. The trade effect of this treatment is minimal since the Aland Islands are part of EFTA tariff area.

Finland has also introduced EU practices on imports of agricultural products. Some agricultural goods are subject to the standard import licensing system, EU-wide quotas, import taxes or other provisions. Finland, along with other new members, is permitted to take measures, accepted by the EU, to shelter its agriculture or foodstuff sector during a limited transition period. In a temporary exception to general EU procedure, Finland may impose higher tariffs than the EU level on the following items: footwear, rubber, plastic, metals, raw hides & skins and some electric machinery. The transition period ended in 1998. As of July 1, 1996 higher tariffs on textiles, clothing and headgear were abolished.

In mid-1996 the Finnish government's inter-ministerial licensing authority began selectively to oppose within the EU American company applications for commercialization of genetically modified organisms (GMOs) such as insect resistant corn. Finland's attitude towards biotechnology is markedly more open than many other EU Member States and Embassy Helsinki has been working actively with Finnish partners to distribute accurate and scientific information on this emotional issue.

TARIFF RATES

Duties and other import taxes are levied on the customs value of the goods at the point of importation. The customs value is based on the transaction value of the goods imported. In practice, the C.I.F. value is commonly used as the customs value. To assess customs value, the place of importation must be indicated. In the case of sea and air cargo, the place of importation is the unloading location. In surface transportation, it is the Customs Office at the frontier. The customs value is determined according to the GATT Valuation Agreement and the Community Customs Code (Council regulation 2913/92) and the Regulation Laying down Provisions for Implementation of the Customs Code (Commission regulation 2454/93).

PROHIBITED IMPORTS

Finnish law prohibits the import of the following products:

- PCB and PCT chemicals used in transformers and condensers causing problem wastes
- whale meat

EXPORT CONTROLS

Finland is an active participant in all export control regimes, notably the Nuclear Suppliers Group (NSG), the NPT Exporters Committee (Zangger Committee), the Missile Technology Control Regime (MTCR), the Australia Group (AG) and the Wassenaar Arrangement (WA). Finland chaired the Zangger Committee in 1989-93 and the NSG in 1995-96 and will chair the MTCR in 2004-01.

A basic principle of Finland's export control policy is that there is no published or unpublished "black list" of undesired destinations except those subject to sanctions by the UN or the EU. All license applications are considered on a case-by-case basis, taking into account the information exchanged within the relevant export control regime.

- Export Control Authorities -

Ministry for Foreign Affairs is in charge of Finnish non-proliferation policy as well as the security and trade policy aspects of export controls.

Ministry of Trade and Industry is in charge of the national implementation of the European Union's system of export controls on dual-use goods. The Trade Department of the MTI is the authority granting export licenses for exports of dual-use goods. The MTI's Energy Department grants licenses for exports of nuclear materials, facilities and equipment.

Ministry of Defense is in charge of export licenses for exports of defense material (i.e. military goods and technologies).

The Ministry of the Interior is responsible for export and import licenses for non-military firearms and ammunition as well as for national implementation of the relevant EU directives.

IMPORT TAXES AND LICENSE REQUIREMENTS

Finland follows import-licensing procedures of the EU. Licenses can be applied for from the National Board of Customs. Certain agricultural products are subject to import duties and/or fees imposed in accordance with EU rules and regulations. Among the products subject to these duties and fees are cereals, flour, certain fats and oils, fishery products, butter, cheese, eggs, poultry, meat, cattle and hogs. The transitional period that allowed Finland to maintain its stricter (than EU) import regulations on certain agricultural products (primarily meat and livestock) expired in 1998.

CUSTOMS REGULATIONS AND CONTACT INFORMATION

Customs duties are levied on goods imported to Finland. As a member of the EU, Finland is part of the EU wide Customs Territory and applies EU Customs legislation.

You can consult Customs Information for customs related matters.

Suomen Tulli (Finnish Customs)
PL 512
FIN-00101 Helsinki, Finland
Tel: +358 9 614 3800
Fax: +358 9 614 3813

TEMPORARY GOODS ENTRY REQUIREMENTS

Temporary exemption from duty can be granted, for instance, to the following:

- Goods intended for public displays at exhibitions and fairs
- Commercial samples
- Professional tools and equipment

If the goods are put to unauthorized use or are not exported within the prescribed time (maximum one-year) they must go through normal customs clearance and become liable for relevant duties and taxes.

In Finland, the ATA-Carnet, the international customs documentation for temporary duty-free admission is issued by the Chamber of Commerce. The ATA-Carnets are frequently used for temporary imports e.g. samples, exhibition materials, and professional equipment (laptop computers, software), and are valid for one year.

SPECIAL IMPORT/EXPORT REQUIREMENTS AND CERTIFICATIONS

Certain import/export items need to meet with special requirements and certifications set by the EU or national standards. These are mostly articles that might damage health, welfare or the country's economy, or result in the spread of animal and plant diseases.

The following items, among others, are subject to restrictions:
- Foodstuffs, fodder and fertilizers, alcoholic beverages and other products containing alcohol, pharmaceuticals, narcotics and dangerous drugs, some chemicals, nuclear and radioactive substances, explosives, blade knives firearms and ammunition, obscene publications, pressure vessels.

LABELING

Labeling and marking requirements in Finland are based on the Act on Product Safety, which was enacted in accordance with the EU Directive on general product safety. The following information should be included in retail packaging, or otherwise marked on the product (a sticker, label, etc.):

- Name of the product (indicating clearly the contents of the package)
- Name of the manufacturer or the name of the company that had the product manufactured
- Amount of contents (weight or volume of the contents to be specified, measures in metric system).

If warranted by safety considerations or economic security of the consumer, the following information should also be included on the retail packaging or otherwise clearly identified on the product: contents of the product, care instructions, operating instructions, and a warning of possible danger related to the use or disposal of the product.

Finland has precise labeling requirements for foodstuff. A retail-size food package must show the name of the manufacturer, packer or importer, commercial name of the product, net metric weight or volume, ingredients in descending order of weight, last recommended date of sale, and storage instructions if perishable or intended for infants. Mandatory information described above must be provided in Finnish and Swedish.

FREE TRADE ZONES/WAREHOUSES

Finland has one free port in Hanko. Hanko is located at the southernmost tip of the country. The port has a year-round railway-ferry link with Turku. In addition, there are 20 storage areas in other locations in the country. The duty free storage areas, which are usually run by municipal corporations, are available to domestic and foreign-owned companies. Warehousing, assembly and manufacturing are allowed in these areas, with permission from the Board of Customs.

TRADE AND PROJECT FINANCING

THE BANKING SYSTEM

In the last few years, the Finnish banking system has undergone rapid change. The initial impetus for this process was the step-by-step deregulation of financial markets and capital movements in the 1980s as part of the overall financial integration in Europe. Then the recession in the early 1990s and a severe banking and financial sector crisis, aggravated by bad lending practices in the late 1980s, touched off a consolidation of excess banking capacity. Tighter competition ensued from Finland's EU entry, accelerating cost cutting in the sector. Financial consolidation has been accomplished by reducing personnel, closing branch offices and introducing modern banking technology.

The Finnish banking system is dominated by three major groups of deposit banks: Merita Nordbanken, the result of the merger between Merita and Swedish Nordbanken, as well as Okobank (the Cooperative Bank Group) and the 100% government-owned Leonia (former Postipankki). At the end of 1999, a total of 337 domestic banks were operating in Finland, eight of theses being commercial banks, 246 co-operative banks part of the OKO bank group, 43 local co-operative banks and 40 savings banks. The market share of the three largest bank groups was 85 percent of all Euro deposits and 87 percent of all Euro lending. In addition to domestic banks, six foreign banks have branches in Finland: Banque Indosuez Helsinki Branch, Citibank International, Skandinaviska Enskilda Banken, Handelsbanken, Unibank, Hambros Bank and Den Danske Banken. Nine foreign banks have representative offices in Finland.

Early in 2004, MeritaNordbanken and the Danish Unidanmark agreed on a merger. The new bank group will be the largest bank group in the Nordic countries and the total of its balance sheet is calculated to be EUR 186 billion.

The second largest bank group in Finland, Leonia, and the insurance company Sampo announced their merger as the new Sampo-Leonia Group.

Finnish banks have been providing their corporate and retail customers with on-line services for nearly 25 years. In 1998, 80% of all payment transactions reached the banks in electronic form.

The Finnish OKO bank group was the first in the world to offer banking transaction services on the Internet in 1996

Most of Finnish banks offer banking services through WAP (wireless application protocol). Customers are able to handle bank transfers, pay bills, ask for accounting info, send/receive customer mail, do shopping and even buy shares on the Finnish stock market using a WAP phone. First bank in the world to offer WAP banking services was Merita Nordbanken. The service has been available since October 1999.

FOREIGN EXCHANGE CONTROLS AFFECTING TRADE

All Finnish foreign exchange controls have been abolished.

GENERAL AVAILABILITY OF FINANCING

The Finnish financial market is a typically European environment where banks and financing institutions have the dominant role, although insurance institutions play a major role in credit supply. Insurance companies, through their management of compulsory insurance schemes of the public social security system, lend a substantial part of the money back to the companies that pay the compulsory premiums. Financing is also available through the stock exchange and the government's financing systems.

Today, there are about thirty venture capital companies in Finland. They can be divided into five main groups; publicly financed, private, regional, those tied to a bank and those tied to some large-scale enterprise. At the end of 1998, the capital administered by venture capitalists stood at FIM 8 billion, FIM 3 billion of which was invested.

HOW TO FINANCE EXPORTS/METHODS OF PAYMENT

Government-owned companies or agencies provide for financing and guarantees for exports. Depending on the nature of the goods exported and on the risks connected to trading partners, a portion of the export costs must be provided by the company in question. Finland prefers that, in subsidized export financing, (where Finland adheres to OECD principles), international arrangements be made with a minimum of government involvement. In addition to government activities, commercial banks provide financing, with guarantees when possible, for exports. The banks advise their customers on bank loans as well as on loans granted by other credit institutions.

TYPES OF AVAILABLE EXPORT FINANCING AND INSURANCE

Financing and guarantees for exports are provided for by the government-owned Leonia Corporate Bank and Finnvera. Major Finnish government and other programs are detailed below.

Leonia Corporate Bank: In October 1997, the Finnish government decided to combine two state owned Financial institutions – Postipankki Ltd and Finnish Export Credit – under a single holding company called Leonia Group. In the new group Finnish Export Credit became Leonia Corporate Bank (LCB) and sells banking services to large Finnish companies and their foreign investors. LCB is a specialist financial institution providing long-term finance. The company finances exports, industrial and infrastructure investments and other long-term corporate funding requirements. Apart from exports from Finland, the company finances domestic and overseas investments, focusing mainly on the forest and engineering industries, energy production and telecommunications sector. LCB also promotes Finnish exporting with officially supported credits,

credits granted on OECD consensus terms and under the OECD understanding on export credits for ships, and concessional (mixed) credits for developing countries. LCB operates on commercial terms, is founded on good profitability and has a strong capital structure, sophisticated risk management and a first-class credit rating. It is 100 percent owned by the Finnish government (www address: www.leonia.fi)

Finnfund - The Finnish Fund for Industrial Cooperation: Similar to the U.S. government-sponsored OPIC, Finnfund promotes investments in developing countries. Finnfund acts as an agent in Finland for EU programs for the financing of investment in emerging continents. It has recently become very active in the former Soviet Union, particularly Russia and the Baltic countries. Finnfund provides equity capital as well as long term investment loans and also participates in guarantee arrangements. In addition to financing the corporation offers a broad range of fund management and advisory services. Finnfund is owned by the State of Finland, business and industry, and Leonia Corporate Bank (www address: www.finnfund.fi).

NIB - Nordic Investment Bank: NIB is a multilateral financial institution owned by the five Nordic countries. Its head office is located in Helsinki. NIB extends loans and provides guarantees on normal banking terms for export and investment projects in line with Nordic interests. Loans and guarantees are given to investments that assure energy supply, improve infrastructure or support research and development. The core of NIB's international lending consists of project investment loans, which are granted to projects with Nordic participation, usually with a government guarantee. For the last three years, NIB has granted loans to private sector infrastructure projects outside the Nordic region, co-financed with other multilateral financial institutions. It also grants long-term collateralized loans (www address: www.nibank.org)

Finnvera: Finnvera is a specialized financing company promoting Finnish exports by offering export credit guarantees and supporting domestic operations of small and medium sized companies by offering risk financing and guarantees. Owned entirely by the Finnish State, Finnvera was formed by merging the activities of Kera Corporation and the Finnish Guarantee Board (FGB) on January 1, 1999. Finnvera's domestic development and financing solutions are particularly geared towards small and medium- sized companies, and thus Finnvera also helps to promote the government's regional policy objectives. Finnvera is the official Finnish export credit agency (ECA) providing export guarantees and insurance. Finnvera's export credit guarantee and insurance commitments are fully guaranteed by the state of Finland (www.address: www.finnvera.fi).

SITRA and TEKES: SITRA (the Finnish National Fund for Research and Development) and TEKES (the Technology Development Center) are public financing institutions with the purpose of strengthening the role of research in economic life and promoting new products with the aim of introducing internationally competitive high-technology products and production methods. SITRA makes equity-related investments in high-tech companies during their start up and growth stages and finances management buy-outs, spin-offs from large and medium-sized companies (corporate venturing) and the corporation of these new businesses. TEKES stimulates and coordinates research and development projects between Finnish companies, universities and research institutes and their foreign counterparts. Activities should diversify production structures, increase production and exports, and create a foundation for employment and well being (www.address: www.sitra.fi & www.tekes.fi)

Ministry of Trade and Industry: The ministry and its regional Business Service Offices offer subsidies for investment in the form of regional investment aid, aid for small businesses or development aid for small and medium size enterprises (SMEs). Special investment and start-up aid is available for small companies in the whole country, especially in rural areas and structural adjustment areas. This subsidy can be up to 45 percent of the investment in development areas and up to 15 percent elsewhere in the country. SMEs can obtain special development aid for improving their competitiveness in the long run or operations increasing internationalization. The ceiling of aid for product development projects is 35 percent which, however, can be exceeded by 5 percentage points inside the development area. The ceiling of aid for using experts is 50 percent, which is available throughout the country (www.address: www.vn.fi/ktm).

PROJECT FINANCING AVAILABLE

Leonia Corporate Bank and Finnfund provide financing for overseas projects. Participation of third country firms in projects is possible. The Nordic Investment Bank grants investment loans for Nordic projects, and also finances projects in third countries.

BANKS WITH CORRESPONDENT U.S. BANKING ARRANGEMENTS

All principal Finnish banks have extensive correspondent relationships with U.S. banks, maintaining relationships with banks in every state as well as with all of the larger financial center banks. Further information on correspondent relationships can be obtained from the Finnish Bankers' Association, P.O. Box 1009, FIN-00101 Helsinki; Tel: 358-9-4056 120, fax: 358-9-40561-291.

IMPORTANT PRACTICAL INFORMATION RELATED TO CUSTOMS OPERATIONS

EXCISE TAXATION

Harmonised and national excise duties Taxable goods and suspension of excise duty Taxable amounts and tax-free products Moving products subject to suspension of excise duty Tax declaration and taxation Licence and guarantee procedure Products taxed in another EU member state Repayment of excise duty Bookkeeping, submission of information and inspections Advance ruling Appeals

HARMONISED EXCISE DUTIES

EXCISE DUTY ON ALCOHOL AND ALCOHOLIC BEVERAGES

Alcohol and alcoholic beverages are subject to harmonised excise taxation in the member states of the European Union. In Finland, the national provisions are contained in the Act on Excise Duty on Alcohol and Alcoholic Beverages (1471/1994). Excise duty on alcohol and alcoholic beverages is levied on beer, wine, other fermented alcoholic beverages, intermediate products and ethyl alcohol. Taxable products are alcoholic beverages and ethyl alcohol containing alcohol more than 1.2% by volume, intended for human consumption, as well as beer containing alcohol more than 0.5% by volume. The products are classified by alcohol content into categories with different tax rates. Exempt from excise duty are e.g. strongly denatured ethyl alcohol as well as lightly denatured products which are used for the production of goods not intended for human consumption.

Customer Bulletin No. 16, National Board of Customs, April 2010

EXCISE DUTY ON TOBACCO

Excise duty on tobacco products is levied on cigarettes, cigars, cigarillos, smoking tobacco and fi ne-cut tobacco for the rolling of cigarettes. This excise duty is also levied on other products containing tobacco and on products comparable with tobacco products but manufactured of substances other than the tobacco plant. A national excise duty is levied on cigarette paper. The taxation is based on the Act on Excise Duty on Tobacco (1470/1994).

EXCISE DUTY ON LIQUID FUELS

Excise duty on liquid fuels is levied e.g. on petrol and diesel oil as well as on light and heavy fuel oil, aviation petrol and jet fuel. The taxation is based on the Act on Excise Duty on Liquid Fuels (1472/1994). In addition, any products used as motor fuels are subject to this excise duty. Thus, all fuels delivered for use in spark-ignition engines are taxed as petrol (e.g. motor petrol, carburettor spirit, biofuels and special fuels). Correspondingly, also fuels other than normal diesel oil are taxed as diesel oil when delivered for use in diesel engines. The duty is also levied on mineral oils and hydrocarbons used for heating purposes (e.g. paraffi n oil).

Liquefied petroleum gas is not subject to excise duty but using the EMCS system is obligatory also when these products are moved between EU member states (see section "Moving products subject to suspension of excise duty" below). Liquid fuels used for the production of electricity are likewise exempted. Part of the excise duty paid for light and heavy fuel oil used in professional greenhouse cultivation may, on application, be refunded on certain conditions (more information available in Finnish in customer bulletin No. 2 on tax refund to greenhouse growers).

In connection with excise taxation, a strategic stockpile fee is collected on liquid fuels. Both the stock pile fee and the excise duty are assessed on the basis of the volume of the product with a temperature of + 15 °C (so-called normal litre).

On conditions provided by law, repayment of the amount of excise duty and stockpile fee paid may be applied for in respect of fuel used by vessels in merchant shipping or other comparable commercial or administrative operations and in respect of fuel used by vessels in professional fi shing. The maximum return of excise duty that can be repaid for fuel used by vessels equipped with a diesel engine is the equivalent of excise duty on light fuel oil. Vessels specified in the Decree on Excise Duty on Liquid Fuels are entitled to obtain fuel free of excise duty directly from tax warehouses of authorised warehouse keepers (more information available in Finnish in customer bulletin No. 12 on tax exemption regarding vessel fuels).

>> Customer bulletins are available on the Customs website www.tulli.fi/en>Finnish Customs>Publications>Customer instructions

EXCISE DUTY ON ELECTRICITY AND CERTAIN FUELS

Excise duty is levied on electricity and certain fuels used for heat production, such as coal, natural gas and tall oil. The taxation is based on the Act on Excise Duty on Electricity and Certain Fuels (1260/1996). A strategic stockpile fee is levied also on natural gas, electricity and coal. Natural gas coming from outside the EU is taxed in connection with customs clearance and in accordance with the provisions on the customs clearance procedure. In the case of combined production of electricity and heat, only the fuels used for generating heat are taxed.

Liable to pay excise duty on electricity are mainly electricity producers and (electricity) network operators, who have to register with the customs district of the area in which they have their domicile. The excise duty on electricity is graded into a lower (II) and a higher (I) category. The lower duty is charged on electricity which is used in industrial manufacturing or professional greenhouse cultivation and measured separately. Network operators pay excise duty for the electricity they deliver for consumption during a tax period. Electricity producers are taxed on the basis of the electricity produced during a tax period, from which the electricity used by their own machinery and that delivered to networks is deducted. Those liable to pay excise duty on electricity are subject to the provisions on registered consignees contained in the Excise Taxation Act, except as regards the authorisation and guarantee procedure.

Subsidies for electricity production are, on certain conditions, granted for electricity generated by energy sources or fuels specified in law, e.g. for electricity generated by wind power or forest chips. The amounts of subsidies vary according to type of power plant. In addition, energy-intensive companies may be refunded 85% of the excise duties paid by them for certain products specified in the Act on Excise Duty on Electricity and Certain Fuels or of the excise duties included in the acquisition prices of those products. No refund is paid for light or heavy fuel oil as such, although they are taken into account in the calculation. However, only the part of the calculated refund exceeding 50 000 euros is repaid. More information on energy subsidies is available in a separate brochure in Finnish (customer bulletin No. 4 on subsidies for the production of electricity and tax returns of energy-intensive companies).

NATIONAL EXCISE DUTIES

EXCISE DUTY ON SOFT DRINKS

A national excise duty is levied on soft drinks on the basis of the Act on Excise Duty on Soft Drinks (1474/1994). Excise duty on soft drinks is paid, for example, for lemonade, mineral water, various juices, juice concentrate and solid drink materials (powders). Certain products specified in law are exempt from tax. For example, soft drinks used in the manufacture of sweets are, on certain conditions, exempt from excise duty.

EXCISE DUTY ON BEVERAGE CONTAINERS

A national excise duty is levied on retail containers of alcoholic beverages and soft drinks. The purpose of the tax is to steer the use of beverage containers in a more ecologically benefi cial direction. The taxation is based on the Act on Excise Duty on Certain Beverage Containers (1037/2004).

Excise duty on beverage containers has been levied since the beginning of 2008 on all containers of beverages classified in Chapter 22 of the customs tariff nomenclature and intended for consumption as beverages. Taxable containers may be of different materials, e.g. glass, plastic or aluminium. However, containers which are included in a deposit-based, functional return system and which can be refilled or used for the recovery of raw material are exempt from the excise duty, as are also containers made entirely of liquid packaging board. Exemption from beverage container tax requires that the Centre for Economic Development, Transport and the Environment for Pirkanmaa has approved the recycling system in its register of producers. Åland has a respective register of its own.

OIL WASTE DUTY

Oil waste duty, comparable to excise duty, is levied on lubricating oils and preparations to cover the expenses of the treatment of oil waste in accordance with the Act on Oil Waste Duty (894/1986). It is collected in accordance with the same procedures as excise duties.

OIL DAMAGE DUTY

Oil damage duty is levied on oils specified in the Act on the Oil Pollution Compensation Fund (1406/2004) which are imported into or transported through Finland. Oil damage duty is collected in accordance with the provisions on registered consignees in the Excise Taxation Act.

TAX ON WASTE

Waste delivered to landfill sites is subject to tax on waste on the basis of the Waste Tax Act (495/1996). Liable to pay tax on waste are landfill site operators, who have to register with the customs district of the area in which the site is situated. The tax is assessed on the basis of the weight or volume of waste. Cases of exemption from the tax are laid down in Section 5 of the Waste Tax Act (1157/1998).

The above Act is not applied e.g. to areas outside landfill sites where only soil or materials of bedrock origin are placed or where waste is utilised. Nor is the Act applicable to sites where separately collected biowaste or sludge from sewage treatment plants is composted or otherwise biologically treated separately from other waste.

The tax period is three months (January–March etc.). A tax declaration has to be lodged with the customs district no later than on the 12th day of the month following the tax period and the tax must be paid on the 27th day at the latest. Tax on waste removed from the landfill site during the tax period may be deducted. In other respects the taxation procedure is carried out in accordance with the Excise Taxation Act.

TAXABLE GOODS AND SUSPENSION OF EXCISE DUTY

The procedure to be observed in excise taxation is laid down in the Excise Taxation Act. The Act is applied primarily to products subject to harmonized excise duties but also, as appropriate, to those subject to national excise duties.

Excise duties are levied on products produced in Finland, received from another EU member state or imported to Finland from outside the EU. The suspension of excise duty allows excise products to be produced, processed, held and moved without paying any tax. The purpose of the arrangement is to facilitate the free movement of products between member states. The suspension of excise duty allows products to be moved only between licence holders. These include authorised warehouse keepers, registered consignors and registered consignees. Furthermore, the arrangement allows a temporarily registered consignee to receive a specific consignment of products. Excise duty must be paid when an excise product is released for consumption in Finland. The release for consumption takes place when the suspension of excise duty is no longer applied to the products.

AUTHORISED WAREHOUSE KEEPER AND TAX WAREHOUSE

An authorised warehouse keeper is a natural person or a legal person authorised by the customs authority to produce, process, hold, receive and dispatch excise products in the course of his business under a duty suspension arrangement.

A tax warehouse is the location where the authorised warehouse keeper conducts these activities.

In other words, the activities must take place in a tax warehouse. The excise duty is paid later when the goods are released from the warehouse for consumption.

REGISTERED CONSIGNEE

A registered consignee is entitled only to receive excise products under a duty suspension arrangement from another EU member state or from a place of import located in Finland. This means that a registered consignee may not store or forward products under the arrangement, but pays excise duties according to tax period for the products received during each calendar month.

TEMPORARILY REGISTERED CONSIGNEE

Natural persons or legal persons who receive products in the course of their business can operate as temporarily registered consignees.

A temporarily registered consignee is entitled to receive excise products under suspension of excise duty. This right applies only to a specific period of time and a specific number of products which an operator, of which Customs has been notified in advance, sends to the consignee from another EU member state or a place of import located in Finland.

Such a taxpayer must pay the taxes for each received consignment.

REGISTERED CONSIGNOR

A registered consignor is a natural or legal person authorised by the competent authorities of the importing member state to dispatch excise products in the course of his business and under a duty suspension arrangement after the release of goods into free circulation referred to in the Community Customs Code.

A registered consignor can be, for example, the forwarder who looks after the customs clearance of the products. A person operating as an authorised warehouse keeper or as a registered consignee can also be granted authorisation to operate as a registered consignor. Authorised warehouse keepers can operate as registered consignors without separate authorisation until 30 June 2010.

Only an authorised consignor can forward products subject to the harmonised excise duty from the place of import under suspension of excise duty. The registered consignor status is not necessary for moving goods subject to national excise duties.

EXCISE TAXATION OF PRODUCTS FROM OUTSIDE THE EU

The import of excise products refers to their arrival in the EU territory when the products are not placed under a customs suspensive procedure or arrangement. It also refers to the removal of goods from under a customs suspensive procedure or arrangement. The place of import is the location where the goods are upon release into free circulation. A registered consignor can forward products from the place of import under suspension of excise duty. If products are not placed under a duty suspension arrangement in the place of import, excise duties are to be paid before the goods are released into free circulation. In such cases, customs legislation is applied in the taxation and other procedures, where applicable. An exception to this are situations where the taxpayer, i.e. the party who lodges a declaration upon import or on whose behalf a declaration is lodged, is a registered customer of Customs. In these cases, excise duties are not collected in connection with customs clearance, but under the excise taxation procedure so that a separate tax declaration is lodged for the products within four working days and the excise duties are paid within ten days of the release of the goods into free circulation. This applies, for example, to situations where the forwarder acts as an indirect representative.

TAXPAYERS

An authorised warehouse keeper and other holders of excise duty licences are obliged to pay excise duty when the products are removed from under suspension of excise duty. Therefore, an authorised warehouse keeper, for example, is liable to pay taxes for products released for consumption from a tax warehouse. Other persons are also liable to pay taxes when they remove products from under suspension of excise duty, also when another party does so on their behalf.

An authorised warehouse keeper is liable to pay taxes for taxable loss, i.e. for the unexplained consumption of products observed in a tax warehouse. An authorised warehouse keeper is liable to pay taxes also after taking products into personal use from a tax warehouse, or after removing products from a tax warehouse against regulations. A person who participates in the above activity is also liable to pay excise duty.

If a breach of regulations occurs when products are moved while under a duty suspension arrangement, and this leads to the removal of products from under the arrangement, the persons who have participated in the breach will be liable to pay excise duty. Furthermore, the person who has lodged a guarantee for moving the goods, or the person who should have lodged such a guarantee, is responsible for paying excise duty.

Moreover, if excise products for which excise duty has not been paid are held in Finland without them being under suspension of excise duty, this results in the liability to pay taxes. Manufacturing or processing excise products in a location other than a tax warehouse also results in tax liability. In such cases, the holder of the products or any party that has participated in holding the products, or manufactured or processed the products or taken part in these activities is responsible for paying the excise duty.

The party that lodges a customs declaration upon import of goods from outside the European Union is liable to pay the excise duty. The person on whose behalf the declaration is lodged is also liable to pay taxes. A party that imports products from a third territory that is a part of the EU customs territory (for example, the Canary Islands and the Åland Islands) is liable to pay taxes. In import that breaches regulations, all parties that have participated in the import are liable to pay taxes.

Products imported from another EU member state or from outside the EU and subject to national excise duty can be moved as temporarily exempt from tax in Finland. If the products are removed from under suspension of excise duty as a result of breaches of regulations, tax liability will fall upon the person who took part in the removal and who knew or should have known about a breach of regulations occurring. The declarant and the party on whose behalf the declaration was lodged are also liable to pay taxes. In import that breaches regulations, all persons that have participated in the import are liable to pay taxes. In addition to the above parties, tax liability will fall upon the authorised warehouse keeper into whose warehouse the products are moved or should have been moved, and on the registered consignee who is supposed to receive the products.

When there are several parties liable to pay taxes, they will be jointly responsible for the tax. Tax liability in certain cases is provided for by the relevant acts on excise duty. The chapter of this instruction on products taxed in another EU member states contains information e.g. on tax liability in distance selling.

TAXABLE AMOUNTS AND TAX-FREE PRODUCTS

TAXABLE AMOUNTS

An authorised warehouse keeper is required to pay taxes for the products released for consumption from a tax warehouse during the tax period. A registered consignee and tax representative are required to pay taxes for products received during the tax period (more information on operating as a tax representative is available in the paragraph on distance selling and tax representatives of distance sellers, and in the chapter focusing on licences and securities). Other taxpayers are required to pay taxes for each received consignment.

Products completely destroyed or irreversibly lost while under suspension of excise duty are not regarded as released for consumption, and therefore no tax is required for such products. It is required that the products become destroyed or lost because of their inherent nature, i.e. due to aging, vaporisation or corresponding reason relating to the qualities of the products, or as a result of a force majeure or an unforeseen event such as a fire, breakage or a similar occurrence. Products are considered completely destroyed or irreversibly lost if it is no longer possible to use them as excise products. Furthermore, the disposal of products under suspension of excise duty is not regarded as release for consumption if the disposal has taken place with the permission of the customs authority. A further requirement is that the disposal takes place under the supervision of the customs authority or in another acceptable manner.

DEDUCTIONS

An authorised warehouse keeper is entitled to deduct the excise duty paid or due to be paid for products returned to the tax warehouse during the tax period, i.e. calendar month, from the amount of excise duty paid for the tax period. The right of deduction does not, however, concern such goods returned to the warehouse that are completely destroyed or irreversibly lost due to their inherent nature or basic qualities.

An authorised warehouse keeper and a registered consignee can deduct the amount of tax paid or due to be paid for goods released for consumption that are, however, completely destroyed or irreversibly lost as a result of an unforeseen event or a force majeure. If a product has become destroyed due to its inherent nature, e.g. due to aging, it is not possible to make a deduction. The products for which a deduction is made must be destroyed under the supervision of a customs authority or in a manner approved by a customs authority.

If it has not been possible to make a deduction in full, the amount not deducted can be deducted in the declarations for the current calendar year's subsequent tax periods and the following year's tax periods.

TAX-FREE PRODUCTS

Products intended for sale or consumption onboard vessels and aircraft in professional international traffic as well as fuels and lubricating substances that such vessels and aircraft bring with them to the customs territory of Finland or which are delivered to them in Finland are exempt from excise duty on certain conditions. Products placed under a customs warehousing or export procedure are likewise exempt from excise duty.

Products delivered in the context of diplomatic and consular relations and to international organisations are also exempt from excise duty. Products can be sold tax-free only from tax warehouses to parties to which the Excise Taxation Act grants an exemption from excise duty based on tax-free use.

As for energy products and electricity, the exemption is implemented by refunding the excise duty.

Exempt from excise duty are also products which are exempt from value added tax on the basis of agreements with non-EU countries or international organisations. Moreover, the individual excise acts contain provisions on exemptions from the excise duty concerned.

MOVING PRODUCTS SUBJECT TO SUSPENSION OF EXCISE DUTY

EMCS AND THE ELECTRONIC ADMINISTRATIVE DOCUMENT

A computerised control system, EMCS (Excise Movement and Control System), is used in moving products subject to the harmonised excise duty within the framework of suspension of excise duty. EMCS will be in the full-scale use of all EU member states as of 2011. The authorised warehouse keeper or the registered consignor who dispatches the products drafts an electronic administrative document (e-AD) for the products. The document is sent to the consignee through EMCS. After receiving the products, the authorised warehouse keeper, registered consignee or temporarily registered consignee must lodge a report through EMCS on receiving the products. This is to be done without delay and no later than five days after the movement of the products has been completed. EMCS transmits the report of receipt to the consignor. During the transitional period of 1 April–31 December 2010, some EU member states, including Finland, will use EMCS only for lodging reports of receipt. Products are sent from Finland using a printed administrative accompanying document (AAD) during the transitional period.

An authorised warehouse keeper or a registered consignor who dispatches products under temporary suspension of excise duty must give the person accompanying the products a print-out of the e-AD or a commercial document that clearly states the administrative reference code (ARC) used to identify the transport. The document is to be presented to the competent authorities upon request when the products are moved.

When excise products are moved for export outside the EU, the e-AD will be left to wait for the export report. When the customs authority at the customs office of exit has confirmed that the export has taken place, an export report that verifies the departure of the products from EU territory is delivered to the consignor.

DIRECT DELIVERY

Direct delivery refers to excise goods being received within the framework of suspension of excise duty in a location other than the tax warehouse of an authorised warehouse keeper or the facilities of a registered consignor. An authorised warehouse keeper or a registered consignee is to notify the customs authorities on starting the use of direct delivery. The right of using direct delivery is entered into the FINSEED register at Customs. It is not necessary to name the places of direct delivery in advance. Direct delivery can be used when products are sent from a tax warehouse located in another EU member state or from a place of imported located in Finland. For example, products can be delivered directly to the consignee's customers. When the products have been received in the place of direct delivery, the authorised warehouse keeper or the registered consignee must lodge a report of receipt through EMCS.

PROCEDURE FOR MOVING GOODS IN FINLAND

EMCS or a simplified procedure where the e-AD is replaced with a consignment note or invoice containing the necessary information can be used when moving goods subject to the harmonised excise duty between tax warehouses in Finland. An authorised warehouse keeper is to draft the document in two copies, one of which will be attached to the consignor's books and the other delivered to the consignee along with the transport. If the received products are different from what is stated in the document, the consignee must notify the consignor about the matter without delay.

The simplified procedure is used also when products subject to national excise duties are moved between tax warehouses in the territory of Finland. Likewise, movements of goods between mainland Finland and Åland can take place either through EMCS or under the simplifi ed procedure.

If products subject to national excise duties are imported to Finland from outside the EU, the authorised warehouse keeper must enter the number of the tax warehouse to where the products are moved in the customs declaration for release into free circulation. The authorised warehouse keeper or registered consignee must also enter the reference number of the import consignment in the customs declaration. After the goods have been received, they must enter the number of the customs declaration and the reference number of the import consignment in their books.

TAX DECLARATION AND TAXATION

Authorised warehouse keepers, registered traders and tax representatives have to file a tax declaration for every tax period, i.e. one calendar month, no later than the on the 18th day of the month following the tax period. The tax declaration is to be given on a form. Other taxpayers are to fi le their declarations within four weekdays (Monday–Friday) after the receipt of the products. If it appears at a check or otherwise that the products have been imported or received without observing the provisions on taxation and control contained in the Excise Taxation Act, the four-day declaration period is not applied.

If there are several tax warehouses, separate declarations have to be filed for each. However, it is possible to apply to the National Board of Customs for permission to file a joint tax declaration.

When the Customs District has received the tax declaration, it assesses the amount of excise duty and gives a tax decision.

Parties who declare their taxes according to tax period have to pay the excise duty for each month no later than on the 27th day of the following month. Other taxpayers have to pay the tax within ten weekdays after the receipt of the products.

If excisable products have been received or imported for commercial or other business purposes without observing the provisions on taxation and control, the obligation to pay the excise duty arises immediately at the moment when the products are received or imported contrary to the provisions or when a breach of regulations is otherwise detected.

If no tax declaration is filed, taxation is carried out by appraisal. Excise duty is assessed by appraisal also in situations where the tax declaration, even if rectified, cannot be used as the basis of taxation.

If the excise duty has not been imposed because the taxpayer has neglected to declare taxes in part or entirely, the customs authority will carry out an additional assessment and impose the tax which has not been paid. Tax which has not been imposed will be collected through additional assessment also when a tax declaration has been lodged, but has been insufficient, misleading or false. This also applies to situations where other false information or document provided by the taxpayer has resulted in taxes not being imposed.

The tax imposed on the taxpayer can be raised if the tax declaration is lodged after its time limit or not until the taxpayer is requested to lodge it. The amount of tax can also be raised when the information provided by the taxpayer is insufficient or erroneous or when the taxpayer has failed to lodge the tax declaration partly or entirely. A penalty fee can be imposed for errors related to the procedure. When a tax increase and penalty fee are imposed, it is considered how reprehensible or repeated a procedure the taxpayer has undertaken, along with other related facts.

LICENCE AND GUARANTEE PROCEDURE

An authorised warehouse keeper, a registered consignee, a registered consignor and a tax representative need a licence from the National Board of Customs for their operations. Likewise, a separate licence is required for keeping a tax warehouse. The authorisation can be applied for in connection with applying for the licence of authorised warehouse keeper.

For the authorised warehouse keeper's licence to be granted, the applicant must meet the following requirements:

In the course of his business, the applicant is to

- produce or process excise products
- conduct the wholesale of excise products continuously and in a signifi cant scope
- use or release for consumption excise products for a purpose deemed as exempt from excise duty by excise legislation continuously and in a signifi cant scope
- run a shop of excise goods
- let out storage space and services for the above activity
- conduct other activity corresponding to the above activity.

The licence for a tax warehouse can be granted if the warehouse, facility or area is administered by the applicant and can be controlled by the customs authority. The warehouse should also be suitable and used for the activity for which the applicant is granted the licence of authorised warehouse keeper. There must be an acceptable and substantiated need for keeping the warehouse.

The licence of a registered consignee is granted to a person who, in the course of his business, receives excise products from another EU member state or from a place of import located in Finland. The licence of a registered consignor concerns the dispatch of excise products for gainful employment after the goods are released into free circulation.

The licence of a tax representative is granted to a person authorised by a distance seller operating in another EU member state to act as its tax representative in Finland as regards products sold in distance selling.

The National Board of Customs grants the licence upon application to a person who is regarded as reliable on the basis of reports received in the matter, and as having sufficient economic and operational prerequisites for conducting the activity for which the licence is granted. It is also required for granting the licence that the applicant is not bankrupt. If the applicant is a natural person, it is also required for the licence that the applicant is of age and not of limited capacity. The licence must be valid upon the start of the activity and during it.

If the application concerns alcohol products, the applicant is to contact the National Supervisory Authority for Welfare and Health (Valvira) in order to obtain the licences required by the legislation on alcohol.

The licence application and appendices are to be lodged with the customs district, which will deliver the application along with its statement to the National Board of Customs. The application is to be made using the form available at customs districts and on the website of Finnish Customs.

Before the licence is granted, the applicant is to lodge a guarantee imposed by the Tax Collection and Credit Management Unit of the National Board of Customs for the payment of excise duties. The most common form of guarantee is an absolute suretyship of a bank or insurance institution. A general bank account pledge is also accepted as a guarantee (a certificate of pledge/waiving the right of setoff from the bank is required). The use of real securities must be agreed on separately with the Tax Collection and Credit Management Unit of the National Board of Customs.

The decision on granting the licence confirms the conditions essential to control and taxation which the licence holder must comply with. A service charge is collected for the decision according to the decree of the Ministry of Finance. The licence conditions can be changed when necessary. The licence holder must notify the customs authorities if substantial changes occur in the information stated in the licence application. The licence can be cancelled later if there is cause for it. The licence is considered terminated if the licence holder is declared bankrupt.

Persons who receive excise products randomly in the course of their business do not require a special licence from Customs for their operations. However, if products under the harmonised excise duty are ordered, a one-off guarantee must be lodged for taxes collected for each import consignment before the products are sent to Finland. This applies also to the Finland-based consignee of products already taxed in another EU member state. The one-off guarantee is imposed by the customs district of the taxpayer's place of domicile.

PRODUCTS TAXED IN ANOTHER EU MEMBER STATE

POSSESSION FOR COMMERCIAL PURPOSES

Finland levies excise duties for products released for consumption in another EU member state which are moved to and kept in possession in Finland for commercial purposes of release or consumption. All parties in possession of products under this arrangement are liable to pay taxes.

PROCEDURE IN COMMERCIAL TRANSFERS

When products subject to the harmonised excise duty which have already been taxed are moved from one EU member state to another for release into commercial use, the simplifi ed administrative accompanying document is used instead of EMCS. This is necessary because the products are taxed again in the member state where they are consumed.

The consignor is to complete the simplified accompanying document in three copies, one of which is enclosed to the consignor's books. The second copy of the accompanying document follows the products in their transport and is to be kept by the consignee. The third copy also follows the products. The consignee is to return the copy with entries of receipt to the consignor.

Before initiating movement of products, the consignor must send a notifi cation to the customs authorities about the products that are to be sent to Finland and provide a guarantee for the payment of the excise duties. When goods under national taxation are moved, it is not necessary to notify the customs authorities about the goods to be sent. A guarantee is not required either.

DISTANCE SELLING AND THE DISTANCE SELLER'S TAX REPRESENTATIVE

Distance selling refers to trade where a private person purchases, from another EU member state, excise products which are sent or transported to Finland by the seller or a party acting on its behalf either directly or indirectly. The products are already taxed in the country of departure once they are released for consumption.

Excise duties for products sold to Finland through distance selling are collected in Finland. The distance seller is liable to pay taxes as regards the excise duty to be paid in Finland. The distance seller is to notify the customs authorities and provide a guarantee before dispatching the products from another EU member state to Finland.

A distance seller operating in another member state can have a tax representative in Finland. A tax representative in distance selling is a person based in Finland who is appointed by a distance seller operating in another EU member state and to whom the customs authority has granted the right to pay excise duty on behalf of the seller for products received in Finland. If the distance seller has a tax representative in Finland, it is not necessary to notify the customs authorities about the dispatch of the products. The tax representative appointed by the distance seller is also liable to pay taxes on behalf of the seller. However, the seller is jointly responsible for the excise duty to be paid by the tax representative.

IMPORT BY PRIVATE PERSONS

Private persons bringing duty-paid goods into Finland from another EU member state do not have to pay excise duty, provided that the goods are intended for personal use. However, the exemption from excise duty of motor fuels brought in by a private person for personal use is restricted by law as regards quantities and ways of import.

If a private person acquires the products for commercial purposes or other business purposes, or if he does not bring the products to Finland personally, he is liable to pay the duty laid down by the relevant act on excise duty. In such cases, private persons have to observe the provisions on the taxation and control of products delivered for commercial purposes.

Products brought in by a private person travelling to Finland from outside the EU are exempt from excise duty under certain requirements and restrictions laid down by law. Excise duty is collected on products exceeding the quantitative limits and an increase of excise duty may also be imposed (see "Customs Instructions for Passengers").

>> Customer instructions for passengers are available on the Customs website www.tulli.fi/en>Finnish Customs>Publications>Customer instructions

REPAYMENT OF EXCISE DUTY

Paid excise duties are refunded on application

- **to a party who has used or released products for tax-free purposes**
- **to the exporter for products placed under an export or customs warehousing procedure and** delivered to countries outside the EU (except for products exported by passengers)
- to the consignor when products taxed in Finland are moved to another member state for delivery for other than private use
- to the seller in distance selling from Finland to another member state when excise duty on the products has been paid in the member state of destination
- to the authorised warehouse keeper who has dispatched the products, in respect of products for which the warehouse keeper has been taxed on the basis of Section 82 of the Excise Taxation Act (for example when the return copy of the accompanying document is missing) and for which excise duty has been paid in another member state where a breach of regulations has occurred or been observed

If the tax refund requires that the excise duty has been paid in another member state, the applicant must indicate the payment. The tax refund is to be applied for from the customs authority within three years from the end of the calendar year during which taxes were imposed on the products in Finland.

BOOKKEEPING, SUBMISSION OF INFORMATION AND INSPECTIONS

An authorised warehouse keeper's bookkeeping must show the quantities of the products produced, processed, stored, taken into personal use, received, completely destroyed or irreversibly lost in a tax warehouse and of products dispatched and released for consumption from the warehouse, as well as the quantities of products received through direct delivery. In addition, the books must indicate other facts required for assessment of excise duty and control of excise taxation. The authorised warehouse keeper is to maintain a chronological archive of documents which have accompanied products imported under suspension of excise duty and which have not been entered in the EMCS.

Other taxpayers and distance sellers have to keep books that show the quantities of the products received, held, moved and sold as well as other necessary details. Registered consignees and temporarily registered consignees are to maintain a chronological archive of documents which have accompanied products imported under suspension of excise duty and which have not been entered in the EMCS.

The books must also indicate the quantities and use of the products acquired exempt from excise duty and the quantities stored.

The bookkeeping material, which comprises receipts, accompanying documents and guarantee documents including appendices, must be kept for four years. If the material is both in normal readable written form and on a computerised data medium, it must be preserved in both formats for the above-mentioned period.

The authorities may inspect the bookkeeping, correspondence and stocks of taxpayers, including those who have acquired products exempt from excise duty. Taxpayers have to give the details of purchases and sales if required. The authorities may also stop and check means of transport.

The bookkeeping material must be presented to the authorities for inspection in the form requested by them. The inspection is carried out either with traditional manual methods or with computer-aided methods. For excise tax inspections, the company must preserve the files and data concerning individual transactions stored in their computerised systems for financial management, production and stock records etc. in a generally readable form not bound to any specific software or hardware.

Anyone who has acquired products for purposes exempt from excise duty must, at the inspection, be able to prove the delivery or use of the products for such purposes. Otherwise excise duty is collected. Those who have delivered or acquired products for victualling purposes must give to the customs authorities the details of purchases, use, quantities stored and deliveries of the products as well as other facts necessary for the control of taxation, as prescribed by the National Board of Customs.

ADVANCE RULING

Anyone who wishes to find out in advance the amount of excise duty payable may apply to the National Board of Customs for an advance ruling. The advance ruling is binding for the excise taxation of the applicant during one year from the beginning of the calendar month following the date of issue. An advance ruling may be cancelled only if the relevant provisions or their interpretation are amended (e.g. by virtue of a decision by the Supreme Administrative Court) or if there is another special reason, but even in that case the advance ruling has to be observed for two months if demanded by the applicant. The advance ruling is subject to a charge prescribed by decree.

APPEALS

RECTIfiCATION IN FAVOUR OF THE TAXPAYER

If the customs authority concludes that too much tax has been imposed, the decision on taxation can be rectified. A tax refund decision can also be rectified if too little tax has been returned. The rectifi cation can be based on e.g. a claim for rectification, a complaint, or the fact that the customs authority itself concludes that too much tax has been imposed or too little tax has been refunded.

APPEALING A DECISION BY THE CUSTOMS AUTHORITY

An appeal against a decision by the customs authority can be made to the Helsinki Administrative Court. However, a decision on no advance ruling cannot be appealed.

The appeal period in matters concerning the imposition of excise duties and tax refunds is three years from the start of the calendar year following the imposition, however no less than 60 days from the receipt of the decision. For other decisions, the appeal period is 30 days from the date when the decision is served. The appeal period of a customs attorney is 30 days from the date when the decision is made.

A decision by the Administrative Court can be appealed further to the Supreme Administrative Court if it grants a permission to appeal. The appeal period is 60 days from the receipt of the decision by the Administrative Court.

In spite of a pending appeal, the excise duty must be paid within the prescribed time.

OCCASIONAL IMPORTATION OF PRODUCTS SUBJECT TO EXCISE DUTY

TEMPORARY REGISTERED CONSIGNEE

In excise legislation, the term temporary registered consignee refers to a business or private person who, for business purposes, may occasionally receive products sent under a duty suspension arrangement. The products may be received from another Member State or from a place of importation located in Finland.

A temporary registered consignee is obliged to pay excise duty on the products in Finland.

To act as a temporary registered consignee, the trader must be temporarily registered by Customs in respect of one receipt of a product consignment. This registration is only carried out when products subject to harmonised excise duties are received.

OTHER OCCASIONAL CONSIGNEES

Other occasional consignees are not required to obtain a specific authorisation from Customs and need not be registered, but should nevertheless observe the procedures described below. The consignee is also liable to pay excise duty in Finland when products for which excise duty has already been paid in another EU country are received in Finland.

Information on the tax treatment of excisable products received by private persons is available in the Customer Bulletin "Customs and tax treatment of gifts received from outside Finland" (No. 10).

Information about the licences required for importing alcohol can be obtained from the National Supervisory Authority for Welfare and Health, Valvira (www.valvira.fi).

>> Customer bulletins are available on the Customs website www.tulli.fi/en>Finnish Customs>Publications>Customer instructions

Customer Bulletin No. 6, National Board of Customs, April 2010

WHICH PRODUCTS ARE SUBJECT TO EXCISE DUTY

Excise duties harmonised within the EU

1. EXCISE DUTY ON ALCOHOL AND ALCOHOLIC BEVERAGES

- beer
- wine and other fermented alcoholic beverages
- intermediate products (e.g. fortified wines containing alcohol not more than 22 per cent by volume)
-

ethyl alcohol (e.g. spirits and liquors).

2. EXCISE DUTY ON MANUFACTURED TOBACCO

- cigarettes
- cigars and cigarillos – other smoking tobacco
- in addition, national excise duty is levied on other products containing tobacco and on cigarette paper.

3. EXCISE DUTY ON LIQUID FUELS

- motor spirit (leaded and unleaded motor spirit and blend leaded – unleaded)
- diesel oil
- light fuel oil
- heavy fuel oil
- jet fuel
- aviation spirit.

4. EXCISE DUTY ON ELECTRICITY AND CERTAIN ENERGY SOURCES

- electricity
- coal
- natural gas.

NATIONAL EXCISE DUTIES

1. EXCISE DUTY ON SOFT DRINKS

– soft drinks (e.g. juices and lemonades).

2. BEVERAGE CONTAINER TAX

– containers of beverages intended to be consumed as such and classified in Chapter 22 of the customs tariff nomenclature (except containers made of liquid packaging board, containers with a capacity of more than five litres and containers of beverages delivered for consumption by small producers referred to in the Act on Beverage Container Tax).

3. TAX ON LUBRICANTS

- lubricating oils (see customs tariff heading 2710)

– lubricating preparations (see customs tariff heading 3403).

4. Oil damage duty

– oil damage duty is levied for oil imported into or transported through Finland. (Oils subject to oil damage duty are the liquid products listed under headings 2707, 2709 and 2710. These include crude oil and its derivative products, as well as petroleum oils and oils obtained from bituminous minerals.)

HOW TO PROCEED

1) Receipt of products from the EU area

Commercial movements

Temporary registered consignees may, for business purposes, at a specific time receive a specifi c quantity of products subject to harmonised excise duties moving under temporary duty suspension from another Member State or from a place of importation located in Finland. They may not hold or dispatch untaxed products. Before the products are dispatched, the trader is to notify the customs authority of the products to be dispatched and to provide a guarantee for the payment of the excise duty. After receiving the notification and the guarantee, the customs authority authorises the trader to act as a temporary registered consignee. The authorisation is issued for one specific consignment received.

When moving products subject to harmonised excise duties under a duty suspension arrangement, traders are required to use a computerised system and an electronic administrative document. More information about the procedure can be found in the Customer Bulletin on EMCS and the movement of goods under duty suspension.

When products subject to harmonised excise duties and released for consumption in another Member State are moved to Finland, excise duties are levied on the products in Finland. The consignor must enclose a simplified accompanying document with the products in the Member State of dispatch. Before the products are dispatched, a notification about their consignment must be sent to the customs authority and a guarantee be provided for them.

No prior notification or guarantee is required when products subject to national excise duties are received.

Acquisitions made by private persons

A private person can only acquire products that have been released for consumption.

If a private person acquires, for personal use, products from another Member State which are subject to excise duty and are transported to Finland by another private person or a professional trader, and their movement is not a case of passenger import or distance selling, the person must pay excise tax in Finland for the products received.

Before initiating a movement of products subject to harmonised excise duties, the private person must send a notification to the customs authorities about the products that are to be sent to Finland and provide a guarantee for the payment of the excise duties.

No prior notification or guarantee is required for movements of products subject to national excise duties.

Providing a guarantee

Customs requires a guarantee for products subject to harmonised excise duties which is equivalent to the amount of the excise duty to be collected later. The guarantee form can be filled in at the offi ces of the Customs Districts and is also available on the Customs website.

A proforma invoice or a commercial invoice and an order or a confirmation of order containing the necessary details about the consignor and the goods must be enclosed with the form. The guarantee must be provided and paid to the Customs District's pay office or bank account. The guarantee may also be furnished by fax or post, if appropriate.

If the guarantees are provided for products subject to harmonised excise duties, and the products are moved under a duty suspension arrangement, the excise number of the buyer's authorisation is required for transporting the products within the EMCS system. The temporary registered consignee will receive this number from Customs' excise authorities after providing the guarantee.

In the case of products subject to harmonised excise duties that have been released for consumption, a guarantee is provided as described above; however, the excise number of the buyers authorisation is not required. The guarantee should be provided immediately after the products have been ordered, as the seller may not send the products until he has received the first copy of the guarantee form (see annex) endorsed by Finnish Customs.

No guarantee is required when receiving products subject to national excise duties (see above).

2) IMPORTATION FROM OUTSIDE THE EU

If a temporary registered consignee receives products from a registered consignor who places the goods under a duty suspension arrangement after the import, the temporary registered consignee is required to provide a guarantee for the products that he is to receive.

If products are imported from outside the Community and not immediately placed under duty suspension after their importation, the provisions and regulations regarding customs duty will, as a rule, be applied when carrying out the taxation and the procedure as a whole. Customs collects the excise duty in accordance with the provisions on customs clearance at the service points for cash customers and does not hand over the products to the customer until he has paid the excise duty.

However, this procedure is not applied if the taxpayer is a registered customer referred to in the Finnish Customs Act. In such cases, the Excise Sections of the Customs Districts will carry out the excise taxation.

Customs does not require guarantees for imports received from outside the EU area.

TAX DECLARATION

A temporary registered consignee or other occasional importer has to file a tax declaration with the Customs District in the area in which he has his domicile. The declaration must be filed within four working days (Mon-Fri) from the day of receipt of the products or the day on which the obligation to pay excise duty otherwise arose, including that day. He may also send the tax declaration by post within the same time limit.

The declaration time limit of four working days is not applied if it is discovered at a control or otherwise that the products have been imported or received without observing the provisions on taxation and control laid down in the Excise Taxation Act.

Declaration forms, separate for each type of excise duty, are available at customs offices and on the Customs website. A copy of a proforma or commercial invoice must be enclosed with the tax declaration.

The computerised EMCS system is to be used when moving products subject to harmonised excise duties under duty suspension. A temporary registered consignee must by using this system issue a report of receipt for the products no later than five working days from the date the movement ended.

Some of the movements undertaken under a temporary duty suspension arrangement will in 2010 still be handled using the traditional paper administrative accompanying document, AAD. When a temporary registered consignee files a tax declaration for products subject to harmonised excise duties that have been received from the EU area and moved using the traditional accompanying document in paper form, he must also enclose the fourth copy of this accompanying document. Other occasional importers should annex a copy of the second copy of the simplified accompanying document or, alternatively, another document accepted by Customs.

The quantities of products should be entered in the declaration as full units (e.g. 55.55 kg => 55 kg). After having received the tax declaration, the Customs District issues a tax decision and mails it to the customer.

HOW EXCISE DUTY IS PAID

A temporary registered consignee or other occasional importer has to pay the excise duty within ten working days of receiving the products. A bank giro form to be used for making the payment is enclosed with the tax decision. If a guarantee has been provided, Customs offsets the excise duty against the guarantee, and in case the guarantee exceeds the amount of the duty, repays the excessive amount to the bank account mentioned by the consignee of the products in the guarantee form.

If the guarantee is insufficient to cover the excise duty, the trader must pay the missing amount within ten working days of receiving the products in accordance with the bank giro form enclosed with the tax decision using the reference number given in the form. If no guarantee has been provided (national excised duties and imports from outside the EU), the excise duty must be paid within ten working days of receiving the excisable products.

FURTHER INFORMATION AVAILABLE FROM

e-mail: name.surname@tulli.fi

SOUTHERN CUSTOMS DISTRICT

Vilhonvuorenkatu 12 B, PO Box 62, 00501 Helsinki, fax 020 492 1347 Advice to cash customers: tel. 020 492 1259

WESTERN CUSTOMS DISTRICT

Satamakatu 22, PO Box 386, 20101 Turku, fax 020 492 4013 Advice to cash customers: tel. 040 332 7550 Tarja Fagerström, tel. 040 332 4053 Tarja Sandell, tel. 040 332 4014

Tampere Customs, Patamäenkatu 18, PO Box 133, 33101 Tampere, fax 020 492 4342 Irma Kettunen, tel. 040 332 4331 Maire Körmöläinen, tel. 040 332 4341

Vaasa Customs, Laivanvarustajankatu 1, PO Box 261, 65101 Vaasa, fax 020 492 4644 Maarit Kosonen, tel. 040 332 4619 Sture Skinnar, tel. 040 332 4604

ÅLAND CUSTOMS DISTRICT

Torggatan 16, Ämbetshuset, PO Box 40, 22101 Mariehamn, fax 020 492 6077, e-mail: atp.acciser@tulli.fi Excise duty advice: 020 492 6058 Mia Boxberg, tel. 020 492 6011 Chlaus Sjöberg, tel. 020 492 6006

EASTERN CUSTOMS DISTRICT

Terminaalinkatu 5, PO Box 66, 53501 Lappeenranta, fax 020 492 5062 Kristiina Ruotsalainen, tel. 040 332 5014 Paula Hjelm, tel. 040 332 5908 Ulla-Maija Toiviainen, tel. 040 332 5911

NORTHERN CUSTOMS DISTRICT

Hallituskatu 1, PO Box 47, 95401 Tornio, fax 020 492 8081 Riitta Könni, tel. 020 492 8020 Marja-Leena Lähteelä, tel. 020 492 8004

Oulu Customs, Poikkimaantie 16, PO Box 56, 90401 Oulu, fax 020 492 8180 Tuula Birstolin, tel. 040 332 8112 Paula Kuosmanen, tel. 020 492 8113

Prices of calls to Customs telephone numbers beginning with 020 492 or 020 391:

- from fixed-line telephones 8.21 cents/call + 6.90 cents/min (incl.VAT 22%)
- from mobile phones 8.21 cents/call + 16.90 cents/min (incl.VAT 22%)

Calls to service numbers beginning with 020 690: no extra charge, the price depends on the subscriber connection used:

- from fixed-line telephones 0 cents/min + local network charge
- from mobile phones 0 cents/min + mobile call charge

SERVICE CONTACTS

Erottajankatu 15-17 00130 Helsinki

CUSTOMS INFORMATION SERVICE

tel. 020 690 600 fax 020 492 1812 Written enquiries can be sent using the enquiry form available at www.tulli.fi /en > Contact us > Enquiry form

STATISTICS SERVICE

tel. 020 690 603 fax 020 492 1860 Written enquiries can be sent using the enquiry form available at www.tulli.fi /en >Contact us>Statistics Service´s enguiry and order form

Tip-off hotline 0800 1 4600 www.tulli.fi

The EU countries are Austria, Belgium, Bulgaria, Cyprus, the Czech Republic, Denmark, Estonia, Finland, France, Germany, Greece, Hungary, Ireland, Italy, Latvia, Lithuania, Luxembourg, Malta, the Netherlands, Poland, Portugal, Romania, the Slovak Republic, Slovenia, Spain, Sweden and the United Kingdom.

The EEA countries are the EU countries, Iceland, Liechtenstein and Norway.

IMPORTATION OF PERSONAL AND HOUSEHOLD EFFECTS AND PRIVATE MOTOR VEHICLES AS REMOVAL GOODS INTO FINLAND

Tip-off hotline 0800 1 4600 (free of charge) **www.tulli.fi**

The EU countries are Austria, Belgium, Bulgaria, Cyprus, the Czech Republic, Denmark, Estonia, Finland, France, Germany, Greece, Hungary, Ireland, Italy, Latvia, Lithuania, Luxembourg, Malta, the Netherlands, Poland, Portugal, Romania, the Slovak Republic, Slovenia, Spain, Sweden and the United Kingdom.

The EEA countries are the EU countries, Iceland, Liechtenstein and Norway.

Importation of Personal and Household Effects and Private Motor Vehicles as Removal Goods into Finland

This bulletin deals with customs duties and car taxation in connection with goods imported by immigrants. The following three basic questions are addressed:

• Importation of removal goods from member states of the European Union

• Importation of removal goods from outside the European Union

• Importation of motor vehicles from abroad as part of removal goods.

The bulletin also contains information for persons moving to the Åland Islands.

There are separate customer bulletins on the tax-free importation of goods and vehicles brought to Finland by temporary visitors ("Customs Instructions for Passengers" and "Temporary Tax-free Use of Motor Vehicles in Finland"). There is also a separate bulletin for used motor vehicles imported into Finland otherwise than as removal goods ("Taxation of Used Motor Vehicles in Finland").

1 WHO IS AN IMMIGRANT?

An immigrant is a person who moves to Finland from abroad and stays as a permanent resident. A person whose permanent place of residence is abroad and who arrives in Finland for a temporary stay, e.g. as a tourist or for studies or temporary employment, is not an immigrant.

People may also take up permanent residence in Finland gradually, so that they originally come to Finland temporarily but later decide to stay permanently. These persons, too, are on certain conditions entitled to bring in a vehicle as part of removal goods within the meaning of the Car Tax Act.

2 WHERE SHOULD REMOVAL GOODS BE DECLARED?

Removal goods, including motor vehicles, imported from outside the EU must be declared for the customs procedure of release for free circulation to the customs authorities of the place of importation.

Importation of removal goods from within the EU is free of customs duty.

A person bringing a vehicle from abroad must notify Customs of the importation of the vehicle as removal goods immediately upon arrival in Finland, irrespective of whether the person is arriving from within or from outside the EU. The vehicle may be used in Finland only if a declaration of use has been submitted to Customs.

3 REMOVAL GOODS IMPORTED FROM EU COUNTRIES

(see also section 5 for importation of motor vehicles as part of removal goods)

When a person moves to Finland from another EU country, his or her personal property is, with certain exceptions, admitted free of taxes and other restrictions applied to importation. For example, VAT is collected on a new means of transport, if the vehicle has been acquired for use in Finland and if the other prerequisites for tax levy are met. Restrictions are imposed by prohibitions justified by e.g. public morality, public policy or public security, or the protection of health of animals or plants.

4 REMOVAL GOODS IMPORTED FROM OUTSIDE THE EU

(see also section 5 for importation of motor vehicles as part of removal goods)

When a person moves to Finland from outside the EU, the EU Regulation on reliefs from customs duty and the Finnish Value Added Tax Act are applied to the removal goods. By virtue of these statutes, the personal property, i.e. the removal goods, of an immigrant arriving from outside the EU may be exempted from customs duty and VAT.

According to the EU Regulation on reliefs from customs duty, personal property means goods intended for the personal use of the persons concerned or for meeting their household needs, i.e. household effects, cycles and motorcycles, private motor vehicles and their trailers, caravans, pleasure boats and private aeroplanes. Household provisions appropriate to normal family requirements, household pets and saddle horses, as well as the portable instruments of the applied or liberal arts, required by the person concerned for the pursuit of his trade or profession, also constitute personal property. Personal property must not be such as might indicate, by its quantity, that it is being imported for commercial reasons.

Household effects are considered to comprise personal effects, household linen, furnishings and equipment intended for the personal use of the persons concerned or for meeting their household needs.

Relief from customs duty and VAT is not granted for alcoholic products, tobacco and tobacco products, commercial means of transport and articles for use in the exercise of a trade or profession, other than portable instruments of the applied or liberal arts.

Certain goods, such as live animals, animal products, plants and parts of plants as well as firearms and ammunition, may be imported only on special conditions. More information on these import restrictions can be obtained from the customs authorities.

Removal goods are exempted from customs duty and VAT on the following conditions:

• Relief from customs duty on removal goods may be granted to persons whose permanent place of residence has been outside the EU for at least 12 months. In justified special cases, if applied for in advance, the National Board of Customs may grant an exception to this rule if the intention of the person concerned was to stay outside the EU for an uninterrupted period of at least 12 months.

• The goods have been under the ownership of the immigrant or in his or her possession under conditions leading to ownership, outside the EU for 6 months. In the case of non-consumable goods, the goods must also have been in his or her use at the previous permanent place of residence for at least 6 months before the date on which he or she ceased to be permanently resident in the country concerned outside the EU. In justified special cases, if applied for in advance, the National Board of Customs may grant exceptions to the time limit.

• The goods are intended for the same use at the new permanent place of residence.

• Relief from customs duty is granted only for removal goods declared to Customs for release for free circulation within 12 months from the removal date. The goods may be imported in several consignments within the period of 12 months. In justified special cases, if applied for, the National Board of Customs may grant exceptions to the time limit. See section 5 for the conditions and time limits regarding reduction of car tax.

The goods may not be lent, given as security, hired out or otherwise transferred to another person, whether for a consideration or free of charge, until 12 months after the date on which their entry for free circulation was accepted. If the immigrant is about to do one of these actions, the Customs District concerned must immediately be informed.

If the goods are lent, given as security, hired out or otherwise transferred before the expiry of the above mentioned time limit of 12 months, customs duty and VAT are collected. See section 5.3.5 for the time limit relating to car tax.

Exceptions

• If a person undertakes to move permanently to Finland within 6 months, he or she can be allowed to import goods free of customs duty and VAT into Finland in advance. This permission is granted by the Customs District through which the goods are imported. The immigrant must provide a security determined by the Customs District.

• If a person leaves his permanent place of residence in a country outside the EU owing to occupational commitments without immediately moving to the customs territory of the EU on a permanent basis, duty-free admission can be granted for his removal goods. This is granted by a Customs District on condition, however, that the person undertakes to move to the customs territory of the EU at a later stage within a period of time of a length set by the Customs District depending on the circumstances. As in the above case, the immigrant may also be required to provide a security.

• If a person has to transfer his permanent place of residence from a country outside the EU to Finland owing to exceptional political circumstances, the National Board of Customs may, on application, grant exceptions to some of the above provisions (e.g. the requirement that the goods have been used for 6 months outside the EU).

5 MOTOR VEHICLES AS REMOVAL GOODS

Motor vehicles imported from within the EU are subject to the Finnish Value Added Tax Act and Car Tax Act. As a rule, VAT is not collected in Finland on vehicles imported as removal goods from within the EU.

Vehicles imported to Finland from outside the EU in connection with removal must be customs cleared upon importation. More information is available at the customs offices.

When vehicles are imported as removal goods from outside the EU, the Value Added Tax Act and the Car Tax Act are applied, but also customs legislation, especially the EU Regulation on reliefs from customs duties. Customs duty and VAT is not collected on vehicles intended for private use that are imported from outside the EU and that are treated as removal goods by virtue of the Regulation on reliefs from customs duties.

Before an imported vehicle is registered or brought into use in Finland, car tax must be paid for it in accordance with the provisions of the Car Tax Act. Car tax must always be paid unless the vehicle is non-taxable by virtue of that Act.

5.1 Use of vehicle in Finland after removal

Motor-driven vehicles that have not been registered in Finland can not be used in traffic in Finland, unless the use is allowed by virtue of the law. Unregistered vehicles can be used in traffic in Finland on certain conditions, for example on account of a transfer permit, a certificate regarding temporary plates or registration abroad.

According to the Decree on Vehicle Registration (893/2007) immigrants may use a vehicle in traffic in Finland for 30 days after the vehicle has been imported, provided that the vehicle is currently registered abroad. If the immigrant has first visited Finland temporarily and later decided to take up permanent residence here, the time limit is calculated from the date on which the owner of the vehicle can be considered to have established him- or herself in Finland permanently. The vehicle must be declared for first registration within the above-mentioned time limit if the vehicle is used in Finland. More information can be obtained from the vehicle inspection stations and from the Finnish Vehicle Administration AKE.

Use of vechicle in Finland before taxation

A person permanently resident in Finland is normally not allowed to use a foreign-registered vehicle in traffic, not even temporarily, if car tax has not been paid for the vehicle. In exceptional circumstances, however, use is permitted. In such cases, a declaration of use must be submitted to Customs. This declaration must be submitted in advance or, at the latest, when the temporary tax-free use begins. The declaration must be submitted on a customs form.

If the vehicle is **currently registered in an EEA country**, the vehicle can be used after a declaration of use has been confirmed by Customs. There must also be a valid motor liability insurance for the vehicle.

If the vehicle is **not currently registered in an EEA country**, use of the vehicle in traffic requires a declaration of use as well as a transfer permit. Transfer permits are granted by the vehicle inspection stations and by Customs. More information on transfer permits is available on the Finnish Vehicle Administration website at www.ake.fi.

A vehicle that is intended to be registered in Finland can be used without paying tax for a maximum of three months, on the condition that a declaration of use has been submitted to Customs on a customs form before the vehicle is used in Finland. If the vehicle is not currently registered in an EEA county or if the registration expires, a transfer permit must also be acquired. The declaration of use must be confirmed by Customs and kept in the vehicle when the vehicle is used. There must also be a valid motor liability insurance for the vehicle. In some respects, the insurance coverage of Finnish motor liability insurance is more exhaustive than in other EEA states.

In order to maintain the right to use the vehicle, a tax declaration must be lodged within five days of the confirmation of the declaration of use. The right to use the vehicle also ends on the day the car tax must be paid, and if the tax declaration or a decision on taxation is withdrawn. In the case of withdrawal, the same sum as for an advance ruling by the National Board of Customs (130 € for private persons in 2009–2010) is collected from the taxpayer, as well as five per cent of the tax amount that would have been collected on the vehicle if the taxation had been carried out. Tax collected due to withdrawal will not be taken into account if the vehicle is taxed later. The right to use the vehicle does not end if the right of ownership is transferred. It should be noted, however, that if the vehicle is covered by Finnish motor liability insurance, the insurance expires when the right of ownership is transferred.

5.2 Taxable and non-taxable vehicles

Taxable vehicles are passenger cars, vans and buses with an unladen mass of less than 1 875 kg, motorcycles (categories L3e and L4e) as well as tricycles and quadricycles (categories L5e and L7e). Mopeds of categories L1e and L2e and certain other three- or four-wheeled vehicles (L6e) with engines with a cylinder capacity not exceeding 50 cubic centimetres, for example, are free of car tax. Details of the categories are given in the Vehicle Act. More detailed information on how the taxable value and the amount of tax are determined as well as examples of calculating the tax are available in the customer bulletin "Taxation of Used Motor Vehicles in Finland".

5.3 Tax reduction for motor vehicles imported as removal goods

5.3.1 General

According to the Finnish Car Tax Act, car tax is collected before the vehicle is registered or taken into use irrespective of whether the vehicle has been imported from within the EU or from outside the EU. The car tax on one taxable private motor vehicle imported by an immigrant in connection with moving to Finland is reduced by a maximum of 13 450 euros provided that

• the immigrant has been abroad for an uninterrupted period of at least one year immediately before moving to Finland

• the vehicle has been under the ownership of the immigrant or his married spouse, or in their possession under conditions leading to ownership, and in the use of the immigrant abroad for a period of at least six months immediately before his or her moving to Finland, and,

• if the immigrant has earlier imported a vehicle with reduced tax or free of tax, the time limit after which that vehicle may be transferred to another person without payment of tax has expired before his or her moving to Finland.

If the immigrant has transferred a vehicle, imported as removal goods, to an insurance company in Finland because of damages or transferred the vehicle for use abroad and later intends to import another vehicle as removal goods, the above time limits concerning importation of the latter vehicle begin to run only after 30 months from the date on which tax reduction was granted for the vehicle brought in earlier.

Unmarried partners are not equivalent to married spouses for the purposes of ownership and use of the vehicle abroad. Therefore an unmarried partner is not allowed to import his or her partner's vehicle from abroad with reduced car tax as removal goods even though he or she has used the vehicle abroad. Persons having registered their partnership are comparable with married couples for the purposes of tax legislation.

If there are questions of interpretation in some respect, it is recommended that the customs office at which the vehicle will be declared for taxation is contacted in advance. In these situations, the National Board of Customs can be asked to give an advance ruling as to how the Car Tax Act will be applied to the case concerned (see section 5.8).

An immigrant may bring in only one taxable vehicle with a reduced tax, e.g. one passenger car or one van or one motorcycle.

Tax reduction can be granted for a taxable vehicle also in the case that the immigrant imports a non-taxable vehicle, e.g. a camper, at the same time.

If the car tax is more than 13 450 euros, the exceeding tax amount is collected.

Example of calculating the reduced tax

General asking price of a similar used car (CO_2 247 g/km) in Finland 50 000.00 €

Usual discounts (5% and 750 €) 3 250.00 €

General retail value 46 750.00 €

Car tax based on CO_2 emissions (35% x general retail value) 16 362.50 €

Tax reduction for importation as removal goods 13 450.00 €

Car tax to be paid 2 912.50 €

5.3.2 Importation of vehicle in connection with removal

The Car Tax Act requires that the vehicle is imported to Finland in connection with the removal. In practice, this means that the importation of the vehicle is caused by the removal and takes place at the same time. It is taken into account, however, that the vehicle and the immigrant cannot always come to Finland at the same time, e.g. because there are problems of transport owing to the distance between Finland and the country concerned.

A vehicle is considered to be imported in connection with removal if it is imported within six months from the person's removal to Finland. If the vehicle is imported before the person's removal, an interval of about 2 to 3 months between the importation and the removal is allowed. However, the vehicle cannot be declared for taxation before the person has arrived in Finland.

5.3.3 Use of vehicle immediately before removal

The requirement concerning the use of a vehicle, which is a condition of granting the car tax reduction at importation as removal goods, is considered to be met if the vehicle has been used by the immigrant or can be deemed to have been in his use for at least six months before the removal. A vehicle is deemed to have been in the immigrant's use if it has been duly registered and insured for use on the road in the former country of residence.

5.3.4 Visits to Finland while living permanently abroad

The immigrant shall have stayed abroad for an uninterrupted period of at least one year immediately before moving to Finland. However, tax reduction is granted also in the case that the immigrant, before moving to Finland, has visited Finland for reasons of acquisition of a residence or work, or for reasons which are to be considered as compelling bearing in mind the situation, or for reasons of an ordinary holiday trip, temporary work or other comparable short visit and after that returned back abroad.

It is an established taxation and legal practice that an average of 72 days stay in Finland owing to a normal holiday trip is allowed during the period of one year preceding moving to Finland. This time limit may usually be exceeded only if the person concerned explains his stay in Finland by reasons that are to be considered as compelling or by other comparable reasons. The days of arrival and departure are also included in the stay in Finland. Accordingly, if a person arrives in Finland on 1 January and returns abroad on 3 January, it is deemed that the stay in Finland has lasted 3 days. A reason has been assessed to be compelling if it has been unforeseeable and beyond the immigrant's control and from a subjective point of view compelled him to stay in Finland. The immigrant's own illness has in some cases been considered to be a compelling reason on certain conditions. This has been possible if the illness has been serious and the patient has been in acute need of medical care. It is also required that the treatment of the illness particularly in Finland is justifiable.

Reasons pertaining to work have not been considered as compelling. Also, a stay allowed for reasons pertaining to work must be occasional and of short duration. According to the established decision practice, a stay of at most 40 to 50 days has been accepted.

A vehicle entered in the export register (for details see section 5.7) may be used for visits to Finland, but not, however, during one month immediately after moving from Finland or one month immediately before moving back to Finland.

5.3.5 Use of vehicle and transfer to another person after moving to Finland

A vehicle which has been granted tax reduction as removal goods may not, without payment of the tax in full, be sold, hired out or otherwise transferred to another person, nor be put at the disposal of persons other than members of the immigrant's family, whether for a consideration or free of charge, before the vehicle has been under the ownership of the immigrant or his spouse or in their possession under conditions leading to ownership and in the use of the immigrant for **in all three years, of which, however, after the removal at least one year in Finland.**

The time during which the vehicle prior to the person's moving to Finland has been in a free zone or elsewhere in Finland is not considered as time of use. However, the use of the vehicle during visits to Finland referred to in section 5.3.4 counts as time of use. If the vehicle has been granted tax reduction by virtue of the provisions on taking up permanent residency after temporary stay (see section 5.4.1), the period from the date of the person's arrival in Finland for a temporary stay to the date of the tax decision granting a reduced tax for the vehicle does not count as time of use.

The period of use in Finland after the person's moving to Finland is considered to begin on the date of the tax decision by which the vehicle was granted the tax reduction referred to in Section 25 of the Car Tax Act. Only that period during which the immigrant and the vehicle are in Finland at the same time counts as time of use. Thus the time limit runs in Finland only when the vehicle is used by the immigrant in Finland. For example, if the vehicle is removed from the register or when the immigrant stays abroad, the time limit ceases to run. It runs, however, during the arrangement that the vehicle is not used in winter between 11 November and 30 April if it was registered for use in Finland before that period. The time limit runs during the arrangement even if a declaration had been made that the vehicle is taken out of traffic. For the running of the time limit during the arrangement, it is also required that the immigrant stays in Finland at the same time.

The family of the immigrant comprises his or her married spouse living in the same household, as well as their unmarried children who also live in the same household. Thus the immigrant's parents, brothers and sisters, for example, do not belong to the immigrant's family even though they live in the same household as the immigrant.

Two persons of the same sex having registered their partnership are considered equivalent to married spouses. A person of the opposite sex who is permanently living together with the immigrant in the same household without their getting married but under circumstances similar to a marriage is in this connection also considered equivalent to a married spouse and is entitled to use the vehicle after the immigrant's moving to Finland also during the ban on transfer of the vehicle.

If the vehicle has been imported from outside the EU, it is also subject to other restrictions on transfer concerning removal goods brought from outside the EU (see section 4 "Removal goods imported from outside the EU").

As an exception from the restrictions on transfer, the immigrant may, before the expiry of the time limit, transfer a vehicle deleted from the register free of tax either to an insurance company if the vehicle has been damaged, or for use abroad. The vehicle has to be deleted from the Finnish register before such transfer. It is also to be noted that if the vehicle is registered again or used in traffic in Finland, normal car tax is collected. In such cases the tax has to be paid by the person who takes the vehicle into use or registers it in Finland.

5.4 Special cases

5.4.1 Persons staying as permanent residents after temporary stay

A person who has stayed in Finland temporarily before moving to Finland permanently is entitled to the tax reduction granted in respect of a vehicle imported as part of removal goods if he or she can show that the requirements for the reduction have been fulfilled immediately before his or her arrival in Finland for a temporary stay. In assessing whether the requirements have been fulfilled, arrival in Finland means the date on which the person arrives in Finland for the first time for a temporary stay.

For getting the tax reduction, it is also required that **the vehicle is declared for taxation as removal goods within six months from the beginning of the temporary stay. If the vehicle has been in Finland temporarily free of tax as a so-called tourist car within the meaning of the sec**ond subsection of Section 2 of the Car Tax Act and the time limit for the tax-free use of the vehicle has been extended by a written permit of the Customs District concerned, the declaration may be lodged before the extended period expires but not later than within 18 months from the beginning of the temporary stay.

The above-mentioned obligation to declare is a condition for granting the vehicle tax treatment as removal goods. Thus a vehicle which has been used in Finland but which has not been declared for taxation as removal goods within the prescribed time is not considered being imported as removal goods.

5.4.2 Students

Tax reduction is not granted to a person who at the time of his moving to Finland is under 18 years old or to a person who has earlier lived in Finland and during the one-year period preceding his or her moving has stayed abroad mainly for study purposes. However, tax reduction is granted to the latter if he or she can prove that the conditions of tax reduction for removal goods have been met during uninterrupted stays abroad during which he or she has not studied.

According to that stated above, a vehicle may be imported as removal goods if the immigrant can prove that he or she has stayed abroad for an uninterrupted period of at least one year for purposes other than studies and that he or she has also owned and used the vehicle without interruption for at least six months during which he or she has not studied. Part of the period required may elapse also during the last year preceding the person's moving to Finland if he or she has not studied during that particular time.

Studies referred to above are studies preparing for a performance within the scope of the curriculum of a university or other educational institute as well as practical training, including on-the-job training, relating to these studies, unless the activity is to be considered as independent research work. For example, preparing a doctoral or licentiate thesis is considered to be independent research work. However, training organised by the labour market authorities and on-the-job learning in that connection are not regarded as studies within the meaning of the relevant provisions.

5.5 Documents needed when importing a vehicle

The immigrant must prove with documents that the conditions for tax exemption or tax reduction are met.

The stay abroad can be proved with any documentary evidence. It is determined case by case whether the evidence is sufficient. As a rule, the stay abroad is proved with a certificate given by the employer. If the person concerned has not been working abroad, the stay can be proved by submitting e.g. account statements, credit card bills or other invoices showing that the person has actually stayed outside Finland. Sometimes even a rental contract concerning lodgings abroad may be accepted as evidence. A notification of moving made to the population information system is generally not considered to be sufficient.

The ownership and possession of a vehicle usually appear from the purchase invoice or other documents on transfer or registration. Moreover, the use of the vehicle must be proved by presenting a certificate of motor liability insurance.

If requested, the immigrant must also produce other evidence to prove eligibility for tax exemption.

5.6 Car tax declaration and collection of tax

Before the vehicle is registered or taken into use in Finland, the immigrant must submit a car tax declaration to the tax authorities. The declaration shall contain details for identifying the vehicle as well as details about the standard of its equipment and about how long the immigrant has owned and used the vehicle. This information is needed e.g. for determining the taxable value of the vehicle.

The person moving must be prepared for the possibility that Customs examines the vehicle when the tax declaration is submitted. The vehicle is always examined if the immigrant uses his or her right to demand that the particular characteristics of the vehicle are taken into account because he or she considers them to be of essential importance for the general retail sale value of the vehicle.

The tax authorities carry out taxation on the basis of the declaration, and after the taxes have been paid, they give permission to register the vehicle.

The vehicle may not be used in Finland before the taxation has been carried out, unless Customs has confirmed a declaration of use for the vehicle. The vehicle must also be insured for use in traffic and registered in an EEA country, or the vehicle must have a transfer permit (for further details see section 5.1).

A car tax declaration must be lodged for all vehicles subject to car tax, i.e. also in cases where no car tax remains to be collected.

Taxation is the responsibility of Customs when a vehicle is registered or brought into use for the first time. After that, the Finnish Vehicle Administration AKE carries out the taxation which may become necessary owing to changes in the construction, purpose of use or ownership of the vehicle. However, if a vehicle imported as removal goods is transferred contrary to the conditions of exemption from tax or the conditions of tax reduction, the taxation is carried out by Customs (see section 5.3.5 "Use of vehicle and transfer to another person after moving to Finland").

5.7 Inspection and registration of vehicle

Information on the technical inspection and the registration of vehicles can be obtained from the **Finnish Vehicle Administration AKE** and the **vehicle inspection stations**. It is recommendable to contact these already prior to moving to Finland and ask for information about e.g. EU type approval and the requirements to be met by the vehicle.

A new vehicle acquired in Finland and intended to be taken into use abroad may be exported from Finland as a so-called export-registered vehicle. Export registration is valid for one year from the end of the month in which the registration decision was given. It depends on the legislation of the country to which the vehicle is taken whether the vehicle must be registered there during the period of one year that the export registration is valid. Information and guidance on export registration can be obtained from the Finnish Vehicle Administration AKE.

If an export-registered vehicle is used for visiting Finland, the visitor must ask the customs authorities to enter the dates of arrival and departure in the documents.

Contact information of the Finnish Vehicle Administration AKE: PO Box 120, 00101 Helsinki, tel. 020 696 300, www.ake.fi.

5.8 Advance ruling and tax relief

If the matter is of special importance to the person concerned, the National Board of Customs may, upon application, give an advance ruling on how the Car Tax Act and the VAT Act are applied to the taxation of his or her vehicle before it is registered for the first time.

Advance rulings are given on questions of interpretation of the law. Advance rulings are given for concrete situations on the basis of the facts presented by the applicant, not on questions of a general nature. No advance ruling is given on the calculation of the amount of car tax or VAT or, because not provided for by the Community legislation, on the amount of customs duty or on exemption from customs duty.

An advance ruling decision given to a private person is subject to a charge, which in 2009–2010 is 130 euros. Advance rulings are appealable.

By virtue of Section 50 of the Car Tax Act, the National Board of Customs may, upon application and on conditions determined by the Board, grant relief from car tax for special reasons. A corresponding provision on relief from VAT is in Section 210 of the VAT Act.

When applying for tax relief, it should be borne in mind, however, that relief can be granted only in certain special cases. Decisions on tax relief are free of charge. They are not appealable. Applications for exceptions provided for by the EU Regulation on reliefs from customs duty are also treated by the National Board of Customs as applications for tax relief (see section 4 "Removal goods imported from outside the EU").

Both advance rulings and tax reliefs can be applied for with freely formulated applications addressed to the National Board of Customs, PO Box 512, 00101 Helsinki.

6 THE ÅLAND ISLANDS AND REMOVAL GOODS

6.1 Declaration of removal goods when moving to the Åland Islands

Persons bringing removal goods, such as household effects, boats or vehicles, to the Åland Islands from the EU or from countries outside the EU shall immediately after their arrival notify the customs authorities of the importation of the goods at the place of arrival. After that the goods are sent to Mariehamn Customs under the customs transit procedure. There the goods are declared for the customs procedure of release for free circulation. The conditions for importation of removal goods are given in section 4.

If the conditions for importation as removal goods are not met, VAT is collected on goods brought in from within the EU territory and also customs duty on goods brought in from outside the EU (see Act No. 1266/1996 laying down exceptions to VAT and excise legislation concerning the Province of Åland). As regards car tax on vehicles imported as removal goods, that stated in section 5 is applied, as appropriate.

6.2 Removal goods between The Åland Islands and mainland Finland

Persons moving from the Åland Islands to mainland Finland, or vice versa, should contact Mariehamn Customs in questions concerning VAT on removal goods (see the Act on exceptions mentioned above). The following basic requirements must be met in order that goods (e.g. household effects, boats and vehicles) can be regarded as removal goods between the Åland Islands and mainland Finland (see also section 4 "Removal goods imported from outside the EU").

• The immigrant must have had his permanent place of residence on the other side of the tax border for at least 12 months

• The goods must have been owned by the immigrant and, with the exception of consumer goods, been in his use for at least 6 months

• The goods may not be lent, given as security, hired out or transferred to another person, whether for a consideration or free of charge, until 12 months after importation.

If these requirements are not met, VAT is collected on the goods.

Further information on inspection and registration of vehicles on the Åland Islands can be obtained from the Motor Vehicle Office of Åland, address Motorfordonsbyrån, Möckelövägen 58, 22120 Mariehamn, tel. (018) 525 840.

7 ENQUIRIES

Further information on importation, customs clearance and car taxation of removal goods and the necessary documents is obtainable e.g. at the customs offices and from the Customs Information Service, tel. 020 690 600. The information service also answers enquiries on the Internet at www.tulli.fi. Texts of acts and decrees (in Finnish and Swedish) can be bought at Edita Oyj and its bookshops. The texts are also available online at www.finlex.fi.

CUSTOMS INFORMATION SERVICE

tel. 020 690 600
fax 020 492 1812
address PO Box 512, 00101 Helsinki
www.tulli.fi
www.ake.fi
Southern Customs District
Car Taxation

Vilhonvuorenkatu 12 B, PO Box 62
00500 HELSINKI
tel. (09) 6141
Hanko Customs
Vapaasatama
10900 HANKO
tel. 020 492 3609
(advice on removal goods
by appointment)
Lahti Customs
Jussilankatu 4, PO Box 110
15100 LAHTI
tel. 020 492 3940
(advice on removal goods
by appointment)
Western Customs District
Turku Customs
Satamakatu 22, PO Box 386
20100 TURKU
tel. 020 492 4133
Tampere Customs
Patamäenkatu 18, PO Box 13
33900 TAMPERE
tel. 020 492 4470
Vaasa Customs
Laivanvarustajankatu 1, PO Box 261
65100 VAASA
tel. 020 492 4600
Åland Customs District
Mariehamn Customs
Torggatan 16, Ämbetshuset, PO Box 40
22100 MARIEHAMN
tel. 020 492 6003
Eastern Customs District
Lappeenranta Customs
Terminaalinkatu 5, PO Box 66
53500 LAPPEENRANTA
tel. 020 391 112
Northern Customs District
Tornio Customs
Hallituskatu 1, PO Box 47
95400 TORNIO
tel. 020 492 8021
Oulu Customs
Poikkimaantie 16, PO Box 56
90400 OULU
tel. 020 492 8105

TEMPORARY TAX-FREE USE OF MOTOR VEHICLES IN FINLAND

Temporary tax-free use of motor vehicle means that a vehicle is used temporarily *free of car tax* or *free of customs duty and value added tax (VAT).*

Temporary use free of car tax is based on the Finnish Car Tax Act. The provisions concerned are applied to both vehicles imported from the EU territory and those imported from outside the EU. Vehicles coming from outside the EU are also subject to the Community legislation on temporary use free of customs duty and VAT. This guide contains information on the conditions of temporary tax-free use both according to the Car Tax Act and the Community legislation.

TEMPORARY USE FREE OF CAR TAX

1 RIGHT OF PERSON NOT PERMANENTLY RESIDENT IN FINLAND TO TEMPORARY TAX-FREE USE OF MOTOR VEHICLE

A person permanently resident outside Finland may, on certain conditions, use a motor vehicle in Finland without having to pay car tax. The extent of the right to tax-free use depends on whether the vehicle has been imported for own use (a so-called tourist car) or whether it is used for business purposes.

USE OF VEHICLE FOR TOURISM PURPOSES

When a private person permanently resident in some other state than Finland imports a vehicle into Finland temporarily free of car tax for his own need the vehicle is considered as a so-called tourist car (see section 1.1.2 "Use of foreign-registered vehicles for business purposes"). The vehicle may be used in Finland temporarily without having to pay car tax on the following conditions:

• The vehicle is registered outside Finland, and the registration is valid.

I The vehicle is allowed to be used for not longer than six months, continuously or interruptedly, during a period of twelve months.

□I The use of the vehicle is not connected with purchasing the vehicle to Finland.

When used in Finland, the vehicle shall be covered by a motor liability insurance valid in Finland.

The conditions of temporary exemption from car tax are the same for persons coming from the territory of the European Union and for those coming from outside the Union.

Provisions on time limits

On application, a Customs District can extend the time limit of six months set for tax-free use

by at most one year and determine the conditions of the extension. The application for the extension shall be lodged at the customs office closest to the applicant´s place of stay before the expiry of the six-month period.

A person who upon his arrival intends to stay in Finland for more than six months shall contact a customs office for finding out about the right to use the car involved. If necessary, Customs Districts give guidance in making the application for an extension of the time limit.

Once the time limit has been extended, the vehicle may be used in Finland again not earlier than after six months from the expiry of the extension.

The time limit explained above in section 1.1.1 is not applied to the vehicle registered abroad of a person permanently residing abroad but working in Finland, if he leaves Finland regularly with the vehicle for his place of residence in another country.

The time limit is not either applied to a vehicle which is registered abroad and imported by a person staying in Finland exclusively for the purpose of studying at a university or other educational establishment but residing permanently in another country. However, the student shall inform the tax authorities of the matter at the latest when the period of six months expires. Furthermore, he has to account for his studies for each study term or at other times determined by the tax authorities.

USE OF FOREIGN-REGISTERED VEHICLES FOR BUSINESS PURPOSES

When a person permanently resident outside Finland brings in a vehicle registered in some other country than Finland to be used in the business of a company situated somewhere else than in Finland, the vehicle may be used in Finland for not more than seven months. Customs Districts cannot extend the time limit. The same also applies to a vehicle that is used in Finland in the activities of an international organization or other corporation established somewhere else than in Finland.

PERMANENT PLACE OF RESIDENCE

With a person´s permanent place of residence, a place is meant where he resides at least 185 days per calendar year, as estimated according to his personal, occupational and other ties.

If the person stays at different places which are located in two or more states, that place where he returns regularly for personal reasons shall be considered his permanent place of residence. When estimating personal reasons, the nature and permanence of work in another country and other special circumstances can also be taken into account. Returning to another state is not required if the person stays in Finland to perform a task of fixed duration. The Customs District concerned may, on conditions which it determines and for not longer than one year at a time, give a decision notifying in which state the person´s place of residence shall be considered to situate according to the produced documents.

A person´s permanent place of residence is not considered to change if he stays in Finland or another country for studying at a university or other educational establishment.

RIGHT OF PERSON PERMANENTLY RESIDENT IN FINLAND TO TEMPORARY TAX-FREE USE OF MOTOR VEHICLE

As a rule, a person permanently resident in Finland is not allowed, not even occasionally, to use a foreign-registered vehicle on the road without paying car tax. There are, however, some exceptions to this rule. In such cases a declaration of use submitted to Customs is usually required and sometimes also a permit to transfer the vehicle.

A vehicle with a valid registration in the EEA area may be used on the basis of a declaration of use confirmed by Customs. A valid motor liability insurance is also required.

When Customs must be informed of the use of the vehicle, the declaration must be lodged in advance or at the latest when the tax-free use is started. The declaration is submitted with customs form No. 83.

When a vehicle does not have a valid registration in the EEA area, a transfer permit is required in addition to the declaration of use. Transfer permits are granted by vehicle inspection stations and Customs upon application.

Further information on transfer permit is available on the Internet sites of the Vehicle Administration AKE at www.ake.fi.

VEHICLES SUBJECT TO CAR TAX AND INTENDED TO BE REGISTERED IN FINLAND

A vehicle which is intended to be registered in Finland may be used for at most three months without paying taxes provided that a declaration of use on customs form No. 83 has been submitted to Customs before the use of the vehicle is started in Finland. If the vehicle does not have a valid registration in the EEA area, a transfer permit is also needed. The declaration of use confirmed by Customs must be kept in the vehicle when the vehicle is used (for the EEA states, see the last page). A vehicle which has earlier been export-registered in Finland may not be used on the road in Finland without a transfer permit after removal back to Finland (for further details, see section 1.3.)

The vehicle must also have a motor liability insurance which is in force in Finland. The insurance coverage of the Finnish insurance is in some respects more extensive than in the other EEA states. If a Finnish motor liability insurance for the vehicle is preferred, a transfer permit must be acquired as well.

In order to keep the right of use, the vehicle must be declared for taxation within five days from the date when the declaration of use was confirmed. The right to tax-free use also expires on the due date of the car tax or if the taxation procedure is cancelled.

If the taxation procedure is cancelled, a charge equivalent to that for an advance ruling of the National Board of Customs (110 euros in 2008) is collected and, in car tax, a charge amounting to five per cent of the car tax which should have been paid if the taxation had been completed. The car tax collected as a result of the cancellation is not taken into account if tax is later assessed on the vehicle.

A declaration of use can be submitted for several vehicles at a time. The right of use does not cease even though the ownership of the vehicle were transferred. However, it is to be noted that if the vehicle has a Finnish motor liability insurance, its validity expires when the ownership is transferred.

BUSINESS VEHICLES

A natural person living permanently in Finland, whose place of work is in a state other than Finland, may on Finnish roads use a vehicle, permanently registered in that other state and owned or controlled by his employer, temporarily free of tax exclusively for purposes of his occupational tasks. The use is considered as temporary if the vehicle is always exported back to the state of registration after the task is completed. However, a continuous use of at most three days can be considered as temporary use. Using the vehicle for travels between the place of residence and the place of work are not considered as use for occupational tasks.

Before taking the vehicle into use on the road, Customs must be notified of the matter with a declaration made on customs form No. 24. The customs authorities confirm the receipt of the declaration. This confirmed declaration must be kept in the vehicle when it is driven.

COMPANY CARS

A company car may be used temporarily free of tax by a cross-border employee who works in a state other than Finland, is resident in Finland and uses the car in both states. According to the relevant provision of the Car Tax Act, a person permanently resident in Finland may, on certain conditions, use a vehicle permanently registered abroad temporarily in Finland without having to pay car tax.

It is required that the person is employed by an employer which has a permanent place of business outside Finland. The vehicle must be owned and controlled by the employer and registered in the country where the employer is established. The right to use the vehicle must be based on an employment contract, e.g. as a car benefit. A motor liability insurance valid in Finland is also required.

As distinct from temporary tax-free use of business vehicles, which may be used for occupational tasks only, company cars may also be used for private purposes.

The use of a company car is subject to a permit given by Customs. The permit must be applied for on customs form No. 17 and can be granted for 12 months. The permit can be renewed if the applicant continues to meet the conditions of temporary tax-free use.

It is also required that a company car in temporary tax-free use is used abroad more than in Finland. The scope of use is determined for a period of 12 months and measured in days. If the vehicle is used both in Finland and abroad during the same day, it is deemed to be used abroad.

The vehicle may not be put at the disposal of any other person permanently resident in Finland, including the family members of the employee. If it is intended that the family members may use the vehicle, the vehicle must be taxed and registered in Finland.

USE FOR RACING PURPOSES

VEHICLES REGISTERED IN ANOTHER EEA STATE AND USED FOR RACING

A vehicle registered in another EEA state is imported temporarily to Finland only for racing purposes for not more than 30 days and is taken out of Finland after that time limit.

I A declaration notifying that the vehicle is taken into use must be submitted to Customs on customs form No. 83. I A transfer permit is not required for using the vehicle.

VEHICLES REGISTERED OUTSIDE THE EEA STATES AND USED FOR RACING

A foreign-registered vehicle is imported temporarily to Finland only for racing purposes for not more than 30 days and is taken out of Finland after that time limit.

I A declaration notifying that the vehicle is taken into use must be submitted to Customs on customs form No. 83. I A transfer permit is required if the vehicle is used by a person permanently resident in Finland.

Unregistered vehicles used for racing

An unregistered vehicle is used in Finland only for racing purposes for not more than seven days uninterruptedly. The vehicle need not be taken out of Finland after that use.

I A declaration notifying that the vehicle is taken into use must be submitted to Customs on customs form No. 83. I A transfer permit is always required for using the vehicle.

Other cases of temporary tax-free use of vehicles

According to the Car Tax Act, there are nine groups of cases in which temporary tax-free use of a vehicle may be applied. In most cases a declaration of use (customs form No. 83) must be submitted to Customs but there are also exceptions. In addition, a vehicle imported from outside the EU must be placed under the relevant customs procedure.

Declaration of use to Customs is required in the following cases:

1. A person permanently resident in Finland imports a vehicle temporarily only for service, repair or other operations.
    1. A vehicle not intended to be registered in Finland is imported or taken into use temporarily and used only for
    2. I trial I research I type inspection I type approval or I demonstration of short duration.
2. A vehicle imported from abroad is moved from the place of importation to some other place in Finland or to the place of exportation without it being registered in Finland.
3. A vehicle not registered in Finland is moved for exportation from the place of delivery to the place of exportation.
4. A vehicle equipped with temporary number plates is moved, the holder of the temporary number certificate or his representative being present in the vehicle, for purposes

I directly connected with testing for research or product development concerning the vehicle of the holder of the temporary number certificate or concerning the vehicle's equipment

I of test driving of the vehicle to get assured of its technical functioning I of short-term sales demonstration to a buyer permanently resident outside Finland I directly connected with other manufacturing, putting up for sales, exportation, repair

or technical inspection of the vehicle.

Use allowed without declaration to Customs

A person permanently resident in Finland may drive a vehicle imported temporarily free of tax over short distances for service, repair or other similar purpose if the importer permanently resident outside Finland is occasionally prevented from driving the vehicle himself.

The right to temporary exemption from car tax is also held by a person studying abroad for at least 185 days per year and visiting Finland for a reason to be considered as compelling under the prevailing circumstances or for an ordinary holiday trip or a similar short stay. A stay not exceeding 72 days is normally deemed to be a short stay.

TEMPORARY TAX-FREE USE OF EXPORT-REGISTERED VEHICLES

As a rule, a vehicle export-registered in Finland may not be used in Finland before exportation but it may be transferred for exportation from the place of delivery to the place of export. The vehicle may also in connection with the owner´s removal abroad be driven to the place of residence of the owner and further to the place of exportation.

A vehicle entered in the export register in Finland may be used in Finland occasionally for a reason to be considered as compelling or for an ordinary holiday trip or a similar short stay. This provision has been interpreted so that the vehicle may be used in Finland for at most 72 days. It is required that the customs authorities are asked to enter the dates of arrival and departure of the vehicle in the export registration documents.

If an export-registered vehicle is used in Finland during one month immediately after removal from Finland or immediately before removal back to Finland, both a declaration of use to Customs (form No. 83) and a transfer permit are required.

PROHIBITION TO TRANSFER VEHICLE

A vehicle which has been imported temporarily free of car tax may not be sold, hired out or otherwise transferred, nor may it be allowed to be used by a person residing permanently in Finland, unless car tax has been paid for the vehicle or unless the tax liability has been transferred as prescribed in Section 4 of the Car Tax Act. Notwithstanding what has been said above, a damaged vehicle may be transferred to an insurance company. This kind of vehicle may not be put into use or registered in Finland, unless the person using or registering it pays car tax for it.

The vehicle may be used by its importer and by the members of his family residing permanently abroad as well as by other persons who themselves would have been or would be entitled to import a vehicle from abroad for temporary use.

However, the steering of the vehicle may be entrusted to another person when the vehicle's possessor permanently resident outside Finland is present in the vehicle.

TAXABLE VEHICLES ACCORDING TO THE CAR TAX ACT

According to law, taxable vehicles are passenger cars, delivery vans, other motor cars with unladen weight of less than 1 875 kg, motorcycles (of categories L3e and L4e) and certain three- or four-wheeled motor vehicles (L5e and L7e). (The complete classification is included in the Vehicle Act 1090/2002.)

VEHICLES RECEIVING THE STATUS OF REMOVAL GOODS AFTER TEMPORARY TAX-FREE USE

The Car Tax Act also contains provisions on tax reduction for vehicles imported into Finland as part of removal goods, see Customer Bulletin No. 8 "Importation of Personal and Household Effects and Private Motor Vehicles as Removal Goods into Finland" of the National Board of Customs. A person moving from abroad to Finland and settling down as a permanent resident has, on certain conditions, the right to bring in a vehicle as removal goods.

A person who has stayed in Finland temporarily before settling down permanently is also entitled to the tax reduction if certain requirements are met (for the requirements, see section 5.4.1 of the above-mentioned Customer Bulletin No. 8). This means that in certain cases the vehicle he has used in Finland temporarily free of tax may receive the status of a vehicle imported as removal goods. It is required that the person has stayed abroad uninterruptedly for at least one year immediately before arriving in Finland. He shall also have had the vehicle abroad under his ownership or in his possession under conditions leading to ownership and in his use for at least six months immediately before his arrival in Finland.

Arrival in Finland refers here to the date on which the person for the first time arrives in Finland for a temporary stay. During the 12 months preceding his arrival in Finland the person shall not have stayed in Finland otherwise than temporarily in the way referred to in the first paragraph of Section 26 of the Car Tax Act.

It is further required that the vehicle is declared for taxation as part of removal goods within six months from the beginning of the temporary stay. If the time limit for temporary use of the vehicle free of tax as a so-called tourist car within the meaning of the second paragraph of Section 2 of the Car Tax Act has been extended by a written permit given by the Customs District concerned, the declaration may be lodged before the extended period expires but not later than within 18 months from the beginning of the temporary stay.

The obligation to declare mentioned above is a precondition for tax treatment of the vehicle as removal goods. Thus a vehicle which has been used in Finland but which has not been declared for taxation as removal goods within the prescribed period is not considered being imported as removal goods.

The regulations on importation of a vehicle as part of removal goods are explained in the above-mentioned Customer Bulletin No. 8 of the National Board of Customs.

TEMPORARY USE FREE OF CUSTOMS DUTY AND VALUE ADDED TAX

1 Vehicles imported from the EU territory

No customs duty or VAT is collected on vehicles which are imported temporarily to Finland from another EU country.

2 Exemption from customs duty and value added tax of vehicles imported for tourist use from outside the EU territory

A vehicle imported from outside the EU for tourist use shall be placed under the customs procedure of temporary importation in order that it can be used free of customs duty and VAT. The provisions on temporary importation are contained in Articles 137–144 of the Community Customs Code [Regulation (EEC) No. 2913/92] and in Articles 553–584 of the provisions for the implementation of the Code [Regulation (EEC) No. 2454/93, as amended by Regulation (EC) No. 993/2001].

For exemption from customs duty and VAT, it is required that the time limits for closing the temporary importation procedure are observed. The time limits for vehicles in private use are:

• I students: the period for which the student stays in the customs territory of the Community only for studies l persons performing tasks of fixed duration: the period for which the person stays in the customs territory of the Community only for performing the task

l other persons: six months.

The time limit for closing the procedure means, as a rule, the period within which the vehicle must be taken out of the EU territory. If necessitated by exceptional circumstances, the customs authorities may extend the time limit upon request. In that case the person concerned shall contact the customs office before the expiry of the period. Private use of vehicle means use for other than commercial purposes.

It must be noted that the vehicle can be in the customs territory only at the same time as the person who has received the authorization to temporary importation. If the holder of the authorization leaves the customs territory temporarily without the vehicle, another customs-approved treatment must be assigned to the vehicle for the time of his absence and the running of the time limit is interrupted.

For the purposes of the temporary importation procedure, leaving the customs territory in this way without the vehicle must, however, be occasional and only a short episode within the intended temporary stay in the customs territory. It is required, for instance, that the traveller must return under the same visa when he makes short visits out of the customs territory.

By contrast, the purpose of the law is not fulfilled if the vehicle is left in the customs territory as if being deposited under another customs-approved treatment whereas the holder of the authorization returns to his permanent place of residence and later comes back to Finland, e.g. for a further holiday the following year.

NOTE! A tourist car imported into Finland is always subject to the provisions on temporary tax-free use of vehicle contained in the Car Tax Act. When the vehicle is imported from outside the EU territory, the above-mentioned provisions on temporary importation procedure contained in the Customs Code and the implementing provisions are also applied. Owing to differences in the provisions, there may be situations where a tourist car may be used free of car tax but not free of customs duty and VAT or vice versa. Further information is available from the customs offices listed in this guide.

3 Vehicles brought in from the Åland Islands

Åland is not covered by the VAT territory of the EU. Therefore vehicles imported from Åland to other parts of Finland are, as appropriate, subject to the same provisions as vehicles brought into Finland from outside the EU. Such provisions are e.g. the time limits on importation. Furthermore, vehicles brought in from Åland may not be used elsewhere in Finland by any person other than one permanently resident in Åland or outside the EU territory.

TO BE NOTED IN CONNECTION WITH TAX-FREE USE

1 Right to temporary tax-free use is proved by documents

In a control situation, a tourist or any other person using a vehicle which has been temporarily exempted from tax shall prove by documents the right to temporary tax-free use of the vehicle. For example, a certificate stating the permanent place of residence abroad may be required. If he hands over the vehicle to be used by another person having legal right to use it, the latter person must have documents proving the right to temporary tax-free use of the vehicle.

2 When conditions of use cease to be fulfilled or time limit expires

If the conditions of temporary tax-free use cease to be fullfilled or the time limit expires, the vehicle shall either be exported, moved to a free zone or other place decided by the authorities, destroyed under the supervision of the authorities, or abandoned to the state without causing expenses to the latter. Otherwise, tax shall be paid for the vehicle.

3 Consequences of non-compliance

The use of a vehicle can be prevented if it is noticed that the vehicle is used contrary to the above provisions, and it can be taken off the road. The procedure is the same if the vehicle is not exported from the country within the time limit. Non-compliance with the provisions may also lead to imposing increased taxes or even to prosecution for tax fraud.

CUSTOMS OFFICES IN CHARGE OF CAR TAXATION

Southern Customs District	Åland Customs District
Car Taxation Vilhonvuorenkatu 12 B PO Box 62, 00501 HELSINKI tel. (09) 6141	Mariehamn Customs Torggatan 16, Ämbetshuset PO Box 40, 22101 MARIEHAMN tel. 020 492 6003 atp.bilbeskattning(at)tulli.fi
Hanko Customs Vapaasatama, 10900 HANKO tel. 020 492 3608 tel. 020 492 3609 (advice on removal goods by appointment)	Eastern Customs District Lappeenranta Customs Terminaalinkatu 5 PO Box 66, 53501 LAPPEENRANTA tel. 020 391 112
Lahti Customs Jussilankatu 4 PO Box 110, 15101 LAHTI tel. 020 492 3940 (advice on removal goods by appointment)	Northern Customs District Tornio Customs Hallituskatu 1 PO Box 47, 95401 TORNIO tel. 020 492 8021
Western Customs District Turku Customs Satamakatu 22 PO Box 386, 20101 TURKU tel. 020 492 4133	Oulu Customs Poikkimaantie 16 PO Box 56, 90401 OULU tel. 020 492 8105
Tampere Customs Patamäenkatu 18 PO Box 133, 33101 TAMPERE tel. 020 492 4400 tel. 020 492 4470	
Vaasa Customs	

Laivanvarustajankatu 1
PO Box 261, 65101 VAASA
tel. 020 492 4600

PRICES OF CALLS TO CUSTOMS TELEPHONE NUMBERS

CALLS TO NUMBERS BEGINNING WITH 020 492 OR 020 391:

–from fixed-line telephones 8.21 cents/call + 2 cents/min (incl.VAT 22%)
–from mobile phones 8.21 cents/call + 14.9 cents/min (incl.VAT 22%)

CALLS TO SERVICE NUMBERS BEGINNING WITH 020 690: NO EXTRA CHARGE, THE PRICE DEPENDS ON THE SUBSCRIBER CONNECTION USED:

–from fixed-line telephones 0 cents/min + local network charge
–from mobile phones 0 cents/min + mobile call charge

Service contacts
Customs Information Service
Erottajankatu 15-17, 00130 Helsinki tel. 020 690 600 fax 020 492 1812
Foreign Trade Statistics, reading room (by appointment)
Erottajankatu 15–17, 00130 Helsinki tel. 020 690 603 fax 020 492 1860
Tip-off hotline 0800 1 4600 (free of charge)
www.tulli.fi

The EU countries are Austria, Belgium, Bulgaria, Cyprus, the Czech Republic, Denmark, Estonia, Finland, France, Germany, Greece, Hungary, Ireland, Italy, Latvia, Lithuania, Luxembourg, Malta, the Netherlands, Poland, Portugal, Romania, the Slovak Republic, Slovenia, Spain, Sweden and the United Kingdom. The EEA countries are the EU countries, Iceland, Liechtenstein and Norway.

TAXATION OF USED MOTOR VEHICLES IN FINLAND

This guide deals with importation of used passenger cars, delivery vans and motorcycles as well as other taxable vehicles of category L into Finland from EU countries and from outside the EU. It contains information on the procedures applied to importation of vehicles and on the assessment of car tax, customs duty and value added tax.

Information on importation of vehicles as part of removal goods is given in the customer bulletin "Importation of Personal and Household Effects and Private Motor Vehicles as Removal Goods into Finland".

The examples given in this guide are intended to clarify the text and they are not binding in final taxation.

1 LIABILITY TO PAY CAR TAX AND TAXABLE VEHICLES

According to the Finnish Car Tax Act, car tax shall be paid to the State for taxable vehicles before they can be registered or taken into use in Finland.

According to Section 1 of the Car Tax Act, taxable vehicles are the following: • l passenger cars (category M_1) • l delivery vans (category N_1) • l buses/coaches with unladen weight of less than 1

875 kg • I motorcycles (categories L_{3e} and L_{4e}) • I tricycles and quadricycles (categories L_{5e} and L_{7e})

On certain conditions, a vehicle may be free of car tax . Details of those conditions are not dealt with in this guide.

The liability to pay car tax lies primarily with the person who is entered in the Finnish vehicle register as the owner of the vehicle. If the vehicle has been sold on hire purchase subject to retention of ownership, the liability lies with the buyer who is entered in the register as the holder of the vehicle. The taxable event is the registration of the vehicle.

The liability to pay car tax remains with the liable person defined above even if the taxation procedure had been taken care of on his behalf by an agent, e.g. the commercial operator who had imported the vehicle. The liable person is not released from the liability to pay the tax although he proved that he had paid the tax amount to the agent or to the agent´s representative.

If the importer of the vehicle is a registered agent for car taxation, the liability lies with the agent and the agent pays the tax on behalf of the liable person. The liability can, however, be transferred by a written contract e.g. to the buyer of the vehicle. The customs authorities must be notified of the transfer. If this notification is not made, the person who handed over the vehicle and the person who received it are responsible together. If the tax cannot be collected from the registered agent, the liability to pay the tax lies with the owner entered in the register, except in the case that he can prove having paid the tax amount to the registered agent or to the agent´s representative.

If the vehicle has been taken into use without registration or no other liable person can be established, the liability to pay the car tax lies with the person who took the vehicle into use. If it is not possible to establish that person or the tax cannot be collected from him, the liability lies with the owner of the vehicle which has been taken into use.

If car tax is not paid to Customs in accordance with the Car Tax Act, the vehicle may not be used on the road in Finland irrespective of who is liable to pay the tax or who is responsible to pay on his behalf.

2 WHAT IS MEANT BY A USED MOTOR VEHICLE

According to the Car Tax Act, a vehicle is considered as used if it has been registered *and* in

use. Use of vehicle means actual use which has an impact on the value of the vehicle and after which the vehicle can no longer be considered as new.

For the tax treatment of vehicles imported as part of removal goods, see customer bulletin of the National Board of Customs "Importation of Personal and Household Effects and Private Motor Vehicles as Removal Goods into Finland".

3 BEFORE BUYING A VEHICLE

Before buying a vehicle it is advisable to find out whether the vehicle can be registered in Finland.

It is especially important to check that the vehicle has the obligatory equipment and whether the EC type approval is required. A vehicle registered in another EU country does not necessarily meet the Finnish registration requirements, e.g. in case it has been accepted to the register in that country under a special national permit.

Information on the registration requirements is available on the website of the Vehicle Administration AKE at www.ake.fi.

Before you buy a used vehicle:

I check that the seller owns the vehicle

I check the chassis number of the vehicle I make sure that you learn the true number of kilometres travelled by the vehicle

I check the compliance of the vehicle with the Finnish requirements, e.g. the EU type

approval and the obligatory equipment

if necessary, contact a vehicle inspection station or the Vehicle Administration AKE to find

out the registration requirements

I take care that the purchase documents are made out properly.

4 USE OF VEHICLES IN FINLAND BEFORE TAXATION

As a rule, a person permanently resident in Finland is not allowed to use, not even occasionally, a foreignregistered vehicle on the road without paying car tax. There are, however, exceptions to this rule. In such cases a declaration of use submitted to Customs is required. The declaration must be lodged in advance or at the latest when temporary taxfree use of the vehicle is started. The declaration is submitted with a customs form.

A vehicle with **a valid registration in the EEA area** may be used on the basis of a declaration of use confirmed by Customs. A valid motor liability insurance is also required.

When a vehicle **does not have a valid registration in the EEA area**, a transfer permit is required in addition to the declaration of use. Transfer permits are granted by vehicle inspection stations and Customs. Further information on transfer permit is available on the website of the Vehicle Administration AKE at www.ake.fi.

VEHICLES INTENDED TO BE REGISTERED IN FINLAND

A vehicle which is intended to be registered in Finland may be used for at most three months without paying tax provided that a declaration of use on a customs form has been submitted to Customs before the use of the vehicle is started in Finland. If the vehicle does not have a valid registration in the EEA area or the validity of the EEA registration expires, a transfer permit is also needed. The declaration of use confirmed by Customs must be kept in the vehicle when the vehicle is used. The vehicle must also have **a motor liability insurance** which is in force in Finland. The insurance coverage of the Finnish insurance is in some respects more extensive than those of the other EEA states.

To keep the right to taxfree use, a tax declaration on the vehicle must be submitted within five days from the date when the declaration of use was confirmed. The right to taxfree use also expires on the due date of car tax or if the tax declaration or a tax decision already issued is cancelled.

As a result of cancellation, a charge equivalent to that for an advance ruling of the National Board of Customs is collected and, in car tax, a charge amounting to five per cent of the car tax which should have been paid if the taxation had been completed. The car tax collected as a result of the cancellation is not taken into account if tax is later assessed on the vehicle. In 2009, the charge for an advance ruling collected from a private person is 130 euros and that collected from a commercial operator 350 euros.

The right of use does not cease even though the ownership of the vehicle were transferred. However, it is to be noted that if the vehicle has a Finnish motor liability insurance, its validity expires when the ownership is transferred.

DEMONSTRATION VEHICLES

A vehicle intended to be sold in Finland may be used temporarily free of tax for a maximum period of nine months for shortterm test driving or demonstration for sales purposes for at most three days per customer in the business of a company importing, manufacturing and selling motor vehicles, provided that, before the use in Finland is started, a declaration on the vehicle has been submitted to the customs authorities in the way determined by these. The declaration confirmed by Customs must be kept in the vehicle when the vehicle is used unless otherwise ordered by Customs.

A transfer permit or a valid EEA registration is required.

5 VALUE ADDED TAX ON INTRA-COMMUNITY ACQUISITION OF NEW MEANS OF TRANSPORT

When a used vehicle is imported into Finland from within the EU territory, it may be possible that a VAT levied on intraCommunity acquisition of new means of transport in accordance with the Finnish Value Added Tax Act must be paid for the vehicle. Although a vehicle were considered as used according to the Car Tax Act, it may, in certain cases, still fulfil the criteria of a new means of transport within the meaning of the Value Added Tax Act.

In the Value Added Tax Act, means of transport means motorized land transport vehicles, aircraft and vessels meeting certain conditions and appropriate for the transport of passengers or goods. Motorized land transport vehicles are means of transport referred to by the Act if they have engines with a cylinder capacity exceeding 48 cc or a power exceeding 7.2kW.

According to the Value Added Tax Act, a vehicle is regarded as a new means of transport if I it has been sold when not more than six months have passed after it was taken into use for the first time, or I it has travelled not more than 6 000 kilometres.

The vehicle is new if one of the two criteria is met. In other words, the vehicle is no longer a new means of transport when both criteria cease to be met. In considering whether the criteria of a new means of transport set out in the Value Added Tax Act are fulfilled, the

date of sale is decisive. This applies to both criteria mentioned above. The owner must be able to show the kilometrage travelled by the vehicle by the time when it is sold.

An essential characteristic of intraCommunity acquisition is that the vehicle is transported from another member state to the buyer in Finland. The transportation may be carried out by the seller, the buyer or a third party by order of the seller or the buyer. It is to be noted that although VAT had been paid in the country of purchase, VAT on intraCommunity acquisition of new means of transport has to be paid in Finland if the buyer intends to import the new vehicle to be used in Finland.

The VAT is 22% of the price of the vehicle agreed between the seller and the buyer. All amounts added to the price and charged by the seller to the buyer, e.g. delivery costs, are included in the acquisition price.

If the vehicle is subject to car tax and the buyer is a private person or otherwise not registered for VAT, the VAT on intraCommunity acquisition of new means of transport is collected by the customs office collecting the car tax.

New means of transport purchased by enterprises liable to pay VAT are treated in taxation as normal intraCommunity acquisitions.

If a new means of transport is free of car tax (e.g. a lorry, a camper), the buyer pays the VAT on intraCommunity acquisition to the Tax Office of his home municipality.

Further information on value added taxation of new means of transport is available e.g. on the website of the Tax Administration at the address www.vero.fi.

6 USED VEHICLES IMPORTED FROM OUTSIDE THE EU

When a vehicle is imported from outside the EU, it must be cleared through Customs for free circulation in the Community. Before the customs duty has been paid, the vehicle may only be moved under a customs procedure, which is usually the external transit procedure involving a guarantee.

Vehicles imported from outside the EU are subject to customs duty and VAT on importation. The customs duty on passenger cars (in January 2009) is 10% and on delivery vans either 10% or 22% depending on the engine. The customs duty on motorcycles is either 6% or 8% depending on the engine.

If the vehicle has been sold for exportation to the Community, its customs value normally consists of the transaction value, i.e. the price actually paid or payable for it, and of certain items defined in the Community Customs Code. Such items are e.g. the transport and insurance costs as well as the costs for loading and handling in connection with transport to the place where the goods are imported into the customs territory of the Community. The provisions on customs value are contained in Articles 28 to 36 of the Customs Code and in Articles 141–181a of the provisions for implementing the Code. More detailed information on determining the customs value can be obtained from the customs office which will be used for the customs clearance and taxation of the vehicle.

The VAT on importation into the EU customs territory is normally calculated on the basis of the customs value, which includes the transport, loading, unloading and insurance costs as well as other costs relating to importation to the first destination in Finland according to the transport contract. If it is known at the time when the liability to pay tax arises that the goods will be transported to another destination in Finland or another EU member state, the above costs to that further destination are taken into account. The customs duty collected is also added to the tax base. Further information on the assessment of VAT can be obtained from customs offices. The VAT on importation of vehicles is 22%.

For the customs clearance of the vehicle, a customs declaration has to be lodged with a customs office within the time limit laid down in the Community Customs Code.

Example 1:	
Used passenger car imported from outside the EU	
Customs duty and VAT on importation	
Customs value of the vehicle	13 400.00 €
10% customs duty	1 340.00 €
Value on which VAT on importation is based	14 740.00 €
22% VAT on importation	3 242.80 €
Customs duty and VAT on importation in total	4 582.80 €
Car tax as below in section 9.	

Example 2:

Used motorcycle imported from outside the EU, cylinder capacity more than 250 cc

Customs duty and VAT on importation

Customs value of the vehicle 5 300.00 €

6% customs duty 318.00 €

Value on which VAT on importation is based 5 618.00 €

22% VAT on importation 1 235.96 €

Customs duty and VAT on importation in total 1 553.96 €

Car tax as below in section 9.

7 CAR TAX DECLARATION

A person liable to pay car tax must submit a car tax declaration to Customs before the vehicle is registered or taken into use in Finland. The declaration may also be submitted by an agent authorized by the liable person to act on his behalf. The declaration must be made in the name of the person who is entered as the owner of the vehicle in the Finnish vehicle register.

The most rapid service is received if the car tax declaration is lodged with one of the customs offices in charge of car taxation. Contact details of these offices are available on the website of Customs www.tulli.fi.

In addition to the car tax declaration, a specification form concerning the vehicle must be filled out giving e.g. the chassis number, make, model and equipment of the vehicle and the number of kilometres travelled by the vehicle. A certificate of the foreign registration of the vehicle and evidence on the right of ownership, usually the purchase contract, must also be annexed.

The vehicle may be examined by Customs, if necessary. The odometer reading, the chassis number and the equipment are checked against the specification form completed by the customer.

The customer has an opportunity to point out such particular characteristics of his vehicle which affect its market value. In these cases the vehicle is always examined. If the customer wants to refer to the condition of the vehicle, this must be done when the car tax declaration is submitted. It is no longer possible in connection with an appeal, if the condition has been declared to be normal or good when submitting the tax declaration.

The odometer reading alone is not regarded as sufficient evidence on the true number of kilometres travelled by the vehicle but further proof is required as well. The condition of the vehicle, its other individual characteristics and the odometer reading can together be considered as sufficient evidence.

As regards passenger cars and delivery vans, evidence on the CO_2 emissions of the car, which affect the tax percentage, can also be presented.

The contact details of the customs offices carrying out car taxation are given at the end of this guide.

The following documents are needed in submitting a car tax declaration:

I specification form concerning used vehicles

I purchase documents

I foreign registration document

I document proving the declarant´s identity

I further documents as may be required by Customs.

A tax decision is not taken immediately but is delivered to the customer by letter. The car tax must be paid within fifteen days from the date of the tax decision.

8 TAXABLE VALUE

The taxable value of a vehicle is its general retail sale value. The general retail sale value of a vehicle means the price, taxes included, which would generally be received for a similar vehicle if it were sold on the Finnish market to a buyer in the position of consumer at the time when the vehicle is, or should have been, declared for taxation. In other words, it is the general selling price from trader to consumer. If no value based on general selling prices is available, the general retail sale value is determined on the basis of the price at which similar vehicles in general are put up for sale, reduced by an appropriate amount for usual discounts. Thus the taxable value can be determined on the basis of the asking price by reducing it with the amount equivalent to the usual discounts.

The general retail sale value of a vehicle covers all consideration which the buyer of the vehicle, directly or indirectly, pays to the seller or to a third party. However, customary financing costs and customary costs, not exceeding 600 euros, for delivery to the client are not included.

For used vehicles, the amount of usual discounts is either 5% of the asking price plus 750 euros, or alternatively 1 500 euros, depending on which alternative gives a larger reduction. However, the maximum amount of discounts is 30% of the asking price. The amounts of usual discounts are changed according to changes on the market.

If the taxable value of a used vehicle cannot be determined in the way described above owing to inadequate information being available from the market, the retail sale value can be determined on the basis of a value which is received by reducing the general retail sale value of a corresponding new vehicle according to the age of the used vehicle by one per cent/month of the residual value calculated at the end of each preceding month. A different calculated amount of value reduction may be applied depending on vehicle model if there are grounds for this in the light of the market information statistics. The age of the used vehicle is determined in full months during which the vehicle has been both registered and used.

AMOUNT OF TAX

1 Passenger cars and delivery vans

The tax percentage for passenger cars and delivery vans is graduated according to the carbon dioxide emissions of the vehicle. Tax percentages determined by carbon dioxide emissions are applied to all passenger cars and vans when these are taxed in Finland for the first time irrespective of when they were taken into use for the first time. Each gramme of carbon dioxide affects the tax rate.

In the taxation of passenger cars, the emission level entered or which should be entered in the technical data of the car in the register is applied. For delivery vans, the applicable emission level is that which was entered or should have been entered in the technical data of the car in the register on 1 January 2008 or should be entered after that.

When there is no information available on the carbon dioxide emissions which should be entered for the car in the register, an estimated level of emissions is determined. In these cases, the tax percentage applicable to the car is determined on the basis of the total mass and motive power of the car in accordance with the tax scale. The estimated level of emissions of sports car type vehicles is determined in another way, as their power and fuel consumption are considerable in relation to the total mass of the vehicle. The tax rate is 12.2 per cent at the minimum and 48.8 per cent at the maximum. The percentages are given in Table 1 annexed to the Car Tax Act.

The tax rate for vans is reduced according to carrying capacity on the following conditions:

I N_1 category

I One row of seats

I Total mass over 2 500 kg

I Carrying capacity (total mass – unladen mass) and relative power (power kW / total mass kg):

– **Carrying capacity 680 – 1 000 kg and relative power at most 0.0**5 or

– Carrying capacity at least 1 000 kg and relative power at most 0.06

The reductions of the tax rate of vans meeting the above requirements vary from a minimum of 6.8% to a maximum of 18.7%. The tax rate is always at least 12.2%. The reductions of the tax rate appear from Table 2 annexed to the Car Tax Act.

Further information on the CO_2based car tax is available from customer bulletin No. 25 of the National Board of Customs "CO_2based car tax " .

Example 1:	
Passenger car taken into use abroad on 1 June 2005	
CO2 emissions according to the EC type approval 100 g/km	
General asking price in Finland	25 000.00 €
Reduction by usual discounts (5% x 25 000 € + 750 €)	2 000.00 €
General retail value i.e. taxable value	23 000.00 €
Car tax (17.1% x 23 000 €)	3 993.00 €

EXAMPLE 2:

Passenger car taken into use abroad on 1 June 1996 CO_2 reading according to the EC type approval not available Total mass of the vehicle: 2 500 kg Motive power: diesel oil General asking price in Finland 16 000.00 € Reduction by usual discounts (5% x 16 000 € + 750 €) 1 550.00 € General retail value i.e. taxable value 14 450.00 € Car tax (32.6% x 14 450 €) 4 710.70 €

Example 3

Delivery van taken into use abroad on 1 June 2008 CO_2 emissions according to the EC type approval 191 g/km Total mass 2 661 kg, carrying capacity 921 kg, relative power < 0.05 Other conditions of tax reduction also satisfied Tax rate according to CO_2 emissions 28.2%, reduction of tax rate 10.8% General asking price in Finland 25 000.00 € Reduction by usual discounts (5% x 25 000 € + 750 €) 2 000.00 € General retail value i.e. taxable value 23 000.00 € Car tax (17.4% x 23 000 €) 4 002.00 €

Example 4

Delivery van taken into use abroad on 1 June 2002 CO_2 reading according to the EC type approval not available Total mass 2 300 kg Motive power: diesel oil Conditions of tax reduction not satisfied General asking price in Finland 9 000.00 € Reduction by usual discounts (5% x 9 000 € + 750 € =1 200 € < 1 500 €) 1500.00 € General retail value i.e. taxable value 7 500.00 € Car tax (29.9 % x 7 500 €) 2 242.50 €

2 MOTORCYCLES AND OTHER TAXABLE VEHICLES OF CATEGORY L

The tax on a motorcycle or other taxable vehicle of category L is calculated as a percentage of the taxable value according to the cylinder capacity of the engine or motive power as follows:

Cylinder capacity	Tax percentage
not more than 130 cc	9.8%
131 – 255 cc	12.2%
256 – 355 cc	15.9%
356 – 505 cc	19.5%
506 – 755 cc	22.0%
756 cc or more	22.4%
Electric vehicle of category L	12.2%

Example:

Motorcycle, taken into use on 1 May 2006

Cylinder capacity 599 cc

General asking price in Finland 21 000.00 €

Reduction by usual discounts (5% x 21 000 € + 750 €) 1 800.00 €

General retail sale value, i.e. taxable value 19 200.00 €

Car tax according to cylinder capacity (22% x 19 200 €) 4 224.00 €

PAYMENT OF TAX AND REGISTRATION OF VEHICLE

Car tax and, if appropriate, value added tax on intraCommunity acquisition of new means of transport must be paid within 15 days from the date of the tax decision. The payment can be made at a bank or a customs office. After the payment has been made, the customs authorities give permission to register the vehicle. The permission is communicated electronically to the data system of the Vehicle Administration AKE.

Before the vehicle is registered, it must be taken to registration inspection.

If in doubt whether a vehicle can be registered in Finland, it is advisable to contact a vehicle inspection station or AKE before deciding to buy the vehicle. Further information on registration is also available on the website of AKE at the address www.ake.fi.

A car tax declaration or a taxation procedure can be cancelled at the customer´s request if the vehicle has not been entered in the Finnish register or taken into use in Finland. If a tax declaration is cancelled before the tax decision is taken, the cancellation is free of charge. In case the decision has already been taken, a payment equal to that for an advance ruling must be made. In 2009, private persons have to pay 130 euros and commercial operators 350 euros. If the vehicle has been used temporarily free of tax for more than five days under a declaration of use, 5% of the tax which would have been levied on the vehicle is also collected.

FURTHER INFORMATION

CUSTOMS INFORMATION SERVICE

www.tulli.fi tel. 020 690 600

VEHICLE ADMINISTRATION AKE

www.ake.fi

Contact details of the customs offices in charge of car taxation are available on

the website of Customs www.tulli.fi.

The EU countries are Austria, Belgium, Bulgaria, Cyprus, the Czech Republic, Denmark, Estonia, Finland, France, Germany, Greece, Hungary, Ireland, Italy, Latvia, Lithuania, Luxembourg, Malta, the Netherlands, Poland, Portugal, Romania, the Slovak Republic, Slovenia, Spain, Sweden and the United Kingdom.

The EEA countries are the EU countries, Iceland, Liechtenstein and Norway.

SERVICE CONTACTS

CUSTOMS INFORMATION SERVICE

Erottajankatu 15-17, 00130 Helsinki tel. 020 690 600 fax 020 492 1812

FOREIGN TRADE STATISTICS, READING ROOM (BY APPOINTMENT)

Erottajankatu 15–17, 00130 Helsinki tel. 020 690 603 fax 020 492 1860

TIP-OFF HOTLINE 0800 1 4600 (FREE OF CHARGE)

www.tulli.fi

TRAVEL TO FINLAND

US STATE DEPARTMENT SUGGESTIONS

COUNTRY DESCRIPTION: Finland is a highly developed democracy with a modern economy. It is a member of the European Union. Tourist facilities are widely available.

ENTRY REQUIREMENTS: A passport is required. A visa is not required for tourist or business stays up to 90 days. For additional information concerning entry requirements, travelers may contact the Embassy of Finland at 3301 Massachusetts Avenue, N.W., Washington, D.C. 20048, tel. (202) 298-5800, or the Finnish Consulate General in Los Angeles or New York. Additional information is available via the Internet at http://www.finland.org.

CRIME INFORMATION: Although the crime rate in Finland is low compared to the U.S. and most European countries, it has increased approximately 15 percent since 1998. However, Finland remains relatively safe. Americans visiting Finland are seldom victims of crime, but visitors should not be complacent regarding personal safety or the protection of valuables. The same precautions employed in the U.S. should be followed in Finland. Finnish police services are excellent; however, some police officers speak little English. The telephone number for police and other emergency services throughout Finland is 112. All forms of public transportation are considered safe. Street crimes such as muggings and pickpocketing remain relatively uncommon, but they do occur. The loss or theft of a U.S. passport should be reported immediately to the local police (112) and the U.S. Embassy (171-931 ext. 271). U.S. citizens may refer to the Department of State's pamphlet *A Safe Trip Abroad* for ways to promote a more trouble-free journey. The pamphlet is available from the Superintendent of Documents, U.S. Government Printing Office, Washington, D.C. 20402, via the Internet at http://www.access.gpo.gov/su_docs, or via the Bureau of Consular Affairs home page at http://travel.state.gov.

MEDICAL FACILITIES: Medical facilities are widely available for emergency services. The public hospital system and many private hospitals honor foreign credit cards. Serious medical problems requiring hospitalization and/or medical evacuation to the United States can cost thousands of dollars or more.

MEDICAL INSURANCE: U.S. medical insurance is not always valid outside the United States. U.S. Medicare and Medicaid programs do not provide payment for medical services outside the United States. Uninsured travelers who require medical care overseas may face extreme difficulties. Please check with your own insurance company to confirm whether your policy applies overseas, including provision for medical evacuation. Please ascertain whether payment will be made to the overseas hospital or doctor or whether you will be reimbursed later for expenses that you incur. Some insurance policies also include coverage for psychiatric treatment and for disposition of remains in the event of death. Useful information on medical emergencies abroad, including overseas insurance programs, is provided in the Department of State's Bureau of Consular Affairs brochure, *Medical Information for Americans Traveling Abroad*, which is available via its home page.

OTHER HEALTH INFORMATION: Information on vaccinations and other health precautions may be obtained from the Centers for Disease Control and Prevention's hotline for international travelers at 1-877-FYI-TRIP (1-877-394-8747), via CDC's autofax service at 1-888-CDC-FAXX (1-888-232-3299), or via CDC's Internet site at http://www.cdc.gov.

TRAFFIC SAFETY AND ROAD CONDITIONS: While in a foreign country, U.S. citizens may encounter road conditions that differ significantly from those in the United States. The information below concerning Finland is provided for general reference only, and may not be totally accurate in a particular location or circumstance.
Safety of Public Transportation: Excellent
Urban Road Condition/Maintenance: Excellent
Rural Road Condition/Maintenance: Excellent
Availability of Roadside Assistance: Excellent

Finland has an extensive network of highways throughout the country, as well as excellent public transportation services. Travelers should be aware that drunk driving laws are strict, and acceptable blood alcohol levels are much lower in Finland than in the United States. Police strictly enforce all traffic laws and institute random roadside breathalyzer tests. Those drivers who register a .05 or above alcohol content are subject to immediate arrest. Driving regulations and traffic signs differ significantly from those in the United States. Visitors should be familiar with both prior to operating a vehicle in Finland. Driving in Finland during the winter months can be hazardous. Icy road conditions are common. Vehicles are required to be winterized and have studded snow tires, and engine heaters are strongly recommended. When driving at night, drivers must be alert to moose wandering onto major roadways. There have been incidents of moose being struck by vehicles, causing severe damage to the vehicle and even death to the occupants. For specific information concerning Finnish driver's permits, vehicle inspection, road tax and mandatory insurance, please contact the Finland National Tourist Organization offices in New York via the Internet at http://www.mek.fi. The e-mail address is med@mek.fi.

AVIATION SAFETY OVERSIGHT: The U.S. Federal Aviation Administration (FAA) has assessed the Government of Finland's Civil Aviation Authority as Category 1 -- in compliance with international aviation safety standards for oversight of Finland's air carrier operations. For further information, travelers may contact the Department of Transportation within the U.S. at tel. 1-800-322-7873, or visit the FAA Internet home page at http://www.faa.gov/avr/iasa/. The U.S. Department of Defense (DOD) separately assesses some foreign air carriers for suitability as official providers of air services. For information regarding the DOD policy on specific carriers, travelers may contact the DOD at tel. (618) 229-4801.

CUSTOMS REGULATIONS: Finland's customs authorities encourage the use of an ATA (Admission Temporaire/Temporary Admission) Carnet for the temporary admission of professional equipment, commercial samples, and/or goods for exhibitions and fair purposes. ATA Carnet Headquarters, located at the U.S. Council for International Business, 1212 Avenue of the Americas, New York, NY 10036, issues and guarantees the ATA Carnet in the United States. For additional information, please call 212-354-4480, send an e-mail to atacarnet@uscib.org, or visit http://www.uscib.org for details.

CRIMINAL PENALTIES: While in a foreign country, a U.S. citizen is subject to that country's laws and regulations, which sometimes differ significantly from those in the United States and may not afford the protections available to the individual under U.S. law. Penalties for breaking the law can be more severe than in the United States for similar offenses. Persons violating Finland's laws, even unknowingly, may be expelled, arrested or imprisoned. Penalties for possession, use, or trafficking in illegal drugs in Finland are strict and convicted offenders can expect jail sentences and heavy fines.

CHILDREN'S ISSUES: For information on international adoption of children and international parental child abduction, please refer to our Internet site at http://travel.state.gov/children's_issues.html or telephone (202) 736-7000.

REGISTRATION AND EMBASSY LOCATION: U.S. citizens are encouraged to register and obtain updated information on travel and security in Finland at the Consular Section of the U.S. Embassy in Helsinki. It is located at Itainen Puistotie 14B; tel: 358-9-171931 or after hours: 358-9-605414; fax: 358-9-652057; e-mail address: consular@usembassy.fi; home page: http://www.usembassy.fi.

BUSINESS TRAVEL

BUSINESS CUSTOMS

Finland is a modern, commercially mature country that enjoys close relations with its Nordic neighbors. Social and business protocol is similar to that in the United States and requires no special mentions of taboos. It is worth noting that relationships are important within the social and business world as Finns prefer to deal with people they know and trust.

VISA REQUIREMENTS AND BUSINESS MOBILITY GENERALLY

With the exception of Nordic (Sweden, Norway, Denmark, Iceland) citizens, citizens of EU countries (except Greece), and citizens of Switzerland, San Marino and Liechtenstein, foreigners entering Finland must have a valid passport. A tourist or business visa is not required for stays of up to three months. For non-EU citizens a visa is needed for stays exceeding 90 days. Visa applications should be submitted to a Finnish diplomatic mission before entry into Finland.

A foreigner needs a residence permit in order to stay in Finland for a longer period of time. However, residence permits are also needed for short stays of less than three months if the purpose of the stay is to work in Finland. Residence permits require either a valid passport or a travel document. Foreigners must have work permits if they intend to work in Finland. Exceptions are citizens of the Nordic countries or citizens of EU/EEA countries. EU-citizens outside the Nordic countries need to apply for an EEA-card from the local police for stays exceeding 90 days. An EEA-card is a combined work and residence permit.

HOLIDAYS

The national holidays are: New Year's Day (January 1); Epiphany (January 6); Good Friday (April 13); Easter (April 15-16); May Day (May 1); Ascension Day (May 24); Mid-Summer (June 23); All Saints' Day (November 3); Independence Day (December 6); Christmas (December 25-26).

Workweek

The average Finnish workweek is 40 hours per week, with annual leave of 25 days, 12.5 free days, and 9 paid holidays. Part-time employment averages to 17.8 hours per week.

BUSINESS INFRASTRUCTURE

- Transportation and communications - see section Economic Trends and Outlook - Infrastructure

LANGUAGE

The two official languages in Finland are Finnish and Swedish. About 92.5 percent of the population speak Finnish and 5.6 percent speak Swedish. Both languages are compulsory at school. English is widely spoken in Finland, especially among younger people and in major cities.

EDUCATION

Finland invests more in education that the EU countries on average. All children aged 7-15 – even handicapped – attend school in Finland. Comprehensive school is a nine-year compulsory general schooling for all children aged 7-16. The municipalities pay teachers' salaries, books, health care, and school meals. After completing comprehensive school, students may attend high schools for three years or receive vocational education. High school prepares students for university studies. Tuition at universities is minimal. Helsinki has international, English, German, Russian, French, and Jewish schools in which classes are taught partly in foreign languages and partly in Finnish. The International, English, German and Jewish schools are private and charge tuition. University level education is mainly in Finnish, with exception of English language BBA and MBA programs in certain universities and polytechnics.

MEDICAL SERVICES

Medical facilities are widely available. The public hospital system will not honor foreign credit cards and/or U.S. insurance coverage. However, private hospitals and clinics that accept major credit cards are widely available. Travelers have found that, in some cases, a letter from their carrier describing supplemental medical insurance with specific overseas coverage has proved useful. A foreigner is usually covered by the Finnish social security after moving to Finland, with health care as one of the benefits. Services are provided within each municipality. The quality of public health care is equivalent to care given by private doctors. In addition, the employers subsidize occupational health care.

HOUSING

Most people in Finland own their own housing. The cost to rent an apartment varies depending on the size, age, condition and location. Rents are generally quite high, especially within the Helsinki area, and most places come unfurnished.

FOOD

Despite prices converging with other EU levels, Finland's price structure regarding food and household needs is the lowest of the Nordic countries and only slightly above the OECD average. Finnish food is consistent to produce that is in season, which provides an array of berries, mushrooms, seafood etc. Potatoes are a main staple and accompany most evening dishes. Temporary Entry of Goods - see section Trade Regulations, Customs, and Standards

CONTACT INFORMATION

The Commercial Service staff in Helsinki provides several services for U.S. companies interested in doing business in Finland or using Finland as a gateway to Russia and the Baltic countries, especially Estonia. Please contact us at the following address to set up an appointment prior to your visit to Finland:

Commercial Service Helsinki
American Embassy
It. Puistotie 14 B
FIN-00140 Helsinki, Finland
Tel: (358-9) 171 931
Fax: (358-9) 635 332
E-mail: Helsinki.Office.Box@mail.doc.gov

SUPPLEMENTS

CUSTOMS DISTRICTS

Northern District Tornio
Kajaani
Karigasniemi
Kilpisjärvi
Kivilompolo
Kuusamo
Muonio
Neiden / Näätämö
Oulu
Polmak
Raahe
Raja-Jooseppi
Rovaniemi
Salla
Utsjoki
Vartius
Western District
Turku
Kaskinen
Kokkola
Jyväskylä
Pietarsaari
Pori
Tampere
Rauma
Vaasa
Eastern District

Lappeenranta
Hamina
Imatra
Kotka
Kouvola
Kuopio
Niirala
Nuijamaa
Parikkala
Vaalimaa
Vainikkala
Åland District Customs Laboratory Southern District Mariehamn Helsinki
41. Espoo
Eckerö 3. Hanko
Långnäs 4. Hämeenlinna
Lahti
Loviisa
Vantaa

National Board of Customs, Statistics Unit
P.O.Box 512, 00101 Helsinki, Finland
Erottajankatu 15-17 A, 00130 Helsinki
Statistics service Tel. +358 20 690 603 Fax +358 20 492 1860 Email: statistics@tulli.fi
www.tulli.fi

CONTACTS FOR ESTABLISHING BUSINESS

ESTATE AGENTS

Helsingin Liiketeollinen Kiinteistönvälitys Oy, www.liiketeollinen.fi
Mikonkatu 13 G 186, 00100 Helsinki
Tel. +358 9 684 0680, Fax +358 9 6840 6840

Catella Property Consultants Ltd, www.catella.fi
Aleksanterinkatu 15 B, 00100 Helsinki
Tel. +358 10 522 0100, Fax +358 10 522 0218

Suomen SKV-Yrityspalvelu Oy,www.skv.fi/yrityspalvelu/
Panuntie 4, 00610 Helsinki
Tel. +358 9 8629 1230, Fax +358 9 8629 1250

The Finnish Real Estates Agents' Association, www.asuntoverkko.com
Malminkaari 5, 00700 Helsinki
Tel. +358 9 530 8500, Fax +358 9 5308 5050

The Finnish Association of Building Owners and Construction Clients, www.rakli.fi
Annankatu 24, 00100 Helsinki
Tel. +358 9 4767 5711, Fax +358 9 4767 5700
Representatives of Foreign Auditing Firms

BDO
www.bdo.fi

BDO Finland Oy
Vattuniemenranta 2, 00210 Helsinki
Tel. +358 207 432 920
Fax +358 9 4780 8210

PricewaterhouseCoopers
www.pwcglobal.com SVH
PriceWaterhouseCoopers Oy
Itämerentori 2, P.O.Box 1015, 00101 Helsinki
Tel. +358 9 228 00
Fax +358 9 174 102

Deloitte Touche Tohmatsu International
www.deloitte.com
Deloitte & Touche Oy
Munkkiniemen puistotie 25,
P.O.Box 94, 00331 Helsinki
Tel. +358 20 755 500
Fax +358 20 755 507

Ernst & Young International
www.ey.com
Ernst & Young Oy
Elielinaukio 5 B, 00100 Helsinki
Tel. +358 9 172 771
Fax +358 9 1727 7700

Grant Thornton International
www.revico.fi
Revico Grant Thornton Oy
Paciuksenkatu 27, P.O.Box 18, 00271 Helsinki
Tel. +358 9 512 3330
Fax +358 9 458 0250

KPMG International
www.kpmg.fi
KPMG: Investment in Finland KPMG Wideri Oy Ab
Mannerheimintie 20 B, P.O.Box 1037, 00101 Helsinki
Tel. +358 9 693 931
Fax +358 9 6939 3399

Midsnell Group International
www.mgimidsnell.com
Tilintarkastustoimisto Kalervo Ariluoma Oy
Keskustie 4, 01900 Nurmijärvi or
Mannerheimintie 16 A 3, 00100 Helsinki
Tel. +358 9 250 9595
Fax +358 9 250 9715

RECRUITMENT CONSULTANTS

Amrop Hever Finland,
Yrjönkatu 16 A, 00120 Helsinki
tel. +358 9 622 9360, fax +358 9 6229 3619, www.amrop.fi

Boyden Finland,
Mikonkatu 17 A, 00100 Helsinki
tel. +358 9 622 6860, fax +358 9 6226 8666, www.boyden.fi

Heidrick & Struggles,
Kasarmikatu 46-48 B, 00130 Helsinki
tel. +358 9 2511 250, fax +358 9 2511 2511, www.heidrick.com
Horton International Finland,
Annankatu 25, 5th floor, 00100 Helsinki
tel. +358 9 6829 110, fax +358 9 6829 1115, www.horton.fi

HRD Group,
Yrjönkatu 27 A, 00100 Helsinki
tel. +358 9 4763 770, fax +358 9 4780 3333, http://www.hrd-group.fi/eng_index.php

IBI Executive Search,
Karvaamokuja 6, 00380 Helsinki
tel. +358 9 506 1899, fax +358 9 556 787, www.ibi.fi
IMS Oy International Management Search
Urho Kekkosen katu 5 C
00100 I lelsinki
tel +358 (0) 9 694 00 44, fax +358 (0) 9 694 55 44, http://www.imssearch.fi

Intersearch Finland,
Iso Roobertinkatu 1 A 5, 00120 Helsinki
tel. +358 9 612 9090, fax +358 9 612 1390, www.intersearch.fi

JL Consultants,
Laulukuja 4, 00420 Helsinki
tel. +358 9 348 3200, fax +358 9 3483 2323, www.jaakkolehto.fi

J. Friisberg & Partners,
Keilasatama 3, 02150 Espoo
tel. +358 9 612 9910, fax +358 9 621 5521, www.friisberg.com (IIC-partners)

Korn/Ferry International Oy,
Eteläesplanadi 24 A, 00100 Helsinki

tel. +358 9 612 2560, fax +358 9 6122 5656, www.kornferry.com

Mercuri Urval,
Mannerheimintie 15 A, 00260 Helsinki
tel. +358 9 476 1700, fax +358 9 476 17777, www.mercuriurval.com

MPS Management Consulting,
Metsänneidonkuja 8, SPEKTRI TRIO, P.O.Box 44, 02131 Espoo
tel. +358 9 430 000, fax +358 9 43 000 301, www.mps.fi

Open Management Oy,
Aleksanterinkatu 17 (WTC), 00100 Helsinki
tel. +358 9 6969 4090, fax +358 9 6969 4099, www.openmanagement.fi

Personnel,
Hitsaajankatu 6,00810 Helsinki
tel. +358 9 7591455, fax +358 9 784627, www.pib.fi

Psyko,
Annankatu 42 C, 00100 Helsinki
tel. +358 9 613141, fax +358 9 6131 4200, www.psyko.fi

S & S Consulting Oy,
Melkonkatu 28 D, 00210 Helsinki
tel. +358 9 686 0570, fax 6860 5769, www.ssconsulting.fi

Selektio Consulting Oy, Accord Group,
Aleksanterinkatu 17 (WTC), 00100 Helsinki
tel. +358 9 6969 2989, fax +358 9 6969 2988, www.accordgroup.net

TEMP-TEAM Finland Oy, Juhler Group,
Fredrikinkatu 47, 00100 Helsinki
tel. +358 207 414 850, fax +358 207 414 851, www.juhlergroup.com
Contacts

THE FINNISH BAR ASSOCIATION

Simonkatu 12 B 20, 4th floor
FI-00100 Helsinki, Finland
Tel. +358 9 6866 120
Fax +358 9 6866 1299
info@barassociation.fi
email: firstname.lastname@barassociation.fi

Bus ID 0202096-1

President
Advocate, LL.M. with court training
Kari Lautjärvi
firstname.lastname@hannessnellman.fi

Vice President
Advocate, LL.M. with court training
Riitta Leppiniemi
firstname.lastname@susiluoto.com

Administration and Development
Secretary General Markku Ylönen

Advocate LawDisciplinary matters
LL.M. with court training Martti Ojala
LL.M. with court training Minna Melender

US AND COUNTRY CONTACTS

U.S. Embassy Trade Personnel

Commercial Service of the United States
It. Puistotie 14 B
FIN-00140 Helsinki, Finland
or
PSC 78, Box H
APO AE 09723
Tel: (358-9) 171 931
Fax: (358-9) 635 332
E-mail: Helsinki.Office.Box@mail.doc.gov
Mr. Thomas Kelsey, Senior Commercial Officer (Stockholm)
Mr. Harri Makinen, Commercial Section Chief
Ms. Tarja Kunnas, Commercial Specialist
Ms. Mia Maki, Commercial Specialist
Ms. Heidi Day, Commercial Assistant

Economic Section
It. Puistotie 14 B
FIN-000140 Helsinki, Finland
Tel: (358-9) 171 931
Fax: (358-9) 174 681
Ms. Ingrid Kollist, Economic Section Chief

Ms. Beatrice Soila, Economic Officer
Ms. Riikka Aho, Economic Assistant

Defense Attache Office
It. Puistotie 14 B
FIN-00140 Helsinki, Finland
Tel: (358-9) 171 931
Fax: (358-9) 171 396
Colonel James R. Luntzel, Defense & Air Attache/Chief, Security Assistance Office
Colonel John M. O'Sullivan, Jr., Army Attache/SAO Officer
Commander Roy N. Peterson, Naval Attache/SAO Officer

Foreign Agricultural Service
Dag Hammarskjolds Vag 31
S-115 89 Stockholm, Sweden
Tel: (46-8) 783 5390
Fax: (46-8) 662 8495
E-mail: agstockholm@fas.usda.gov
Mr. Robert C. Tetro, Agricultural Counselor (for Sweden, Finland, Norway, Estonia and Latvia)
Ms. Asa Lexmon, Agricultural Specialist
Ms. Inger Gozalbez, Agricultural Marketing Specialist
Ms. Bettina Dahlbacka, Agricultural Marketing Assistant
Ms. Ann-Charlotte Bjorkegren, Administrative Assistant

Chambers of Commerce

Mr. Kari Jalas
Managing Director
Central Chamber of Commerce
P.O. Box 1000 (Aleksanterinkatu 17, WTC Helsinki)
FIN-00101 Helsinki, Finland
Tel: (358-9) 696 969
Fax: (358-9) 650 303
Internet: www.keskuskauppakamari.fi
E-mail: keskuskauppakamari@wtc.fi

Mr. Timo Vuori
Secretary General
International Chamber of Commerce (ICC)
Aleksanterinkatu 17, WTC Helsinki
FIN-00100 Helsinki, Finland
Tel: (358-9) 669 459
Fax: (358-9) 6969 6647
Internet: www.iccwbo.fi
E-mail: timo.vuori@wtc.fi

Mr. Heikki J. Perala
Managing Director
Helsinki Chamber of Commerce
Kalevankatu 12
FIN-00100 Helsinki, Finland
Tel: (358-9) 228 601
Fax: (358-9) 2286 0228
Internet: www.helsinki.chamber.fi
E-mail: kauppakamari@helsinki.chamber.fi

Mr. Matti Sundberg
Chairman
Finnish-American Chamber of Commerce
Arkadiankatu 2
FIN-00100 Helsinki, Finland
Tel: (358-9) 4695 539
Fax: (358-9) 695 553
Ms. Sirpa Rissa-Anttilainen
Managing Director
World Trade Center Helsinki
P.O. Box 800 (Aleksanterinkatu 17)
FIN-00100 Helsinki, Finland
Tel: (358-9) 696 911
(358-9) 6969 2021 (trade information)
Fax: (358-9) 6969 2027
Internet: www.wtc.fi
E-mail: noora.salo@wtc.fi

Country Trade Associations

Mr. Guy Wires
Managing Director
Federation of Finnish Commerce and Trade
Mannerheimintie 76 A
FIN-00250 Helsinki, Finland
Tel: (358-9) 531 560
Fax: (358-9) 4315 6302
Internet: www.kaupankl.fi
E-mail: guy.wires@kaupankl.fi

Central organization for 40 branch associations

Ms. Airi Vaaranto
Head of Secretariat
Finnish Foreign Trade Agents' Federation
Elimaenkatu 29
FIN-00510 Helsinki, Finland
Tel: (358-9) 8683 1650
Fax: (358-9) 8683 1651

Internet: www.agenttiliitto.fi
E-mail: fftaf@agenttiliitto.fi

Mr. Sakari Virtanen
Managing Director
Finnish Direct Marketing Association
Lonnrotinkatu 11 A
FIN-00120 Helsinki, Finland
Tel: (358-9) 2287 7400
Fax: (358-9) 6121 039
Internet: www.ssml-fdma.fi
E-mail: sakke@ssml-fdma.fi

Mr. Johannes Koroma
Director General
Confederation of Finnish Industry and Employers
P.O. Box 30 (Etelaranta 10)
FIN-00130 Helsinki, Finland
Tel: (358-9) 686 81
Fax: (358-9) 6868 2316
Internet: www.tt.fi
E-mail: tt@tt.fi

Mr. Harri Malmberg
Director General
Federation of Finnish Metal, Engineering and Electrotechnical Industries (FIMET)
P.O. Box 10 (Etelaranta 10)
FIN-00130 Helsinki, Finland
Tel: (358-9) 192 31
Fax: (358-9) 624 462
Internet: www.met.fi
E-mail: harri.malmberg@met.fi

Mr. Timo Poranen
Managing Director
Finnish Forest Industries' Federation
P.O. Box 336 (Snellmaninkatu 13)
FIN-00170 Helsinki, Finland
Tel: (358-9) 132 61
Fax: (358-9) 1324 445
Internet: www.forestindustries.fi
E-mail: timo.poranen@forestindustries.fi

Mr. Seppo Harkonen
Managing Director
Finpro
P.O. Box 908 (Arkadiankatu 2)
FIN-00100 Helsinki, Finland
Tel: (358-204) 6951
Fax: (358-204) 695 535
Internet: www.finpro.fi
E-mail: info@finpro.fi

Ms. Sirkka Aura
Chief Executive
Invest in Finland Bureau
Aleksanterinkatu 17, WTC Helsinki
FIN-00100 Helsinki, Finland
Tel: (358-9) 6969 125
Fax: (358-9) 6969 2530
Internet: www.investinfinland.fi
E-mail: investinfinland@wtc.fi

Country Government Offices

Dr. Jaana Husu-Kallio
Veterinary Department
Ministry of Agriculture and Forestry
Kluuvikatu 4 A, 6th fl.
FIN-00100 Helsinki, Finland
Tel: (358-9) 1603 385
Fax: (358-9) 1603 338
Internet: www.mmm.fi
E-mail: jaana.husu-kallio@mmm.fi

Ms. Elina Lehto
Director
Employment and Economic Development Center
P.O. Box 15 (Maistraatinportti 2)
FIN-00240 Helsinki, Finland
Tel: (358-9) 2534 2401
Fax: (358-9) 2534 2410
Internet: www.te-keskus.fi
E-mail: elina.lehto@te-keskus.fi

Dr. Osmo Maki-Petays
Head of Meat Hygiene Unit
National Veterinary and Food Research Institute
P.O. Box 368 (Hameentie 57)
FIN-00230 Helsinki, Finland
Tel: (358-9) 3931 899
Fax: (358-9) 3931 811
Internet: www.mmm.fi/hallinnonala/eela
E-mail: osmo.maki-petays@mmm.fi

Mr. Veikko Koskela
Senior Customs Inspector
The Board of Customs
P.O. Box 512 (Erottajankatu 2)
FIN-00120 Helsinki, Finland
Tel: (358-9) 6141

Fax: (358-9) 6142 256
Internet: www.tulli.fi
E-mail: veikko.koskela@tulli.fi

Mr. Timo Relander
Director General
Statistics Finland
Tyopajankatu 13
00033 Tilastokeskus (Helsinki)
Tel: (358-9) 173 41
Fax: (358-9) 1734 2279
Internet: www.stat.fi
E-mail:
kirjasto.tilastokeskus@tilastokeskus.fi

Mr. Heikki Partanen
Chief Inspector
Office of Data Protection Ombudsman
P.O. Box 315 (Albertinkatu 25 A, 3rd fl.)
FIN-00180 Helsinki, Finland
Tel: (358-9) 182 51
Fax: (358-9) 1825 7835
Internet: www.tietosuoja.fi
E-mail: tietosuoja@om.vn.fi

Mr. Jyrki Alanko
Manager, Information Services
Finnish Standardization Association (SFS)
Maistraatinportti 2 A, 3rd fl.
FIN-00240 Helsinki, Finland
Tel: (358-9) 1499 331
Fax. (358-9) 1464 925
Internet: www.sfs.fi
E-mail: info@sfs.fi or jyrki.alanko@sfs.fi

Mr. Tuomo Ilomaki
Managing Director
Finnish Electrotechnical Standard
Association (SESKO)
P.O. Box 134 (Sarkiniementie 3)
FIN-00210 Helsinki, Finland
Tel: (358-9) 696 391
Fax: (358-9) 677 059
Internet: www.sesko.fi
E-mail: myynti@sesko.fi or sales@sfs.fi

Mr. Martti Enajarvi
Director General
National Board of Patents and Registration
Arkadiankatu 6 A
FIN-00100 Helsinki, Finland
Tel: (358-9) 6939 500
Fax: (358-9) 6939 5328
Internet: www.prh.fi
E-mail: martti.enajarvi@prh.fi

Ms. Eeva Kelloniemi
Engineer – Product Safety
National Consumer Administration
P.O. Box 5 (Haapaniemenkatu 4)
FIN-00530 Helsinki, Finland
Tel: (358-9) 772 61
Fax: (358-9) 7726 7557
Internet: www.kuluttajavirasto.fi
E-mail: posti@kuluttajavirasto.fi

Country Market Research Firms

Mr. Ari Heino
Managing Director
Research International RI Finland
(member of Research Int. Group Ltd.)
Lapinlahdenkatu 3 A
FIN-00180 Helsinki, Finland
Tel: (358-9) 6859 930
Fax: (358-9) 6859 9333
Internet: www.research-int.com

Mr. Jyri Seppa
Managing Director
A.C. Nielsen Finland Oy (specialized in retail trade)
Tietajantie 14
FIN-02130 Espoo, Finland
Tel: (358-9) 430 030
Fax: (358-9) 463 628
Internet: www.acnielsen.fi
E-mail: acn@acnielsen.fi

Ms. Tiina Myllykangas-Suonto
Publicist
Agricultural Economics Research Institute
P.O. Box 3
FIN-00411 Helsinki, Finland
Tel: (358-9) 504 471
Fax: (358-9) 563 1164
Internet: www.mttl.fi
E-mail: tiina.myllykangas-suonto@mttl.fi

COUNTRY COMMERCIAL BANKS

Mr. Pertti Voutilainen
President
Merita Pankki Oyj (Merita Bank Plc.)
Aleksanterinkatu 30
FIN-00020 Merita (Helsinki), Finland

Tel: (358-9) 1651
Fax: (358-9) 1654 2838
Internet: www.merita.fi

Mr. Mikael Silvennoinen
Managing Director
Okopankkien Keskuspankki Oyj (Okobank)
Teollisuuskatu 1 b
FIN-00510 Helsinki, Finland
Tel: (358-9) 4041
Fax: (358-9) 4043 703
Internet: www.osuuspankki.fi

Mr. Pentti Hakkarainen
President
Leonia Pankki Oyj (Leonia Bank Plc.)
Etelaesplanadi 8
FIN-00007 Leonia (Helsinki), Finland
Tel: (358-204) 2511
Fax: (358-204) 252 608
Internet: www.leonia.fi

Mr. Stephen L. Dwyre
Managing Director
Citibank International Plc.
Finland Branch
Aleksanterinkatu 48 A
FIN-00100 Helsinki, Finland
Tel: (358-9) 348 871
Fax: (358-9) 3488 7388
Internet: www.citicorp.com

Washington-Based USG Country Contacts

Ms. Leaksmy Norin
International Trade Specialist
U.S. Department of Commerce
Office of European Union and Regional Affairs
Washington, D.C. 20230
Tel: (202) 482-4414
Fax: (202) 482-2897
E-mail: leaksmy_norin@ita.doc.gov

Mr. Andrew Burst
Area Officer – Eastern Europe & Eurasia
Foreign Agricultural Service
U.S. Department of Agriculture
Washington, D.C. 20250
Tel: (202) 690-4053
Fax: (202) 690-2909
E-mail: BurstA@fas.usda.gov

U.S. Department of Agriculture
Foreign Agricultural Service
Trade Assistance and Promotion Office
Tel: (202) 720-7420
Fax: (202) 690-4374
Internet:
www.fas.usda.gov/agexport/tapohome.html
E-mail: TAPO@fas.usda.gov

TIC Trade Information Center in Washington
Tel: 1-800-USA-TRADE
Internet: infoserv2.ita.doc.gov/tic.nsf
E-mail: TIC@ita.doc.gov

U.S. Department of State
Office of the Coordinator for Business Affairs
2201 C Street NW
Washington, D.C. 20520-7512
Tel: (202) 647-1625
Fax: (202) 647-3953
Internet:
www.state.gov/www/about_state/business/index.html
E-mail: cbaweb@state.gov

Oveseas Private Investment Corporation (OPIC)
1100 New York Avenue, NW, 12th fl.
Washington, D.C. 20527
Tel: (202) 336-8799
Fax: (202) 408-9859
Internet: www.opic.gov
E-mail: info@opic.gov

GOVERNMENT OF FINLAND

Ministry of Trade and Industry
Aleksanterinkatu 4
00170 Helsinki
Tel: +358-9-160 3666

Ministry of Foreign Affairs
Laivastokatu 22
PL 176
00161 Helsinki
Tel: +358-9-135151

Competition Office
PL 332
00531 Helsinki
Tel: +358-9-731 41

Immigration Office
Siltasaarenkatu 12 A
PL 92
00531 Helsinki
Tel: +358-9-476 5500

Financial Supervision Authority
PL 159
Kluuvikatu 5
00101 Helsinki
Tel: +358-9-18 351

EMBASSIES AND CONSULATES

Embassy of Finland
3301 Massachusetts Avenue, NW
Washington, DC 20048
USA
Tel: +202-298 5800

Office of the Counselor
for Science and Technology
Embassy of Finland
3301 Massachusetts Avenue, NW
Washington, DC 20048
USA
Tel: +202-298 5837

Consulate of Finland
1900 Avenue of the Stars
Suite 1025
Los Angeles, CA 90067
Tel: +310-203 9903

Consulate of Finland
15 Long Common Road
Riverside
Chicago, IL 60546
Tel: +708-442 0635

Consulate of Finland
Pinewold Circle
Houston, TX 77056
Tel: +552-1722

FINANCIAL INSTITUTIONS

BANKS

Bank of Finland
Snellmanin aukio
00170 Helsinki
Tel: +358-9-1831

Citibank International plc, Finland Branch
Aleksanterinkatu 48
00100 Helsinki
Tel: +358-9-348 871

Crédit Agricole Indosuez
Keskuskatu 7
00100 Helsinki
Tel: +358-9-69 6991

Den Danske Bank
Aleksanterinkatu 44
00100 Helsinki
Tel: +358-9-7514 5000

Handelsbanken
Eteläranta 8
00130 Helsinki
Tel: +358-9-166 771

Leonia
Unioninkatu 22
00007 Helsinki
Tel: +358-9-42 511

Merita Bank (MeritaNordbanken)
Aleksanterinkatu 30
00100 Helsinki
Tel: +358-9-1651

Okopankki Oy
Arkadiankatu 23
00100 Helsinki
Tel: +358-9-12901
Skandinaviska Enskilda Banken
Unioninkatu 30
00100 Helsinki
Tel: +358-9-6162 8900

BANKING ORGANIZATIONS

Central Union of Cooperative Banks
Arkadiankatu 23
00100 Helsinki
Tel: +358-9-4041

Finnish Bankers' Assn.
Kansakoulukatu 1 A
00100 Helsinki
Tel: +358-9-694 8422

Finnish Savings Banks Assn.
Pohjoisesplanadi 35 A
00100 Helsinki
Tel: +358-9-13341

OTHER FINANCIAL ORGANIZATIONS

Helsinki Exchanges (HEX)
Fabianinkatu 14
00100 Helsinki
Tel: +358-9-616 671

COMMERCIAL INSTITUTIONS

Chambers of Commerce
Central Chamber of Commerce
Aleksanterinkatu 17
PL 1000
00101 Helsinki
Tel: +358-9-696 969
Helsinki Chamber of Commerce
Kalevankatu 12
00100 Helsinki
Tel: +358-9-228 601

The Finnish section of the
International Chamber of Commerce
Aleksanterinkatu 17
PL 1000
00101 Helsinki
Tel: +358-9-696 969
Espoo Chamber of Commerce
Ahlbergin kartano
Sokerilinnantie 7
02600 Espoo
Tel: +358-9-512 3220
Turku Chamber of Commerce
Puolalankatu 1
20100 Turku
Tel: +358-2-274 3400

Tampere Chamber of Commerce
Kehräsaari
33200 Tampere
Tel: +358-3-2141 444
Lahti Chamber of Commerce
Rauhankatu 10
15110 Lahti
Tel: +358-3-871 2500

THE FINNISH-AMERICAN CHAMBER OF COMMERCE

http:// www.finlandtrade.com/

Finland Office
Arkadiankatu 2
00100 Helsinki
Tel: +358-9-69 651

Midwest Office
710 Remmington Road
Schaumburg, IL 60173
Tel: +847-885 3200

New York Office
866 United Nations Plaza
Suite 249
New York, NY 10017
Tel: +212-821 0255

Northwest Office
11045 S.E.
28th Place
Bellevue, WA 98004
Tel: +425-451 3983

Southeast Office
2310 Peachford Road
Atlanta, GA 30338
Tel: +470-457 8795

Southwest Office
1300 Post Oak Boulevard
Suite 1990
Houston, TX 77056
Tel: +713-627 9700

West Coast Office
1900 Avenue of the Stars
Suite 1060
Los Angeles, CA 90067
Tel: +310-203 9903

CONFEDERATION OF FINNISH INDUSTRIES

Eteläranta 10
00100 Helsinki
Tel: +358-9-68 681

FINNISH ASSN. OF CONSULTING FIRMS

Pohjantie 12
02100 Espoo
Tel: +358-9-460 122
Finnish Fair Corp.

HELSINKI EXHIBITION & CONGRESS CENTER

P.O. Box 21
00521 Helsinki
Tel: +358-9-15091
Finnish Foreign Trade
Association

Arkadiankatu 2
PL 908

00101 Helsinki
Tel: +358-9-46 951

MAJOR NEWSPAPERS:

Helsingin Sanomat Aamulehti
P.O. Box 975 Pieni Roobertinkatu 11 A
FIN-00101 Helsinki, Finland FIN-00120 Helsinki, Finland
Tel: 358-9-1221, Fax: 358-9-605 709 Tel: 358-9-853 9560, Fax: 358-9-853 9579

BUSINESS MAGAZINES/JOURNALS:

Kauppalehti (Business daily) Taloussanomat (Business daily)
P.O.Box 189 P.O. Box 1230
FIN-00101 Helsinki, Finland FIN-00101 Helsinki, Finland
Tel: 358-9-507 81, Fax: 358-9-660 383 Tel: 358-9-1221, Fax: 358-9-122 4119

Talouselama (Business weekly)
P.O.Box 920
FIN-00101 Helsinki, Finland
Tel: 358-9-148 801, Fax: 358-9-685 6650

E-Commerce Websites: www.soneraplaza.net, www.elisa.com, www.saunalahti.fi, sirkus.com

TRADE PROMOTION

The main fair centers in Finland are located in the cities of Helsinki, Jyvaskyla, Turku, Tampere and Lahti. In 1999, they had approximately 1.5 million visitors. For further information, please contact:

The Finnish Fair Corporation Jyvaskyla Fair Ltd.
P.O. Box 21 P.O. Box 127
FIN-00521 Helsinki, Finland FIN-40101 Jyvaskyla, Finland
Tel: 358-9-150 91 Tel:358-14-334 0000
Fax: 358-9-142 358 Fax: 358-14-610 272

Turku Fair Center Ltd. Lahti Fair Ltd.
P.O. Box 57 P.O. Box 106
FIN-20201 Turku, Finland FIN-15141 Lahti, Finland
Tel: 358-2-337 111 Tel: 358-3-525 820
Fax: 358-2-2401 440 Fax: 358-3-525 8225

Tampere Trade Fairs Ltd.
33201 Tampere, Finland
Tel: 358-3-2516 111
Fax: 358-3-2123 888

GLOSSARY

Council for Mutual Economic Assistance (CMEA, CEMA, or Comecon).
Members in 1988 included Bulgaria, Cuba, Czechoslovakia, the German Democratic Republic (East Germany), Hungary, Mongolia, Poland, Romania, the Soviet Union, and Vietnam. Its purpose is to further economic cooperation among members.

Council of Europe

Founded in 1949 to foster parliamentary democracy, social and economic progress, and unity among its member states. Membership is limited to those European countries that respect the rule of law and the fundamental human rights and freedoms of all those living within their boundaries. As of 1988, its membership consisted of twenty-one West European countries.

European Community (EC--also commonly called the Community).

The EC comprises three communities: the European Coal and Steel Community (ECSC), the European Economic Community (EEC, also known as the Common Market), and the European Atomic Energy Community (Euratom). Each community is a legally distinct body, but since 1967 all the members have shared common governing institutions. The EC forms more than a framework for free trade and economic cooperation: the signatories to the treaties governing the communities have agreed in principle to integrate their economies and ultimately to form a political union. Belgium, France, Italy, Luxembourg, the Netherlands, and the Federal Republic of Germany (West Germany) are charter members of the EC. Britain, Denmark, and Ireland joined on January 1, 1973; Greece became a member on January 1, 1981; and Portugal and Spain entered on January 1, 1986.

European Economic Community

See European Community.

European Free Trade Association (EFTA)

Founded in 1961, EFTA aims at supporting free trade among its members and increasing the liberalization of trade on a global basis, but particularly within Western Europe. In 1988 the organization's member states were Austria, Finland, Iceland, Norway, Sweden, and Switzerland.

Finnish mark (Fmk)

Also called Finnmark. Consists of 100 *pennia* (singular: *penni*). In terms of the United States dollar, the average annual exchange rate was Fmk3.22 in 1965, Fmk3.86 in 1975, Fmk3.85 in 1980, Fmk5.30 in 1982, Fmk6.54 in 1984, Fmk5.42 in 1995, Fmk4.79 in 1986, Fmk3.95 in 1987, and Fmk4.17 in 1988.

General Agreement on Tariffs and Trade (GATT)

An international organization established in 1948 and headquartered in Geneva that serves as a forum for international trade negotiations. GATT members pledge to further multilateral trade by reducing import tariffs, quotas, and preferential trade agreements, and they promise to extend to each other any favorable trading terms offered in subsequent agreements with third parties.

gross domestic product (GDP)

The total value of goods and services produced by the domestic economy during a given period, usually one year. Obtained by adding the value contributed by each sector of the economy in the form of profits, compensation to employees, and depreciation (consumption of capital). Most GDP usage in this book was based on GDP at factor cost. Real GDP is the value of GDP when inflation has been taken into account.

gross national product (GNP)

Obtained by adding GDP (*q.v.*) and the income received from abroad by residents, less payments remitted abroad to nonresidents. GNP valued at market prices was used in this book. Real GNP is the value of GNP when inflation has been taken into account.

International Monetary Fund (IMF)

Established along with the World Bank (*q.v.*) in 1945, the IMF is a specialized agency, affiliated with the United Nations, that takes responsibility for stabilizing international exchange rates and payments. The main business of the IMF is the provision of loans to its members when they experience balance-of-payment difficulties. These loans often carry conditions that require substantial internal economic adjustments by the recipients.

Organisation for Economic Co- operation and Development (OECD)

Established in 1961 to replace the Organisation for European Economic Co-operation, the OECD is an international organization composed of the industrialized market economy countries (twenty-four full members as of 1988). It seeks to promote economic and social welfare in member countries as well as in developing countries by providing a forum in which to formulate and to coordinate policies.

World Bank

Informal name used to designate a group of three affiliated international institutions: the International Bank for Reconstruction and Development (IBRD), the International Development Association (IDA), and the International Finance Corporation (IFC). The IBRD, established in 1945, has the primary purpose of providing loans to developing countries for productive projects. THe IDA, a legally separate loan fund administered by staff of the IBRD, was set up in 1960 to furnish credits to the poorest developing counties on much easier terms than those of conventional IBRD loans. The IFC, founded in 1956, supplements the activities of the IBRD through loans and assistance designed specifically to encourage the growth of productive private enterprises in less developed countries. The president and certain senior officers of the IBRD hold the same positions in the IFC. The three institutions are owned by the governments of the countries that subscribe their capital. To participate in the World Bank group, member states must first belong to the IMF (*q.v.*).

BASIC TITLES ON FINLAND

IMPORTANT!

All publications are updated annually!

Please contact IBP, Inc. at ibpusa3@gmail.com for the latest ISBNs and additional information

TITLE
Finland A "Spy" Guide - Strategic Information and Developments
Finland A Spy" Guide"
Finland Air Force Handbook
Finland Air Force Handbook
Finland Army Weapon Systems Handbook
Finland Army Weapon Systems Handbook
Finland Army Weapon Systems Handbook
Finland Army, National Security and Defense Policy Handbook
Finland Army, National Security and Defense Policy Handbook
Finland Aviation and Aerospace Industry Handbook
Finland Aviation and Aerospace Industry Handbook
Finland Banking & Financial Market Handbook
Finland Banking & Financial Market Handbook
Finland Business and Investment Opportunities Yearbook
Finland Business and Investment Opportunities Yearbook
Finland Business and Investment Opportunities Yearbook Volume 1 Strategic Information and Opportunities
Finland Business and Investment Opportunities Yearbook Volume 2 Leading Export-Import, Business, Investment Opportunities and Projects
Finland Business Intelligence Report - Practical Information, Opportunities, Contacts
Finland Business Intelligence Report - Practical Information, Opportunities, Contacts
Finland Business Law Handbook - Strategic Information and Basic Laws
Finland Business Law Handbook - Strategic Information and Basic Laws
Finland Business Law Handbook - Strategic Information and Basic Laws
Finland Business Law Handbook - Strategic Information and Basic Laws
Finland Business Law Handbook Volume 2 Investment and Trade Laws Volume 2 Investment and Trade Laws
Finland Clothing & Textile Industry Handbook
Finland Clothing & Textile Industry Handbook
Finland Company Laws and Regulations Handbook
Finland Constitution and Citizenship Laws Handbook - Strategic Information and Basic Laws
Finland Country Study Guide - Strategic Information and Developments
Finland Country Study Guide - Strategic Information and Developments
Finland Country Study Guide - Strategic Information and Developments Volume 1 Strategic

TITLE
Information and Developments
Finland Customs, Trade Regulations and Procedures Handbook
Finland Customs, Trade Regulations and Procedures Handbook
Finland Diplomatic Handbook - Strategic Information and Developments
Finland Diplomatic Handbook - Strategic Information and Developments
Finland Ecology & Nature Protection Handbook
Finland Ecology & Nature Protection Handbook
Finland Ecology & Nature Protection Laws and Regulation Handbook
Finland Economic & Development Strategy Handbook
Finland Economic & Development Strategy Handbook
Finland Education System and Policy Handbook
Finland Energy Policy, Laws and Regulation Handbook
Finland Export-Import Trade and Business Directory
Finland Export-Import Trade and Business Directory
Finland Fishing Industry Business Intelligence Report - Practical Information, Opportunities, Contacts
Finland Fishing Industry Business Intelligence Report - Practical Information, Opportunities, Contacts
Finland Foreign Policy and Government Guide
Finland Foreign Policy and Government Guide
Finland Gold Mining Industry Business Opportunities Handbook
Finland Gold Mining Industry Business Opportunities Handbook
Finland Government and Business Contacts Handbook
Finland Government and Business Contacts Handbook
Finland Healthcare Sector Organization, Management and Payment Systems Handbook - Strategic Information, Programs and Regulations
Finland Immigration Laws and Regulations Handbook - Strategic Information and Basic Laws
Finland Industrial and Business Directory
Finland Industrial and Business Directory
Finland Insolvency (Bankruptcy) Laws and Regulations Handbook - Strategic Information and Basic Laws
Finland Intelligence & Security Activities & Operations Handbook
Finland Intelligence & Security Activities & Operations Handbook
Finland Intelligence, Security Activities & Operations Handbook
Finland Intelligence, Security Activities & Operations Handbook
Finland Internet and E-Commerce Investment and Business Guide - Strategic and Practical Information: Regulations and Opportunities
Finland Internet and E-Commerce Investment and Business Guide - Strategic and Practical Information: Regulations and Opportunities
Finland Investment and Business Guide - Strategic and Practical Information
Finland Investment and Business Guide - Strategic and Practical Information
Finland Investment and Business Guide - Strategic and Practical Information
Finland Investment and Business Guide - Strategic and Practical Information
Finland Investment and Business Guide Volume 2 Business, Investment Opportunities and Incentives

TITLE
Finland Investment and Trade Laws and Regulations Handbook
Finland Justice System and National Police Handbook
Finland Justice System and National Police Handbook
Finland Labor Laws and Regulations Handbook - Strategic Information and Basic Laws
Finland Land Ownership and Agriculture Laws Handbook
Finland Medical & Pharmaceutical Industry Handbook
Finland Medical & Pharmaceutical Industry Handbook
Finland Mineral & Mining Sector Investment and Business Guide - Strategic and Practical Information
Finland Mineral & Mining Sector Investment and Business Guide - Strategic and Practical Information
Finland Mining Industry Business Intelligence Report - Practical Information, Opportunities, Contacts
Finland Mining Industry Business Intelligence Report - Practical Information, Opportunities, Contacts
Finland Mining Laws and Regulations Handbook
Finland Recent Economic and Political Developments Yearbook
Finland Recent Economic and Political Developments Yearbook
Finland Recent Economic and Political Developments Yearbook
Finland Research & Development Policy Handbook
Finland Research & Development Policy Handbook
Finland Research & Development Policy Handbook
Finland Space Agency and Programs Handbook
Finland Space Agency and Programs Handbook
Finland Starting Business (Incorporating) in Finland Guide
Finland Starting Business (Incorporating) in....Guide
Finland Tax Guide
Finland Tax Guide
Finland Taxation Laws and Regulations Handbook
Finland Telecom Laws and Regulations Handbook
Finland Telecommunication Industry Business Opportunities Handbook
Finland Telecommunication Industry Business Opportunities Handbook
Finland Transportation Policy and Regulations Handbook
Finland: How to Invest, Start and Run Profitable Business in Finland Guide - Practical Information, Opportunities, Contacts

BASIC LAWS AND REGULATIONS AFFECTING BUSINESS[1]

COUTRY	LAW TITLE
Finland	Act Amending the Child Welfare Act 2006
Finland	Act of the Medical Use of Human Organs and Tissues
Finland	Act on Assisted Fertility Treatments

[1] For ordering texts of specific laws in English, French or other languages, please contact Global Investment Center USA at ibpusa3@gmail.com

Finland	Act on Background Checks
Finland	Act on Book-Entry Accounts(17.5.1991/827)
Finland	Act on checking the criminal backround of persons working with children
Finland	Act on Collective Marks
Finland	Act on Commercial Banks and other Limited Credit Institutions (28.12.2001/1501)
Finland	Act on Communications Administration 29.6.2001/625
Finland	Act on Compensation for Environmental Damage 1994
Finland	Act on Competition Restrictions (480/1992), incl. amendment (318/2004)
Finland	Act on Conciliation in Criminal and Certain Civil Cases
Finland	Act on Conciliation in Criminal and Certain Civil Cases (2005)
Finland	Act on Confirmation of General Applicability of Collective Agreements (2001)
Finland	Act on Confirmation of General Applicability of Collective Agreements (2001)
Finland	Act on Co-operation within Finnish and Community-wide Groups of Undertakings 2007
Finland	Act on Co-operation within Undertakings
Finland	Act on Cooperation within Undertakings (1978, amended 2005)
Finland	Act on Cooperative Banks and other Cooperative Credit Institutions (28.12.2001/1504)
Finland	Act on Credit Institutions
Finland	Act on Disclosure of Election Financing (2000)
Finland	Act on District Prosecutors
Finland	Act on Electronic Services and Communication in the Public Sector
Finland	Act on Electronic Signatures
Finland	Act on Environmental Permit Authorities 2000
Finland	Act on European Schooling Helsinki 2007
Finland	Act on Extradition on the Basis of an Offence Between Finland and Other Member States of the European Union 2003
Finland	Act on Food Hygiene of Foodstuffs of Animal Origin
Finland	Act on Foreign Credit and Financial Institutions in Finland (30.12.1993/1608)
Finland	Act on Foreign Investment Firms' Right to Provide Investment Services in Finland (26.7.1996/580)
Finland	Act on Health Care Professionals
Finland	Act on Implementation of the Legislation on Environmental Protection
Finland	Act on International Legal Assistance in Criminal Matters
Finland	Act on Inventions of Importance to the Defense of the Country
Finland	Act on Involvement of Employees in European Companies (2004)
Finland	Act on Job Alternation Leave
Finland	Act on Jointly Owned Forests
Finland	Act on Labour Council and Derogation Permits concerning Labour Protection (2004)
Finland	Act on Licenses for Roadworthiness Test of Vehicles
Finland	Act on Measures to Restrict Tobacco Smoking 1976
Finland	Act on Mediation in Labour Disputes (1962, amended 1993)
Finland	Act on Military Crisis Management 2006
Finland	Act on Mortgage Credit Banks
Finland	Act on Mortgage Societies (8.12.1978/936)
Finland	Act on National Aid for Agriculture and Horticulture 2002
Finland	Act on Occupational Safety and Health Enforcement and Cooperation on Occupational Safety and Health at Workplaces (2006)

Finland	Act on Openness of Government Activities (1999 as amended 2002)
Finland	Act on Plant Variety Rights (789/1992; amendments up to 651/2000)
Finland	Act on Preventing and Clearing Money Laundering
Finland	Act on Preventing and Investigating Money Laundering and Personal Data (30.1.1998/68)
Finland	Act on Public Contracts 2007
Finland	Act on Public Prosecutors
Finland	Act on Registered Partnerships 2001
Finland	Act on Registering of Ship's Crew 2006
Finland	Act on Registration Services of Vehicles
Finland	Act on Social Assistance 1998
Finland	Act on Social Enterprises
Finland	Act On State Indemnity For Art Exhibitions (30 May 1986/411)
Finland	Act on Television and Radio Operations 9.10.1998/744
Finland	Act on the Autonomy of Aland
Finland	Act on the Book-Entry System (17.5.1991/826)
Finland	Act On The Classification Of Audiovisual Programs
Finland	Act on the Conformity of Certain Technical Devices to Relevant Requirements 2004
Finland	Act on the Contractor's Obligations and Liability when Work is Contracted Out 2006
Finland	Act on the Exclusive Right in the Layout-Design (Topography) of an Integrated Circuit
Finland	Act on the Exercise of Freedom of Expression in Mass Media 13.6.2003/460
Finland	Act on the Financial Supervision Authority (27.6.2003/587)
Finland	Act on the Finnish Board of Film Classification
Finland	Act on the Finnish Red Cross
Finland	Act on the Government Guarantee Fund (30.4.1992/379)
Finland	Act on the Ice Classes of Ships and Icebreaker Assistance 2005
Finland	Act on the Integration of Immigrants and Reception of Asylum Seekers (1999)
Finland	Act on the Labor Court (1974, amended 2006)
Finland	Act on the Land Information System and Related Information Service 2002
Finland	Act on the Market Court 2001
Finland	Act on the Openness of Government Activities 2003
Finland	Act on the Operations of a Foreign Management Company in Finland
Finland	Act on the Protection of Privacy and Data Security in Telecommunications 22.4.1999/565
Finland	Act on the Protection of Privacy in Electronic Communications
Finland	Act on the Protection of Privacy in Working Life
Finland	Act on the public disclosure and confidentiality of tax information 1999
Finland	Act on the Public Employment Service 2002
Finland	Act on the Right in Employee Inventions
Finland	Act on the Right to Transfer State Real Estate Assets
Finland	Act on the Sami Parliament 1995
Finland	Act on the State Television and Radio Fund 9.10.1998/745
Finland	Act on the Status and Rights of Patients 1992
Finland	Act on the Statutes of Finland
Finland	Act on the Supervision of Financial and Insurance Conglomerates (30.7.2004/699)
Finland	Act on the Supervision of Occupational Safety and Health and Appeal in Occupational

	Safety and Health Matters (131/1973)
Finland	Act on the Temporary Interruption of the Operations of a Deposit Bank 2001
Finland	Act on Trade in Forest Reproductive Material
Finland	Act on Transport of Dangerous Goods
Finland	Act on Utility Model Rights
Finland	Act on Verification and Notification of Origin of Electricity 2003
Finland	Act on Water Resources Management 2004
Finland	Act on Water Services (119/2001)
Finland	Administrative Judicial Procedure Act 1996
Finland	Administrative Procedure Act 2003
Finland	Adoption Act
Finland	Advocates Act 1958
Finland	Alcohol Act
Finland	Aliens Act (1991, amended 2001)
Finland	Aliens Decree (1994, amended 2000)
Finland	Animal Transport Act 2006
Finland	Animal Welfare Decree
Finland	Annual Holidays Act 2005
Finland	Arbitration Act
Finland	Archives Act
Finland	Archives Act (1994)
Finland	Assembly Act (1999, 2001)
Finland	Associations Act (1989, amended 2002)
Finland	Auditing Act 2007
Finland	Bankruptcy Act
Finland	Basic Education Act
Finland	Code of Inheritance
Finland	Code of Judicial Procedure
Finland	Code of Real Estate 1995
Finland	Coins act 216/1998
Finland	Collective Agreements Act (1946, amended 2001)
Finland	Communicable Diseases Act 1986
Finland	Communications Market Act 1997
Finland	Constitution of Finland 1999
Finland	Consumer Protection Act
Finland	Contracts Act
Finland	Co-operatives Act
Finland	Copyright Act
Finland	Credit Institutions Act (30.12.1993/1607)
Finland	Criminal Procedure Act
Finland	Criminal Records Act
Finland	Decree concerning the Aliens Ombudsman (1991)
Finland	Decree of the Ministry of Social Affairs and Health on the medical use of radiation
Finland	Decree on Marine Equipment
Finland	Decree on the Financing of Sustainable Forestry

Finland	Decree on the Sami Parliament
Finland	Decree on the Transport of Dangerous Goods by Air
Finland	Decree on the Vehicle Registration 1995
Finland	Decree on Utility Model Rights 1991
Finland	Domain Name Act
Finland	Election Act
Finland	Electricity Market Act (386/1995)
Finland	Electricity Market Act (386/1995)
Finland	Emergency Powers Act
Finland	Employment Contracts Act 2001
Finland	Environmental Damage Insurance Act
Finland	Environmental Protection Decree
Finland	Finnish Companies Act 2006
Finland	Firearms Act
Finland	Food Act 23/2006
Finland	Forest Act 1996
Finland	Forest Management Association Act
Finland	Foundations Act (1930 as amended 2001)
Finland	Gene Technology Act
Finland	Government Decision on the Safety of Construction Work
Finland	Government Decree on Auditing
Finland	Government Decree on European Schooling Helsinki 2008
Finland	Government Decree on Joint Procurement in Central Government 2006
Finland	Government Decree on Substances Dangerous and Harmful to the Aquatic Environment 2006
Finland	Government Decree on Television and Radio Operations
Finland	Government Decree on the Assessment of Soil Contamination and Remediation Needs
Finland	Government Decree on the sulphur content of heavy fuel oil, light fuel oil and marine gas 2006
Finland	Government Decree on the Transport and Temporary Storage of Dangerous Goods in a Port Area
Finland	Government Decree on Urban Waste Water Treatment 2006
Finland	Government Decree on Vessel Traffic Service 2005
Finland	Government Decree on Youth Work 2002
Finland	Highways Act
Finland	Housing Companies Act
Finland	Hunting Act 1993
Finland	Insurance Companies Act (28.12.1979/1062)
Finland	Insurance Contracts Act 1994
Finland	Investment Firms Act (26.7.1996/579)
Finland	Land Use and Building Act (132/1999)
Finland	Land Use and Building Decree
Finland	Language Act 2003
Finland	Legal Aid Act
Finland	Library Act 904/1998
Finland	Limited Liability Companies Act 2006

Finland	Local Government Act 1995
Finland	Lotteries Act
Finland	Marriage Act
Finland	Medical Research Act
Finland	Medicines Act
Finland	Mental Health Decree
Finland	Mining Act
Finland	Money Collection Act 2006
Finland	Mortgage Bank Act (23.12.1999/1240)
Finland	Mutual Funds Act (29.1.1999/48)
Finland	Narcotics Act
Finland	Nationality Act 359/2003 (2003)
Finland	Natural Gas Market Act
Finland	Nature Conservation Act (1096/1996)
Finland	Non-Discrimination Act
Finland	Nuclear Energy Act (1987)
Finland	Occupational Safety and Health Act 738/2002
Finland	Parliamentary Ombudsman Act 2002
Finland	Patents act
Finland	Penal Code
Finland	Personal Data Act
Finland	Personal Data Act (1999)
Finland	Police Act (1995, amended 2001)
Finland	Postal Services Act
Finland	Pressure Equipment Act 1999
Finland	Private Security Services Act
Finland	Product Liability Act
Finland	Public Procurement Act
Finland	Radiation Act (592/1991)
Finland	Radiation and Nuclear Safety Authority
Finland	Radio Act 16.11.2001/1015
Finland	Railway Act
Finland	Real Estate Funds Act (19.12.1997/1173)
Finland	Regional Development Act
Finland	Register of Ships Decree
Finland	Registered Designs Decree
Finland	Sale of Goods Act
Finland	Sámi Language Act
Finland	Savings Bank Act (28.12.2001/1502)
Finland	Seamen's Act (1978, amended 2006)
Finland	Securities Markets Act (26.5.1989/495)
Finland	Ship and Port Facility Security Act
Finland	Statistics Finland Act 24.1.1992/48
Finland	Supreme Court Act
Finland	Telecommunications Market Act

Finland	The Act on Plant Breeder's Right (No. 789/1992)
Finland	The Act on the Finnish Competition Authority (711/1988), amended by (482/1992)
Finland	The Market Court Act (1527/2001)
Finland	The Regulation of the Parliamentary Ombudsman (10 January 1920/2, with later amendments)
Finland	Tort Liability Act
Finland	Trademarks Act
Finland	Trademarks Decree 1964
Finland	Travel Agency Act (1080/1994)
Finland	Universities Act 1967
Finland	Value Added Tax Act
Finland	Vehicles Act 1090/2002
Finland	Vehicular and Driver Data Register Act
Finland	Vessel Traffic Service Act
Finland	Waste Decree 1993
Finland	Waste Oil Charge Act (894/1986)
Finland	Waste Tax Act
Finland	Working Hours Act
Finland	Working Hours Act
Finland	Youth Act (72/2006)
Finland	Youth Work Act

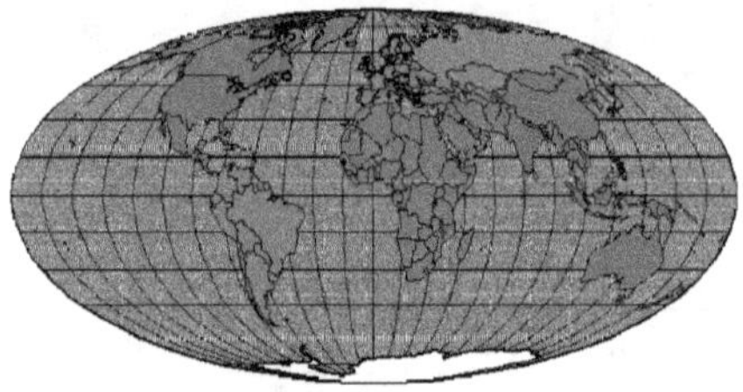

WORLD BUSINESS AND INVESTMENT OPPORTUNITIES YEARBOOK LIBRARY

World Business Information Catalog, USA: http://www.ibpus.com
Email: ibpusa3@gmail.com

Price: $99.95 Each

TITLE
Abkhazia (Republic of Abkhazia) Business and Investment Opportunities Yearbook Volume 1 Strategic, Practical Information and Opportunities
Afghanistan Business and Investment Opportunities Yearbook Volume 1 Strategic, Practical Information and Opportunities
Aland Business and Investment Opportunities Yearbook Volume 1 Strategic, Practical Information and Opportunities
Albania Business and Investment Opportunities Yearbook Volume 1 Strategic, Practical Information and Opportunities
Algeria Business and Investment Opportunities Yearbook Volume 1 Strategic, Practical Information and Opportunities
Andorra Business and Investment Opportunities Yearbook Volume 1 Strategic, Practical Information and Opportunities
Angola Business and Investment Opportunities Yearbook Volume 1 Strategic, Practical Information and Opportunities
Anguilla Business and Investment Opportunities Yearbook Volume 1 Strategic, Practical Information and Opportunities
Antigua and Barbuda Business and Investment Opportunities Yearbook Volume 1 Strategic, Practical Information and Opportunities
Antilles (Netherlands) Business and Investment Opportunities Yearbook Volume 1 Strategic, Practical Information and Opportunities
Argentina Business and Investment Opportunities Yearbook Volume 1 Strategic, Practical Information and Opportunities
Armenia Business and Investment Opportunities Yearbook Volume 1 Strategic, Practical Information and Opportunities
Aruba Business and Investment Opportunities Yearbook Volume 1 Strategic, Practical Information and Opportunities
Australia Business and Investment Opportunities Yearbook Volume 1 Strategic, Practical Information and Opportunities
Austria Business and Investment Opportunities Yearbook Volume 1 Strategic, Practical Information and Opportunities
Azerbaijan Business and Investment Opportunities Yearbook Volume 1 Strategic, Practical Information and Opportunities
Bahamas Business and Investment Opportunities Yearbook Volume 1 Strategic, Practical Information and Opportunities
Bahrain Business and Investment Opportunities Yearbook Volume 1 Strategic, Practical Information and Opportunities
Bangladesh Business and Investment Opportunities Yearbook Volume 1 Strategic, Practical Information and Opportunities
Barbados Business and Investment Opportunities Yearbook Volume 1 Strategic, Practical Information and Opportunities
Belarus Business and Investment Opportunities Yearbook Volume 1 Strategic, Practical Information and Opportunities

For additional analytical, business and investment opportunities information,
Please contact Global Investment & Business Center, USA
at (202) 546-2103. Fax: (202) 546-3275. E-mail: ibpusa3@gmail.com

TITLE
Belgium Business and Investment Opportunities Yearbook Volume 1 Strategic, Practical Information and Opportunities
Belize Business and Investment Opportunities Yearbook Volume 1 Strategic, Practical Information and Opportunities
Benin Business and Investment Opportunities Yearbook Volume 1 Strategic, Practical Information and Opportunities
Bermuda Business and Investment Opportunities Yearbook Volume 1 Strategic, Practical Information and Opportunities
Bhutan Business and Investment Opportunities Yearbook Volume 1 Strategic, Practical Information and Opportunities
Bolivia Business and Investment Opportunities Yearbook Volume 1 Strategic, Practical Information and Opportunities
Bosnia and Herzegovina Business and Investment Opportunities Yearbook Volume 1 Strategic, Practical Information and Opportunities
Botswana Business and Investment Opportunities Yearbook Volume 1 Strategic, Practical Information and Opportunities
Brazil Business and Investment Opportunities Yearbook Volume 1 Strategic, Practical Information and Opportunities
Brunei Business and Investment Opportunities Yearbook Volume 1 Strategic, Practical Information and Opportunities
Bulgaria Business and Investment Opportunities Yearbook Volume 1 Strategic, Practical Information and Opportunities
Burkina Faso Business and Investment Opportunities Yearbook Volume 1 Strategic, Practical Information and Opportunities
Burundi Business and Investment Opportunities Yearbook Volume 1 Strategic, Practical Information and Opportunities
Cambodia Business and Investment Opportunities Yearbook Volume 1 Strategic, Practical Information and Opportunities
Cameroon Business and Investment Opportunities Yearbook Volume 1 Strategic, Practical Information and Opportunities
Canada Business and Investment Opportunities Yearbook Volume 1 Strategic, Practical Information and Opportunities
Cape Verde Business and Investment Opportunities Yearbook Volume 1 Strategic, Practical Information and Opportunities
Cayman Islands Business and Investment Opportunities Yearbook Volume 1 Strategic, Practical Information and Opportunities
Central African Republic Business and Investment Opportunities Yearbook Volume 1 Strategic, Practical Information and Opportunities
Chad Business and Investment Opportunities Yearbook Volume 1 Strategic, Practical Information and Opportunities
Chile Business and Investment Opportunities Yearbook Volume 1 Strategic, Practical Information and Opportunities
China Business and Investment Opportunities Yearbook Volume 1 Strategic, Practical Information and Opportunities
Colombia Business and Investment Opportunities Yearbook Volume 1 Strategic, Practical Information and Opportunities
Comoros Business and Investment Opportunities Yearbook Volume 1 Strategic, Practical Information and Opportunities
Congo Business and Investment Opportunities Yearbook Volume 1 Strategic, Practical Information and Opportunities
Congo, Democratic Republic Business and Investment Opportunities Yearbook Volume 1 Strategic, Practical Information and Opportunities
Cook Islands Business and Investment Opportunities Yearbook Volume 1 Strategic, Practical Information and Opportunities
Costa Rica Business and Investment Opportunities Yearbook Volume 1 Strategic, Practical Information and Opportunities

TITLE
Cote d'Ivoire Business and Investment Opportunities Yearbook Volume 1 Strategic, Practical Information and Opportunities
Croatia Business and Investment Opportunities Yearbook Volume 1 Strategic, Practical Information and Opportunities
Cuba Business and Investment Opportunities Yearbook Volume 1 Strategic, Practical Information and Opportunities
Cyprus Business and Investment Opportunities Yearbook Volume 1 Strategic, Practical Information and Opportunities
Czech Republic Business and Investment Opportunities Yearbook Volume 1 Strategic, Practical Information and Opportunities
Denmark Business and Investment Opportunities Yearbook Volume 1 Strategic, Practical Information and Opportunities
Djibouti Business and Investment Opportunities Yearbook Volume 1 Strategic, Practical Information and Opportunities
Dominica Business and Investment Opportunities Yearbook Volume 1 Strategic, Practical Information and Opportunities
Dominican Republic Business and Investment Opportunities Yearbook Volume 1 Strategic, Practical Information and Opportunities
Ecuador Business and Investment Opportunities Yearbook Volume 1 Strategic, Practical Information and Opportunities
Egypt Business and Investment Opportunities Yearbook Volume 1 Strategic, Practical Information and Opportunities
El Salvador Business and Investment Opportunities Yearbook Volume 1 Strategic, Practical Information and Opportunities
Equatorial Guinea Business and Investment Opportunities Yearbook Volume 1 Strategic, Practical Information and Opportunities
Eritrea Business and Investment Opportunities Yearbook Volume 1 Strategic, Practical Information and Opportunities
Estonia Business and Investment Opportunities Yearbook Volume 1 Strategic, Practical Information and Opportunities
Ethiopia Business and Investment Opportunities Yearbook Volume 1 Strategic, Practical Information and Opportunities
Falkland Islands Business and Investment Opportunities Yearbook Volume 1 Strategic, Practical Information and Opportunities
Faroes Islands Business and Investment Opportunities Yearbook Volume 1 Strategic, Practical Information and Opportunities
Fiji Business and Investment Opportunities Yearbook Volume 1 Strategic, Practical Information and Opportunities
Finland Business and Investment Opportunities Yearbook Volume 1 Strategic, Practical Information and Opportunities
France Business and Investment Opportunities Yearbook Volume 1 Strategic, Practical Information and Opportunities
Gabon Business and Investment Opportunities Yearbook Volume 1 Strategic, Practical Information and Opportunities
Gambia Business and Investment Opportunities Yearbook Volume 1 Strategic, Practical Information and Opportunities
Georgia Business and Investment Opportunities Yearbook Volume 1 Strategic, Practical Information and Opportunities
Germany Business and Investment Opportunities Yearbook Volume 1 Strategic, Practical Information and Opportunities
Ghana Business and Investment Opportunities Yearbook Volume 1 Strategic, Practical Information and Opportunities
Gibraltar Business and Investment Opportunities Yearbook Volume 1 Strategic, Practical Information and Opportunities
Greece Business and Investment Opportunities Yearbook Volume 1 Strategic, Practical Information and Opportunities

TITLE
Greenland Business and Investment Opportunities Yearbook Volume 1 Strategic, Practical Information and Opportunities
Grenada Business and Investment Opportunities Yearbook Volume 1 Strategic, Practical Information and Opportunities
Guam Business and Investment Opportunities Yearbook Volume 1 Strategic, Practical Information and Opportunities
Guatemala Business and Investment Opportunities Yearbook Volume 1 Strategic, Practical Information and Opportunities
Guernsey Business and Investment Opportunities Yearbook Volume 1 Strategic, Practical Information and Opportunities
Guinea Business and Investment Opportunities Yearbook Volume 1 Strategic, Practical Information and Opportunities
Guinea-Bissau Business and Investment Opportunities Yearbook Volume 1 Strategic, Practical Information and Opportunities
Guyana Business and Investment Opportunities Yearbook Volume 1 Strategic, Practical Information and Opportunities
Haiti Business and Investment Opportunities Yearbook Volume 1 Strategic, Practical Information and Opportunities
Honduras Business and Investment Opportunities Yearbook Volume 1 Strategic, Practical Information and Opportunities
Hungary Business and Investment Opportunities Yearbook Volume 1 Strategic, Practical Information and Opportunities
Iceland Business and Investment Opportunities Yearbook Volume 1 Strategic, Practical Information and Opportunities
India Business and Investment Opportunities Yearbook Volume 1 Strategic, Practical Information and Opportunities
Indonesia Business and Investment Opportunities Yearbook Volume 1 Strategic, Practical Information and Opportunities
Iran Business and Investment Opportunities Yearbook Volume 1 Strategic, Practical Information and Opportunities
Iraq Business and Investment Opportunities Yearbook Volume 1 Strategic, Practical Information and Opportunities
Ireland Business and Investment Opportunities Yearbook Volume 1 Strategic, Practical Information and Opportunities
Israel Business and Investment Opportunities Yearbook Volume 1 Strategic, Practical Information and Opportunities
Italy Business and Investment Opportunities Yearbook Volume 1 Strategic, Practical Information and Opportunities
Jamaica Business and Investment Opportunities Yearbook Volume 1 Strategic, Practical Information and Opportunities
Japan Business and Investment Opportunities Yearbook Volume 1 Strategic, Practical Information and Opportunities
Jersey Business and Investment Opportunities Yearbook Volume 1 Strategic, Practical Information and Opportunities
Jordan Business and Investment Opportunities Yearbook Volume 1 Strategic, Practical Information and Opportunities
Kazakhstan Business and Investment Opportunities Yearbook Volume 1 Strategic, Practical Information and Opportunities
Kenya Business and Investment Opportunities Yearbook Volume 1 Strategic, Practical Information and Opportunities
Kiribati Business and Investment Opportunities Yearbook Volume 1 Strategic, Practical Information and Opportunities
Korea, North Business and Investment Opportunities Yearbook Volume 1 Strategic, Practical Information and Opportunities
Korea, South Business and Investment Opportunities Yearbook Volume 1 Strategic, Practical Information and Opportunities

TITLE
Kosovo Business and Investment Opportunities Yearbook Volume 1 Strategic, Practical Information and Opportunities
Kurdistan Business and Investment Opportunities Yearbook Volume 1 Strategic, Practical Information and Opportunities
Kuwait Business and Investment Opportunities Yearbook Volume 1 Strategic, Practical Information and Opportunities
Kyrgyzstan Business and Investment Opportunities Yearbook Volume 1 Strategic, Practical Information and Opportunities
Laos Business and Investment Opportunities Yearbook Volume 1 Strategic, Practical Information and Opportunities
Latvia Business and Investment Opportunities Yearbook Volume 1 Strategic, Practical Information and Opportunities
Lebanon Business and Investment Opportunities Yearbook Volume 1 Strategic, Practical Information and Opportunities
Lesotho Business and Investment Opportunities Yearbook Volume 1 Strategic, Practical Information and Opportunities
Liberia Business and Investment Opportunities Yearbook Volume 1 Strategic, Practical Information and Opportunities
Libya Business and Investment Opportunities Yearbook Volume 1 Strategic, Practical Information and Opportunities
Liechtenstein Business and Investment Opportunities Yearbook Volume 1 Strategic, Practical Information and Opportunities
Lithuania Business and Investment Opportunities Yearbook Volume 1 Strategic, Practical Information and Opportunities
Luxembourg Business and Investment Opportunities Yearbook Volume 1 Strategic, Practical Information and Opportunities
Macao Business and Investment Opportunities Yearbook Volume 1 Strategic, Practical Information and Opportunities
Macedonia Business and Investment Opportunities Yearbook Volume 1 Strategic, Practical Information and Opportunities
Madagascar Business and Investment Opportunities Yearbook Volume 1 Strategic, Practical Information and Opportunities
Madeira Business and Investment Opportunities Yearbook Volume 1 Strategic, Practical Information and Opportunities
Malawi Business and Investment Opportunities Yearbook Volume 1 Strategic, Practical Information and Opportunities
Malaysia Business and Investment Opportunities Yearbook Volume 1 Strategic, Practical Information and Opportunities
Maldives Business and Investment Opportunities Yearbook Volume 1 Strategic, Practical Information and Opportunities
Mali Business and Investment Opportunities Yearbook Volume 1 Strategic, Practical Information and Opportunities
Malta Business and Investment Opportunities Yearbook Volume 1 Strategic, Practical Information and Opportunities
Man Business and Investment Opportunities Yearbook Volume 1 Strategic, Practical Information and Opportunities
Marshall Islands Business and Investment Opportunities Yearbook Volume 1 Strategic, Practical Information and Opportunities
Mauritania Business and Investment Opportunities Yearbook Volume 1 Strategic, Practical Information and Opportunities
Mauritius Business and Investment Opportunities Yearbook Volume 1 Strategic, Practical Information and Opportunities
Mayotte Business and Investment Opportunities Yearbook Volume 1 Strategic, Practical Information and Opportunities
Mexico Business and Investment Opportunities Yearbook Volume 1 Strategic, Practical Information and Opportunities

TITLE
Micronesia Business and Investment Opportunities Yearbook Volume 1 Strategic, Practical Information and Opportunities
Moldova Business and Investment Opportunities Yearbook Volume 1 Strategic, Practical Information and Opportunities
Monaco Business and Investment Opportunities Yearbook Volume 1 Strategic, Practical Information and Opportunities
Mongolia Business and Investment Opportunities Yearbook Volume 1 Strategic, Practical Information and Opportunities
Montserrat Business and Investment Opportunities Yearbook Volume 1 Strategic, Practical Information and Opportunities
Montenegro Business and Investment Opportunities Yearbook Volume 1 Strategic, Practical Information and Opportunities
Morocco Business and Investment Opportunities Yearbook Volume 1 Strategic, Practical Information and Opportunities
Mozambique Business and Investment Opportunities Yearbook Volume 1 Strategic, Practical Information and Opportunities
Myanmar Business and Investment Opportunities Yearbook Volume 1 Strategic, Practical Information and Opportunities
Nagorno-Karabakh Republic Business and Investment Opportunities Yearbook Volume 1 Strategic, Practical Information and Opportunities
Namibia Business and Investment Opportunities Yearbook Volume 1 Strategic, Practical Information and Opportunities
Nauru Business and Investment Opportunities Yearbook Volume 1 Strategic, Practical Information and Opportunities
Nepal Business and Investment Opportunities Yearbook Volume 1 Strategic, Practical Information and Opportunities
Netherlands Business and Investment Opportunities Yearbook Volume 1 Strategic, Practical Information and Opportunities
New Caledonia Business and Investment Opportunities Yearbook Volume 1 Strategic, Practical Information and Opportunities
New Zealand Business and Investment Opportunities Yearbook Volume 1 Strategic, Practical Information and Opportunities
Nicaragua Business and Investment Opportunities Yearbook Volume 1 Strategic, Practical Information and Opportunities
Niger Business and Investment Opportunities Yearbook Volume 1 Strategic, Practical Information and Opportunities
Nigeria Business and Investment Opportunities Yearbook Volume 1 Strategic, Practical Information and Opportunities
Niue Business and Investment Opportunities Yearbook Volume 1 Strategic, Practical Information and Opportunities
Northern Cyprus (Turkish Republic of Northern Cyprus) Business and Investment Opportunities Yearbook Volume 1 Strategic, Practical Information and Opportunities
Northern Mariana Islands Business and Investment Opportunities Yearbook Volume 1 Strategic, Practical Information and Opportunities
Norway Business and Investment Opportunities Yearbook Volume 1 Strategic, Practical Information and Opportunities
Oman Business and Investment Opportunities Yearbook Volume 1 Strategic, Practical Information and Opportunities
Pakistan Business and Investment Opportunities Yearbook Volume 1 Strategic, Practical Information and Opportunities
Palau Business and Investment Opportunities Yearbook Volume 1 Strategic, Practical Information and Opportunities
Palestine (West Bank & Gaza) Business and Investment Opportunities Yearbook Volume 1 Strategic, Practical Information and Opportunities
Panama Business and Investment Opportunities Yearbook Volume 1 Strategic, Practical Information and Opportunities

TITLE
Papua New Guinea Business and Investment Opportunities Yearbook Volume 1 Strategic, Practical Information and Opportunities
Paraguay Business and Investment Opportunities Yearbook Volume 1 Strategic, Practical Information and Opportunities
Peru Business and Investment Opportunities Yearbook Volume 1 Strategic, Practical Information and Opportunities
Philippines Business and Investment Opportunities Yearbook Volume 1 Strategic, Practical Information and Opportunities
Pitcairn Islands Business and Investment Opportunities Yearbook Volume 1 Strategic, Practical Information and Opportunities
Poland Business and Investment Opportunities Yearbook Volume 1 Strategic, Practical Information and Opportunities
Polynesia French Business and Investment Opportunities Yearbook Volume 1 Strategic, Practical Information and Opportunities
Portugal Business and Investment Opportunities Yearbook Volume 1 Strategic, Practical Information and Opportunities
Qatar Business and Investment Opportunities Yearbook Volume 1 Strategic, Practical Information and Opportunities
Romania Business and Investment Opportunities Yearbook Volume 1 Strategic, Practical Information and Opportunities
Russia Business and Investment Opportunities Yearbook Volume 1 Strategic, Practical Information and Opportunities
Rwanda Business and Investment Opportunities Yearbook Volume 1 Strategic, Practical Information and Opportunities
Sahrawi Arab Democratic Republic Volume 1 Strategic Information and Developments
Saint Kitts and Nevis Business and Investment Opportunities Yearbook Volume 1 Strategic, Practical Information and Opportunities
Saint Lucia Business and Investment Opportunities Yearbook Volume 1 Strategic, Practical Information and Opportunities
Saint Vincent and The Grenadines Business and Investment Opportunities Yearbook Volume 1 Strategic, Practical Information and Opportunities
Samoa (American) A Business and Investment Opportunities Yearbook Volume 1 Strategic, Practical Information and Opportunities
Samoa (Western) Business and Investment Opportunities Yearbook Volume 1 Strategic, Practical Information and Opportunities
San Marino Business and Investment Opportunities Yearbook Volume 1 Strategic, Practical Information and Opportunities
Sao Tome and Principe Business and Investment Opportunities Yearbook Volume 1 Strategic, Practical Information and Opportunities
Saudi Arabia Business and Investment Opportunities Yearbook Volume 1 Strategic, Practical Information and Opportunities
Scotland Business and Investment Opportunities Yearbook Volume 1 Strategic, Practical Information and Opportunities
Senegal Business and Investment Opportunities Yearbook Volume 1 Strategic, Practical Information and Opportunities
Serbia Business and Investment Opportunities Yearbook Volume 1 Strategic, Practical Information and Opportunities
Seychelles Business and Investment Opportunities Yearbook Volume 1 Strategic, Practical Information and Opportunities
Sierra Leone Business and Investment Opportunities Yearbook Volume 1 Strategic, Practical Information and Opportunities
Singapore Business and Investment Opportunities Yearbook Volume 1 Strategic, Practical Information and Opportunities
Slovakia Business and Investment Opportunities Yearbook Volume 1 Strategic, Practical Information and Opportunities

TITLE
Slovenia Business and Investment Opportunities Yearbook Volume 1 Strategic, Practical Information and Opportunities
Solomon Islands Business and Investment Opportunities Yearbook Volume 1 Strategic, Practical Information and Opportunities
Somalia Business and Investment Opportunities Yearbook Volume 1 Strategic, Practical Information and Opportunities
South Africa Business and Investment Opportunities Yearbook Volume 1 Strategic, Practical Information and Opportunities
Spain Business and Investment Opportunities Yearbook Volume 1 Strategic, Practical Information and Opportunities
Sri Lanka Business and Investment Opportunities Yearbook Volume 1 Strategic, Practical Information and Opportunities
St. Helena Business and Investment Opportunities Yearbook Volume 1 Strategic, Practical Information and Opportunities
St. Pierre & Miquelon Business and Investment Opportunities Yearbook Volume 1 Strategic, Practical Information and Opportunities
Sudan (Republic of the Sudan) Business and Investment Opportunities Yearbook Volume 1 Strategic, Practical Information and Opportunities
Sudan South Business and Investment Opportunities Yearbook Volume 1 Strategic, Practical Information and Opportunities
Suriname Business and Investment Opportunities Yearbook Volume 1 Strategic, Practical Information and Opportunities
Swaziland Business and Investment Opportunities Yearbook Volume 1 Strategic, Practical Information and Opportunities
Sweden Business and Investment Opportunities Yearbook Volume 1 Strategic, Practical Information and Opportunities
Switzerland Business and Investment Opportunities Yearbook Volume 1 Strategic, Practical Information and Opportunities
Syria Business and Investment Opportunities Yearbook Volume 1 Strategic, Practical Information and Opportunities
Taiwan Business and Investment Opportunities Yearbook Volume 1 Strategic, Practical Information and Opportunities
Tajikistan Business and Investment Opportunities Yearbook Volume 1 Strategic, Practical Information and Opportunities
Tanzania Business and Investment Opportunities Yearbook Volume 1 Strategic, Practical Information and Opportunities
Thailand Business and Investment Opportunities Yearbook Volume 1 Strategic, Practical Information and Opportunities
Timor Leste (Democratic Republic of Timor-Leste) Business and Investment Opportunities Yearbook Volume 1 Strategic, Practical Information and Opportunities
Togo Business and Investment Opportunities Yearbook Volume 1 Strategic, Practical Information and Opportunities
Tonga Business and Investment Opportunities Yearbook Volume 1 Strategic, Practical Information and Opportunities
Trinidad and Tobago Business and Investment Opportunities Yearbook Volume 1 Strategic, Practical Information and Opportunities
Tunisia Business and Investment Opportunities Yearbook Volume 1 Strategic, Practical Information and Opportunities
Turkey Business and Investment Opportunities Yearbook Volume 1 Strategic, Practical Information and Opportunities
Turkmenistan Business and Investment Opportunities Yearbook Volume 1 Strategic, Practical Information and Opportunities
Turks & Caicos Business and Investment Opportunities Yearbook Volume 1 Strategic, Practical Information and Opportunities
Tuvalu Business and Investment Opportunities Yearbook Volume 1 Strategic, Practical Information and Opportunities

TITLE
Uganda Business and Investment Opportunities Yearbook Volume 1 Strategic, Practical Information and Opportunities
Ukraine Business and Investment Opportunities Yearbook Volume 1 Strategic, Practical Information and Opportunities
United Arab Emirates Business and Investment Opportunities Yearbook Volume 1 Strategic, Practical Information and Opportunities
United Kingdom Business and Investment Opportunities Yearbook Volume 1 Strategic, Practical Information and Opportunities
United States Business and Investment Opportunities Yearbook Volume 1 Strategic, Practical Information and Opportunities
Uruguay Business and Investment Opportunities Yearbook Volume 1 Strategic, Practical Information and Opportunities
Uzbekistan Business and Investment Opportunities Yearbook Volume 1 Strategic, Practical Information and Opportunities
Vanuatu Business and Investment Opportunities Yearbook Volume 1 Strategic, Practical Information and Opportunities
Vatican City (Holy See) Business and Investment Opportunities Yearbook Volume 1 Strategic, Practical Information and Opportunities
Venezuela Business and Investment Opportunities Yearbook Volume 1 Strategic, Practical Information and Opportunities
Vietnam Business and Investment Opportunities Yearbook Volume 1 Strategic, Practical Information and Opportunities
Virgin Islands, British Business and Investment Opportunities Yearbook Volume 1 Strategic, Practical Information and Opportunities
Wake Atoll Business and Investment Opportunities Yearbook Volume 1 Strategic, Practical Information and Opportunities
Wallis & Futuna Business and Investment Opportunities Yearbook Volume 1 Strategic, Practical Information and Opportunities
Western Sahara Business and Investment Opportunities Yearbook Volume 1 Strategic, Practical Information and Opportunities
Yemen Business and Investment Opportunities Yearbook Volume 1 Strategic, Practical Information and Opportunities
Zambia Business and Investment Opportunities Yearbook Volume 1 Strategic, Practical Information and Opportunities
Zimbabwe Business and Investment Opportunities Yearbook Volume 1 Strategic, Practical Information and Opportunities

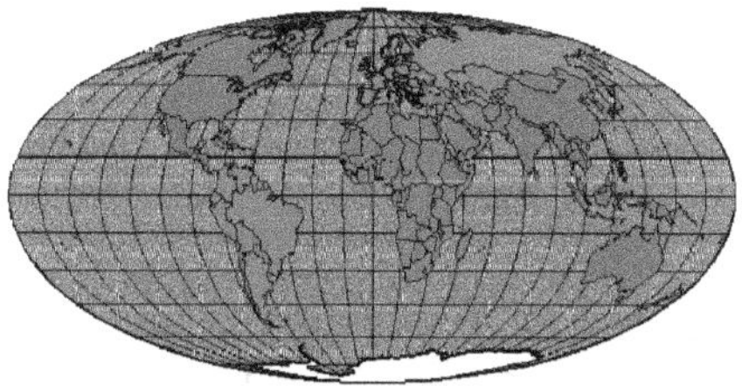

TITLE
Cape Verde Investment and Business Guide Volume 1 Strategic and Practical Information
Cayman Islands Investment and Business Guide Volume 1 Strategic and Practical Information
Central African Republic Investment and Business Guide Volume 1 Strategic and Practical Information
Chad Investment and Business Guide Volume 1 Strategic and Practical Information
Chile Investment and Business Guide Volume 1 Strategic and Practical Information
China Investment and Business Guide Volume 1 Strategic and Practical Information
Colombia Investment and Business Guide Volume 1 Strategic and Practical Information
Comoros Investment and Business Guide Volume 1 Strategic and Practical Information
Congo Investment and Business Guide Volume 1 Strategic and Practical Information
Congo, Democratic Republic Investment and Business Guide Volume 1 Strategic and Practical Information
Cook Islands Investment and Business Guide Volume 1 Strategic and Practical Information
Costa Rica Investment and Business Guide Volume 1 Strategic and Practical Information
Cote d'Ivoire Investment and Business Guide Volume 1 Strategic and Practical Information
Croatia Investment and Business Guide Volume 1 Strategic and Practical Information
Cuba Investment and Business Guide Volume 1 Strategic and Practical Information
Cyprus Investment and Business Guide Volume 1 Strategic and Practical Information
Czech Republic Investment and Business Guide Volume 1 Strategic and Practical Information
Denmark Investment and Business Guide Volume 1 Strategic and Practical Information
Djibouti Investment and Business Guide Volume 1 Strategic and Practical Information
Dominica Investment and Business Guide Volume 1 Strategic and Practical Information
Dominican Republic Investment and Business Guide Volume 1 Strategic and Practical Information
Ecuador Investment and Business Guide Volume 1 Strategic and Practical Information
Egypt Investment and Business Guide Volume 1 Strategic and Practical Information
El Salvador Investment and Business Guide Volume 1 Strategic and Practical Information
Equatorial Guinea Investment and Business Guide Volume 1 Strategic and Practical Information
Eritrea Investment and Business Guide Volume 1 Strategic and Practical Information
Estonia Investment and Business Guide Volume 1 Strategic and Practical Information
Ethiopia Investment and Business Guide Volume 1 Strategic and Practical Information
Falkland Islands Investment and Business Guide Volume 1 Strategic and Practical Information
Faroes Islands Investment and Business Guide Volume 1 Strategic and Practical Information
Fiji Investment and Business Guide Volume 1 Strategic and Practical Information
Finland Investment and Business Guide Volume 1 Strategic and Practical Information
France Investment and Business Guide Volume 1 Strategic and Practical Information
Gabon Investment and Business Guide Volume 1 Strategic and Practical Information
Gambia Investment and Business Guide Volume 1 Strategic and Practical Information
Georgia Investment and Business Guide Volume 1 Strategic and Practical Information
Germany Investment and Business Guide Volume 1 Strategic and Practical Information
Ghana Investment and Business Guide Volume 1 Strategic and Practical Information
Gibraltar Investment and Business Guide Volume 1 Strategic and Practical Information
Greece Investment and Business Guide Volume 1 Strategic and Practical Information
Greenland Investment and Business Guide Volume 1 Strategic and Practical Information
Grenada Investment and Business Guide Volume 1 Strategic and Practical Information
Guam Investment and Business Guide Volume 1 Strategic and Practical Information
Guatemala Investment and Business Guide Volume 1 Strategic and Practical Information
Guernsey Investment and Business Guide Volume 1 Strategic and Practical Information
Guinea Investment and Business Guide Volume 1 Strategic and Practical Information

TITLE
Guinea-Bissau Investment and Business Guide Volume 1 Strategic and Practical Information
Guyana Investment and Business Guide Volume 1 Strategic and Practical Information
Haiti Investment and Business Guide Volume 1 Strategic and Practical Information
Honduras Investment and Business Guide Volume 1 Strategic and Practical Information
Hungary Investment and Business Guide Volume 1 Strategic and Practical Information
Iceland Investment and Business Guide Volume 1 Strategic and Practical Information
India Investment and Business Guide Volume 1 Strategic and Practical Information
Indonesia Investment and Business Guide Volume 1 Strategic and Practical Information
Iran Investment and Business Guide Volume 1 Strategic and Practical Information
Iraq Investment and Business Guide Volume 1 Strategic and Practical Information
Ireland Investment and Business Guide Volume 1 Strategic and Practical Information
Israel Investment and Business Guide Volume 1 Strategic and Practical Information
Italy Investment and Business Guide Volume 1 Strategic and Practical Information
Jamaica Investment and Business Guide Volume 1 Strategic and Practical Information
Japan Investment and Business Guide Volume 1 Strategic and Practical Information
Jersey Investment and Business Guide Volume 1 Strategic and Practical Information
Jordan Investment and Business Guide Volume 1 Strategic and Practical Information
Kazakhstan Investment and Business Guide Volume 1 Strategic and Practical Information
Kenya Investment and Business Guide Volume 1 Strategic and Practical Information
Kiribati Investment and Business Guide Volume 1 Strategic and Practical Information
Korea, North Investment and Business Guide Volume 1 Strategic and Practical Information
Korea, South Investment and Business Guide Volume 1 Strategic and Practical Information
Kosovo Investment and Business Guide Volume 1 Strategic and Practical Information
Kurdistan Investment and Business Guide Volume 1 Strategic and Practical Information
Kuwait Investment and Business Guide Volume 1 Strategic and Practical Information
Kyrgyzstan Investment and Business Guide Volume 1 Strategic and Practical Information
Laos Investment and Business Guide Volume 1 Strategic and Practical Information
Latvia Investment and Business Guide Volume 1 Strategic and Practical Information
Lebanon Investment and Business Guide Volume 1 Strategic and Practical Information
Lesotho Investment and Business Guide Volume 1 Strategic and Practical Information
Liberia Investment and Business Guide Volume 1 Strategic and Practical Information
Libya Investment and Business Guide Volume 1 Strategic and Practical Information
Liechtenstein Investment and Business Guide Volume 1 Strategic and Practical Information
Lithuania Investment and Business Guide Volume 1 Strategic and Practical Information
Luxembourg Investment and Business Guide Volume 1 Strategic and Practical Information
Macao Investment and Business Guide Volume 1 Strategic and Practical Information
Macedonia Investment and Business Guide Volume 1 Strategic and Practical Information
Madagascar Investment and Business Guide Volume 1 Strategic and Practical Information
Madeira Investment and Business Guide Volume 1 Strategic and Practical Information
Malawi Investment and Business Guide Volume 1 Strategic and Practical Information
Malaysia Investment and Business Guide Volume 1 Strategic and Practical Information
Maldives Investment and Business Guide Volume 1 Strategic and Practical Information
Mali Investment and Business Guide Volume 1 Strategic and Practical Information
Malta Investment and Business Guide Volume 1 Strategic and Practical Information
Man Investment and Business Guide Volume 1 Strategic and Practical Information
Marshall Islands Investment and Business Guide Volume 1 Strategic and Practical Information

TITLE
Mauritania Investment and Business Guide Volume 1 Strategic and Practical Information
Mauritius Investment and Business Guide Volume 1 Strategic and Practical Information
Mayotte Investment and Business Guide Volume 1 Strategic and Practical Information
Mexico Investment and Business Guide Volume 1 Strategic and Practical Information
Micronesia Investment and Business Guide Volume 1 Strategic and Practical Information
Moldova Investment and Business Guide Volume 1 Strategic and Practical Information
Monaco Investment and Business Guide Volume 1 Strategic and Practical Information
Mongolia Investment and Business Guide Volume 1 Strategic and Practical Information
Montserrat Investment and Business Guide Volume 1 Strategic and Practical Information
Montenegro Investment and Business Guide Volume 1 Strategic and Practical Information
Morocco Investment and Business Guide Volume 1 Strategic and Practical Information
Mozambique Investment and Business Guide Volume 1 Strategic and Practical Information
Myanmar Investment and Business Guide Volume 1 Strategic and Practical Information
Nagorno-Karabakh Republic Investment and Business Guide Volume 1 Strategic and Practical Information
Namibia Investment and Business Guide Volume 1 Strategic and Practical Information
Nauru Investment and Business Guide Volume 1 Strategic and Practical Information
Nepal Investment and Business Guide Volume 1 Strategic and Practical Information
Netherlands Investment and Business Guide Volume 1 Strategic and Practical Information
New Caledonia Investment and Business Guide Volume 1 Strategic and Practical Information
New Zealand Investment and Business Guide Volume 1 Strategic and Practical Information
Nicaragua Investment and Business Guide Volume 1 Strategic and Practical Information
Niger Investment and Business Guide Volume 1 Strategic and Practical Information
Nigeria Investment and Business Guide Volume 1 Strategic and Practical Information
Niue Investment and Business Guide Volume 1 Strategic and Practical Information
Northern Cyprus (Turkish Republic of Northern Cyprus) Volume 1 Strategic Information and Developments
Northern Mariana Islands Investment and Business Guide Volume 1 Strategic and Practical Information
Norway Investment and Business Guide Volume 1 Strategic and Practical Information
Oman Investment and Business Guide Volume 1 Strategic and Practical Information
Pakistan Investment and Business Guide Volume 1 Strategic and Practical Information
Palau Investment and Business Guide Volume 1 Strategic and Practical Information
Palestine (West Bank & Gaza) Investment and Business Guide Volume 1 Strategic and Practical Information
Panama Investment and Business Guide Volume 1 Strategic and Practical Information
Papua New Guinea Investment and Business Guide Volume 1 Strategic and Practical Information
Paraguay Investment and Business Guide Volume 1 Strategic and Practical Information
Peru Investment and Business Guide Volume 1 Strategic and Practical Information
Philippines Investment and Business Guide Volume 1 Strategic and Practical Information
Pitcairn Islands Investment and Business Guide Volume 1 Strategic and Practical Information
Poland Investment and Business Guide Volume 1 Strategic and Practical Information
Polynesia French Investment and Business Guide Volume 1 Strategic and Practical Information
Portugal Investment and Business Guide Volume 1 Strategic and Practical Information
Qatar Investment and Business Guide Volume 1 Strategic and Practical Information
Romania Investment and Business Guide Volume 1 Strategic and Practical Information
Russia Investment and Business Guide Volume 1 Strategic and Practical Information
Rwanda Investment and Business Guide Volume 1 Strategic and Practical Information
Sahrawi Arab Democratic Republic Volume 1 Strategic Information and Developments
Saint Kitts and Nevis Investment and Business Guide Volume 1 Strategic and Practical Information

TITLE
Saint Lucia Investment and Business Guide Volume 1 Strategic and Practical Information
Saint Vincent and The Grenadines Investment and Business Guide Volume 1 Strategic and Practical Information
Samoa (American) A Investment and Business Guide Volume 1 Strategic and Practical Information
Samoa (Western) Investment and Business Guide Volume 1 Strategic and Practical Information
San Marino Investment and Business Guide Volume 1 Strategic and Practical Information
Sao Tome and Principe Investment and Business Guide Volume 1 Strategic and Practical Information
Saudi Arabia Investment and Business Guide Volume 1 Strategic and Practical Information
Scotland Investment and Business Guide Volume 1 Strategic and Practical Information
Senegal Investment and Business Guide Volume 1 Strategic and Practical Information
Serbia Investment and Business Guide Volume 1 Strategic and Practical Information
Seychelles Investment and Business Guide Volume 1 Strategic and Practical Information
Sierra Leone Investment and Business Guide Volume 1 Strategic and Practical Information
Singapore Investment and Business Guide Volume 1 Strategic and Practical Information
Slovakia Investment and Business Guide Volume 1 Strategic and Practical Information
Slovenia Investment and Business Guide Volume 1 Strategic and Practical Information
Solomon Islands Investment and Business Guide Volume 1 Strategic and Practical Information
Somalia Investment and Business Guide Volume 1 Strategic and Practical Information
South Africa Investment and Business Guide Volume 1 Strategic and Practical Information
Spain Investment and Business Guide Volume 1 Strategic and Practical Information
Sri Lanka Investment and Business Guide Volume 1 Strategic and Practical Information
St. Helena Investment and Business Guide Volume 1 Strategic and Practical Information
St. Pierre & Miquelon Investment and Business Guide Volume 1 Strategic and Practical Information
Sudan (Republic of the Sudan) Investment and Business Guide Volume 1 Strategic and Practical Information
Sudan South Investment and Business Guide Volume 1 Strategic and Practical Information
Suriname Investment and Business Guide Volume 1 Strategic and Practical Information
Swaziland Investment and Business Guide Volume 1 Strategic and Practical Information
Sweden Investment and Business Guide Volume 1 Strategic and Practical Information
Switzerland Investment and Business Guide Volume 1 Strategic and Practical Information
Syria Investment and Business Guide Volume 1 Strategic and Practical Information
Taiwan Investment and Business Guide Volume 1 Strategic and Practical Information
Tajikistan Investment and Business Guide Volume 1 Strategic and Practical Information
Tanzania Investment and Business Guide Volume 1 Strategic and Practical Information
Thailand Investment and Business Guide Volume 1 Strategic and Practical Information
Timor Leste (Democratic Republic of Timor-Leste) Investment and Business Guide Volume 1 Strategic and Practical Information
Togo Investment and Business Guide Volume 1 Strategic and Practical Information
Tonga Investment and Business Guide Volume 1 Strategic and Practical Information
Trinidad and Tobago Investment and Business Guide Volume 1 Strategic and Practical Information
Tunisia Investment and Business Guide Volume 1 Strategic and Practical Information
Turkey Investment and Business Guide Volume 1 Strategic and Practical Information
Turkmenistan Investment and Business Guide Volume 1 Strategic and Practical Information
Turks & Caicos Investment and Business Guide Volume 1 Strategic and Practical Information
Tuvalu Investment and Business Guide Volume 1 Strategic and Practical Information
Uganda Investment and Business Guide Volume 1 Strategic and Practical Information
Ukraine Investment and Business Guide Volume 1 Strategic and Practical Information
United Arab Emirates Investment and Business Guide Volume 1 Strategic and Practical Information

TITLE
United Kingdom Investment and Business Guide Volume 1 Strategic and Practical Information
United States Investment and Business Guide Volume 1 Strategic and Practical Information
Uruguay Investment and Business Guide Volume 1 Strategic and Practical Information
Uzbekistan Investment and Business Guide Volume 1 Strategic and Practical Information
Vanuatu Investment and Business Guide Volume 1 Strategic and Practical Information
Vatican City (Holy See) Investment and Business Guide Volume 1 Strategic and Practical Information
Venezuela Investment and Business Guide Volume 1 Strategic and Practical Information
Vietnam Investment and Business Guide Volume 1 Strategic and Practical Information
Virgin Islands, British Investment and Business Guide Volume 1 Strategic and Practical Information
Wake Atoll Investment and Business Guide Volume 1 Strategic and Practical Information
Wallis & Futuna Investment and Business Guide Volume 1 Strategic and Practical Information
Western Sahara Investment and Business Guide Volume 1 Strategic and Practical Information
Yemen Investment and Business Guide Volume 1 Strategic and Practical Information
Zambia Investment and Business Guide Volume 1 Strategic and Practical Information
Zimbabwe Investment and Business Guide Volume 1 Strategic and Practical Information

www.ingramcontent.com/pod-product-compliance
Lightning Source LLC
LaVergne TN
LVHW080033210926
848481LV00011B/3176

9781438767574